The Recovery-Stress Questionnaires

The Recovery-Stress Questionnaires (RESTQs) identifies the current recovery-stress states and provides a complete picture of the actual extent of stress and recovery. Written to support those using the RESTQ, this manual offers advice on scope and application, facets of stress and recovery, versions and scoring, interpretation of results, and reliability and validity for each of the five forms of the questionnaire.

The questionnaire is based on the hypothesis that an accumulation of stress in different areas of life, with insufficient opportunity for recovery, leads to a critical psychophysiological state. The RESTQ measures the frequency of current stress symptoms along with the frequency of recovery-associated activities to offer a differentiated picture of the current recovery-stress state. There are five forms of the RESTQ: a general version (RESTQ-Basic) with seven stress scales and five recovery scales is the foundation for the specific versions for athletes (RESTQ-Sport), for coaches (RESTQ-Coach), for children and adolescents (RESTQ-CA), and for the work context (RESTQ-Work). All versions take a modular structure and contain scales measuring specific aspects of stress and recovery in their field. These scales provide valuable information immediately on areas where improvement is needed in stress and recovery research across a range of applied settings.

Drawing on experiences and scientific findings from sport to make them usable for an expanded understanding of recovery in the fields of health, work, and other related areas, this manual is written for the scientific community, applied psychologists and health scientists, and interested readers.

Michael Kellmann is Professor of Sport Psychology at the Faculty of Sport Science at Ruhr University Bochum, Germany. He is also an Honorary Professor in the School of Human Movement and Nutrition Sciences at The University of Queensland, Australia.

K. Wolfgang Kallus is a retired Professor of Work and Organisational Psychology in the Department of Psychology, Faculty of Natural Sciences at the University of Graz, Austria.

Advances in Recovery and Stress Research: Multi-Disciplinary Approaches

Series Editors

Michael Kellmann, Ruhr University Bochum, Germany, and The University of Queensland, Australia

Jürgen Beckmann, Technical University of Munich, Germany, and The University of Queensland, Australia

Advances in Recovery and Stress Research: Multi-Disciplinary Approaches covers a broad range of areas in which recovery plays a crucial role, providing the current status of research on recovery and stress. In particular, it aims to be unique in addressing fields in which recovery and stress play an important role, but recovery has not received adequate attention, for example, in the areas of health promotion as well as performance promotion in work settings. Another feature of the series is that it contains both up-to-date theoretical and applied perspectives from multi-disciplinary approaches.

Recovery and Well-being in Sport and Exercise
Interdisciplinary Insights
Edited by Michael Kellmann and Jürgen Beckmann

The Importance of Recovery for Physical and Mental Health
Negotiating the Effects of Underrecovery
Edited by Michael Kellmann, Sarah Jakowski, and Jürgen Beckmann

Fostering Recovery and Well-being in a Healthy Lifestyle
Psychological, Somatic, and Organizational Prevention Approaches
Edited by Michael Kellmann and Jürgen Beckmann

The Recovery-Stress Questionnaires
A User Manual
Edited by Michael Kellmann and K. Wolfgang Kallus

For more information about this series, please visit: www.routledge.com/Advances-in-Recovery-and-Stress-Research/book-series/ARSR

The Recovery-Stress Questionnaires

A User Manual

Edited by
Michael Kellmann
and K. Wolfgang Kallus

Routledge
Taylor & Francis Group
LONDON AND NEW YORK

Designed cover image: ©Getty Images\liuzishan

First published 2025
by Routledge
4 Park Square, Milton Park, Abingdon, Oxon OX14 4RN

and by Routledge
605 Third Avenue, New York, NY 10158

Routledge is an imprint of the Taylor & Francis Group, an informa business

British Library Cataloguing-in-Publication Data
A catalogue record for this book is available from the British Library

ISBN: 9781032643373 (hbk)
ISBN: 9781032620503 (pbk)
ISBN: 9781032643380 (ebk)

DOI: 10.4324/9781032643380

Typeset in Bembo
by codeMantra

Access the Support Material: www.routledge.com/9781032643373

Contents

Contributors

Sebastian Altfeld works as an applied sport psychologist and as a trained psychotherapist with athletes, coaches, and referees in different kind of sports. He graduated with a master's degree in clinical psychology and has published in the area of coaches' burnout during his PhD studies. He has been admitted to the pool of sport psychological experts of the *German Association of Sport Psychology* (asp). Moreover, he is part of the team of sport psychologists in the project www.mentaltalent.de, which offers sport psychology to young talented athletes, their coaches, and parents in Germany. E-mail: mail@sebastian-altfeld.de

Jens Brandt is Head of Business Psychology Department and Program Director of B.Sc. Business Psychology and M.Sc. Work and Organisational Psychology at the International School of Management (Dortmund & Frankfurt/Main, Germany). He studied psychology at the University of Würzburg (diploma/master degree) and Graz (doctoral degree). His research focuses on questionnaire development, Work Psychology (especially stress and resources), and Personnel Psychology (especially leadership). E-mail: jens.brandt@ism.de

Anita Bregenzer is Research Associate at the University of Graz (Austria) in the sub-division of Work and Organisational Psychology. Anita graduated with a master's degree in work and organizational psychology in job satisfaction. She continued her research at the University of Graz, working in different fields of Work- and Organizational Psychology. Her main field of research includes health-promoting leadership, workplace health promotion, burnout and work-related strain, stress, and recovery. Anita works in different national and international projects and achieved her PhD on health-promoting leadership and its effects on the employees' health. E-mail: anita.bregenzer@uni-graz.at

Petra Hampel is Professor of Health Psychology and Health Education, Europe-University Flensburg (Germany). Prior to her current role, she was guest Professor of Developmental Psychology at the Department of Psychology, Karl-Franzens University of Graz (Austria), Professor of Rehabilitation Psychology at the Department of Psychology, University of Bremen (Germany) and Professor of Rehabilitation in Children and Adolescents at the Faculty of Social Work and Health, University of Applied Sciences Kiel (Germany). Petra is a member of the German Psychological Association, the German Association of Neuropsychology, and the German Association of Rehabilitation Sciences. Petra's research interests include stress and coping in childhood and adolescence among healthy students as well as students with chronic diseases; health promotion in children and adolescents; cognitive-behavioural management training for patients with chronic low-back pain and depressive symptoms; participatory health research, and culturally sensitive community health promotion among elderly people with social inequality. E-mail: petra.hampel@uni-flensburg.de

Paulino Jiménez works at the University of Graz (Austria) in the sub-division of Work and Organisational Psychology. He is a member of the leading team of Work-, Industrial-, and Organizational Psychology of the Austrian Professional Association of Psychologists (BÖP). Here he also serves as delegate for Austria for the Board of Assessment in the European Federation of Psychological Associations, EFPA. In the field of standardization, he works in the Austrian Standards Institute as full member of the committee of ergonomics and as vice head of the committee services and processes of human resources development. He was funder of the consulting company research-team for consulting and research in Work, Organizational, and Economic Psychology, Evaluation which is now Jiménez-Schmon-Höfer GmbH, currently being in the role as scientific head. His main field of research is occupational health promotion, especially work-related stress and recovery, as well as job satisfaction, burnout, and leadership. E-mail: paul.jimenez@uni-graz.at

K. Wolfgang Kallus is a retired Professor of Work and Organisational Psychology in the Department of Psychology, Faculty of Natural Sciences at the University of Graz (Austria). His research in the past years focused on stress and regeneration especially in aging workers, applied methods, and Human Factors with a focus on Aviation Psychology. He is a member of different national and international scientific organisations and is past president of the board of the IEA-Group 'Psychophysiology in Ergonomics (PIE)', past-president of the Austrian Aviation Psychology Association, and since 1995 director of the institute for evaluation research (Institut für Begleitforschung, IfB). In 2012, he received the biannual award of the European Association of Aviation Psychology. E-mail: wolfgang.kallus@uni-graz.at

Michael Kellmann is Professor of Sport Psychology at the Faculty of Sport Science at Ruhr University Bochum, Germany. He is also an Honorary Professor in the School of Human Movement and Nutrition Sciences at the University of Queensland, Australia. He has been on the editorial boards of the *German Journal of Sport Psychology* (2001–2007), the *German Journal of Sport Medicine* (2002–today), and *The Sport Psychologist* (1999–2023). He served on the executive board of the *German Association of Sport Psychology* (2001–2007) and was the chair of the education, training, and certification programme 'Sport psychology in high performance sport' for German sport psychologists. Michael's current research activities include overtraining prevention and recovery enhancement, regeneration management in elite sports, sport psychological diagnostics and intervention, as well as the development of research tools for the assessment of recovery. E-mail: michael.kellmann@rub.de

Verena Wagner-Hartl is Professor for Engineering Psychology at Furtwangen University (Germany). She studied psychology at the University of Graz (diploma [equivalent to a master's degree] and doctoral degree) and instrumental/vocal education at the J.J. Fux Konservatorium, Graz (diploma/teaching certificate) and University of Music and Performing Arts Graz (bachelor degree). Prior to her current role, Verena worked in the Customer Research Center of the Daimler AG (Germany) and in the Global HMI Team of the Ford Werke GmbH (Germany). During her time as research associate at the Department of Psychology of the University of Graz and the Institut für Begleitforschung (IfB), she worked on different projects within the research field of Work-, Organizational and Environmental Psychology. From 2012–2018 she was lecturer at the Ruhr West University (Bottrop), Germany (degree programs: Human-Machine Interaction; Safety Engineering), and since 2020 lecturer of Engineering Psychology at Offenburg University. Verena's research activities include sound perception and sound design, hearing impairment in (older) employees/elderly people, Occupational Health Psychology, Human Factors, and Human-Machine-Interaction. E-mail: verena.wagner-hartl@hs-furtwangen.de

Series foreword

This manual is published in the series *Advances in Recovery and Stress Research: Multi-Disciplinary Approaches* edited by Michael Kellmann and Jürgen Beckmann. This series covers a broad range of areas in which recovery plays a crucial role, providing the status of research on recovery and stress. It is the idea of the series to publish a volume each year. We started with *Recovery and Well-being in Sport and Exercise* (Volume 1), followed by *The Importance of Recovery for Physical and Mental Health: Negotiating the Effects of Underrecovery* (Volume 2), and by Volume 3 *Fostering Recovery and Well-being in a Healthy Lifestyle: Psychological, Somatic, and Organizational Prevention Approaches. The Recovery-Stress Questionnaires: A User Manual* (Volume 4) and *Creating Urban and Workplace Environments for Recovery and Well-being: New Perspectives on Urban Design and Mental Health* (Volume 5) are on the way, and Volume 6 is already organized but the title is not finalized. Always current information on the series can be found at www.routledge.com/Advances-in-Recovery-and-Stress-Research/book-series/ARSR.

We thank Routledge for the flexibility and engagement for this adventure to develop the series *Advances in Recovery and Stress Research: Multi-Disciplinary Approaches.*

Michael Kellmann
Jürgen Beckmann

Preface

Moving publishers is not always a joy, and often a lot of obstacles occur. In our case, however, we felt always appreciated and supported even if we came up with a lot of 'uncommon' ideas and approaches. *The Recovery-Stress Questionnaires* were published with Pearson Assessment in Germany in 2016, and this manual has now been modified and updated to offer the reader up-to-date knowledge on *The Recovery-Stress Questionnaires*. We thank Routledge for the engagement for this journey.

The structure of the manual changed slightly but the biggest modification is the creation of a download hub on the websites of Routledge. To gain access to the resources for this manual, please visit the Routledge Resource Centre.

The Routledge Resource Centre offers advantages to the owners of the original manual:

A) The English and German versions of the Recovery-Stress Questionnaires can be directly downloaded.
B) There will be no additional costs for unlimited duplication and use of the Recovery-Stress Questionnaires.
C) Further selected international versions in different languages will be added to the download hub free of charge. A short summary, documentation, and the instruments will be available for download. Be aware that this is a step-by-step process and the availability of the international versions will not start before January 2025.

This manual is intended to provide the background for a professional work with the Recovery-Stress Questionnaires. Due to different modular versions and different areas of application, a broad range of validities could be empirically substantiated. An overview across versions and validities allows a professional interpretation of results from a specific sample in a specific area and possibly for specific occasions. The manual provides the background for interpretation. The questionnaires described in the chapters are versions with a specific time frame, which can vary depending on the version used (e.g., Basic, Sport).

While this manual is written in English, it is designed to serve for the English and German versions of the Recovery-Stress Questionnaires. For differentiation, the

English first part of the abbreviation is RESTQ (Recovery-Stress Questionnaire) and for the German questionnaires EBF (Erholungs-Belastungs-Fragebogen), respectively. However, the second part of the abbreviation (e.g., Basic, Sport) is kept in English.

English version	*German version*
RESTQ-Basic	EBF-Basic
RESTQ-Sport	EBF-Sport
RESTQ-Coach	EBF-Coach
RESTQ-Work	EBF-Work
RESTQ-CA	EBF-CA
	EBF-Student

In the manual, we only use the term RESTQ for all versions of the RESTQ, respectively EBF. Which questionnaire was used when collecting data can be derived from the description of the samples. Samples in this manual are abbreviated with a letter for the language used in the questionnaire (e.g., G: German) and the version of the RESTQ (e.g., B: Basic, C: Coach, CA: Children and Adolescents).

The guidelines for the administration, scoring, and interpretation apply to all available languages of the version we are referring to in each chapter, and not only to the language we are directly discussing.

This consistent terminology provides guidance for the reader and hopefully improves understanding.

Michael Kellmann
K. Wolfgang Kallus

Acknowledgements

Large projects, such as *The Recovery-Stress Questionnaires* (RESTQs), can only be realized with the unremitting effort of creative and motivated people. Our special thanks for the groundwork and help during the first studies of the RESTQ goes to Wilhelm Janke (1933-2011). The development and concept are closely tied to his bio-psychological research and his study groups for the theme of stress, coping, and emotion.

For the sport-specific version, we were glad to be able to win Hans Eberspächer (1943-2014), Hans-Dieter Hermann, and Jürgen Steinacker for establishing the recovery-stress model in high-performance sport. Therefore, the spectrum of the RESTQ-Sport has been completed by the valuable possibility of enlightening psychological and physical factors of overtraining and underrecovery.

For the RESTQ-Basic, the RESTQ for Children and Adolescents, and the RESTQ-Work many motivated students contributed with their diploma theses and master theses. Thanks to all of them for their valuable contribution. The compilation of the data from these studies and the preparation for the manual was in the busy hands of Kerstin Gaisbachgrabner, who successfully assisted to finish the final version together with Denise Tautenhahn in Bochum. Special thanks from Wolfgang Kallus to his colleges and coworkers, who used the RESTQ in our applied studies and who collaborated with me over decades. I am deeply indebted to Christa Kolodej, Katharina Göttlicher, Anita Gratzl-Baumberger, Thomas Uhlig, Peter Hoffmann, and the first editor of this manual Michael Kellmann.

We are glad to introduce the whole family of *The Recovery-Stress Questionnaires*. Thank you to all the people involved in the development process.

Michael Kellmann
K. Wolfgang Kallus

User information for *The Recovery-Stress Questionnaires*

Dear User,

Purchasing *The Recovery-Stress Questionnaires* (RESTQs) includes access to the assessment tools, which are hosted on the Routledge Resource Centre. These assessment tools can be downloaded and used without limitation. The only requirement is that you have purchased the original manual from Routledge.

If you use the RESTQ in your studies or in applied settings, the authors would appreciate feedback on your experience in working with these instruments. For further development of these instruments, we would be grateful if you could send us a copy of the original data set, a sample description, and information about the study or intervention approach used.

If you have further questions or comments, please contact:

Prof. Dr. Michael Kellmann
Ruhr University Bochum, Faculty of Sport Science
Gesundheitscampus-Nord 10, 44801 Bochum, Germany
E-mail: michael.kellmann@rub.de
https://sport.ruhr-uni-bochum.de/de/sportpsychologie

Once purchased, you may use the RESTQ as research or monitoring tool in sports, at the workplace, or in the health context. **However, you should not use the RESTQ for selection purposes!** Although there is a slight tendency to use the results of psychological assessments for selection decisions, this practice is unethical and may destroy the trusting relationship between all people involved. Furthermore, the consultation with a trained psychologist or counselling centre, as well as medical advice is highly recommended if a serious long-lasting and unhealthy recovery-stress state is detected.

Please be aware that the authors hold the copyright for all languages, except the ones given away. In case you are interested in obtaining permission to translate and validate *The Recovery-Stress Questionnaires* into other languages, please contact the authors for the respective version by e-mail. In addition, you must have a background in psychometrics and you need to follow the translation procedure described by Vallerand (1989). Also, the 2018 International Test

Commission *Guidelines for Translating and Adapting Tests #1 to #11* (regarding Pre-Condition Guidelines, Test Development Guidelines, Confirmation Guidelines) must be realized.

Also keep in mind that using items, scales, or the RESTQ as a whole instrument in the internet or other media by third parties without written permission is a violation of copyright and will be persecuted.

As a guideline for validating the RESTQ in another language, we propose the following steps:

- First step: A team of researchers (3–5) should come up with individually different translations for each item.
- Second step: You will combine/compare these different translations, the ones which match the others are ready for the next step. The other items need some more consideration and maybe a recheck with the translators to identify which translation is the best. Also, test with some persons of the target population if the primary version is understandable.
- Third step: Get 2–3 back-translations of the items. These will be checked by the authors of the respective RESTQ version if the back-translations match the English/German original and if the translated versions are consistent.
- Fourth step: A linguist is extremely helpful to refine the version regarding grammatical issues.
- Fifth step: Collect a sample of 100 persons of the target population and run the first preliminary analysis checking the reliability of the translated version. Depending on the results, maybe some items need to be modified, and another sample of this size is needed again.

Summary: We have learned from Vallerand (1989) that one linguist might be worth many 'bilingual' researchers, and that the meaning of each subscale is more important than a proper grammatical translation. Also, various steps are supposed to be correct – but we have learned to modify these steps and emphasized some of them [i.e., checking that items (wording and vocabulary) are well understood by the target population].

Furthermore, for the validation of the RESTQs at least two cross-sectional studies and one longitudinal study must be realized. The first cross-sectional study should include more than 300 participants; the second study should include more than 600 participants to run the Exploratory and Confirmatory Factor Analysis. The longitudinal study should be the monitoring approach in a 7–10-day training camp (in sports) or a working week (RESTQ-Work).

Sometimes, researchers just translate an instrument without validation and without receiving permission from the authors. Besides breaching the copyright, this may lead to difficulties in the development and interpretation of the instrument.

Furthermore, in some languages a direct translation of terms (without considering the content with the specific cultural background) leads to an unreliable translation. Therefore, the validation process needs to be solid and well documented.

References

International Test Commission. (2018). *Guidelines for translating and adapting tests* (Second Edition, Version 2.4). Retrieved December 12, 2023 from https://www.intestcom.org/files/guideline_test_adaptation_2ed.pdf

Vallerand, R. J. (1989). Vers une méthodologie de validation trans-culturelle de questionnaires psychologiques: Implications pour la recherche en langue française [Toward a methodology for the transcultural validation of psychological questionnaires: Implications for research in the French language]. *Canadian Psychology/Psychologie Canadienne, 30*(4), 662–680.

1 General Background of the Recovery-Stress Questionnaires

Michael Kellmann and K. Wolfgang Kallus

Introduction

This chapter will give an introduction to the concept and the theoretical background of the Recovery-Stress Questionnaire (RESTQ) and its versions and will present a first overview of the broad range of applications. A person can be met in a wide range of physical, cognitive, and motivational states, which determine how the person will act and react to a task or a treatment in a certain situation. The recovery-stress state is an important aspect of the persons' state and is reflected in emotion, motivation, activation, and cognition as well as psychophysical symptoms and in current social activities. The recovery-stress state is assessed by the RESTQ, to draw a picture of the current psychophysical state or 'bio-psycho-social' state of the person. This state changes with impaired well-being and illness, with normal day-to-day demands, hassles, and uplifts specifically during high-performance situations.

The current manual is intended to support scientists and practitioners to work with the RESTQ professionally and to measure/monitor the impact of the recovery-stress state of their participants and clients. This will allow a diagnosis of the bio-psycho-socially founded recovery-stress state and thus allow a sound derivation of necessary additional information and interventions. The manual provides the psychological background for the different scales in detail and allows developing an understanding of the background, which goes deeper than the partly ambiguous and (over-)simplifying labels of the scales. Every scale of the RESTQ and its modules is theoretically and empirically well founded in psychological research. These concepts should be considered for any interpretation of results. A good basic knowledge of the concepts is necessary to use the full potential of the RESTQ, as the pattern or profile reveals the relevant information in most instances. The RESTQ is useful not only to check for critical stress states but also to detect performance potential and options to optimize the recovery of resources. The background concepts will be at least briefly outlined in this manual. For further information, a detailed list of references is provided.

Kellmann, M., & Kallus, K.W. (2025). General background of the Recovery-Stress Questionnaires. In M. Kellmann & K.W. Kallus (Eds.), *The Recovery-Stress Questionnaires: A User Manual* (pp. 1–27). Routledge.

DOI: 10.4324/9781032643380-1

General description

The current recovery-stress state of a person is assessed by measuring the frequency of stress and recovery-related activities and states in the past days and nights. The basic version of the RESTQ (RESTQ-Basic) assesses a recovery-stress profile with twelve scales, which can be grouped into two basic dimensions: *Overall Stress* and *Overall Recovery*. The stress dimension encompasses two subdimensions which are labelled as *Social-Emotional Stress* and *Performance(-related) Stress*. The *Overall Stress* value is especially recommended when using a short version of the RESTQ. *Stress and recovery should not be combined into a single value, as they constitute two conceptually independent dimensions as far as the frequency in the past days/nights is concerned.* The relationship between the scales for recovery and stress is neither linear nor symmetrical. ***Consequently, the calculation of one overall single score of all stress and recovery scales does not make sense and is strongly prohibited.*** This result was obtained with the first versions of the RESTQ (Kallus, 1992, 1995) and could be replicated in different areas of application.

The basic version (RESTQ-Basic) with seven stress scales and five recovery scales is the basis for the specific versions for athletes (RESTQ-Sport), coaches (RESTQ-Coach), students (RESTQ-Student), and working people (RESTQ-Work). In clinical contexts, a short version had been developed (RESTQ-Risco), which is combined with a measure for resignative coping style and state anxiety. However, the information on the patients' recovery-stress state provided interesting validities in research contexts even for parameters like stay in hospitals but it could not be incorporated into the clinical routines of hospitals in the long run. Thus, this version was not further developed or translated as the other versions were.

For all long forms of the RESTQ, short versions are available, which can be used for screening purposes or to check for a 'flashlight' in monitoring applications or for orientation purposes in organizations. With reference to ISO 10075, the short screening versions allow an interpretation of the values for the dimensions and not for the scales, as reliabilities partly fall below critical thresholds due to the reduced number of items (Jiménez et al., this volume, Chapter 5). Thus, the restriction of the interpretations to the dimensions is recommended for the short versions. For the RESTQ-Basic, the standard version comprises 48 items (RESTQ-Basic-48), and the short version consists of 24 items (RESTQ-Basic-24). Additional information on the time frame of reference should always be given, when it deviates from the standard, which is *in the past (3) days/nights* for the RESTQ-Basic. The time frame is given in the instruction and depicted in the header of the questionnaire. It is different for each kind of the specific modules but stable within each version. Other time frames than *(3) days/nights* are added for the RESTQ-Basic, as different time frames are possible. Mind that the frequency of states and events changes when the time window is opened or restricted, which implies a change in scale values.

The RESTQ can be tailored to the actual research question or measurement purpose. Short versions allow a quick and less detailed assessment of the recovery-stress state. Longer versions are recommended when interventions or counselling are required. Recommendations on which version should be used for which purpose are given at the end of most chapters. The more detailed view of different facets of recovery and stress allows deriving specific interventions. An even more detailed view of the recovery-stress state will be provided by the specific modules, which can be added to the basic version of the RESTQ. In addition, different time frames in the heading of each page evolved during the application of the RESTQ in different areas. The shorter the time frame the stronger the influence of interventions or specific events. Scores reflect less state and more trait variance with longer time frames. The scores are comparable to 'moving averages' which are less affected by a stressful event or a recovery period with a longer reference period and are stronger affected by a short reference time.

The standard version of the RESTQ assesses states and activities during the past three days/nights. This time frame of three days is also recommended for athletes and children/adolescents. It can be modified to seven days/nights (e.g., for organizational and work applications) or up to 14 days/nights for medical context, which proved to be useful to assess the pre-operative state of patients. Psychometric quality and factorial structure are only affected marginally by changing time frames, while the mean scores of the scales can change with longer time frames. Even longer time intervals (four weeks) have been used in applied contexts (Stelzhammer, 2008) but are not recommended as internal consistency drops below acceptable limits for some scales.

The second possible modification in the modular set of RESTQs is to use one of the area-specific versions of the RESTQ. Most of them are available in standard and short form. The area-specific versions cover work and organizations (RESTQ-Work), athletes (RESTQ-Sport), coaches (RESTQ-Coach), and children/adolescents (RESTQ-CA). These specific versions will be presented in the respective chapters. For some areas of applications, quick short forms were developed for orienting and screening purposes only. The short forms provide a first view on the recovery-stress state with only a few items. Especially when large samples are at hand and only sub-samples need a detailed diagnosis, the screening versions allow identifying the person(s) for further diagnosis and intervention.

In addition to the different areas of application, versions of the RESTQs are available in various languages (e.g., English, German, Portuguese, Spanish, French) but only the English, German, and Portuguese versions of the RESTQ-Sport and the German version of the RESTQ-Basic have been published in a manual. At least for the RESTQ-Basic and the RESTQ-Sport, data on reliabilities are available in a broad range of different languages. The present manual and the download options via the Routledge Resource Centre allow to bring together all different versions into one compact hub (for details, see Kellmann & Kallus, this volume, Preface).

Results of the RESTQs can be displayed in a recovery-stress profile. Reference values are provided to allow an interpretation with respect to the recovery-stress balance. For high stress, high recovery is needed, while for low stress moderate recovery will be sufficient. In the case of unbalanced states over a longer period with high stress and low recovery, a high risk for chronic stress, burnout, performance decrements, and health problems occurs. The state of reduced activity (low stress) with low recovery might also be an indication of a dysfunctional state. As short-term disbalance can even be functional (e.g., in training situations), long-term phases of non-recovery impair resources and indicate a risky state. This is best evaluated by repeated measurements with the RESTQ.

Validation studies show convergent and discriminant validity as well as high predictive validity for non-questionnaire measures, such as performance data and health indicators. The broad range of validities of the RESTQ and its different versions allow a sound interpretation of results. In many instances, there is a great benefit from looking into another area of application or a different domain of validities. Predictive validities range from biological markers of stress and recovery, via state and health questionnaires to behavioural and medical outcome measures and into various areas of performance and social behaviour. The main purpose of this manual is to allow users of the RESTQ to incorporate this empirical evidence into their research or daily work. An overview of empirically substantiated validation criteria is given in the respective chapters.

The modular structure of the RESTQ

The concept of a modular-structured questionnaire (Kallus, 2016) endeavours to solve the problem that global scores allow only a parsimonious classification and comparison to norms, which does not allow a detailed diagnosis. Thus, very general questions are often considered as not relevant in a specific area of application by the participants or even by the researcher. This calls for rather specific items. However, specific items cannot be used with different populations without adaptation. This restricts the options to draw comparisons between sub-groups or different populations. A prominent example with population-specific formulated items is the original version of Maslach's Burnout Inventory (MBI; Maslach & Jackson, 1986). The MBI has been transferred from the helping professions towards a broad range of applications. This causes problems, as some items referred directly to 'my patients', which cannot be used with subordinates, teachers, or coaches. An obvious solution to the dilemma would be using global and specific questionnaires together or to use a combination of global scores and specific scores within one questionnaire. This combination within one questionnaire results in a modular-structured questionnaire (Kallus, 2016). With different areas of application, the modular RESTQs constitute a set (questionnaire family), which is documented in this manual.

A modular-structured questionnaire combines the requirement of usability and comparison in and with a broad population with the requirement of specific questions, which are needed to derive specific interventions or to give a specific diagnosis in a well-defined area of application.

Consequently, the basic module of the RESTQ consists of global items, which can be answered without modifications by a wide population. Global items will result in rather global scores. Global scores allow a normative comparison across populations and a diagnosis with reference to a global construct like stress.

In most instances, a global score like high body temperature calls for more specific investigation. This can either be achieved by additional population-specific scales or in some instances with adaptive item generation. Therefore, specific items were developed for the RESTQ in different areas of application and for different populations. For the RESTQ the specific scales are always combined with the basic module. This allows us to address specific areas (e.g., for athletes) simultaneously with a global comparison and/or reference to validation studies with different populations. In some instances, even project-specific items for project-specific scales can be added, which, for example, has been done for the RESTQ to assess the role of the recovery-stress state for variables from the organizational area of social capital (Blattner, 2006; Stelzhammer, 2008), or for student-specific topics (Brandt & Kallus, 2023).

Table 1.1 provides an overview of the psychometrically tested specific versions of the RESTQs available in this manual. For the RESTQ-Basic, psychometric data are available for different time frames (3, 7, 14 days).

Thus, different forms can be applied; deviations from three days/nights are depicted in the header. Former versions of the RESTQ-Coach used three days/nights, and for RESTQ-CA some researchers tried out a five-day/night time frame. A careful check of the correct and identical time frame of the version and the reference value is recommended, whenever using reference values.

The modular character of the RESTQ conflicts with the economic principle in test construction to use as few items as possible for measurement of individual differences (Rammstedt & John, 2007). This development led to very economic tools to assess personality for classification purposes. However, these global measures are far away from tools, which allow deriving specific interventions. The specific versions of the RESTQ offer a detailed picture of the basic non-specific recovery-stress state as well as the area-specific aspects

Table 1.1 Versions, item numbers, and standard time frame of the Recovery-Stress Questionnaires.

Standard time frame	*RESTQ-Basic* *3 days*	*RESTQ-Sport* *3 days*	*RESTQ-Coach* *7 days*	*RESTQ-Work* *7 days*	*RESTQ-CA* *7 days*	*RESTQ-Student* *7 days*
Long	48	76 (48+28)	76 (48+28)	92 (48+44)		—
Short	24	—	52 (24+28)	—		—
Modified	—	36	—	27 (7+20)	40 (32+8)	30 (12+18)

of stress and recovery. This combination provides valuable and relevant information for interventions. The basic scales provide most useful background information for any area of application, as the basic aspects of stress and recovery are assessed, and a broad range of validation studies are available for these basic areas. The RESTQ is sensitive to changes and reflects a detailed picture of change in the recovery-stress state especially with its area-specific versions. Thus, the modular structure should only be questioned or given up with very good reasons, as it is a strategic fault in most instances. One of the most probable questions in any area of application is 'and how are the values to be interpreted with reference to …'. This question can be answered with the data from the basic module, while the derivation of specific advice or intervention is supported by more specific scales. Therefore, the conception of a modular structure allows reaching partly divergent goals.

As the wording in various areas of application and in publications on the RESTQ differs, the following terminology is proposed and will be used in the manual to denote the values of scales and dimensions (Table 1.2).

Scores that combine *Overall Stress* and *Overall Recovery* as well as scores that combine *Area-specific Stress* and *Area-specific Recovery* should be avoided, as valuable information is lost and a valid interpretation of the score (see above) is almost impossible. Recovery is much broader and much more than just the absence or opposite of stress. A pattern diagnosis, which combines recovery and stress

Table 1.2 Terminology of scales and dimensions.

Score	*RESTQ-Basic*	*Area-specific versions*
Scale	Scale, e.g., *Emotional Stress*	Scale, e.g., *Self-Efficacy*
Sub-dimensions	*Social-Emotional Stress* *Performance(-related) Stress*	
Dimensions	*Overall Stress* (global score for stress)	*Sport-specific Stress* *Coach-specific Stress* *Work-specific Stress*
	Overall Recovery (global score for recovery)	*Sport-specific Recovery* *Coach-specific Recovery* *Work-specific Recovery*
Mean of basic and specific stress scores	*Total Stress**	
Mean of basic and specific recovery scores	*Total Recovery**	

Note: *An aggregation of overall and specific values might cause values, which are not easy to interpret, as the sums are not justified by structural equations modelling (SEM). SEM indicates conceptual problems with total scores, which means high scores that originate from high *Overall Stress* and middle *Area-specific Stress* values indicate not the same as a high score resulting from middle *Overall Stress* and high *Area-specific Stress* values. The same applies to recovery.

scores in a 2×2 matrix or in a 3×3 matrix (Kellmann & Kallus, this volume, Chapter 3) is much better.

The interesting area between state and trait

As already described, the RESTQ assesses the frequency of events and states in a defined time frame, which can be adapted to the area of application. Mood states and behaviour-oriented concepts are assessed by frequency scales, while current states are measured with respect to intensity in most instances. Traits are normally assessed by scaling the amount of agreement to relevant statements by Likert-type scales. The current recovery-stress state is comparable to a mood-like state (Diener & Emmons, 1984) with high short-term stability. In contrast to traits, fluctuations are to be expected in the course of weeks.

The distribution of scale values for frequency scales is dependent on the time frames. The increase in scale values with increasing time is not linear but seems to follow a logarithmic or root function. The hypothesis was derived from an analysis of the early versions of the RESTQ-Basic (Kallus, 1992, 1995), in which the time frame was not specified but termed *in the past days*, and subjects had to fill in an answer to the question *how many days were included in the past days*. The answers were multi-modal and varied from three days to four weeks. This result of multi-modal time frames of reference for different subjects led to the definition of fixed time frames in the header of the questionnaire in the construction phase of the RESTQ. In an empirical study with 131 participants and three measurement occasions (Wagner, 2000), the time of measurement as well as the time frames of the RESTQ (3, 14, and 28 days) were varied systematically (Figure 1.1).

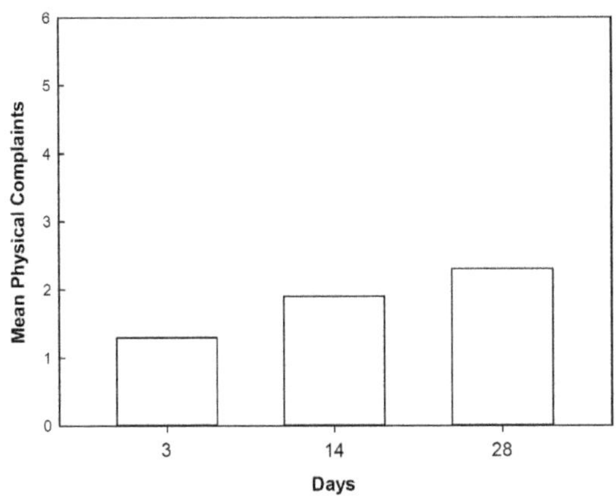

Figure 1.1 Means of the RESTQ-Basic scale *Physical Complaints* with changing time frames of reference (N=131).

Table 1.3 Consistency (Con) and specificity (Spe) of the RESTQ with different time frames from Latent State-Trait-Models (*N*=131; Wagner, 2000).

		Stress	*Recovery*
3 days	Con	.37	.41
	Spe	.14	.15
14 days	Con	.39	.48
	Spe	.13	.13
28 days	Con	.41	.51
	Spe	.07	.09

Measures were collected at four different times (baseline, 3, 14, and 28 days after baseline measurement). The analysis allowed checking how scale values and psychometric properties change with changing reference times. The results for different scales were not homogeneous. For *Physical Complaints*, the expected increase could be observed. For other scales, no change or even a decrease of means appeared (e.g., *General Well-being*). Thus, different evaluative processes seem to change the scores with changing time of reference.

Consistency and specificity were analysed in the *Latent-State-Trait Model* with LISREL, a statistical analysis program for linear structural relations (Steyer et al., 1999). The result in Table 1.3 shows increasing trait variance (consistency) and decreasing state variance (specificity) with the long-time frames of 28 days. This indicates that time frames up to 14 days are possible without changing the measurement in direction of trait scales.

Exploratory Factor Analysis showed a comparable factor structure for 3 and 14 days in this study, while the time frames of four weeks resulted in a different structure, indicating that the long-term state perspective might be assessed with a two-week time reference, while with longer time frames aspects of chronic stress (see the Trier Inventory of Chronic Stress; Schulz et al., 2004) or personality have increasing influence on the scores. For different areas of application, different default time frames were selected, as shown in Table 1.1.

Demands, strain, stress, recovery, and resources

The main purpose of the RESTQ is to assess the individual's current recovery-stress state. The logic of the recovery-stress state claims that measuring the stress-state should always take recovery into account, which implies to assess stress and recovery simultaneously. However, unequivocal concepts are neither available for stress nor for recovery. On the contrary, conflicting terminology and concepts are found in different areas of research and in different applied contexts. Therefore, the conceptual background for the terminology of the RESTQ is outlined in the following paragraphs, and arguments will be reviewed, which explain the use of the term stress and the naming of the RESTQs.

Load, task load, workload, strain, and stress

Regarding the terms and concepts of stress and recovery there is no full agreement within the scientific community. There has been a never-ending debate on the use of terms on stress (Cooper, 2000; Hancock & Desmond, 2019; Laux, 1983), and especially there is still no agreement in the different fields of application. Thus, load, strain, and stress are used with partly overlapping and interchanged meaning.

In ergonomics, the basic model from physics is used, which differentiates between load, resulting in stress in the material, and which can produce deformation of the material, which is termed strain. This basic stress-strain terminology from ergonomics is also used in the international norms on stress at work. Between 2000 and 2004, the International Organization for Standardization (ISO) published an international norm for the assessment of mental workload. Norms EN-ISO 10075 part 1 to part 3 covering the *Ergonomic principles related to mental workload* define mental stress and strain, contrary to most scientific authors, as follows:

> Mental (or psychological) stress, defined as the sum of all variables impacting on an operator, will lead to mental strain within the operator, depending on her/his resources, capacities or experience. This strain can lead to positive outcomes, e.g. warming up or learning, or to impairing effects, e.g. fatigue, monotony, reduced vigilance or satiation.
>
> (ISO 10075-1, 2004, p. 3)

As EN-ISO 10075 is based on DIN 33400, the errors in translation can easily be followed. The German word 'Belastung' (load) was translated with mental stress instead of task load, demand, or pressure. This is misleading and indicates a very inaccurate and global use of the term stress. Stress should not be used interchangeably with load, as it normally denotes a tense state of a system. Conversely, the term load should not be used to name a state of a system, as 'load' refers to external factors. The use of the term strain to refer to the state of a person is very popular in British Work and Organizational Psychology (Cooper, 2000). In human factors-oriented textbooks, task load is used to characterize the impacting variables, and workload is used as a term for the resulting state in the operator (Hancock & Desmond, 2019; Hilburn & Jorna, 2019; Wickens, 2008). In Work and Organizational Psychology, 'stress' is one form of inadequate workload (Hacker & Sachse, 2014).

Implicitly or explicitly, the term stress is used to indicate a process, which is caused by a load or demand beyond the level of normal functioning. Janke and Wolffgramm (1995) as well as Janke and Erdmann (2002) explained that stress refers to a state of the organism, which is beyond homeostatically regulated normal functioning. Thus, stress in bio-psychological concepts encompasses a more tense state than just strain. While strain in physics is automatically set back, when the load is removed, stress is defined as a more prolonged process or state, due to long-term effects of intense stressors or due to enduring or intermittent stressors. Stress in the bio-psychological sense starts beyond the threshold of automatic recovery. This view is in accordance with the basic mechanical stress models. Three different perspectives justify using the term stress in recovery-stress states to characterize the state of the individual by the RESTQ. This seems to be worthwhile as some authors use the term strain to characterize the reaction of the individual even to highly demanding conditions and use the term stress either to denote the demand/load or the overall process (Cooper, 2000).

First, the term stress in recovery-stress state is in accordance with the process definition of stress (i.e., stress in the wording of Cooper, 2000), as the recovery-stress approach focuses on the process, and the items are not just symptoms but drawn from different process perspectives. Therefore, stress is the adequate term for the RESTQ. However, Cooper uses the term strain in addition, which is possible for low demands in the light of the mechanical view of stress and strain in material sciences (Callister & Rethwisch, 2009).

From material sciences, an integral framework for the stress-strain terminology can be derived for the use in bio-psychological/clinical stress research, sport psychology, and most fields of work and organizational psychology.

As already mentioned, the term stress is adopted from physics where stress (German 'Spannung') is basically introduced in mechanics, e.g., in Hook's Law (Mayr, 2012) or Boyle Mariotte's Law (Kuchling, 2010). In Hook's Law load acts on an object (spring) and causes a change in shape (elongation) which is termed strain. This change in shape is accompanied by an energetic change within the spring: stress. Stress (the energy) will cause the spring to switch back to its basic length when the load is removed. Thus, stress is a force stored in the material. In this model, it is not stress which causes strain, but both strain (elongation) and stress (state of the object) are caused by the load. When the load is removed, the spring returns to its original shape if the elastic limit (stress limit) has not been reached. Beyond the stress point, a non-reversible deformation takes place. In physics, strain is the change in shape of the spring referenced to its original length. Stress results from the load referenced to the elasticity or the surface.

The critical load for the spring is the point which goes beyond elasticity and causes a change in the structure of the spring, which is not set back, when the load is removed. Beyond the set point, the spring is either deformed or broken. This point is of central importance, when transferring the analogy to biological sciences (e.g., concept of training, overreaching, overtraining, see Meeusen & De Pauw, 2022; Meeusen et al., 2013). Thus, the state of tension should be referred to as stress state, while the change of shape is strain. Most interesting is, whether full recovery is to be expected when the load is removed, or whether the load was too large and goes beyond the stress point. Before reaching the critical load, strain and stress are directly proportional and thus, the terms can be used interchangeably. Beyond this point, stress is the crucial variable, and strain and stress are no more interchangeable because their direct proportional relation is restricted to the strain below the proportionality limit. Note that strain is defined

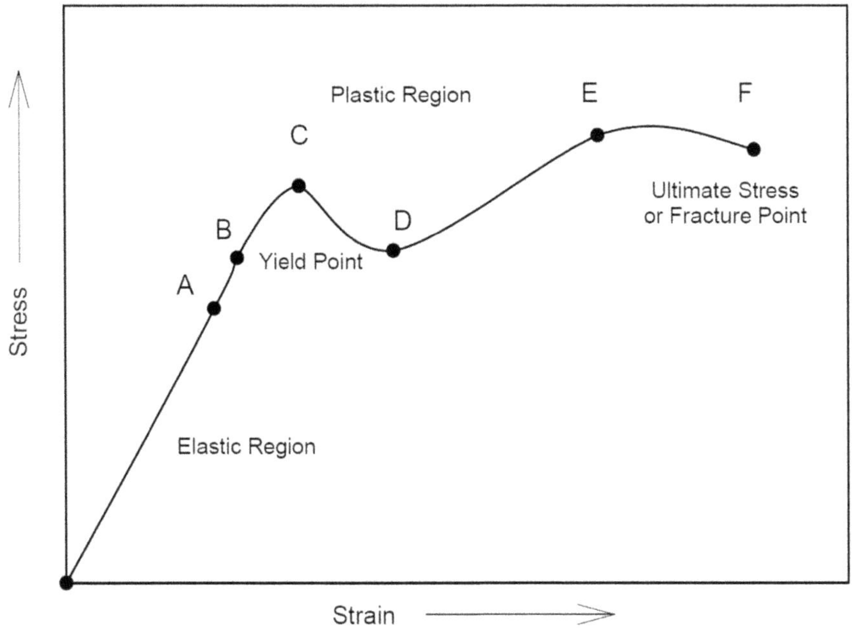

Figure 1.2 Strain-stress diagram for materials like metals.

as a change in length of the spring referenced to the initial length, and stress is an energetic term of pressure with reference to basic pressure, i.e., the energetic state of the spring.

Figure 1.2 shows a strain-stress diagram which is drawn from material sciences. It describes the changes in a material (e.g., a spring) with increasing load. In the elastic region, stress and strain describe the situation interchangeably due to their direct proportionality according to Hook's law. Thus, in the elastic region the confusion of the terms 'stress' and 'strain' is just a look at the independent variable strain or the dependent variable stress, which both are proportional to the load. In the elastic region, full recovery takes place when the load is removed. Beyond the elasticity limit or yield point (B), the proportionality vanishes and non-recoverable change in the material occurs (C) with increasing load. This area is called the plastic region. Between points C and D different forms of deformation occur until the final point F is reached. Stress does not substantially increase beyond point E because increases in load are fully transformed into changes in the material.

Finally, with additional load beyond point E the material might break. This point is termed stress or fracture point in material sciences. The simple analogy to mechanics is most valuable for terminological clarification. One could extend the analogy a bit, as the effect of a load might change, when material fatigue develops. In addition, the process of elongation and recovery does not follow the same dynamic in time but results in a hysteresis process. The analogy shows already that stress process and recovery process are much more different than one would expect at a first glance. Characteristics in the course of time differ markedly even in mechanical systems.

Differences between mechanics and biological systems are multifold and are most relevant in the plastic region and beyond the stress point. The damaged mechanical system must be repaired or replaced while biological systems have the capacity for regeneration, repair, and adaptation. The first part of the plastic region parallels the state of acute stress in biological systems, in which removal of the load is still directly answered by removal of strain and stress. The point, when the spring deforms finally and breaks might be the limit of the analogy because complex adaptation, coping, recovery as well as short-term or long-term damage and impairment can occur in biological systems under stress. The only point which might cause debate is that strain in accordance with applied physics is close to load and visible on the material, while stress is an energetic state. This state, however, is not the cause of strain.

A third argument to use the term stress to characterize the resulting dynamic state of the individual stems from the terminology in Biological Psychology. Following the research of Selye (1936), the term load is replaced by the term stressor.

The term stress describes the state of the organisms. Conditions that cause stress are termed stressors in Selye's terms. This biopsychological view on stress is also shared with Health Psychology and in Clinical Psychology. Modern psychological concepts of stress, which follow a bio-psychological approach and/or system view, also use the term stress for a resulting state of an organism characterized by homeostatic (or allostatic) dysregulation, which is caused by stressors or inadequate demands. This terminology will be used throughout the manual.

The above analogy to physics allows clarifying the use of the term stress. However, the 'stress state' of the individual is far different from a passive energetic state but should be viewed as a highly dynamic transactional process, which allows the individual to cope with demands and the own stress reaction and finally to recover and adapt the taxed or damaged resources.

Stress and allostatic 'load'

Whether demands act as stressors depends on appraisal processes in most instances (Lazarus, 1966, 1999). Depending on the relation between coping capacity and demand, the situation is classified as not relevant for coping, or either as challenge or as threat (Lazarus & Launier, 1978; McGrath, 1981). Threat will cause a stress state which can be defined as a state of disbalance of the organism, which is close to or beyond the 'stress point', i.e., beyond the 'elasticity' or in other words beyond the automatically working recovery processes of the individual.

Hobfoll (1989) states that threats should be specified and proposes that threatening the persons' subjective or objective resources is the main factor to provoke a stress response. McEwen's (1998) contributions to bio-psychological stress research increase the confusion in terminology in his attempt to avoid the negative connotations of the term stress. He introduced the concept of allostatic load, which denotes a state of the organism like the stress state in bio-psychological models following Selye's (1936, 1981) concept. Allostatic 'load' is used as a term to denote chronic stress as it can result in vulnerability, dysfunction, and disease, if it is prolonged and no opportunities for adaptation and/or recovery are given. In this manual, stress is used as a global term addressing a dynamic state of the organism, which is characterized by an acute or chronic functional unbalance due to threats, functional exhaustion, or loss of meaningful resources. As long as acute stress has no risk of becoming chronic, it can be coped with rather effectively by the organism. In other words, if full recovery is easy to achieve, there is no enhanced risk of damaged resources.

The RESTQ is based on a bio-psycho-social approach. Stress in Biological Psychology, Clinical Psychology, and Health Psychology is used as a concept to explain stress-health-illness relationships. Physiological and biochemical pathways of these relationships could be detected in psychophysiological, neuroendocrine, neuro-immunological, and metabolic systems in the past decades. These biological pathways allow tracking the ways in which stressful encounters lead from adaptation and maladaptation to pathophysiological effects (Hellhammer et al., 2010; Kubo et al., 2024; Picard et al., 2014) and disease. The biopsychological stress approach can be viewed as the central theoretical basis for the development of the basic form of the RESTQ. In addition, this research is of paramount importance for Work Psychology and other fields of Psychology, together with Biology, Sociology, and Neuroscience. The new results on stress-health pathways along with classical results on stress and coping as well as stress and performance serve as background to interpret the results from the stress-related scales of the RESTQ. Stress and recovery are basic bio-psychological processes, which affect the whole organism on different functional levels: physiological, psychological, and social (Janke & Wolffgramm, 1995).

Figure 1.3 outlines the concept of the recovery-stress balance. The model integrates classical cognitive stress concepts (Lazarus, 1966) with an action-oriented approach: the 'redefinition' of an objective task to a subjective task. This process is well known in Work Psychology and overlaps with cognitive appraisals in psychological stress concepts. The model can easily be extended to reactions in critical situations. In this instance, the 'redefinition' is a perceptual appraisal process (primary and secondary appraisal; Lazarus & Launier, 1978).

The model includes mediators (left side) and moderators (right side) and implicitly the representation of time (Janke, 1976). The bases are resources which demonstrate the importance of recovery (Kallus, 1995). Recovery should be triggered by appropriate task execution (mastering) as well as by the stress process itself (like fatigue triggers sleep). However, the complex systemic interactions of social, cognitive, emotional, and motivational aspects are not represented explicitly. In addition, it must be pointed out that from research on stress and anxiety, different psycho-physiological pathways have been discovered, which moderate or mediate the stress-resources-health relationships. Hopefully, research on recovery processes will add further and new evidence to this area.

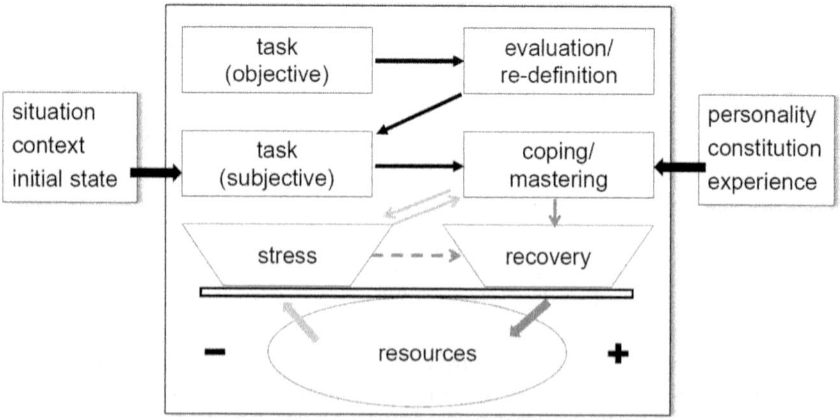

Figure 1.3 Stress process with recovery loop.

Chronic stress, which depletes resources, has a high potential of pathogenesis (Hellhammer et al., 2010). While acute stress is primarily mediated by the hypothalamus-adrenomedullar system (Henry & Stephens, 1977), effects of chronic stress are mediated primarily by the hypothalamus-pituitary-adrenocortical system. Changes in cortisol (the most prominent hormone of the adrenal cortex) affect immune function, inflammatory processes, and metabolism. The metabolic effects of cortisol allow understanding of pathophysiological mechanisms in metabolism, which can be tracked down to the level of intracellular biochemical processes including ribonucleic acid processes. However, system-specific damages might also be of high relevance and need more biopsychological foundation as the data on Karoshi (Kubo et al., 2024) suggest. However, epidemiologic data need experimental and longitudinal data as support.

Stress, resources, and coping

The potential of recovery from stress and exhaustion is the most important feature of biological systems (Blasche, 2020). Recovery as well as stress is a process. The question in what area recovery is needed leads to the resources, which have been taxed, used, or lost during demanding periods. Finally, the relation between recovery and 'the ability to recover readily' or 'the ability to properly adapt to stress and adversity' and adaptation or resilience needs more attention in the future. Implicitly or explicitly, authors agree on the fact that stress is linked to resources. Resources were introduced explicitly into the field of stress research by Schönpflug (1983, 1987). The economic distinction between consumptive and permanent resources can help to understand the different facets of recovery. Acute stress affects consumptive resources in the first instance as the stress response mobilizes and utilizes our resources to allow an effective coping or adaptation. Cannon (1932) used the metaphor of a 'fight-or-flight' response. Chronic stress is more prone to have negative effects on permanent resources. In addition, permanent resources are at stake and can be taxed or hurt even in acute stress situations.

Stress can come up when resources are affected beyond their functional fluctuations. This situation can be threatening for the individual. The concept of threat is key to understanding the role of the appraisal process in the classical stress conception of Lazarus (1966, 1999). According to his conception, stress originates from an appraisal that demands are relevant for the person, and individual resources might not be sufficient to meet the demands. Thus, implicitly the threat of resources is relevant in the *Lazarus Model* of *Stress and Coping*. Schönpflug (1983, 1987) was one of the first psychologists, who highlighted the relevance of resources for stress explicitly. He pointed out that consumptive and permanent resources are taxed during stress. While consumptive resources can be recovered easily, wear and tear or damage on permanent resources needs repair or regeneration, which implies a demand for longer time intervals and effort to recover. Also, in the 1980s, Hobfoll (1989) explicitly addressed the importance of resources for the understanding of stress. *Hobfoll's Model* of *Conservation of Resources* states that threat of resources causes (anticipatory) stress, and that acute stress is always associated with a loss or damage of resources. Hobfoll integrates research on anxiety in his concepts and criticizes the tautological problem in demand-resource balance models. He proposes a functional distinction of resources into object resources like a home, conditions like living with someone, personal characteristics like sense of coherence and energies, which include time, money, and knowledge. Knowledge, however, seems rather arbitrary as energy. Social support is addressed separately as it does not fit in his classification. Hobfoll's explicit classification of resources differs from the implicit classification of resources in the RESTQ, which includes only the area of personal resources and uses the basic distinction into physical, psychic, and social resources, while environmental, economic, cultural, and other external resources are only considered selectively in specific modules of the RESTQ.

The RESTQ considers resources primarily as the basis, while stress and recovery are functional processes which act on and with resources. Schönpflug's (1983, 1987) distinction of permanent and consumptive resources is helpful for deriving ways to optimize the recovery of resources based on a RESTQ profile. Resources can be mobilized and used by the individual. The physiology of the human lung allows understanding the distinction between working capacity and reserve capacity, which can well be transferred to consumptive resources. In the range of working capacity, recovery is easy or takes place even automatically (comparable to the elastic region of an elastic material). Especially for more permanent resources, additional effort can make resources from the area of reserve capacities available, comparable to the reserve capacity in our respiratory system. In addition, some resources can be enlarged by training and learning processes (like the oxygen capacity of the blood). Excessive demands are sometimes covered by adaptive systems like the anaerobic metabolism in muscles. The more the resources are taxed, the more recovery and regeneration are necessary. In some instances, even organismic repair processes have to be initiated, to make the resources available again.

Recovery

Recovery from these adaptive processes can differ markedly from standard recovery and might include maintenance and repair mechanisms, which follow different timelines. The stress response itself can be viewed as an adaptive process to excessive demands, which tax our resources beyond the homeostatically regulated capacities and/or beyond our physical, psychic, social, or economic limits.

Additional adaptive responses often fall back on permanent resources, which can result in long-term effects on physiological systems and health – either in the form of adaptation or damage. Adaptation is often a recovery process with additional overcompensation of the preceding loss in resources.

The RESTQ in its original form implicitly used the concept of resources to explain the balance of recovery and stress. Recovery and stress are in balance, when the depleted resources during stress episodes are adequately restored in the recovery phases. This is reflected in full functional capacity and (dynamic) homeostatic state of the individual. The interplay of recovery and stress, tension and relaxation, activity and rest, work and leisure, etc., constitutes a basic biological phenomenon. However, recovery from stress is rarely addressed explicitly and systematically in stress conceptions and theories. Often simple physical metaphors imply that recovery from stress is a simple passive process, which takes place more or less automatically. Thus, Frankenhaeuser (1971) uses the metaphor of 'unwinding', Picard et al. (2014) refers to 'bouncing back' and Rau (2006) uses the term 'reset process' or 'set back process'. These terms suggest that recovery is a more or less passive mechanical process, when the demand is removed or the stress ends. This is by far a wrong model as a look at concepts illustrates, such as on physical training, on post-stress research, or at the basic biological recovery process 'sleep' (Kullik & Kiel, 2024; Walsh et al., 2021). Taking a glance at the broad variety of terms for recovery like rest, relaxation, recreation, restoring, restoration, regeneration, recuperation, repose, revival, rebounce, rebound, rehabilitation, repair, reconditioning, reinstatement, restock, refill, refuel, redress, demanding reparation, recompose, amend, apologize, excuse, fill-up, comeback, or maintenance shows that different processes on different levels with different time frames should be addressed when talking about recovery.

Regeneration in Sport Psychology stresses the facet of active components in regeneration as a motivated and controlled action, which reinstates full performance capacity of the athlete (Kellmann & Beckmann, 2022; Kellmann et al., 2018). Recovery in the narrower sense of the word refers primarily to the restoration of consumptive resources on the physical and psychological level. But even social, economic, cultural, and environmental resources can recover – like fresh air in the office. Hobfoll's (1989) view on resources focusses on resource replacement (like replacing a lost job) and skips the options of recovery in bio-psycho-social systems. In addition, active restoration of depleted resources as well as enabling physiological recovery processes must be considered.

Recovery is used as a global term, which encompasses not only simple recovery processes in an exponential way like the recovery of muscular performance capacity after muscular exhaustion. Fatigue already shows that recovery may take considerable time, and even muscular strength is impaired after extensive load due to muscle soreness. Therefore, recovery research might structure the field with respect to different recovery functions, describing the relations between recovery and repair, looking at relations of speed of recovery with psychological and physical fitness, and clarifying the relation of recovery and grooming, which could be considered as a kind of 'maintenance' process.

In a publication by Kallus and Kellmann (2000), the basic features of recovery (based on Kallus, 1995) were listed, which still are to be considered (Table 1.4). The characteristics of recovery show that recovery is much more than eliminating fatigue or restarting the system. Only differentiated and longitudinally oriented observations can reflect the complex individual recovery process. Based on former approaches to define recovery (Kallus, 1992; Kellmann & Kallus, 2001), a definition which includes the aspect of resources is proposed: Recovery is an inter- and intraindividual multilevel (e.g., psychological, physiological, social) process in time for the re-establishment of personal resources and their full functional capacity. Recovery includes a broad range of physiological processes like sleep, motivated behaviour (like eating and drinking) and goal-oriented components (like relaxation or meeting friends).

Furthermore, Kellmann (2002) distinguishes between passive, active, and pro-active approaches to recovery. Passive methods may range from the application of external methods (e.g., massage) to implementing a state of rest

Table 1.4 Characteristics of recovery according to Kallus and Kellmann (2000, p. 210).

- Recovery is a process in time.
- Recovery is related to the type of and duration of stress.
- Recovery depends on a reduction of, a change of, or a break from stress.
- Recovery is individually specific and depends on individual appraisal.
- Recovery ends when a psychophysical state of restored efficiency and homeostatic balance is reached.
- Recovery includes purposeful action (active recovery), as well as automated psychological and biological processes restoring the initial state (passive recovery).
- Recovery can be described on various levels (e.g., physiological level, psychological level, social level, socio-cultural level, environmental level).
- Recovery processes can be displayed in various organismic subsystems.
- Various sub-processes of recovery can be dissociated.
- Recovery is closely tied to boundary conditions (e.g., sleep, social contact, etc.).

Source: Reprinted by permission from K. W. Kallus, and M. Kellmann, "Burnout in Athletes and Coaches," in *Emotions in Sport*, edited by Y.L. Hanin (Champaign, IL: Human Kinetics, 2000), 210.

characterized by inactivity. Active recovery (e.g., cooldown jogging) involves mainly physical activities aimed at compensating the metabolic responses of physical fatigue. Pro-active recovery (e.g., social activities) implies a high level of self-determination by choosing activities customized to individual needs and preferences (Kellmann & Beckmann, 2022). Recovery is used as a superordinate concept, which also includes the recreation of lost resources. In many instances, full recovery (e.g., from illness like COVID) is not possible without long-term regeneration of physical, psychic, and social resources.

Hobfoll (1989) does not address the dynamics of recovery. Instead, he claims that people will search to replace lost resources as soon as possible. The processes of coping with stress and the replacement of lost resources are not included in the recovery concept. Coping with stress is often a prerequisite for effective recovery. Replacement of resources is necessary when recovery is no more possible. Recovery, however, often includes optimization of situational conditions, which allow to build up and to refill personal resources.

The conceptual symmetry between stress and recovery structured the initial item pool for the basic RESTQ but could not be maintained during test construction as stress and recovery constitute different functional systems with different characteristics, which results in different covariance matrixes of stress and recovery facets. Note that the hypothalamic pituitary adrenal (HPA) axis as a stress system has no counterpart in the recovery area.

Stress and recovery

Acute stress results in chronic stress if coping and recovery are not possible or not successful. Thus, chronic stress results from stress without adequate recovery.

Chronic stress might either result from long-term stress without adequate recovery or adaptation or from acute high-intensity stress, which can lead to prolonged stress reactions up to post-traumatic stress disorders. Thus, coping and recovery play a central role in the distinction of 'normal' demands, acute bio-psycho-social stress and chronic stress, which is characterized by changes in the HPA-axis, immune function, and maybe metabolic dysregulation. This view stresses the central role of recovery to define chronic stress, which has by far received less interest than the stress process itself. One of the links between stress and recovery is coping with stress. Effective coping will allow adequate recovery, while ineffective coping will impair recovery, and by this the acute stress response turns into a prolonged one, which might be a first step to become chronic. But even with inadequate coping strategies, certain processes of recovery will take place, especially basic physiological recovery processes will start after changes in the situation (e.g., finishing work or going to sleep). In some instances, even these basic recovery processes will suffer from stress. This can tax the resources beyond their limits. As a conclusion, stress and recovery must be balanced, which might depend on functional coping.

The recovery-stress balance

Resources are used and taxed during stress and must be either re-established or even be adapted to the current demands. The problem of underrecovery (Kellmann, 2002; Kellmann et al., 2018, 2023; Kellmann & Beckmann, 2022) is a topic in Sport Psychology, but is hardly addressed in stress research or in Work- and Organizational Psychology (Kuntz, 2024; Kubo et al., 2024). A disbalance manifests itself in stress symptoms in the case of high stress and underrecovery. However, demands can be too low and the disbalance can be due to a low stress/low recovery-state. A very basic and generic approach to reflect the recovery-stress balance is to delineate a 2×2 matrix for stress and recovery.

The typology in Table 1.5 simplifies the situation. Simultaneous median splits for *Overall Stress* and *Overall Recovery* scores normally result in a distribution of 2/3 of the subjects in the main diagonals (*high stress – low recovery, low stress – high recovery*) and 1/3 of the subjects in the secondary diagonal, at least for large samples. Thus, the patterns *high stress – high recovery* and *low stress – low recovery* occur each in about 1/6th of the population (Kellmann & Kallus, this volume, Chapter 3).

The concept of the recovery-stress balance directs our attention to the fact that life without activity is a no go. Selye (1981) emphasized the view that humans need some basic stress (at least some activities) for life, and our biological rhythms reflect the principles of activity-rest cycles.

Sleep as one of the basic processes in the recovery domain occurs even after lazy days and during our holidays. Thus, recovery is a basic element of biological life, which is organized in biological rhythms, one of which is the circadian sleep-wake-cycle. Even during sleep and while being awake during the day, humans experience bio-psycho-social changes in activity, our ultradian rhythms like Kleitman's (1969) *Basic Rest Activity Cycle*. Therefore, recovery encompasses a broad range of processes, with a set of biologically based rhythms. Life, like a swing, needs continuous switches between acceleration and deceleration, activation and deactivation, as well as stress and recovery. In the case of intelligent manipulation, growth can be introduced, in the case of passivity, the 'swing' tends to lose dynamic.

Note that recovery activities and processes are not restricted to the basic biological and 'natural' cycles. Our social life, our culture, and our health system provide a wide range of options to restore, recover, regenerate, and repair our resources. One of the most effective activities for occupational stress is physical activity and sports.

Table 1.5 Prototypical recovery-stress patterns.

	Stress low	**Stress high**
Recovery low	Inactivity/depression	Chronic stress/risk of burnout
Recovery high	Vacancies/dolce vita	Top performance

The parallel between stress and energy brings an interesting view on the effects of sports on the recovery-stress balance, as sport allows spending surplus energy, which has been accumulated due to stress states. With increasing stress, the individual is more activated, and an increasing energy level can be measured especially in psychophysiological measures. A simple picture of this increased energy level can be drawn from the atom model. In the *Bohr-Sommerfeld Model* (Kragh, 2012) on atomic structure, electrons circle round the 'nucleus' on a defined shell. The atom is in a basic state if electrons are on the closest shells. This state can be viewed as the recovered state. In the case of increasing energy, the electrons jump on more distant shells, and the atom is in a different functional state with increased reactivity. This parallels with the increased metabolic (oxidative) stress in persons under chronic stress and/or with an upregulated recovery-stress balance (Kraxner, 2002). Switching back to lower shells is a kind of recovery process. For the atom, it is accompanied by photon emission. Thus, energy-consuming activities ('active recovery') might have a special recovery potential (Kellmann et al., 2018).

Kellmann (2002) has proposed a model describing the interrelation between stress states and recovery demands (Figure 1.4). The basic assumption is that with increasing stress, increased recovery is necessary. Limited resources (e.g., time) initiate a vicious cycle: under increased stress and the inability to meet increased recovery demands, the athlete experiences more stress. Athletes may be stressed to the point where they fail to find time to recover adequately or to consider better ways of coping with the situation.

In this model, the simplest case is a symmetrical increase in stress and recovery demands: the two axes drift apart with elevated stress levels ('scissors' function). With intermediate levels of stress, one can find an area of optimal performance and thus an area of adequate recovery (continuous arrows in Figure 1.4). Beyond this point, one cannot meet recovery demands without additional recovery activities. Stress will accumulate, and without intervention, burnout or overtraining symptoms will likely develop. The state of balanced stress and recovery is related to optimal performance and perhaps to the performance-related bio-psycho-social states and their emotional correlations within the *Individual Zones of Optimal Functioning* (IZOF) model (Hanin, 2000).

In a state of adequate recovery, the individual can react appropriately and cope successfully with stress without additional recovery activities. Lack of recovery can trigger a process that brings on a state of elevated stress. As increasing stress limits the possibility of recovery, the athlete must be given special opportunities for recovery to reestablish an optimal level of performance (Kallus & Kellmann, 2000; Kellmann, 2002; Kellmann et al., 2018; Kellmann & Beckmann, 2022, 2024). In summary, the model suggests that it is not bad to be high on stress as long as the individual knows how to recover optimally.

Health and performance capacities, as part of modern health definitions, are the meta-resources, which are of central importance to understand why the recovery-stress balance is of paramount importance for the individual. Performance

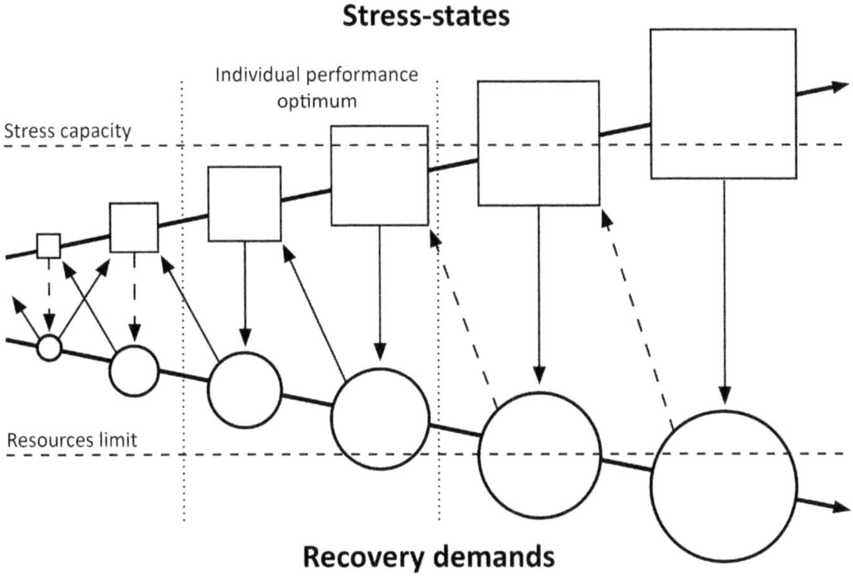

Figure 1.4 The *Scissors-Model* of the interrelation of stress-states, and recovery demands. *Source:* Reprinted by permission from K. W. Kallus, and M. Kellmann, "Burnout in Athletes and Coaches," in Emotions in Sport, edited by Y.L. Hanin (Champaign, IL: Human Kinetics, 2000), 212.

capacity and health-related variables turned out to be the most interesting areas of application and validation for the recovery-stress state, which is reflected by the RESTQ.

Exploratory analysis and linear structural modelling

Exploratory analysis and linear structural modelling will be performed for most of the RESTQ versions throughout the manual. Some considerations are addressed in the following section.

Exploratory Factor Analysis

Exploratory Factor Analysis has become very popular in test construction. Areas of application are as follows: 1) statistical development of scales, 2) empirical support of a theoretical item structure, and 3) empirical support of scale structure (dimensional structure), which is an important part in construct validation.

A methodological problem of item factor analysis is due to the sometimes very low item reliability. This is the basic reason why items are combined to scales in *Classical Test Theory*. Scale reliabilities can be estimated by methods from *Classical or Probabilistic Test Theory* (Bühner, 2010; Kallus, 2016; Lord & Novick,

1968). For scales with low reliability, the communalities cannot be assumed to be $h^2 = 1$ and have to be estimated (e.g., by the squared multiple correlation of items) which has already been discussed in detail by Cattell (1952). Therefore, no Principal Component Analysis but Principal Axis Method must be used, and the number of factors cannot be determined by Kaiser's logic of an Eigenvalue of 1. Instead, the Scree Test can be used – but it yields no exact measure of the number of factors. In addition, the applicability of factor analysis must be checked (Bühner, 2010), while large samples of subjects and a representative set of items must be developed. This could be omitted for the RESTQ, as stress research allowed deriving the central areas from a theoretical basis.

Exploratory Factor Analysis is only reported for scales or dimensions in this manual. For the RESTQ the different facets of stress and recovery could be derived from work on stress and the multilevel approach in stress theory. This was transferred to the area of recovery. The method of linear structural equation modelling (SEM) was used in the development and validation of the RESTQ. In this approach, the structural model and the measurement model are distinguished (Anderson & Gerbing, 1988). Measurement models were computed for each scale and for each dimension of the RESTQ. For the structural models, scales were used as the basic variables (manifest variables) subsequently.

Evaluation of model fit in Linear Structural Models

Linear Structural Models (SEM) are evaluated by statistics of model fit. For model fit, the following criteria were used: Chi-square statistics (χ^2) are calculated routinely to evaluate the fit of SEM. As the χ^2-statistic is very sensitive to sample size, large samples will most likely show a significant result, indicating almost always that the empirically found model is significantly different from the hypothetical model. To prevent a possible misinterpretation, it is common to interpret fit indices instead of the χ^2 (Byrne, 2001). The fit indices, which are calculated as standard and the critical values for evaluation of the model fit are given in Table 1.6.

However, as both GFI and AGFI tend to be sensitive to sample size, it is suggested to have higher cut-offs (GFI > .95; AGFI > .90; Hooper et al., 2008). The CFI should be greater than .95 (Beauducel & Wittmann, 2005) and the RMSEA should be lower than .08 or .06 to indicate a good or very good model fit (Hu & Bentler, 1999). For the measurement models, an acceptable fit is assumed as long as three out of four fit indices exceed the above-mentioned limits.

AMOS provides modification indices to improve model fit (Byrne, 2001). These additional correlations were accepted in cases where theoretical arguments could be provided. They will be commented in the text. For measurement models, correlated residuals (errors of measurement) were accepted if item content or formal item characteristics justify this correlation. This is, of course, a violation of the assumptions of *Classical Test Theory* – but it indicates characteristics of the scales.

Table 1.6 Fit indices to evaluate the model fit in structural equation modelling.

Name	*Short*	*Critical value*	*References*
Goodness of Fit Index	GFI	0.90	Schermelleh-Engel and Moosbrugger (2003)
Adjusted Goodness of Fit Index	AGFI	0.85	Schermelleh-Engel and Moosbrugger (2003)
Comparative Fit Index	CFI	0.95	Beauducel and Wittmann (2005)
Root Mean Square Error of Approximation	RMSEA	0.08	Hu and Bentler (1999)

Areas of application and research with high relevance of the recovery-stress balance

The large field of regeneration from injury and sickness in top athletes or from injury and sickness in the normal population including elderly received a lot of interest due to the problem of incomplete recovery as in long-term COVID or burnout or increasing allergy reactions (Altfeld & Kellmann, 2015; Haunhorst et al., 2023a, 2023b). However, common concepts like the recovery-stress state are sparse.

Research on posttraumatic stress disorders or methods of prevention like critical incident stress management (Mitchell, 2020) received attention for research on rescue personnel and disaster helpers, but detailed knowledge of the impact of the recovery-stress state is still sparse. Due to the validity studies with the RESTQ, it can be inferred from the recovery-stress state to long-term risk factors for health and active life. In addition, a sound body of data is necessary to prepare helpers and professionals for upcoming disasters, as disasters will further increase exponentially.

The problem of switching off after work or within different shift blocks in unfavourable conditions is one of the areas of research in the group of Sonnentag (e.g., Sonnentag & Niessen, 2020).This should receive more systematic research. The RESTQ family is on its way to become a valuable research tool and diagnostic instrument. It should be used for the benefit of researchers, athletes, and people at risk.

References

Altfeld, S., & Kellmann, M. (2015). Are German coaches highly exhausted? A study of differences in personal and environmental factors in relation to emotional exhaustion. *International Journal of Sports Science and Coaching, 10*(4), 637–654.

Anderson, J. C., & Gerbing, D. W. (1988). Structural equation modeling in practice: A review and recommended two-step approach. *Psychological Bulletin, 103*(3), 411–423.

Beauducel, A., & Wittmann, W. W. (2005). Simulation study on fit indexes in CEA based on data with slightly distorted simple structure. *Structural Equation Modeling, 12*, 41–75.

Blasche, G. (2020). *Erholung 4.0* [Recovery 4.0]. Facultas.

Blattner, A. (2006). *Der Zusammenhang psychologischer Variablen des Erholungs-Beanspruchungs-Zustands mit Fehlzeiten und körperlichen Beschwerden* [The relationship between psychological variables of the recovery-stress state and physical complaints; Unpublished diploma thesis]. University of Graz, Austria.

Brandt, J., & Kallus, K. W. (2023). Messung von Stress im Studium. Der Erholungs-Belastungs-Fragebogen für das Studium (EBF-Student) [Measuring student stress. The Recovery-Stress Questionnaire for Students (RESTQ-Student)]. *Diagnostica, 69*(3), 111–120.

Bühner, M. (2010). *Einführung in die Test- und Fragebogenkonstruktion* [Introduction into test- and questionnaire construction]. Pearson Studium.

Byrne, B. M. (2001). *Structural equation modeling with AMOS. Basic concepts, applications, and programming*. Erlbaum.

Callister, W. D., & Rethwisch, D. G. (2009). *Materials science and engineering: An introduction*. John Wiley and Sons.

Cannon, W. B. (1932). *The wisdom of the body*. Norton.

Cattell, R. B. (1952). *Factor analysis*. Harper.

Cooper, C. L. (Ed.). (2000). *Theories of stress*. Oxford University Press.

Diener, E., & Emmons, R. A. (1984). The independence of positive and negative affect. *Journal of Personality and Social Psychology, 47*, 1105–1117.

Frankenhaeuser, M. (1971). Behavior and circulating catecholamines. *Brain Research, 31*, 241–262.

Hacker, W., & Sachse, P. (2014). *Allgemeine Arbeitspsychologie. Psychische Regulation von Tätigkeiten* [General work psychology. The psychological regulation of action]. Hogrefe.

Hancock, P. A., & Desmond, P. A. (2019). *Stress, workload and fatigue*. Routledge.

Hanin, Y. L. (2000). Individual Zones of Optimal Functioning (IZOF) model: Emotion-performance relationships in sport. In Y. L. Hanin (Ed.), *Emotions in sport* (pp. 65–89). Human Kinetics.

Haunhorst, S., Bloch, W., & Puta, C. (2023a). Recovery and the immune system. In M. Kellmann, S. Jakowski, & J. Beckmann (Eds.), *The importance of recovery for physical and mental health: Negotiating the effects of underrecovery* (pp. 125–140). Routledge.

Haunhorst, S., Bloch, W., & Puta, C. (2023b). Impact of long COVID on recovery in sport and exercise. In M. Kellmann, S. Jakowski, & J. Beckmann (Eds.), *The importance of recovery for physical and mental health: Negotiating the effects of underrecovery* (pp. 203–222). Routledge.

Hellhammer, D. H., Stone, A. A., Hellhammer, J., & Broderick, J. (2010). Measuring stress. In G. F. Koob, M. Le Moal, & R. F. Thompson (Eds.), *Encyclopedia of behavioral neuroscience* (pp. 186–191). Academic Press.

Henry, J. P., & Stephens, P. M. (1977). *Stress, health, and the social environment. A sociobiological approach to medicine*. Springer.

Hilburn, B., & Jorna, P. (2019). Workload and air traffic control. In P. A. Hancock & P. A. Desmond (Eds.), *Stress, workload and fatigue: Theory, research and practice* (pp. 384–394). Routledge.

Hobfoll, S. E. (1989). Conservation of resources: A new attempt at conceptualizing stress. *American Psychologist, 44*(3), 513–524.

Hooper, D., Coughlan, J., & Mullen, M. R. (2008). Structural equation modelling: Guidelines for determining model fit. *The Electronic Journal of Business Research Methods, 6*(1), 53–60.

Hu, L., & Bentler, P. M. (1999). Cutoff criteria for fit indexes in covariance structure analysis: Conventional criteria versus new alternatives. *Structural Equation Modeling, 6*, 1–55.

International Organisation for Standardization. (ISO). (2004). *ISO 10075-3. Ergonomic principles related to mental workload part 3: Principles and requirements concerning methods for measuring and assessing mental workload.* Retrieved April 22, 2024 from https://www.iso.org/standard/27571.html

Janke, W. (1976). Psychophysische Grundlagen des Verhaltens [Psychophysic fundamentals of behaviour]. In M. von Kerekjarto (Ed.), *Medizinische Psychologie* (pp. 1–101). Springer.

Janke, W., & Erdmann, G. (2002). *SVF-78. Eine Kurzform des Stressverarbeitungsfragebogens SVF-120* [SVF-78. A shortened version of the German Coping Questionnaire SVF-120]. Hogrefe.

Janke, W., & Wolffgramm, J. (1995). Biopsychologie von Streß und emotionalen Reaktionen: Ansätze interdisziplinärer Kooperation von Psychologie, Biologie und Medizin [Biopsychology of stress and emotional reactions: Starting points of an interdisciplinary cooperation of psychology, biology, and medicine]. In G. Debus, G. Erdmann, & K. W. Kallus (Eds.), *Biospsychologie von Streß und emotionalen Reaktionen* (pp. 293–349). Hogrefe.

Kallus, K. W. (1992). *Beanspruchung und Ausgangszustand* [Stress and initial state]. PVU.

Kallus, K. W. (1995). *Der Erholungs-Belastungs-Fragebogen* [The Recovery-Stress Questionnaire]. Swets & Zeitlinger.

Kallus, K. W. (2016). *Erstellung von Fragebogen* [Construction of questionnaires]. Facultas.

Kallus, K. W., & Kellmann, M. (2000). Burnout in athletes and coaches. In Y. L. Hanin (Ed.), *Emotions in sport* (pp. 209–230). Human Kinetics.

Kellmann, M. (2002). Underrecovery and overtraining: Different concepts – Similar impact? In M. Kellmann (Ed.), *Enhancing recovery: Preventing underperformance in athletes* (pp. 3–24). Human Kinetics.

Kellmann, M., & Beckmann, J. (Eds.). (2022). *Recovery and well-being in sport and exercise.* Routledge.

Kellmann, M., & Beckmann, J. (Eds.). (2024). *Fostering recovery and well-being in a healthy lifestyle: Psychological, somatic, and organizational prevention approaches.* Routledge.

Kellmann, M., Bertollo, M., Bosquet, L., Brink, M., Coutts, A., Duffield, R., Erlacher, D., Halson, S., Hecksteden, A., Heidari, J., Kallus, K. W., Meeusen, R., Mujika, I., Robazza, C., Skorski, S., Venter, R., & Beckmann, J. (2018). Recovery and performance: Consensus statement. *International Journal of Sports Physiology and Performance, 13*, 240–245.

Kellmann, M., Jakowski, S., & Beckmann, J. (Eds.). (2023). *The importance of recovery for physical and mental health: Negotiating the effects of underrecovery.* Routledge.

Kellmann, M., & Kallus, K. W. (2001). *The Recovery-Stress Questionnaire for Athletes. User manual.* Human Kinetics.

Kleitman, N. (1969). Basic rest activity cycle in relation to sleep and wakefulness. In A. Kales (Ed.), *Sleep physiology and pathology* (pp. 33–38). Lippincott.

Kragh, H. (2012). *Niels Bohr and the quantum atom: The Bohr model of atomic structure 1913–1925.* Oxford University Press.

Kraxner, M. (2002). *Erholungs-Beanspruchungszustand und oxidativer Stress* [Recovery-stress state and oxidative stress; Unpublished doctoral dissertation]. University of Graz, Austria.

Kubo, T., Liu, X., & Matsuo, T. (2024). Death due to overwork: Problems and solutions. In M. Kellmann & J. Beckmann (Eds.), *Fostering recovery and well-being in a healthy lifestyle: Psychological, somatic, and organizational prevention approaches* (pp. 199–217). Routledge.

Kuchling, H. (2010). *Taschenbuch der Physik* [Pocketbook on physics]. Carl Hanser.

Kullik, L., & Kiel, A. (2024). Sleep well! A key strategy beyond sports. In M. Kellmann & J. Beckmann (Eds.), *Fostering recovery and well-being in a healthy lifestyle: Psychological, somatic, and organizational prevention approaches* (pp. 143–162). Routledge.

Kuntz, J. (2024). Building recovery into organizations to foster resilience. In M. Kellmann & J. Beckmann (Eds.), *Fostering recovery and well-being in a healthy lifestyle: Psychological, somatic, and organizational prevention approaches* (pp. 182–198). Routledge.

Laux, L. (1983). Psychologische Streßkonzeptionen [Psychological stress concepts]. In H. Thomae (Ed.), *Theorien und Formen der Motivation. Enzyklopädie der Psychologie* (Part IV/1, pp. 453–535). Hogrefe.

Lazarus, R. S. (1966). *Psychological stress and the coping process*. McGraw-Hill.

Lazarus, R. S. (1999). *Stress and emotion: A new synthesis*. Springer.

Lazarus, R. S., & Launier, R. (1978). Stress-related transactions between person and environment. In L. A. Pervon & M. Lewis (Eds.), *Perspectives in interactional psychology* (pp. 287–327). Plenum.

Lord, F. M., & Novick, M. R. (1968). *Statistical theories of mental test scores*. Addison-Wesley.

Mayr, M. (2012). *Technische Mechanik* [Technical mechanics]. Carl Hanser.

Maslach, C., & Jackson, S. E. (1986). *Maslach Burnout Inventory*. Consulting Psychologists Press.

McEwen, B. S. (1998). Stress, adaption and disease. Allostasis and allostatic load. *Annals of the New York Academy of Sciences, 840*, 33–44.

McGrath, J. E. (1981). Methodological problems in research on stress. In H.W. Krohne & L. Laux (Eds.), *Achievement, stress, and anxiety* (pp. 19–48). Hemishpere.

Meeusen, R., & De Pauw, K. (2022). Overtraining – What do we know? In M. Kellmann & J. Beckmann (Eds.), *Recovery and well-being in sport and exercise* (pp. 51–62). Routledge.

Meeusen, R., Duclos, M., Foster, C., Fry, A., Gleeson, M., Nieman, D., Raglin, J., Rietjens, G., Steinacker, J., Urhausen, A., European College of Sport Science, & American College of Sports Medicine. (2013). Prevention, diagnosis, and treatment of the overtraining syndrome: Joint consensus statement of the European College of Sport Science and the American College of Sports Medicine. *Medicine and Science in Sports and Exercise, 45*, 186–205.

Mitchell, J. T. (2020). Critical incident stress management: A comprehensive, intergrative, systematic, and multi-component program for supporting first responder psychological health. In C. A. Bowers, D. C. Beidel, & M. R. Marks (Eds.), *Mental health intervention and treatment of first responders and emergency workers* (pp. 103–128). Medical Information Science Reference/IGI Global.

Picard, M., Juster, R. P., & McEwen, B. S. (2014). Mitochondrial allostatic load puts the 'gluc' back in glucocorticoids. *Nature Reviews. Endocrinology, 10*(5), 303–310.

Rammstedt, B., & John, O. P. (2007). Measuring personality in one minute or less: A 10-item short version of the Big Five Inventory in English and German. *Journal of Research in Personality, 41*, 203–212.

Rau, R. (2006). Learning opportunities at work as predictor for recovery and health. *European Journal of Work and Organizational Psychology, 15*(2), 158–180.

Schermelleh-Engel, K., & Moosbrugger, H. (2003). Evaluating the fit of structural equation models: Tests of significance and descriptive goodness-of-fit measures. *Methods of Psychological Research Online, 8*, 23–74.

Schönpflug, W. (1983). Coping efficiency and situational demands. In R. Hockey (Ed.), *Stress and fatigue in human performance* (pp. 299–326). Wiley.

Schönpflug, W. (1987). Beanspruchung und Belastung bei der Arbeit – Konzepte und Theorien. Arbeitspsychologie [Strain and stress during work – Concepts and theories]. In U. Kleinbeck & J. Rutenfranz (Eds.), *Arbeitspsychologie. Enzyklopädie der Psychologie* (Part III/1, pp. 131–184). Hogrefe.

Schulz, P., Schlotz, W., & Becker, P. (2004). *TICS – Trierer Inventar zum chronischen Stress* [Trier Inventory of Chronic Stress]. Hogrefe.

Selye, H. (1936). A syndrome produced by diverse nocuous agents. *Nature, 138*, 32.

Selye, H. (1981). Geschichte und Grundzüge des Stresskonzepts [History and ground concept of the stress concept]. In J. R. Nitsch (Ed.), *Stress – Theorien, Untersuchungen, Maßnahmen* (pp. 163–187). Bern.

Sonnentag, S., & Niessen, C. (2020). To detach or not to detach? Two experimental studies on the affective consequences of detaching from work during non-work time. *Frontiers in Psychology, 11*, 560156. https://doi.org/10.3389/fpsyg.2020.560156

Stelzhammer, J. (2008). *Sozialkapital in Organisationen: Entwicklung und Validierung des Social Capital Questionnaires* [Social capital in organisations: Development and validation of the Social Capital Questionnaires (RESTQ-SCQ); Unpublished diploma thesis]. University of Graz, Austria.

Steyer, R., Schmitt, M., & Eid, M. (1999). Latent state-trait theory and research in personality and individual differences. *European Journal of Personality, 13*, 389–408.

Wagner, G. (2000). *Die Latent-State-Trait-Eigenschaften des Erholungs-Belastungs-Fragebogens* [The latent-state-trait concept of the Recovery-Stress Questionnaire; Unpublished diploma thesis]. University of Graz, Austria.

Walsh, N. P., Halson, S. L., Sargent, C., Roach, G. D., Nédélec, M., Gupta, L., Leeder, J., Fullagar, H. H., Coutts, A. J., Edwards, B. J., Pullinger, S. A., Robertson, C. M., Burniston, J. G., Lastella, M., Le Meur, Y., Hausswirth, C., Bender, A. M., Grandner, M. A., & Samuels, C. H. (2021). Sleep and the athlete: Narrative review and 2021 expert consensus recommendations. *British Journal of Sports Medicine, 55*, 356–368.

Wickens, C. D. (2008). Multiple resources and mental workload. *Human Factors, 50*(3), 449–455.

2 RESTQ-Basic

The general version of the Recovery-Stress Questionnaire

K. Wolfgang Kallus

Main concept of the Recovery-Stress Questionnaire

The Recovery-Stress Questionnaire (RESTQ) is an instrument that allows measuring the recovery-stress state of persons systematically. The recovery-stress state indicates the extent to which persons are stressed emotionally, socially, mentally, or physically, and whether or not compensatory recovery states or activities occurred in the past days. Thus, the recovery-stress state reflects the current state of the person's resources.

The basic RESTQ module was developed to assess the current psychophysical state of a person and first published by Kallus (1995) in German. It has been continuously developed starting from fundamental bio-psychological research in the area of initial state in recovery-stress sequences (Kallus, 1989). For specific areas of application, the basic RESTQ module was later extended by additional sets of scales and the concept of a modular questionnaire evolved. These additional scales allow for assessing the specific complexities of stress and recovery in different areas of application. The basic module is always included, and it allows comparisons across different areas of application. The modular concept brings a lot of advantages, especially from the research perspective, as there is always the basic part, which allows comparisons between different domains. However, from a more practical point of view it has been questioned or violated repeatedly. Specific questions can be answered quickly and easily. This advantage can cause problems in the stage of interpreting the results, when comparisons with other results or other domains are required. Even on an individual level, it might be valuable to know if a problem in a specific area is specific or an expression of a more global problem.

The RESTQ was constructed to obtain a detailed and valid answer to the question *"How are you?"*. Initially, a primary objective in compiling the items was to look for ways to predict the stress reactions of individuals from their

Kallus, K. W. (2025). RESTQ-Basic: The general version of the Recovery-Stress Questionnaire. In M. Kellmann & K. W. Kallus (Eds.), *The Recovery-Stress Questionnaires: A User Manual* (pp. 28–75). Routledge.

DOI: 10.4324/9781032643380-2

present state. Additionally, this idea followed the everyday observation that individuals who are tired and in need of a vacation obviously react differently to demands than individuals who currently have a high degree of psychological and physical fitness.

The RESTQ outlines a differentiated picture of the actual extent of different demand-oriented facets of stress that constitute the overall stress state. The questionnaire is based on the hypothesis that an accumulation of stress from different demands in different areas of life will lead to a changed psychophysical state of acute or even chronic stress, at least in cases with insufficient recovery possibilities. As the initial state changes, the person's capacity to act and perform will vary, along with their potential for adapting to further stressors (Kallus, 1992). The RESTQ endeavours to represent the recovery-stress state as a temporary state, including physical, emotional, behavioural, and social aspects, with certain persistence in time (Bradburn, 1969; Brodsky, 1988; Emmons, 1986; Emmons & Diener, 1985). Therefore, the recovery-stress state, in contrast to the actual condition, is stable in the face of short-term temporary functional fluctuations. The scores obtained should be considered independently of temporary and negligible conditional changes of state by means of a representation in the degree of stress and the extent of recovery in the *past (3) days/nights*. Consequently, the scales show a high short-term stability, at least in the period of one to two days. In addition, items were used that relate closely to observable states and behaviour. Simultaneously, the RESTQ is conceived as an instrument that allows for the sensitive assessment of changes in a person's recovery-stress state and clearly monitors changes in stress and recovery, respectively.

As a multidimensional questionnaire, the RESTQ is especially suitable for clarification of the interdependencies of stress and recovery processes. For this purpose, the questionnaire records the frequency of stress and recovery states and activities. By recording recovery and stress at the same time, the RESTQ closes a theoretically as well as practically important gap in the interplay of stress and recovery (Kellmann & Kallus, this volume, Chapter 3; Kenttä & Hassmén, 1998).

Recovery and regeneration have gained a lot of interest and attention in the recent decades. This is reflected in new academic fields and educations with regeneration topics like rehabilitation, Health Psychology, and nutrition. Mind that nutrition is closely related to recovery as it is a basic way to fill used consumptive resources and recover basic biological functions after exhaustion.

Scope and application

The RESTQ assumes that the current recovery-stress state depends primarily on preceding stress and recovery-related states and activities. Thus, the items assess the frequency of current stress-related states and activities along with the frequency of recovery-associated states and activities. Through the simultaneous assessment of stress and recovery, a differentiated profile on different functional levels of the current recovery-stress state can be provided. The specific characteristics of the RESTQ allow a systematic and direct measurement of appraised events, states, and activities regarding their frequency, while simultaneously considering stress and recovery processes on different levels of resources (physical, emotional, mental, social).

With twelve scales, the RESTQ-Basic assesses potentially stressful and restful events and their subjective consequences during the past three days/nights. Without essential changes in the internal consistency of the scales, the period of reference can be extended to seven days and up to two weeks, depending on the research question (Kallus, 1995, 2002). The questionnaire considers subjectively appraised events and states, while items, which addressed objective demands or activities, were discarded during item selection (Kallus, 1995, 2016). Thus, the concept of appraisal is well represented in the RESTQ. This fits perfectly into cognitive concepts of psychological stress (Lazarus, 1966, 1993), which highlight the transactional relationship between demanding conditions and actively appraising persons. Positive appraisal seems to be a basic characteristic of most recovery processes. However, recovery is closely related to resources (Hobfoll et al., 2018). The RESTQ-Basic can be used well between 11 and 88 years.

Facets of stress and recovery

The RESTQ assesses symptoms of stress and recovery on different functional levels, which are related to different resources: psychophysiological symptoms, motivational and emotional symptoms, behaviour, and performance as well as social aspects.

Facets of stress

From a system-oriented viewpoint, stress is a destabilization or deviation from the normal functional state or rhythm in a biological/psychological system, which shows a dynamic psychophysical balance in normal conditions. Deviations from the psycho-physical balance lead to critical psychological states. Stress occurs when demands are too high or lead to a misfit with the person's capabilities. Demands that are too low result in additional fatigue, sleepiness, monotony, or psychological saturation (Hacker & Sachse, 2014). Stress is used as a term which characterizes the internal state of the person (Kellmann & Kallus, this volume, Chapter 1) and is a result from a transactional process, which is accompanied by coping and adaptation processes. In addition, the RESTQ follows a time-oriented view (Roe, 2014) which implies that recovery processes should always be taken into account. The term strain, which is used in Applied Psychology (cf. Cooper, 2000), is not used in this manual; the reasons are outlined by Kellmann and Kallus (this volume, Chapter 1). The term stressor or demand will be used when the external conditions or the situational aspects are addressed.[1]

From a psychological viewpoint, the mediating subjective appraisal processes of a person play a predominant role in a stress process (Lazarus, 1966, 1991; Lazarus & Launier, 1978). Depending on the subjective perception of objective facts, the same stressor can cause different stress. The individual is not passively exposed to stressors and demands but can influence them in their quality and quantity, depending on the goal of action, and can even redefine or avoid them. In addition, the person influences the stress state actively by different ways of coping (Janke & Erdmann, 2002; Lazarus, 1966, 1991), and, of course, by ongoing or initiated recovery processes and activities.

Resources, coping, and recovery

Functional coping or the distribution of demands in time either allows recovery of resources or adaptation. Dysfunctional coping and very intense, prolonged, or uncontrollable stressors or demands can prohibit recovery and result in underrecovery of resources (Kellmann, 2002) and/or chronic stress.

Stress can have positive and negative effects on the person's resources (Selye, 1981), depending on the state of the person and the recovery processes. Stress, coping, and recovery determine the state of the person, which, in turn, determines the reactions to subsequent demands (Kallus, 1992). Thus, the recovery-stress state plays a key role in the understanding of stress effects, changing performance potential, and changing psychological as well as physical fitness. The recovery-stress approach takes the state of resources of the person on different levels into account, as resources determine the person's resilience (Hollnagel et al., 2013; Weick & Sutcliffe, 2001; Werner, 1971), and the ability to cope with subsequent stressors.

The reactions to stress depend on the availability of consumptive and permanent resources, which can provide a person with resistance to stress (Schönpflug, 1983, 1987). Consumptive resources are dependent on regeneration and recovery, whereas permanent resources like health need development, training, maintenance, repair, or replacement in order to be available in a stress-prone situation. Consumptive resources refer to energetic and motivational processes like effort, tension, will, power, and energy. Consumptive resources have limited reserves and show clearly increasing reduction in time. They activate, keep up, and support the permanent resources, which include long-term internal performance requirements such as talent, competence, and capacity. Limited capacities, or the inability to refill the consumptive resources, negatively affect the immediate and mid-term regeneration of the permanent resources. Consequently, the risk of exhaustion of resources increases. Therefore, the goal should always be to create, care for, use wisely, repair after use, and replace both consumptive and permanent resources when diminished (Hobfoll, 1989; Schönpflug, 1987).

Besides the intensity of stress, the duration and the distribution in time determine the necessity and the options of regeneration and recovery. The possible positive consequences of action latitude on stress (Karasek, 1979; Meijman & Mulder, 1998) are discussed in action psychological models (Frese & Zapf, 1994; Schönpflug, 1987) and in publications on the biopsychology of stress (Janke & Wolffgramm, 1995). Stress, as a transactional process, can neither be examined nor validly diagnosed without considering adaptation and coping processes and the individual recovery. Although many methods are available for the recording of coping processes (Carver, 2011; Erdmann & Janke, 2010; Folkman & Lazarus, 1988; Rüger et al., 1990), there was insufficient assessment of the recovery processes until the construction of the first version of the RESTQ. Even today only a very few instruments and models are available to successfully cover the recovery-stress topic. The Meijman and Mulder (1998) model at least incorporates recovery, and the Need for Recovery Scale (van Veldhoven & Meijman, 1994) is one of the most frequently used measures with respect to recovery in work and organizational psychology. More recent instruments address sleep, resilience, switching off and detachment from work as well as life domain balance (Parker et al., 2020; Sonnentag & Fritz, 2007). The repeatedly reported validities for performance and health measures emphasize the psychological impact of recovery (Kellmann & Beckmann, 2022, 2024; Kellmann et al., 2018, 2023; Smolders et al., 2012; van Veldhoven & Broersen, 2003). The recently published work on detachment and recovery in the research group of Sonnentag (Binnewies & Sonnentag, 2013; Sonnentag, 2018; Sonnentag & Fritz, 2007, 2015; Sonnentag et al., 2022) also showed a growing interest in the field of recovery. Note that the problem of 'unwinding' has already been discussed in Work Psychology by Frankenhaeuser in the 1970s (Frankenhaeuser & Rissler, 1970) and has already been related to the problem of detachment by Rau and Richter (1996). However, an instrument to assess chronic stress (Trier Inventory of Chronic Stress, TICS; Schulz et al., 2004) addresses facets of chronic stress with a frequency-based scale format, which is well compatible to the scales of the RESTQ – but recovery is missing in the TICS.

Stress and recovery

The interrelation between the baseline condition and stress has been described in a model derived from stress research (Janke, 1976) by Kallus (1992, 1995) as well as Kallus and Uhlig (2001) as a feedback process (Kellmann & Kallus, this volume, Chapter 1). Stress reactions influence the baseline condition, which on its part influences the reactions to stress. The complete model shows that the baseline condition for further stress reactions is influenced by stress, recovery activities, and coping with antecedent stressors. Note that coping is closely related to (missing) detachment but the relation is still only partly resolved (Karabinski et al., 2021). The interrelation between stress and recovery has also been emphasized by Wieland-Eckelmann and Baggen (1994), who introduced the work-recovery cycle. The work-recovery cycle is determined by the (task-related) demand/capacity relation, the (recovery-related) expense/return relation, and the relation between the need for recovery and the possibility of recovery. A similar view on the development of chronic stress can be found in Kuiper's model (Kuiper et al., 1993) and in recent models on the development of burnout (Schaufeli & Bakker, 2004) and the related concept like work engagement (Bakker, 2011) or psychological detachment (Sonnentag & Fritz, 2015).

Many definitions describe recovery as a compensation of deficit conditions of the organism that are determined by activity. Often, the principle of homeostasis has been taken as an explanatory concept in which recovery supposedly leads to restoration of the baseline condition. For example, Allmer and Niehues (1989) labelled recovery with reference to Renzland and Eberspächer (1988) as a process "through which the psychological consequences of stress from preceding activities are balanced and the individual condition to act is restored" (p. 18). The defining characteristics of recovery have already been outlined by Kellmann and Kallus (this volume, Chapter 1). Recovery is a multilevel (e.g., physiological, psychological, social) process in time for the re-establishment of bio-psycho-social resources and performance abilities. Recovery includes biological, psychological, and action-oriented components. Activities, which can be systematically used to optimize situational conditions to build up and to refill personal resources and buffers (pro-active recovery), should also be considered as components of recovery.

The classical concepts seem to underestimate the crucial role of continuous regenerative and repair processes in biological (and maybe psychological and social) systems. At least on the level of organic cells it has been found as a basic physiological process principle, which governs life and adaptation. Comparable to stress, a biopsychological approach will be most appropriate to study and to describe the complexity of recovery processes, as outlined by Kallus and Erdmann (1994). Recovery is much more than unwinding from stress and has to be described with respect to time dynamics, systems, and biological foundation. Recovery encompasses much more than the few self-regulatory and resources-related actions of a person to re-establish the functional fitness of resources. A broad range of simple and complex biological processes is more or less automatically set into action, when homoeostatic balances are upset, or biologically relevant functions are out of their functional range. In addition, motivational needs and emotional processes link the biological processes with behaviour and action. This is especially true for re-establishment of resources. Note that the timing and intensity of compensatory processes is not functional in all instances. Fulfilling needs is often stopped or initiated too late, for example, eating and drinking too late after strong feelings of hunger and thirst. The feeling of tiredness often appears when already fatigued beyond the level of critical performance potential as reflected in the problem of seconds sleep in lorry and bus drivers.

The RESTQ-Basic follows the view that the recovery-stress state is a very general and non-specific state of the person, which has an evolutionary biological basis comparable to the stress response (Janke & Wolffgramm, 1995). A multilevel approach is recommended for the assessment of stress. Consequently, stress and recovery are assessed simultaneously on different functional levels in the RESTQ: a) physical symptoms, b) emotional reactions, c) behaviour (action/performance), d) social activities, and additionally e) holistic processes, which are reflected in non-specific items.

Facet of stress and recovery in the RESTQ-Basic

The first set of items was systematically oriented at the classification of stressors by Janke (1976). Based on this theoretical classification, an item pool was compiled that should reflect stress and recovery for different levels of resources.

Items were selected from an extensive list of observations on various stress and recovery activities, according to the criterion of sufficient frequency of occurrence. The area of stress was overrepresented in the initial set of items. While the basic version of the RESTQ puts a greater emphasis on the area of stress (seven of twelve scales), the specific modules compensate this, as they put a larger weight on recovery and resources. For the RESTQ-Basic, it is of interest that emotional and unspecific aspects of recovery could not be separated well by the initial item pool, as recovery seems to be dependent on positive emotional appraisal and only positively evaluated items could be kept. The asymmetric representation of stress and recovery in a questionnaire might be due to some specific features of recovery. Autonomic and automatic ways of recovery are non-conscious and other recovery processes are at least non-public, deeply private, and shielded by social norms. Thus, they are not suitable for a questionnaire, but should either be private or assessed by personal interview with experts.

The basic RESTQ module was constructed according to the principles of *Classic Test Theory* (Lienert, 1969; Lienert & Raatz, 1994; Lord & Novick, 1968). In the item selection, item variance and corrected item-total correlations were included, as well as indices of item validity regarding stress indicators (current psychological state, blood pressure, and heart rate under experimentally induced stress). As a result, an instrument was created that attempts to achieve not only high internal consistency but also significant item validities (Gulliksen technique; Lienert, 1969). While the first version of the basic module of the RESTQ consisted of six items or more per scale, the version with four items per scale (RESTQ-Basic-48) or the short form with two items per scale (RESTQ-Basic-24) turned out to serve the requirements of the users best. The basic Recovery-Stress Questionnaire (RESTQ-Basic-48) consists of seven stress scales and five recovery scales (Kallus, 1995). Scales 1 through 7 consider global stress/emotional stress, social-emotional stress, performance(-related) stress, and physical aspects of stress. Scales 8 through 12 consider different facets of recovery activities. Table 2.1 provides an overview of the RESTQ-Basic scales.

General Stress covers non-specific stress reactions which manifest themselves after intense and demotivating periods of stress, especially when active control is impossible (Hellhammer et al., 2010; Henry & Stephens, 1977; Seligman, 1979). Items cover motivational consequences of stress periods like depressed mood, demotivation, and listlessness. The motivational state also shows some correspondence to symptoms of burnout in working people (Maslach & Leiter, 1997). This scale was labelled *General Stress* because of its consistently high correlation with the remaining stress scales (Kallus, 1995).

Emotional Stress predominantly is covered by items which deal with anxiety, inhibitions, and irritation in the past few days. Emotional reactions are closely related to stress. Stress research in the 1970s–1990s of the past century was hardly distinguishable from anxiety research as Neufeld (1999) stated. Lazarus (1999) developed an emotion theory based on his stress conception. Anger due to frustrating non-reward is another symptom of emotional stress, which can be related to behavioural inhibition concepts (Gray, 1976, 1982).

Table 2.1 Scales of the basic Recovery-Stress Questionnaire.

Number	*Scale* *Summary*
1	***General Stress*** Subjects with high values describe themselves as being frequently mentally stressed, depressed, unbalanced, and listless.
2	***Emotional Stress*** Subjects with high values experience mood-oriented frequent irritation, aggression, anxieties, and restraints or loneliness.
3	***Social Stress*** High values match subjects with frequent arguments, fights, irritation concerning others, being upset, and lack of humour.
4	***Conflicts/Pressure*** High values are reached if in the past few days conflicts were unsettled, unpleasant things had to be done, goals could not be reached, and certain thoughts could not be dismissed.
5	***Fatigue*** Time pressure in job, training, school, and life, being constantly disturbed during important work, over-fatigue, and lack of sleep characterize this area of stress.
6	***Lack of Energy*** This scale matches ineffective work behaviour like inability to concentrate, lack of energy and decision-making.
7	***Physical Complaints*** Physical indisposition and physical complaints related to the whole body are characterized by this scale.
8	***Success*** Success, pleasure at work, and creativity during the past few days belong to this area.
9	***Social Recovery*** High values are reached by frequent pleasurable social contacts and change combined with relaxation and amusement.
10	***Physical Recovery*** Physical recovery, physical well-being, and fitness are characterized in this area.
11	***General Well-being*** Besides frequent good moods and a high level of well-being, general relaxation and being content are also in this scale.
12	***Sleep Quality*** Enough and recovering sleep, and no sleeping disorders while falling asleep and sleeping through the night characterize recovery sleep.

Social Stress measures the frequency of being upset or irritated and having arguments or fights with others. Social stress is one of the most powerful stress conditions. This is reflected in the high scores of social stress in life event scales (Holmes & Rahe, 1967), in massive reactions to social stress in early childhood, in multiple social stress models in behavioural neuroscience (Henry & Stephens, 1977; Steptoe et al., 2007; von Holst, 1998), and in the massive impact of stress from social aggression and anger.

Conflicts/Pressure assesses whether conflicts were unresolved, unpleasant things had to be done, goals could not be reached, or certain thoughts could not be dismissed. This scale is one of the scales which are related to work and the field of goal-related activity and performance, though this field shows a considerable overlap with social stress. Problems with tasks and performance are exaggerated when the individual has difficulties to switch off or detach (Sonnentag & Zijlstra, 2006) or in distancing from the problem (Rau, 2006). This, of course, is related to non-functional coping (Erdmann & Janke, 2010). Note that for the 2016 versions of the RESTQ, one item in the scale *Conflicts/Pressure* was exchanged to improve the internal consistency, as this scale is the least homogeneous scale in the basic version. The item … *I felt I had to perform well in front of others* was replaced by the item … *I had to do something I did not like to do* from the former version RESTQ-72 (Kallus, 1995). The means of the changed scale result in a slightly increased mean (0.06). However, separate questionnaires have been developed for conflicts and pressure as they are very important domains in work and organisations, in sports, and in social relations (Kolodej et al., 2005, 2013). Note that social support on the resources side belongs to the most powerful stress buffers/stress moderators (Cohen, 1988).

Fatigue deals with feelings of tiredness and exhaustion, with lack of sleep as well as with overfatigue. Fatigue can be viewed as an indication of exhaustion of consumptive resources (Hockey, 2013), which is especially reflected in reduced activation and an increased variability in performance, as decrements are normally compensated by processes like reactive effort (Debus, 1981; Düker, 1963). With increasing fatigue decrements in performance and activation are visible. The feeling of tiredness is a rather late indicator of progredient fatigue. Fatigue is one of the major risk factors in human performance like steering a vehicle, as brief periods of uncontrollable sleep episodes (micro-sleep) can occur. Fatigue is defined as a state, which needs a recovery period like a break or some sleep. The chronic fatigue syndrome (Fukuda et al., 1994; Noor et al., 2021) might be a symptom related to chronic stress and chronic underrecovery. Fatigue also has a motivational component, which is assessed by the scale *Lack of Energy*.

Lack of Energy indicates ineffective work behaviour, such as a lack of concentration, energy, and decision-making. Lack of energy is also part of the burnout syndrome 'emotional exhaustion' and an indication of exhausted resources. It can occur due to exhausted resources or the inability to activate resources in a constructive task-related way. Lack of energy occurs together with emotional exhaustion in burnout (Maslach & Leiter, 1997) as well as in precursors of chronic fatigue (Wolf et al., 2008). Motivational deficits resulting from uncontrollable aversive events (Seligman, 1979) will show effects of lack of energy as well as periods of negative or missing feedback after coping with taxing demands.

Physical Complaints measured by the seventh stress-oriented scale relate to physical stress symptoms and complaints. Physical complaints can occur under stress because of metabolic, autonomous, central activation, and muscular activation (Hancock, 2008; Janke, 1976; McEwen, 1998; Pinel, 2013). Physical complaints and pain, however, can trigger further stress reactions. The selection of items for the RESTQ-Basic with psychophysiological validities puts a specific emphasis on physiological stress responses, which in many instances can be assessed by questionnaire (e.g., self-report) at least indirectly (feeling uncomfortable) or when symptoms become stronger.

Success relates to pleasure at work, having lots of ideas, and achievement. It is the only recovery-oriented scale that is concerned with performance in the basic module of the RESTQ. Success is a factor which might at least indirectly contribute to recovery. After finishing a task successfully, an option for regenerating resources and recovery normally occurs. In addition, success affects the mood state and the motivational state (Dweck, 2006, 2012) and results in behavioural changes like helping behaviour (Isen, 1970). Success is one of the cornerstones of Positive Psychology (Seligman & Csikszentmihalyi, 2000). The rewarding properties of success might also help to re-establish a positive achievement motivation (McClelland, 1988).

Social Recovery assesses the frequency of pleasurable social contacts and change combined with relaxation and amusement. Items include the area of positive mood, which seems to be a most potent factor for recovery. In addition, items like … *I had a good time with my friends* indicate a strong correlation of social recovery with social support and the coping strategy 'need for social support' (Erdmann & Janke, 2010). Social support is a very potent stress buffer (Cohen, 1988, 2004; Lakey & Orehek, 2011); the relation between social recovery and regeneration activities has hardly been discussed.

Physical Recovery covers physiological relaxation and fitness. The feeling of physical fitness seems to be a very good and important indicator for the state of being recovered (for coaches; Kellmann et al., this volume, Chapter 4). Physical relaxation techniques have become a standard procedure to optimise breaks and to cope with stress states (Kellmann et al., 2024). In addition, physical exercise seems to be a very potent buffer for stress illness consequences (Chandola et al., 2008; Salmon, 2001).

Besides the frequency of good mood and the level of well-being, general relaxation and being content are assessed by the *General Well-being* scale. Up to now, only conceptual aspects allow to distinguish between well-being (Brodsky, 1988) and a state of recovered and functionally usable resources. The process of item selection for the RESTQ-Basic showed better statistical properties for the emotionally positive formulated items, which indicates a conceptual overlap between recovery and well-being. Gloria et al. (2013) showed that adaptation to work stress is markedly influenced by positive affect, which is closely related to the unspecific recovery as measured by the scale *General Well-being*. Note that a broad range of effects of physical activity also seems to be related to a positive mood during exercises (Eime et al., 2013; Gerber et al., 2020; Kallus, 1994).

Sleep Quality, the final scale of the RESTQ-Basic, indicates absence of having trouble falling asleep and interrupted sleep (Kallus, 1995). Due to the multiple functions of sleep and the fact that intense or chronic stress is often accompanied by sleep problems (Åkerstedt & Kecklung, 2012; Grote, 2010; Prather et al., 2013; Wiegelmann et al., 2023; Zijlstra et al., 2014), the scale for sleep quality should theoretically be related to both stress and recovery.

The sequence of scales in the RESTQ-Basic is based on the intercorrelations and the scale means, which allows to draw test profile with an easy interpretation. Thus, please do not mix up the sequence.

Stress states, recovery demands, and the recovery-stress balance

Kellmann (2002) has proposed a model describing the interrelation between stress states and recovery demands (for a detailed description see Kellmann & Kallus, this volume, Chapter 1). The basic assumption is that with increasing stress, increased recovery is necessary. Limited resources (e.g., time) initiate a vicious circle: under increased stress and the inability to meet increased recovery demands, the person experiences more stress. In a state of adequate recovery, the individual can react appropriately and cope successfully with stress. This is comparable to the 'elastic phase' in mechanical load-strain-stress models. In a state of underrecovery, permanent resources tend to be taxed or depleted beyond their functional values. In this state, the normal function of recovery in breaks, with an over-proportional recovery in the first minutes (Allmer, 1996), will be changed, as not only consumptive resources are depleted. Instead, longer lasting recovery processes like sleep or even repair or restoring activities are necessary, which often have a timeline just opposite to the well-known recovery function of the muscle. In contrast to recovery, repair starts slowly and becomes more effective over time. In summary, Kellmann's model suggests that it is not bad to be high on stress, if the individual knows how to recover optimally (Kellmann & Kallus, this volume, Chapter 1).

High sensitivity to disturbance and interruptions seems to be one of the key features of recovery, which allows even non-stress events like daily hassles (DeLongis et al., 1988; Holm & Holroyd, 1992) to interfere with recovery processes. An evident example is given by noise, which is not only aversive when intensity is too high but also when it is 'disturbing' (Cohen, 1988; Hellbrück & Fischer, 1999; Kryter, 1970). Recovery is a goal-oriented process, which easily provokes emotional reactions when disturbed, as shown in a laboratory experiment (Kallus & Krauth, 1995; Kellmann & Kallus, this volume, Chapter 3).

As will be outlined in the specific versions, there is a close empirical and theoretical link between the recovery-stress (dis-)balance and burnout. After research on burnout was carried out in the social professions (Pines, 1993), it was expanded to other professional groups, and a recovery-stress imbalance has been proposed as an important source of burnout (Altfeld & Kellmann, 2014, 2015).

Related but alternative models focus on the effort-reward imbalance (Siegrist, 1996), an imbalance of job demands and resources (Schaufeli & Bakker, 2004), or negative organizational burnout factors (Leiter & Harvie, 1998). All these factors are very likely to be accompanied by stress symptoms and will manifest in burnout, in the case that resources are not recovered appropriately.

Thus, symptoms of chronic stress, stress-related health impairment, stress-related performance deficits as well as burnout and chronic fatigue constitute areas for which the RESTQ claims a high validity. The simultaneous inclusion of recovery and stress will result in incremental validity with respect to instruments, which assess only stress, only need for recovery, or only ways of coping.

Versions and scoring

The RESTQ has been developed iteratively and the current standard version comprises 48 items (4 items per scale). This version turned out to be the best compromise between reliability and economy, while the first publication (Kallus, 1995) proposed a version with 72 items (6 items per scale). Due to the additional items in the specific modules, the short version with 24 items (RESTQ-Basic-24 former RESTQ-24A) is also selected in many instances. An overview of the actual items and scales is provided in Online Appendix A.A1.

For the RESTQ-Basic the standard time frame is *in the past (3) days/nights* (RESTQ-Basic-24, RESTQ-Basic-48). For the area of work and for coaches, the time frame has been fixed to *in the past (7) days/nights*. RESTQ-Basic data exist for three different time frames, as the basic module is always included in the specific versions. Two samples on the relation of recovery, resources, and social capital are even available for a time frame of four weeks (Stelzhammer, 2008), as the validity concept 'social capital' is one with a long-term dimension. In addition, a very short 'snapshot version' with seven items has been developed. This brief version has been kept for screening purposes and has also been used in the work context (Goettlicher, 2014).

As items do not change with changing time frames, translations of short versions need not be conducted for short versions but can be adopted without problems. However, any free selection of items from 'the pool' is strongly prohibited and is a violation of copyright and intellectual property, as it presents an act of plagiarism. The items of the RESTQ identify activities or conditions in the form of incomplete sentences. Together with the time frame given at the top of the page (*in the past (3) days/nights*), each item forms a statement. A Likert-type scale is used with values ranging from 0 (*never*) to 6 (*always*) indicating how often the respondent participated in various activities during the *past (3) days/nights* (Table 2.2). The RESTQ includes a warm-up item that is not included in the analysis.

The scale values are calculated by taking the mean of the item values (checked numbers, rounded off to two decimal points). The formation of the mean is appropriate because of the different number of questions in the various versions of the RESTQ. In the case of missing data, the mean should only be calculated

Table 2.2 Sample item and answer mode of the RESTQ-Basic.

In the past (3) days/nights							
... I read a newspaper							
	0	1	2	3	4	5	6
	never	seldom	sometimes	often	more often	very often	always

when at least 50% of the items of each scale have been answered. In the scale for *Sleep Quality*, the items for disturbed sleep first have to be inverted (6 minus item value = raw item score, e.g., 6 → 0; 5 → 1; 4 → 2; 3 → 3; 2 → 4; 1 → 5; 0 → 6). Scoring sheets are available for manual scoring. Additionally, the data can be represented graphically in a *recovery-stress profile*.

The mean of each scale can range from 0 – 6. High scores in the stress-associated activity scales reflect high subjective stress, whereas high scores in the recovery-oriented scales reflect plenty of recovery activities.

- The scales in the area of stress can either be summarized in an overall stress score for the dimension *Overall Stress* (mean of scales 1–7) or into two separate scores for the sub-dimensions: *Social-Emotional Stress* (mean of scales 1–3) and *Performance(-related) Stress* (mean of scales 4–7).
- A total mean for recovery can be formed from the values for *Overall Recovery* dimension (mean of scales 8–12).

Kallus (1995) as well as Kellmann and Kallus (this volume, Chapter 1, p. 2) state that:

> stress and recovery should not be combined to a single value, as they constitute two conceptually independent dimensions as far as the frequency in the past days/nights is concerned. The relationship between the scales for recovery and stress is neither linear nor symmetrical. **Consequently, the calculation of one overall single score of all stress and recovery scales does not make sense and is strongly prohibited.**

Note that the relationships between stress and recovery differ depending on the perspective. For a time-oriented analysis, one would expect a high negative correlation between *Overall Stress* and *Overall Recovery*: The more time is spent under stress the less time will remain for recovery. However, switching the perspective to *resources* will result in a positive correlation of *Overall Stress* and *Overall Recovery*: The more resources are spent under stress the more resources need to be recovered.

Scoring is not affected by the different time frames, which are used for different areas of application, but note that means and standard deviations might change.

Interpretation of results

The RESTQ is constructed in accordance with the *Classical Test Theory* (*Classical-Latent-Additive Model*; Moosbrugger, 1982). Scores from the classical test can be considered as interval scales (Bühner, 2010; Lord & Novick, 1968). Therefore, an interpretation of the scale mean as an absolute value is not possible. Please keep in mind that the impression from the profiles that 'recovery scores' are much higher than 'stress scores' is due to the formulation of items and is neither related to the concepts nor to the state. Thus, it is recommended to base the interpretation of the RESTQ profile on a reference group, on intraindividual changes over time, or on the reference values provided in the Online Appendix A.A2 and A.A3. Moreover, it is important to check if the RESTQ version corresponds to the chosen time frame and the moment of testing to the respective comparison group.

The reference values in the Online Appendix A.A2 and A.A3 can be treated like a kind of norm, as the more than 35 years of using the RESTQ in different areas of application showed that there might be an overall average recovery-stress state. Of course, the recovery-stress state varies during the working week, the weekend, during vacation, and during personal stress periods, different phases of life, and because of specific stress and recovery activities.

Therefore, the means in the Online Appendix A.A2 and A.A3 constitute general situation-unspecific reference values. Norms are useful to compare individuals and groups with respect to stable characteristics like personality characteristics (e.g., extraversion) or performance characteristics (e.g., intelligence). In psychology, norms are only available for long-term functional states (e.g., depression), while for short-term and mid-term functional fluctuations within subjects, change scores are the most common way to evaluate the data. This contrasts with procedures in the medical domain where state indicators like increased body temperature are the most relevant indicators, as there are functional norms available. The norm value of about 37 degrees Celsius could theoretically be obtained and assessed by a large sample procedure and a cross validation over different samples. This way is used for the RESTQ-data, and it could be shown that there are stable values which reflect an 'average recovery-stress state of the population'.

In addition to the data in the first publication of the RESTQ-Basic (Kallus, 1995), additional data are available from a broad range of samples in different areas of application. Many samples were from studies in the occupational area and thus, seven days as reference time were used. Data for the standard version in the *past (3) days/nights* are mostly drawn from the basic part of the RESTQ-Sport or the former versions of the RESTQ-Coach.

Reliability and validity

Data on reliability and validity stem from a broad range of studies. Sample descriptions of the first validation studies with the RESTQ-Basic are given in

Table 2.3 Research samples used to test validity and reliability.

	GB1	*GB2*	*GB3*	*GB3*
Author/ year	Kallus (1995)	Hüppe and Uhlig (1992)	Rauscher (2007)	Gappmaier (2007)
Sample size	*N*=72	*N*=420	*N*=192	*N*=378
Gender distribution	Male=72	Male=140	Male=96	Male=163
		Female=280	Female=96	Female=215
Age	*M*=23.90	*M*=35.82	*M*=41.45	*M*=42.30
	SD=2.74	*SD*=18.42	*SD*=12.33	*SD*=12.41
RESTQ-version			RESTQ-Basic	RESTQ-Basic
Time frame	Past several days	3 days/night	7 days/nights	7 days/nights
Measurements	1	1	1	1
Country	Germany	Germany	Austria	Austria
Special features	Students	Participants of a large sports event	White collar Workers	Workers

	GB4	*GB4*	*GB4*	*GB4*
Author/ year	Kogler (2007)	Schuster (2007)	Lernbeiss (2008)	Windisch (2008)
Sample size	*N*=128	*N*=108	*N*=102	*N*=146
Gender distribution	Male=64	Male=44	Male =19	Male=45
	Female=64	Female=66	Female=83	Female=98
Age	*M*=41.84	*M*=40.67	*M*=40.79	*M*=38.59
	SD=9.24	*SD*=9.61	*SD*=9.73	*SD*=11.44
RESTQ-version	RESTQ-Basic	RESTQ-Basic	RESTQ-Basic	RESTQ-Basic
Time frame	7 days/nights	7 days/nights	7 days/nights	7 days/nights
Measurements	1	1	1	1
Country	Austria	Austria	Austria	Austria
Special features	Workers	Nurses	Nurses	Teachers

Note: For samples GB3 two datasets with the RESTQ-Basic-48/7 were pooled from studies on: 378 white collar workers (Gappmaier, 2007, age: M=42.30; SD=12.41; gender: 215 women, 163 men) and 192 workers (Rauscher, 2007, age: M=41.45; SD=12.33; gender: 96 women, 96 men); GB4 was pooled from 4 studies; Samples are abbreviated with a letter for language (G: German) and the version of the RESTQ (B: Basic); Identical sample labels indicate pooled samples.

Table 2.3. Sample descriptions for the samples of athletes and coaches are given by Kellmann and Kallus (this volume, Chapter 3) and Kellmann et al. (this volume, Chapter 4). Samples GB1 and GB2 are drawn from the first RESTQ publication (Kallus, 1995).

In addition, results from the basic part of the RESTQ-Sport (Kellmann & Kallus, this volume, Chapter 3; samples GS1, ES1), the RESTQ-Coach (Kellmann et al., this volume, Chapter 4; samples GC3.1, EC1), and RESTQ-Work (Jiménez et al., this volume, Chapter 5; sample EW1) were utilized to provide a comparison of reliability measures with different versions, different time frames, different populations, and different languages.

Internal consistency of the RESTQ-Basic

Basic psychometric results from different samples will be given for the RESTQ-Basic-48 and the RESTQ-Basic-24 with time frames of three and seven days in the following section.

For most of the RESTQ-Basic scales, an overview of the reliability coefficients (Table 2.4) shows very good estimations of the accuracy of measurement for most of the scales as long as the 48-item version is used. The values of the German sample are above $\alpha = .74$, most of them above $\alpha = .80$, except for *Conflicts/Pressure* and *Success*.

The internal consistencies for *Conflicts/Pressure* and *Success* turned out to be repeatedly below Cronbach's $\alpha = .70$ (Table 2.4) and depending on the sample, the interpretation for those scales is limited. As Kallus (1995) pointed out, the meaning of the globally formulated items, such as … *I finished important tasks*, is different for persons in different professions and life situations. For the final version the item … *I felt I had to perform well in front of others* was replaced by the item … *I had to do something I did not like to do.* This item had a slightly better part-whole correlation in the construction samples (Kallus, 1995) and covers a broader range of situations and is relevant for almost any person.

Since the item … *I had some good ideas* from the *Success* scale can be a rare event for persons in routine life and jobs, the scale *Success* also shows variable internal consistencies. To sum up, *Success* and *Conflicts/Pressure* as scales have changing relevance depending on the profession, the hobbies, and the life situation at the time of assessment.

Table 2.4 shows overall high scores for Cronbach's α especially for the overall scores. Results are based on different studies from different areas and encompass English versions. The German samples (GB1, GB2) of the first longer version of the RESTQ with 72 items (Kallus, 1995) are included for reference. High consistencies (with repeated exceptions for scale *Conflicts/Pressure*) could be replicated for the pooled German and English athlete samples (GS1, ES1; Kellmann & Kallus, this volume, Chapter 3), the pooled German samples (GB3, GB4), the English RESTQ-Work sample (EW1; Jiménez et al., this volume, Chapter 5), and the English sample of coaches (EC1; Kellmann et al., this volume, Chapter 4) for the RESTQ-Basic-48.

Columns 2–6 in Table 2.4 show results from the RESTQ-Basic with a time frame of three days/nights; columns 7–10 show internal consistencies for the time frame of seven days/nights. Columns 4, 6, 8, and 10 show results for the short version of the RESTQ-Basic with two items per scale. A decline in

Table 2.4 Estimation of reliability (Cronbach's α) for the RESTQ-Basic for German samples (GB1, GB2, GB3, GB4), the RESTQ-Sport (ES1), the RESTQ-Work (EW1), and the RESTQ-Coach (EC1) samples.

Samples	*GB1*	*GB2*	*GS1*	*GS1*	*ES1*	*ES1*	*GB3*	*GB4*	*EW1*	*EC1*
	N = 72	N = 420	N = 820	N = 820	N = 734	N = 734	N = 570	N = 484	N = 195	N = 133
Version/days *RESTQ-Basic scales*	72	72/3	48/3	24/3	48/3	24/3	48/7	24/7	48/7	24/7
1 General Stress	.84	.90	.82	.61	.86	.74	.88	.86	.90	.86
2 Emotional Stress	.71	.92	.74	.74	.78	.77	.82	.74	.87	.73
3 Social Stress	.73	.92	.82	.60	.87	.72	.88	.81	.91	.88
4 Conflicts/Pressure	.77	.89	.60	.62	.69	.58	.55	.61	.78	.56
5 Fatigue	.78	.87	.78	.54	.79	.67	.81	.84	.82	.79
6 Lack of Energy	.78	.89	.75	.52	.73	.60	.80	.75	.83	.55
7 Physical Complaints	.66	.80	.72	.54	.70	.70	.79	.83	.83	.73
8 Success	.68	.91	.61	.40	.68	.65	.73	.69	.73	.81
9 Social Recovery	.83	.95	.80	.57	.80	.72	.85	.85	.83	.80
10 Physical Recovery	.64	.95	.80	.54	.75	.60	.85	.82	.79	.74
11 General Well-being	.84	.97	.85	.79	.89	.82	.91	.90	.92	.87
12 Sleep Quality	—	.95	.80	.69	.81	.66	.87	.70	.82	.71
Overall Stress	—	—	.86	.83	.91	.82	.87	.77	.96	.93
Social-Emotional Stress	—	—	.83	.81	.89	.82	.85	.74	.96	.93
Performance(-related) Stress	—	—	.70	.60	.80	.59	.73	.80	.94	.86
Overall Recovery	—	—	.77	.73	.82	.68	.78	.79	.92	.90

consistency from the 48-item version to the 24-item version appears in most scales and is most pronounced for the sample of athletes GS1 (Kellmann & Kallus, this volume, Chapter 3) and for *Conflicts/Pressure*, and *Lack of Energy* in the other samples. *Overall Stress* shows good values in all samples as well as *Overall Recovery* for the German samples.

While in sample GB1 and GB2, a version with 6 items per scale was used, the shorter version with 4 items per scale (48 items) became the one most frequently used. Compared to the results with sample GB2, which consisted primarily of participants of a gymnastics sports weekend (280 females, 140 males; mean age M=35.8, SD=18.4), the reduction of items in the shorter versions is accompanied by a slight drop of reliability, which follows the principles of *Classical Test Theory*. However, reliabilities are very good to satisfactory even for the RESTQ with 48 items. The short versions with 24 items show a further reduction in internal consistency, which results repeatedly in unsatisfactory values (see the parallel results in sample GS1 for 24 and 48 items in columns 3 and 4, and ES1 in columns 5 and 6, respectively). This implies the recommendation to restrict the interpretation of results from the short versions to scores for dimensions if high reliability is required (as in the case of diagnosing an individual state on the basis of just one assessment).

For English versions, no language-specific reduction in internal consistency appeared, neither in the standard or short version, nor with the changes in time frames from three to seven days.

The risk to find low homogeneity scores is largest within the sub-dimension of *Performance(-related) Stress* (*Conflicts/Pressure*, *Fatigue*, *Lack of Energy*, and *Physical Complaints*). The recovery scales *Success* and *Sleep Quality* approach the critical limit of α=.70 in some samples. The reduction in homogeneity can be explained by sample characteristics in most instances. However, it is advised to relate to the data, which are representative or at least related to the population of the user. If a sample above N=50 is available, the user might briefly check the homogeneity of the sample, as reliability might change with the sample, the background situation, and the time sample. However, reliability of the dimensions is high, even for the short version of the questionnaire (RESTQ-Basic-24).

Item-scale statistics and (corrected) part-whole correlations for the RESTQ-Basic-48 (for three and seven days) are given in Online Appendix A.A4 and A.A5 for the English and German versions. Linear structural models in more recent data sets support the good reliabilities of the RESTQ-Basic. The new measurement models allow to better understand the interrelation of the items of a subtest. Items can be correlated due to formal or formulation similarities and not only due to their content (Kellmann & Kallus, this volume, Chapter 1).

Time frames

Internal consistencies show stable values across the different time frames, which are given in the header of the questionnaire. The study by Wagner (2000) mentioned by Kellmann and Kallus (this volume, Chapter 1) allowed computing the internal consistencies for different time frames from the same subjects. No systematic trend in internal consistencies was found. The same applies for different samples with time frames of three and seven days/nights, which can be inferred from Table 2.4.

For the short version RESTQ-Basic-24 (former RESTQ-24A), the values are less consistent and partly below the threshold of $\alpha = .70$ or even below the critical threshold of $\alpha = .60$ (Table 2.4), indicating that the scales should only be used as an interpretative support of the values for the dimensions in the short forms on the RESTQ.

The internal consistencies are very good for the dimensions and subdimensions if the standard version with 48 items is used, in most instances even if the short version RESTQ-Basic-24 is applied (Table 2.4 bottom).

Test-retest reliability and data from retests

For the first measurement of a repeated measure data set from athletes (columns 1 and 2 of Table 2.5), the Cronbach's α are lower compared to the second measurement. As a rule, internal consistency increases with the subjects' familiarity with the instrument. Consequently, an introductory measurement is valuable in studies with multiple measurements and for the applied use in monitoring studies as discussed by Kellmann and Kallus (this volume, Chapter 3).

Test-retest reliabilities

In the first manual of the RESTQ-Basic (Kallus, 1995), high short-term stabilities were reported for the scales based on sample GB1. Data are reproduced in the last column of Table 2.5. For the RESTQ-Basic-48 repeated measures were available for two samples (GB1, R5). Repetitions within two days, three days, nine days, and with intervals longer than two weeks are provided in Table 2.5.

Table 2.5, drawn from the basic part of the RESTQ-Sport with sample R5 (Kellmann & Kallus, this volume, Chapter 3), displays the test-retest reliability of the RESTQ-Basic-48 with a time frame of three days/nights after two, three, nine, and 37 days.

Stability over time is quite high after 24 hours for an instrument with high sensitivity to changes. This is true for the majority of scales even within a three-day period and for some scales even within nine days. Note, the high stability occurs also for scales with a moderate homogeneity, as in the case of *Conflicts/Pressure* and *Success*. The consistently high short-term stability, however, clearly shows the reliability of all scales of the RESTQ. The test-retest reliability exceeds or approaches values of $r = .70$ in most instances, which implies that interindividual differences in the recovery-stress states can be well reproduced. Moreover, the high test-retest reliability shows that the results of the RESTQ are stable concerning short-term functional fluctuations and minor short-term changes in the recovery-stress state. In addition, one can infer that for most scales the stability of scores exceeds the sampled time frame. However, results indicate

Table 2.5 Test-retest reliability of the RESTQ-Basic-48 in various time spans for the German RESTQ-Sport-76 sample R5 (N=58, see also Table 3.6), last column reproduces the 24-hrs stability from sample GB1 (Kallus, 1995).

	Time between the intervals of testing				
Sample	*R5*				*GB1*
RESTQ-Basic scales	*2 days*	*3 days*	*9 days*	*37 days*	*24-hours*
1 General Stress	.71	.72	.57	.13	.86
2 Emotional Stress	.78	.53	.55	.12	.82
3 Social Stress	.69	.68	.62	.43	.79
4 Conflicts/Pressure	.78	.52	.72	.30	.84
5 Fatigue	.63	.75	.56	.19	.85
6 Lack of Energy	.66	.78	.52	.18	.86
7 Physical Complaints	.61	.65	.51	.10	.83
8 Success	.85	.79	.62	.19	.80
9 Social Recovery	.87	.74	.60	.35	.91
10 Physical Recovery	.81	.78	.52	.51	.85
11 General Well-being	.86	.57	.61	.44	.80
12 Sleep Quality	.74	.66	.56	.43	No data

that high consistency and lower stability can be expected at least with systematic situational changes or longer time intervals.

Table 2.5 shows a considerably high short-term stability of the RESTQ-Basic in the range of one to three days. With increasing time between measures, correlations drop throughout. This is in accordance with the claim of the RESTQ to measure states of a medium temporal stability but not personality traits.

Latent structure measurement models

Two approaches were followed to test the measurement models for the scales of the RESTQ-Basic. In a first step for each scale, the four items of the RESTQ were considered as manifest variables and the scale served as one latent variable. In a second step, the dimension and all scales of the dimensions were included as latent variable, and items served as manifest variables. For the short version RESTQ-24, the sub-dimensions were included, as there were only two items per scale, which is trivial and always allows fitting the measurement-model without modifications.

Measurement models for scales

As can be expected on the basis of the item-total correlations and the internal consistency from *Classical Test Theory*, all scales except *Fatigue* and *Sleep Quality* show a good model fit on most fit indices. Results are based on sample GS2 (N=597 athletes, RESTQ-Basic-48). Figure 2.1 represents the tested model for *General Stress*.

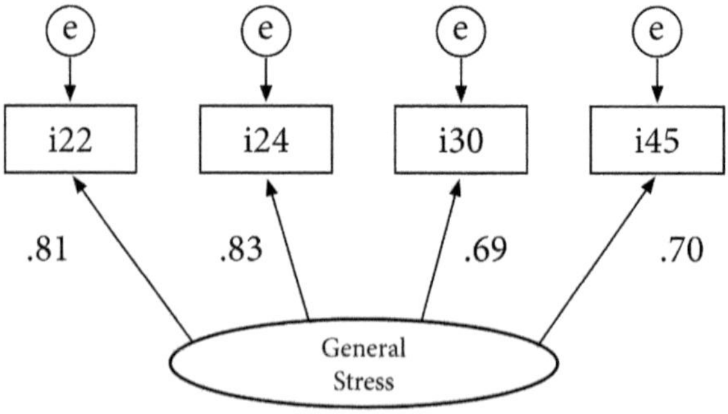

Figure 2.1 Measurement model for *General Stress* (GFI = .98, AGFI = .91, CFI = .97, RMSEA = .13; e = error term, i22 = item 22).

Table 2.6 Fit indices and proposed specific correlations for the RESTQ-Basic scales.

RESTQ-Basic scales		*GFI*	*AGFI*	*CFI*	*RMSEA*	*Modification*
1 General Stress	Initial model	.91	.98	.97	.13	
	Modification	1.00	1.00	1.00	.00	(Item 30 ↔ Item 45)
2 Emotional Stress	Initial model	.89	.99	.96	.15	
	Modification	1.00	1.00	1.00	.00	(Item 5 ↔ Item 28)
3 Social Stress	Initial model	.98	1.00	1.00	.04	
	Modification	.98	1.00	1.00	.04	No modification
4 Conflicts/ Pressure	Initial model	.60	.92	.62	.30	(Item 12 ↔ Item 18)
	Modification	.97	1.00	.99	.07	
5 Fatigue	Initial model	.35	.87	.77	.39	
	Modification	1.00	1.00	1.00	.00	(Item 2 ↔ Item 35)
6 Lack of Energy	Initial model	.77	.95	.93	.22	
	Modification	.98	1.00	1.00	.06	(Item 31 ↔ Item 40)
7 Physical Complaints	Initial model	.99	1.00	1.00	.03	No modification
	Modification	.99	1.00	1.00	.03	
8 Success	Initial model	.90	.98	.90	.14	
	Modification	1.00	1.00	1.00	.00	(Item 3 ↔ Item 17/41)
9 Social Recovery	Initial model	.53	.91	.89	.31	
	Modification	.99	1.00	1.00	.14	(Item 6 ↔ Item 33)
10 Physical Recovery	Initial model	.91	.98	.97	.13	
	Modification	1.00	1.00	1.00	.00	(Item 9 ↔ Item 13/38)
11 General Well-being	Initial model	.96	.99	1.00	.08	
	Modification	.96	.99	1.00	.08	No modification
12 Sleep Quality	Initial model	.64	.93	.91	.27	(Item 36 ↔ Item 46)
	Modification	.98	1.00	1.00	.05	

Note: GFI = Goodness of Fit Index, AGFI = Adjusted Goodness of Fit Index, CFI = Comparative Fit Index, RMSEA = Root Mean Square Error of Approximation.

The model fits satisfactorily without any correlated measurement error and shows relatively high loadings for all items. RMSEA indicates an option for further improvements but as CFI is above .95 the fit is acceptable (Kellmann & Kallus, this volume, Chapter 1). However, modifications result in an overfitting, as shown in Table 2.6, which gives an overview over the fit indices of the RESTQ-Basic scales and the opportunities for improvement, when correlated errors of measurement (i.e., specific variance in two items) are allowed. For most of the scales, the initial model can be kept, as at least two of the fit indices indicate an acceptable initial model.

For the scale *Fatigue*, AGFI and RMSEA indicate a poor model fit, and it is necessary to allow a correlation of items 2 and 35. Both items are not directly related to work as the other two do. Thus, this correlation can be justified by specific item contents.

The recovery scales show a satisfactory model fit except *Sleep Quality*, which requires a specific correlation of item 36 and item 46. This can be explained well by differences in polarity. Items 36 and 46 (inverted items) are formulated negatively (low sleep quality), while the other items address high sleep quality.

Measurement models for the RESTQ-Basic-48 indicate a good model fit for the scales, except for *Fatigue* and *Sleep Quality*, which might require special attention in the structural modelling.

Measurement models with dimensions

In a next step, the measurement models for each sub-dimension were computed, which indicates the structure of the sub-dimensions and is necessary in the case of the two-item scales of the RESTQ-Basic-24. Models depicted in this section are based on an analysis of the scales with items of RESTQ-Basic-24 from the sample GS2.

Two models are possible for the stress dimension, either a direct one-factor solution or a stress dimension with two sub-dimensions. For recovery, no sub-dimensions resulted from the Exploratory Factor Analysis in the development of the RESTQ (Kallus, 1995).

The first stress dimension *Social-Emotional Stress* shows a bad model fit in the first instance with negative variance estimates for *General Stress. Emotional Stress* and *Social Stress* share more common content (Figure 2.2). After fixing the loadings of *Emotional Stress* and *Social Stress* to one and allowing two correlations for 'item errors', a good model fit was obtained. The specific correlations of items i14 (… *I felt down*) ↔ i3 (… *I was in a bad mood*) are due to the depression-oriented item content. The same applies for the specific correlation of items i20 (… *I was annoyed*) ↔ i13 (… *I was annoyed by others*), which both address anger.

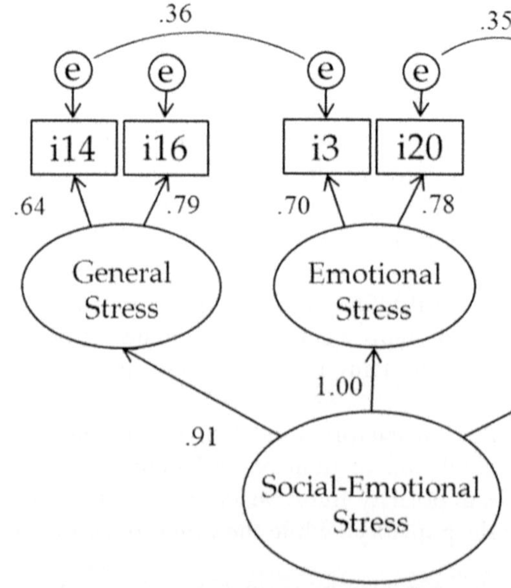

Figure 2.2 Measurement model for *Social-Emotional Stress* (GFI = .99, AGFI = .97, CFI = .99, RMSEA = .05).

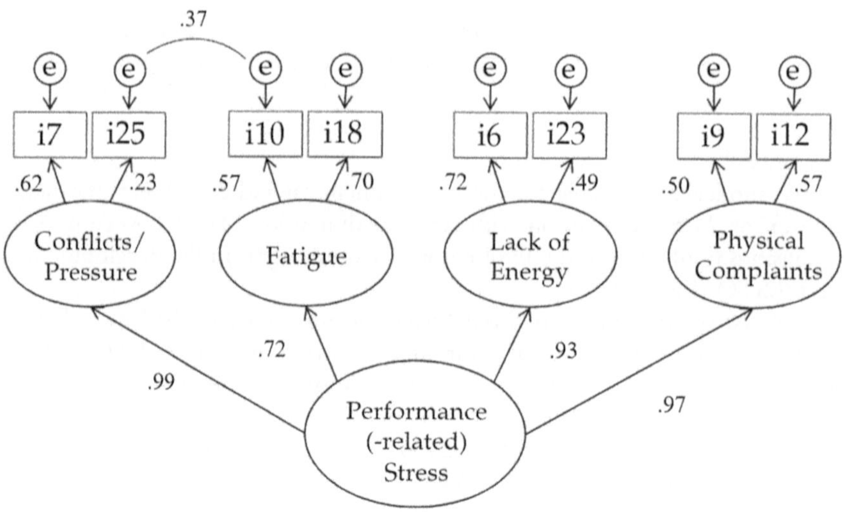

Figure 2.3 Measurement model for *Performance(-related) Stress* (GFI = .97, AGFI = .93, CFI = .92, RMSEA = .08).

The measurement model for the sub-dimension *Performance(-related) Stress* (Figure 2.3) shows satisfactory model fit including correlated measurement errors for item i25 (… *I felt under pressure*) and item i10 (… *I was dead tired after work*). Similar to the analysis with the longer version of the RESTQ, the scale *Fatigue* is not fitting easily into a linear structure.

For *Overall Recovery* (Figure 2.4), a good model fit was obtained after letting items of the scale *Sleep Quality* correlate specifically with item i4 (… *I felt physically relaxed*) from the scale *Physical Recovery*. Furthermore, the very global item i2 (… *I laughed*) from *Social Recovery* shows a specific relation to item i17 (… *I was in a good mood*), which makes sense and indicates a limited specificity of item i2 for *Social Recovery*. In addition, the correlation of *General Well-being* with the score for *Overall Recovery* was set equal to 1.

A comparison of the scale-specific measurement models and the measurement models of the dimensions results in a good model fit after items with similar content were allowed a specific correlation.

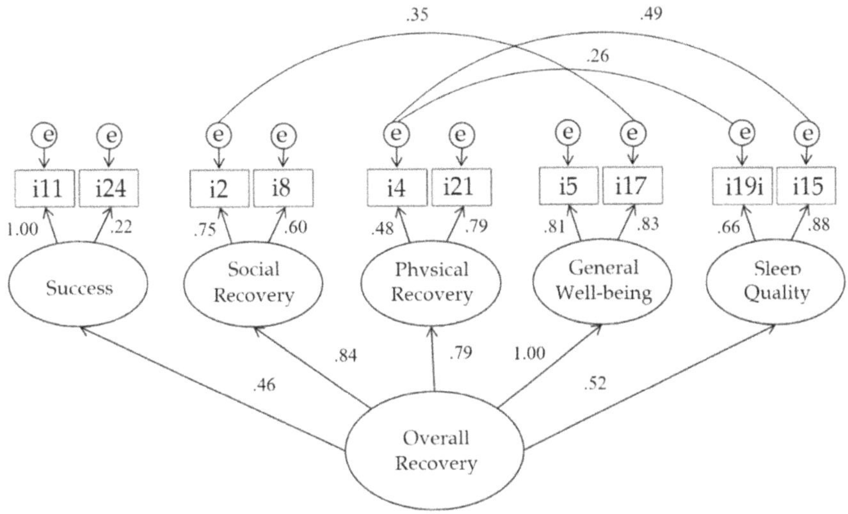

Figure 2.4 Measurement model for *Overall Recovery* (GFI = .96, AGFI = .93, CFI = .96, RMSEA = .07).

Construct validity

For the construct validity scale intercorrelations, Exploratory Factor Analysis and results from linear structural modelling will be reported first. Convergent validity will be reported for stress, recovery measures, and coping scales, and discriminant validity will shortly be addressed by data from studies in which the big five personality factors and anxiety measures were included.

Scale intercorrelations

The height of the scale correlations proved to be only partially stable across different samples; however, the fundamental correlation pattern is almost unchanged across all samples with respect to stress and recovery areas. Both, the stress and the recovery scales correlate positively with the scales of the same area, but they have a negative relationship with the scales of the other areas. This pattern is mainly stable between different samples (Table 2.7), gender, and age. In addition, the time frames only marginally affect the correlations of scales. Moderating variables like gender and age as well as instrumental variables like time frames or length of scales do not seem to influence the relationship between the scales substantially.

Intercorrelations are systematically lower in the pooled sample of top athletes with a time frame of three days/nights. Further examples of intercorrelations including the RESTQ-Basic are given by Kellmann and Kallus (this volume, Chapter 3) as well as Kellmann et al. (this volume, Chapter 4). The basic pattern of high to medium correlation within each dimension and medium negative correlations between the stress and the recovery dimension is stable across different samples and resulted in comparable results in Exploratory and Confirmatory Factor Analysis.

Factorial structure of the scales

Since factor analysis has established itself as a classic instrument for describing the intercorrelational structure, the results will be displayed briefly. Scales of the samples GB3 and GB4 were factor analysed via Principal Component Analysis followed by a Varimax rotation. After the stop criterion (Eigenvalue < 1; Kaiser), two factors could be extracted. The results confirm the two-factor solution published by Kallus (1995). All factor analyses suggest a separation of a stress-related and a recovery-related factor (Tables 2.8a and b).

The basic stress-related factor explains approximately 30%–35% of the variance; the recovery-related factor ranges between 19% and 27%. Thus, stress explains more variance of the RESTQ-Basic than recovery – a fact, which is reversed in the specific versions. However, it is important to note that stress and recovery factors are based on different numbers of scales.

For sample GB3, *Sleep Quality* shows a negative loading on stress. This reflects conceptual and instrumental overlaps. Sleep is a basic physiological process which helps to recover from fatigue and restore resources. At the same time, sleep is negatively affected by stressful events, and ruminative coping is likely to disturb sleep. Furthermore, sleep loss will increase stress reactivity (Grote, 2010; Kallus, 1992).

Table 2.7 Intercorrelations of the RESTQ-Basic-48 for the standard *(3) days/nights* time frame (sample GS2, N=597) and the *(7) days/nights* time frame (sample GC4, N=309).

					Upper data matrix: GS2							
RESTQ-Basic scales	*1*	*2*	*3*	*4*	*5*	*6*	*7*	*8*	*9*	*10*	*11*	*12*
1 General Stress		**.79**	.66	.58	.47	.60	.62	−.06	−.34	−.55	−.62	−.53
2 Emotional Stress	**.78**		**.78**	.59	.38	.57	.53	.01	−.30	−.41	−.57	−.49
3 Social Stress	.66	**.78**		.53	.35	.51	.44	.10	−.18	−.29	−.41	−.45
4 Conflicts/Pressure	.47	.40	.37		.44	.45	.49	.22	−.15	−.31	−.31	−.37
5 Fatigue	.50	.55	.46	.47		.50	.56	.12	−.11	−.45	−.27	−.51
6 Lack of Energy	.52	.59	.47	.31	.52		.52	−.03	−.20	−.42	−.39	−.38
7 Physical Complaints	.62	.60	.52	.42	**.72**	.64		−.05	−.19	−.63	−.42	−.52
8 Success	−.27	−.26	−.24	.18	−.15	−.34	−.23		.27	.31	.34	.13
9 Social Recovery	−.32	−.37	−.26	−.23	−.32	−.13	−.21	.31		.43	.66	.30
10 Physical Recovery	−.45	−.52	−.38	−.30	−.53	−.49	−.54	.57	.53		.69	.55
11 General Well-being	−.61	−.65	−.59	−.34	−.54	−.46	−.53	.53	.68	**.77**		.53
12 Sleep Quality	−.38	−.40	−.34	−.25	−.38	−.28	−.30	.27	.32	.43	.51	
					Lower data matrix: GC4							

Note: $r \geq .70$ are bolded.

Table 2.8a Two-factor-solution (with a > .25) for the RESTQ-Basic-48 for the sample GB3 (N=570).

RESTQ-Basic scales	*Factor 1*	*Factor 2*	h^2
1 General Stress	.78	−.30	.69
2 Emotional Stress	.79		.67
3 Social Stress	.78		.62
4 Conflicts/Pressure	.78		.63
5 Fatigue	.68		.50
6 Lack of Energy	.66		.47
7 Physical Complaints	.61	−.35	.49
8 Success		.68	.49
9 Social Recovery		.75	.58
10 Physical Recovery	−.38	.73	.67
11 General Well-being	−.37	.78	.74
12 Sleep Quality	−.51	.48	.49
Eigenvalue	5.31	1.73	
Variance in %	36.10	22.61	

Table 2.8b Two-factor-solution (with a > .25) for the RESTQ-Basic-48 for the sample GB4 (N= 484).

RESTQ-Basic scales	*Factor 1*	*Factor 2*	h^2
1 General Stress	.67		.49
2 Emotional Stress	.56	−.32	.42
3 Social Stress	.77		.62
4 Conflicts/Pressure	.78		.62
5 Fatigue	.58		.63
6 Lack of Energy	.73		.69
7 Physical Complaints	.65	−.39	.60
8 Success		.81	.65
9 Social Recovery		.77	.60
10 Physical Recovery		.72	.54
11 General Well-being		.59	.42
12 Sleep Quality		.75	.63
Eigenvalue	3.50	2.25	
Variance in %	29.83	18.85	

Three factor solutions with two stress sub-dimensions can be justified by scree plots as well (Kallus, 1995).

Structural modelling

The results from Exploratory Factor Analysis, the basic patterns of intercorrelations, which turned out to be stable across different populations, different versions, and different translations, led to the hypothesis that the basic structure of the RESTQ can well be reproduced by linear structural modelling with good model fit. The structural model for the RESTQ scales used scale values as 'manifest variables', and sub-dimensions were the 'latent variables'. Thus, the measurement models for the scales were considered acceptable. A model with two latent variables representing the dimensions 'stress' and 'recovery' fits the data well, as expected from Exploratory Factor Analysis.

Figure 2.5 shows that a model with one recovery factor and a stress factor with two sub-dimensions gives a good representation of the variance for the sample GS2 (N=597). This model could be replicated with different samples (Wagner-Hartl et al., this volume, Chapter 7) and data from different versions of the RESTQ.

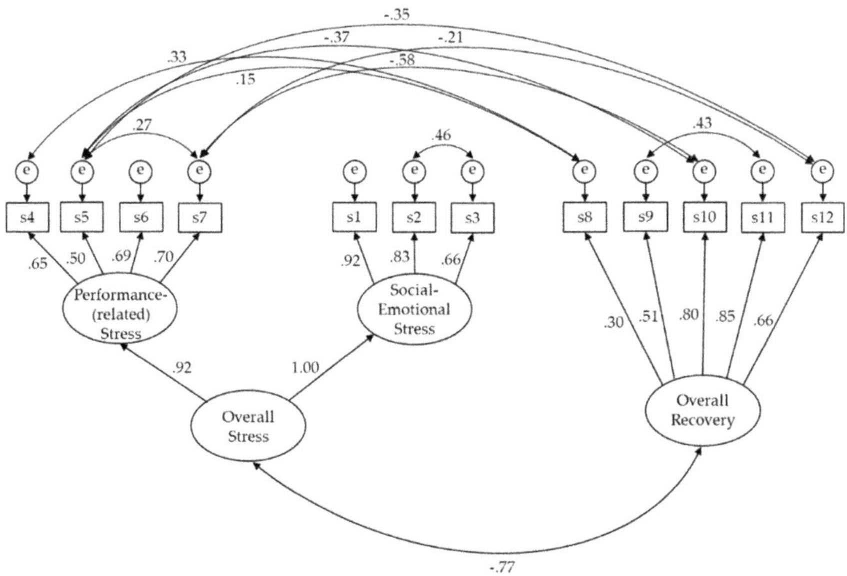

Figure 2.5 Structural model of the RESTQ-Basic scales (GFI=.94, AGFI=.89, CFI=.95, RMSEA=.08).

Note: s1: *General Stress*, s2: *Emotional Stress*, s3: *Social Stress*, s4: *Conflicts/Pressure*, s5: *Fatigue*, s6: *Lack of Energy*, s7: *Physical Complaints*, s8: *Success*, s9: *Social Recovery*, s10: *Physical Recovery*, s11: *General Well-being*, s12: *Sleep Quality*.

The separation of a stress and a recovery factor, which emerges from the correlational structure and the Exploratory Factor Analysis, can be strengthened by the linear structural model of the RESTQ-Basic. The model requires some specific correlations between scales within the sub-dimension: *Fatigue* (s5) and *Physical Complaints* (s7), *Emotional Stress* (s2), and *Social Stress* (s3). The correlation between *Social Recovery* (s9) and *General Well-being* (s11) can also be interpreted well and partly appeared already in the measurement models.

However, Figure 2.5 shows that a couple of specific correlations between dimensions must be allowed to obtain a good structural model of the RESTQ-Basic. No specific correlations from the sub-dimension *Social-Emotional Stress* to other areas are necessary. Specific correlations can be restricted to those between *Performance(-related) Stress* and *Overall Recovery*. As expected, origins of misfit are the scales *Conflicts/Pressure* and *Fatigue*, as these scales already showed problems in the measurement models. In addition, scale *Physical Complaints* is negatively related to the scales *Physical Recovery* and *Sleep Quality*, which makes sense from a functional point of view. *Conflicts/Pressure* is negatively related to *Success*, while *Fatigue* shows negative correlations with *Sleep Quality* and *Physical Recovery* and a small positive correlation to *Success*. These correlations as well as the results from the measurement models indicate that fatigue is a complex concept, which needs further research with respect to its role in the recovery-stress dynamics (Hockey, 2013).

Finally, the correlation between the dimensions and the option of the two sub-dimensions within the stress domain should be commented upon. For the structural model, the two sub-dimensions of stress can be omitted without losing the model fit. Thus, the *Overall Stress* score can well be interpreted. The high negative correlation between stress and recovery indicates that with increasing aggregation of concepts the correlational structure becomes less differentiated. Changes of the correlational pattern with aggregation of concepts have been discussed in Differential Psychology (Asendorpf & Neyer, 2012) and follows the same logic as the aggregation (summing up) of items to obtain reliable scale values (Wittmann, 1988). However, it is recommended not to misinterpret the correlation between the stress and recovery concept as indication to collapse them. This would be a step of oversimplification.

Convergent and discriminant validity

Convergent and discriminant validity of the RESTQ refer to the content of the constructs and to the state-trait aspects.

Correlations with actual condition/state

The expected relationships between the actual state and the RESTQ-Basic have been repeatedly empirically verified. Kallus (1995) published the first correlations between the basic RESTQ scales and various mood dimensions of the German Adjective Checklist (Eigenschaftwörterliste, EWL; Janke & Debus, 1978) and their short forms. For the RESTQ-Basic-48 correlations to state variables have been found in athletes and in coaches repeatedly in combination with the specific scales. Results are reported by Kellmann and Kallus (this volume, Chapter 3) as well as Kellmann et al. (this volume, Chapter 4) for the State-Trait-Anxiety Inventory (Spielberger et al., 1970), the Profile of Mood States (McNair et al., 1971/1992), and the Multidimensional Physical Symptom List (Erdmann & Janke, 1981).

Relationships with other stress and recovery scales

The expected high correlations between the RESTQ stress scales and the Trier Inventory of Chronic Stress (TICS; Schulz & Schlotz, 2002; Schulz et al., 2004) could be shown with a sample of blue-collar workers (Gaisbachgrabner, 2014; Table 2.9). Thus, chronic stress assessed by a frequency-based scaling of stressful events in the past four weeks is highly related to the recovery-stress state. However, there is a certain overlap of items between TICS and the earlier published RESTQ, but the instruments claim to address different facets of stress. The correlations (e.g., for *General Stress*) in Table 2.9 partly exceed reliabilities. Thus, very high convergent validities were shown for all scales of the RESTQ-Basic-24 with a time frame of seven days/nights.

The high values might be because states and events, which were experienced in the past seven days/nights will also be indicated, when asked for the past four weeks. But this part-whole relation is intransitive.

Chronic stress, depression, and burnout are concepts, which are used to explain the increasing prevalence and incidence rates of psychological and psychosomatic sickness rates in Western countries. RESTQ scores show consistent and theoretically expected correlational patterns to burnout, depression, and global health measures as the General Health Questionnaire (GHQ; Golderberg & Williams, 1988) or the Work Ability Index (WAI; Tuomi et al., 1998). These results are presented in detail by Jiménez et al. (this volume, Chapter 5).

In the past years, a couple of recovery-related scales were published. One of the most often used measures is the Need for Recovery Scale from a Dutch research group (van Veldhoven & Broersen, 2003). Table 2.10 presents the results from a sample of Austrian bus and tram drivers ($N=129$; Strohmaier, 2008), which show high correlations between the Need for Recovery Scale and the stress and recovery scales of the RESTQ-Basic.

The highest correlations are found for the RESTQ-Basic scale *Fatigue* (66% common variance). Recovery scales indicate high negative correlations which reach 52% common variance between *Physical Recovery* and the Need for Recovery Scale.

Table 2.9 Correlations between Trier Inventory of Chronic Stress (TICS) and RESTQ-Basic-24 (N= 173; Gaisbachgrabner, 2014).

	TICS-scales									
RESTQ-Basic scales	*1*	*2*	*3*	*4*	*5*	*6*	*7*	*8*	*9*	*10*
1 General Stress	**.86**	**.78**	**.83**	**.95**	**.98**	**.96**	**.74**	**.92**	**.71**	**.86**
2 Emotional Stress	**.75**	.23	.38	.50	.53	.50	.18	.50	.17	.33
3 Social Stress	.65	**.94**	**.91**	**.93**	**.89**	**.92**	**.92**	**.92**	**.89**	**.79**
4 Conflicts/ Pressure	.60	.43	.47	.67	**.70**	.67	.36	.63	.35	.65
5 Fatigue	.46	**.88**	.45	.56	.52	.54	.40	.55	.42	**.83**
6 Lack of Energy	**.74**	**.89**	**.91**	**.88**	**.88**	**.93**	**.88**	**.87**	**.87**	**.80**
7 Physical Complaints	**.76**	−.56	**.91**	**.91**	**.88**	**.89**	**.87**	**.88**	**.86**	**.80**
8 Success	−.40	−.59	−.53	−.61	−.46	−.58	−.55	−.65	−.53	−.56
9 Social Recovery	−.66	−.58	−.60	**−.74**	−.69	**−.70**	−.58	−.64	−.54	**−.71**
10 Physical Recovery	−.64	−.58	−.58	−.69	**−.74**	**−.78**	−.59	**−.71**	−.57	−.66
11 General Well-being	−.53	**−.70**	**−.70**	**−.76**	**−.74**	**−.72**	−.68	−.67	−.65	−.62
12 Sleep Quality	−.46	−.55	−.55	−.58	**−.73**	−.66	−.54	−.52	−.54	−.64

Note: $r \geq .70$ are bolded; 1 = *Work Overload*, 2 = *Social Overload*, 3 = *Pressure to Succeed*, 4 = *Work Dissatisfaction*, 5 = *Excessive Work Demands*, 6 = *Absence of Social Appreciation*, 7 = *Social Stress*, 8 = *Social Isolation*, 9 = *Chronic Worrying*, 10 = *Screening Scale* (Translations by Author).

Table 2.10 RESTQ-Basic-48/7 and Need for Recovery Scale (NfR) for a sample of public transport operators (N= 129; Strohmaier, 2008).

RESTQ-Basic scales	*NfR*
1 General Stress	**.72**
2 Emotional Stress	**.70**
3 Social Stress	.56
4 Conflicts/Pressure	.52
5 Fatigue	**.81**
6 Lack of Energy	**.72**
7 Physical Complaints	**.74**

(*Continued*)

Table 2.10 (Continued)

RESTQ-Basic scales	*NfR*
8 Success	−.46
9 Social Recovery	−.55
10 Physical Recovery	**−.72**
11 General Well-being	−.67
12 Sleep Quality	**−.71**

Note: $r \geq .70$ are bolded.

Table 2.11 Correlations between RESTQ and coping scales of the German Stress-Coping Inventory (SVF; $N = 187$; Kraxner, 2002).

	SVF-scales							
RESTQ-Basic scales	*1*	*2*	*3*	*4*	*5*	*6*	*7*	*8*
1 General Stress	.36	−.06	.41	.04	.18	.18	.33	.27
2 Emotional Stress	.27	−.13	.39	−.05	.12	.08	.28	.18
3 Social Stress	.37	−.09	.41	.00	.09	.05	.33	.15
4 Conflicts/Pressure	.16	.06	.30	.02	.17	.12	.24	.11
5 Fatigue	.32	.04	.30	−.01	.19	.24	.27	.21
6 Lack of Energy	.33	−.12	.31	−.05	.17	.04	.33	.19
7 Physical Complaints	.21	−.19	.19	−.17	−.01	.08	.16	.16
8 Success	−.20	.10	−.11	.01	−.06	−.03	−.24	−.03
9 Social Recovery	−.10	.12	−.20	.13	.02	−.07	−.14	−.03
10 Physical Recovery	−.22	.11	−.30	.04	−.11	−.07	−.23	−.13
11 General Well-being	−.23	.06	−.34	.05	−.13	−.16	−.30	−.11
12 Sleep Quality	.04	.05	−.07	.05	−.02	.13	−.01	.05

Note: 1 = *Self-Aggrandizement by Comparison with Others*, 2 = *Distraction*, 3 = *Situation Control*, 4 = *Positive Self-Instructions*, 5 = *Need for Social Support*, 6 = *Escape*, 7 = *Rumination*, 8 = *Resignation*.

Personality measures

Table 2.11 shows correlations with a short version of the German Stress-Coping Inventory (SVF; Erdmann & Janke, 2010) with data from Kraxner (2002).

Correlations to coping are low but theoretically consistent. This shows that coping and recovery should not be treated as two sides of the same coin. However, there are functional relations. Recovery can be markedly impaired in cases of insufficient coping. Coping strategies which allow switching off stress are needed to allow recovery processes, while ruminating coping strategies or continuing to manage the stress situation will prolong the stress response and block and impair recovery – at least in the short run. Thus, detailed studies which

Table 2.12 RESTQ-Basic and personality characteristics assessed with the NEO Personality Inventory (NEO-PI; N= 32; Streit, 2008).

	Scales of the NEO-PI				
RESTQ-Basic scales	*N*	*E*	*O*	*A*	*C*
1 General Stress	.46	−.01	.22	.07	−.27
2 Emotional Stress	.45	−.08	.03	−.30	−.25
3 Social Stress	.47	−.03	−.13	−.29	−.24
4 Conflicts/Pressure	.31	−.09	.22	−.17	−.25
5 Fatigue	.32	.13	.24	−.02	−.28
6 Lack of Energy	.07	.06	.30	−.16	−.51
7 Physical Complaints	−.01	.01	−.16	.01	−.02
8 Success	−.03	.14	−.02	−.09	−.04
9 Social Recovery	−.27	.29	−.11	.13	.35
10 Physical Recovery	−.31	−.02	−.21	.17	.38
11 General Well-being	−.20	−.09	−.27	.26	.17
12 Sleep Quality	−.39	−.15	−.11	−.04	.27

Note: N = *Neuroticism*, A = *Agreeableness*, E = *Extraversion*, C = *Conscientiousness*, O = *Openness*.

include short-term, mid-term, and long-term measures are needed to build a concept of the interplay of coping and recovery.

A couple of studies used personality questionnaires to describe the sample. From one of these studies correlations between the NEO Personality Inventory (Ostendorf & Angleitener, 2004) are presented in Table 2.12 (N=32; Streit, 2008).

The recovery-stress state is related to *Neuroticism*, particularly *Social Stress* and *Emotional Stress*. *Neuroticism* shows a negative relation to recovery, especially *Sleep Quality*. These correlations fit into the facets of *Neuroticism*. Quite interesting is the pattern for *Conscientiousness*. Here the highest negative correlation of the matrix is with scale *Lack of Energy*, and high correlations with *Social Recovery* and *Physical Recovery* occur. These relations call for more investigations. Note that *Extraversion* is related to *Social Recovery* and *Agreeableness* to low *Emotional Stress* and low *Social Stress*, which results in a theoretically consistent picture.

Studies on different facets of validity

This section will focus on psychophysiological data. Psychological measures have already been presented in the previous section on convergent and discriminant validity, and behavioural data will be presented in the section on case studies. The RESTQ assesses the bio-psycho-social aspects of stress and recovery and claims validity for all three areas.

Psychophysiological criteria

One of the most distinct features of the RESTQ is the high validity with respect to physiological symptoms. RESTQ scores are related to the susceptibility to catch a cold after a stressful period. This result has been published by Deinzer and Schuller (1998) and was also obtained with medical students by Kallus (1995). Both, *Overall Stress* and *Overall Recovery* scores, resulted in significant predictions of somatic symptoms after an examination. These results fit well in the more recent data, which allowed predicting the susceptibility to injuries in athletes (Kellmann & Kallus, this volume, Chapter 3; Steinacker et al., 1999).

Kallus (1995) reported that subjects classified as 'high stress/low recovery' showed increased reactivity in a stress experiment regarding anger in a public speaking situation.

Different physiological stress parameters were studied in the past years, which repeatedly demonstrated high validities of RESTQ scores with respect to the physical state of the subjects. Kraxner (2002) replicated correlations to metabolic processes (increased oxidative stress in females with low recovery scores). This result is depicted in Figure 2.6 (left). The effect could be replicated with a sample of patients, awaiting a surgical intervention (Figure 2.6, right). Note that for males a different picture emerged.

A study by Buchegger (2014) demonstrated that low recovery scores reflect a state of unfavourable metabolism. The result from 131 patients, who received a treatment in a health resort for musculoskeletal problems, is given in Figure 2.7. Patients were grouped into four groups according to high/low *Overall Stress* scores and high/low *Overall Recovery* scores in the RESTQ-Basic with respect to a representative sample of Austrian workers (Jiménez et al., this volume, Chapter 5). Time frame of the RESTQ was seven days/nights in this study. Both groups with low recovery scores show significantly increased low-density lipids values.

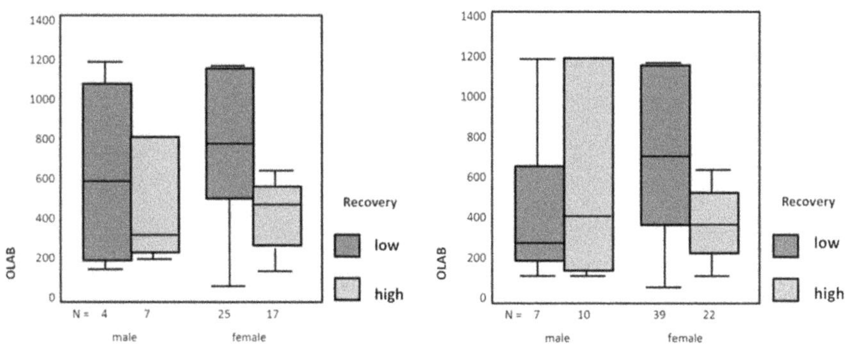

Figure 2.6 Oxidized lipid antibodies (OLAB) in two samples of patients with low/high recovery values in the RESTQ-Basic (boxplots; $N = 187$; Kraxner, 2002).

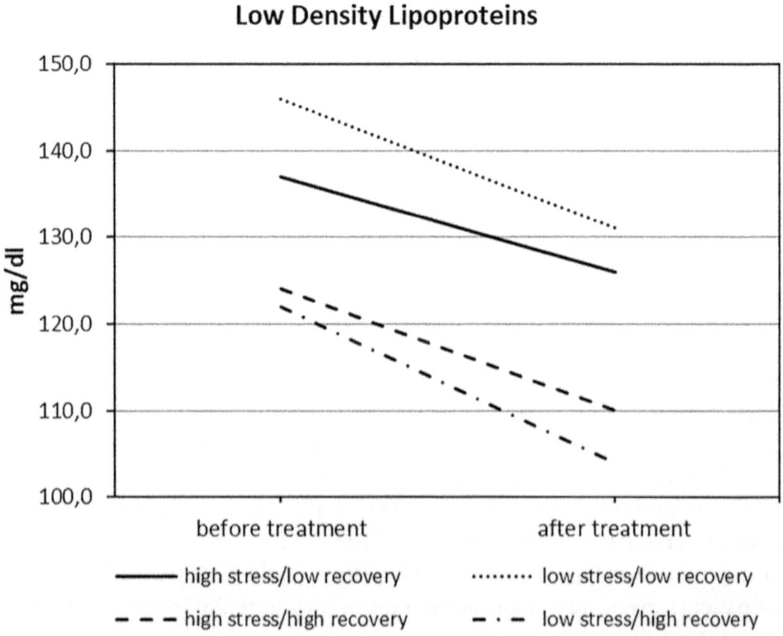

Figure 2.7 Low-density lipids in patients of a health resort ($N = 131$; Buchegger, 2014).

Sleep

Sleep is a physiological state which allows recovery from fatigue, muscular exhaustion, and metabolic as well as humoural dysregulation. *Sleep Quality* is one of the RESTQ-Basic scales and the scale intercorrelations as well as the structural modelling showed that sleep quality is related to both: recovery and stress (Table 2.13).

The results from Grote (2010) demonstrate that theoretically expected relations between different aspects of sleep as assessed by a sleep questionnaire (IND-Sleep Questionnaire; Grote, 2010) show consistent and high correlation to the *Sleep Quality* scale of the RESTQ. Recovery scales show low to moderate positive correlations, while stress scales show only very low negative correlations to the sleep scales. The IND-Sleep Questionnaire integrates different current sleep questionnaires.

Social criteria

Low correlations between RESTQ-Basic scales and *Need for Social Support* from the German Stress-Coping Inventory (Erdmann & Janke, 2010) were shown in Table 2.11.

A couple of social criteria are included in the concept of Social Capital in Organizations (Badura et al., 2008). Stelzhammer (2008) used the RESTQ answer format and the idea of items with close relation to experience and behaviour

Table 2.13 RESTQ scores and sleep quality (N=672; Grote, 2010).

RESTQ-Basic scales	*Sleep quality*	*Sleep attributes*	*Sleep rating*	*Sleep length*
1 General Stress	−.19	−.09	−.24	−.14
2 Emotional Stress	−.14	.05	−.22	−.21
3 Social Stress	−.09	.03	−.16	−.12
4 Conflicts/Pressure	−.12	.02	−.24	−.08
5 Fatigue	−.20	−.00	−.28	−.25
6 Lack of Energy	−.17	−.11	−.23	−.06
7 Physical Complaints	−.19	−.04	−.27	−.19
8 Success	.29	.26	.27	.13
9 Social Recovery	.12	.09	.20	.00
10 Physical Recovery	.28	.09	.36	.26
11 General Well-being	.34	.21	.39	.23
12 Sleep Quality	.55	.35	.56	.43

Table 2.14 Correlations between RESTQ sub-dimensions and the Social Capital Questionnaire (SCQ) scales (N=81; Stelzhammer, 2008).

SCQ scales	*Social-Emotional Stress*	*Performance (-related) Stress*	*Overall Recovery*
Leadership Ability	−.32	−.38	.46
Relationship Quality	−.21	.27	.42
Social Support	−.31	.33	.46
Integration New Staff	−.31	.29	.43
Strategic Cooperation	.36	.38	−.18
Appreciation	−.44	−.43	.47
Impact	−.16	−.16	.35
Communication	−.27	−.31	.54
Trust	−.29	−.28	.43
Identification with Company	−.33	−.32	.42
Involvement	−.40	−.36	.48
Breaks	—	.15	.21

(Kallus, 2016) to assess the different facets of social capital. Especially for the *Overall Recovery* of the RESTQ consistently positive correlations to social criteria like *Social Support*, *Appreciation*, and *Communication* occurred (Table 2.14).

A similar picture was found for *Team Quality* with the Team Quality Questionnaire (TQF; Brandt, 2010), which also uses the format of the RESTQ but with a time frame of four weeks. Fifty items assess the frequency of behaviours and experiences, which indicate good team quality (Table 2.15). Five core dimensions can be derived from TQF. They were correlated with the sub-dimensions of the RESTQ with a seven-day time frame with a sample pooled from rail system operators and management (N=88; Kallus & Brandt, 2011). Especially a good *Team Climate*, *Cooperation*, and *Leadership* are related to low stress and especially to better recovery.

As *Conflicts/Pressure* turned out to be a scale with variable internal consistency specific measures for conflicts at the workplace were developed. One of these instruments assesses the amount of conflict escalation by a frequency-based scale with a reference of four weeks (IKEAr; Kolodej et al., 2005).

High correlations for *Emotional Stress* with *Conflicts/Pressure* were obtained (Essler, 2007) together with negative correlations between recovery and conflict escalation (Table 2.16). However, the RESTQ-Basic scale *Conflicts/Pressure* is not linearly associated with amount of conflict escalation.

Table 2.15 RESTQ-Basic sub-dimensions and Team Quality (TQF; N=88; Kallus & Brandt, 2011).

	TQF 1	*TQF 2*	*TQF 3*	*TQF 4*	*TQF 5*
Social-Emotional Stress	−.32	−.32	−.18	−.12	−.39
Performance(-related) Stress	−.18	−.25	−.05	.03	−.24
Overall Recovery	.37	.42	.29	.25	.38

Note: TQF 1 = *Leadership*, TQF 2 = *Cooperation*, TQF 3 = *Capacity to Act*, TQF 4 = *Productivity*, TQF 5 = *Team Climate*.

Table 2.16 Recovery-stress scales and conflict escalation (IKEAr; N=171; Essler, 2007).

RESTQ-Basic scales	*Conflict escalation*
1 General Stress	.23
2 Emotional Stress	.43
3 Social Stress	.27
4 Conflicts/Pressure	.10
5 Fatigue	.02
6 Lack of Energy	.36
7 Physical Complaints	.25
8 Success	−.00
9 Social Recovery	−.21
10 Physical Recovery	−.32
11 General Well-being	−.30
12 Sleep Quality	−.23

Application studies

The RESTQ scales allow to draw a recovery-stress profile as the sequence of scales was composed based on scale correlations and refined by the means (Kallus, 2016). Thus, changes in the profile reflect changes in the recovery-stress state in an easy picture. The profile is highly sensitive to stress-related or recovery-related activities and interventions. This was already reported in the first manual on the RESTQ for changes in the state of students during a period of examinations and for participation in stress management courses (Kallus, 1995).

A large-scale study by Collatz (2002) on the effects of mother-child health resort interventions for underprivileged mothers used the RESTQ to assess the initial state during admission to the resort, one measurement after the intervention and in a three-month follow-up (dotted line).

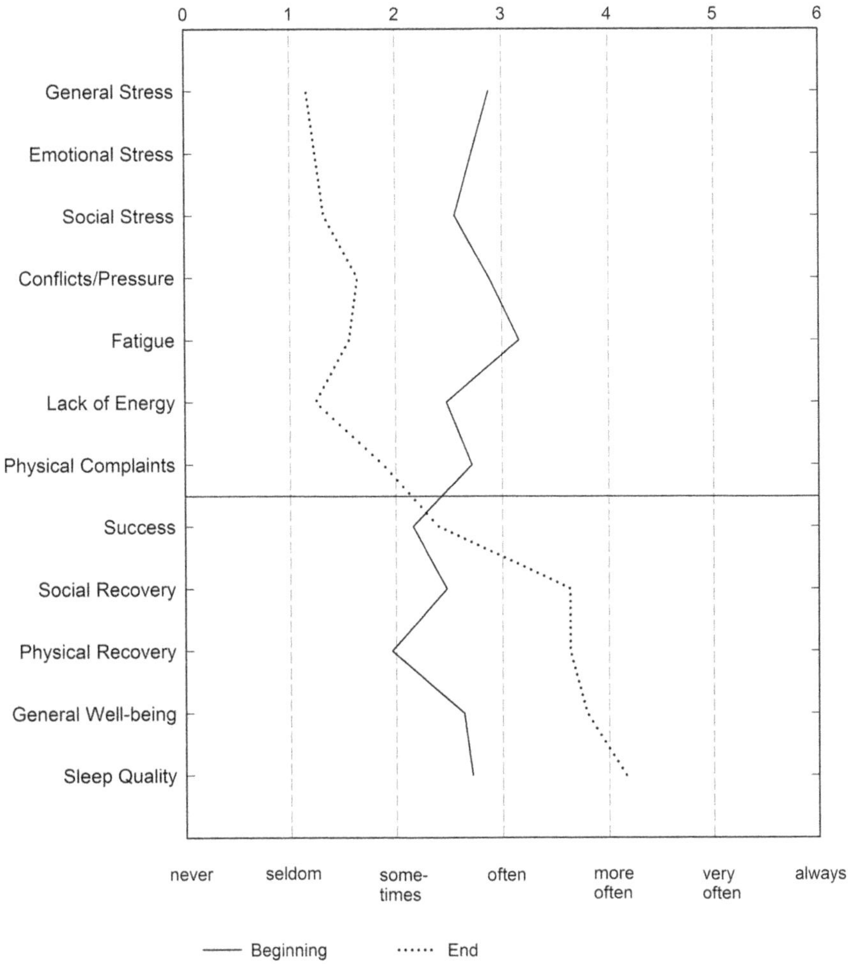

Figure 2.8 Changes during a therapeutic stay of mother and child at a health resort ($N = 2346$; Collatz, 2002).

Figure 2.8 shows overall significant changes from start to end of a mother-child rehabilitation program in which 2346 mothers participated (Collatz, 2002). A total change in the overall profile reflects the high sensitivity of the RESTQ for changes in the psychophysical state.

Areas of application

Areas of application exceed stress and recovery research. As can be seen for the specific forms of the RESTQ, there is always a large proportion of variance in the applied data, which can be explained by the RESTQ-Basic scales. The RESTQ-Basic allows assessing the overall psychophysical state of a person, the psychophysical 'fitness' in a global way. Thus, an important area of application which emerged is occupational health and occupational fitness monitoring. In a couple of projects, the effects of occupational health promotion projects could be well documented by changes in the recovery-stress state of the participants.

Another related area which has become of central importance due to legal regulations is the assessment of occupational stress. In combination with instruments which identify sources of stress, RESTQ-values deliver valuable hints which persons will need support and in which areas resources are still available.

An important area might also be recovery-stress checks for persons who undergo extremely demanding situations (Wagner-Hartl et al., this volume, Chapter 7).

Reference values and norms

These values are summarized in the Online Appendix A.A2 and A.A3 together with standard deviations for English and German samples. Norms were split for gender, as significant differences occurred for some scales.

For the dimensions and sub-dimensions additional values are given from a large sample from pooled online studies (N=3758; Kallus & Brandt, 2011). The sample consists of 1577 females and 1688 males. Values are given for both genders in Online Appendix A.F3.

Summary

- The RESTQ provides clinical and health psychologists, work, and organizational psychologists as well as sport psychologists and developmental psychologists with important information about the current state of a person or group of persons with respect to the basic processes of stress and recovery, which have a basic relevance for the state of the individual's resources.
- Together with the specific modules, the RESTQ profiles allow to derive interventions and to evaluate the effects of interventions or monitor functional changes.
- The high validities to trait like concepts (e.g., chronic stress) allow using the RESTQ even to evaluate more long-term states in larger groups and to check for changes after interventions.

- An increasing field of application seems to open, as the question "is my client, colleague, sports mate, patient, staff, team, operator … fit (enough) for the intended activity or to cope with the challenge or threat" is of increasing relevance in our high-performance society.
- At the same time, the other end of the scale 'how exhausted are the resources' is of central importance after stressful situations. Maybe the diagnosis of burnout is just one facet of a more general 'flat tyre syndrome', which is reflected in low recovery high stress scores in the RESTQ.
- New syndromes like long-term COVID or related ones like chronic fatigue might profit from monitoring the RESTQ profiles.

Note

1 However, the German version of the RESTQ translates 'stress' to 'Belastung' in the title of the questionnaire which is misleading in the light of the terminology in Work Psychology and ISO 10075 (Hacker & Sachse, 2014). Items of the RESTQ address both, situational aspects, the process components, and the states and reactions of the stress process. Scores finally reflect the state of the person which is closer to the reaction-oriented term 'Beanspruchung'. This should be kept in mind when interpreting the scores of the RESTQ.

References

Åkerstedt, T., & Kecklung, G. (2012). Sleep, work, and occupational stress. In C. M. Morin & C. Espie (Eds.), *The Oxford handbook of sleep and sleep disorders* (pp. 248–265). Oxford University Press.

Allmer, H. (1996). *Erholung und Gesundheit. Grundlagen, Ergebnisse und Maßnahmen* [Recovery and health. Fundamentals, results, and interventions]. Hogrefe.

Allmer, H., & Niehues, C. (1989). Individuelle Erholungsmaßnahmen nach mentalen Arbeitsanforderungen unter Berücksichtigung der sportlichen Aktivität [Individual recovery after mental workload while considering the physical activity]. *Brennpunkt der Sportwissenschaft, 3*, 164–183.

Altfeld, S., & Kellmann, M. (2014). Analyse der Beanspruchungs- und Erholungsbilanz deutscher Trainer [Analyses of the stress-recovery balance of German coaches]. *Zeitschrift für Sportpsychologie, 21*, 137–148.

Altfeld, S., & Kellmann, M. (2015). Are German coaches highly exhausted? A study of differences in personal and environmental factors in relation to emotional exhaustion. *International Journal of Sports Science and Coaching, 10*(4), 637–654.

Asendorpf, J. B., & Neyer, F. J. (2012). *Psychologie der Persönlichkeit* [Psychology of personality]. Springer.

Badura, B., Greiner, W., Rixgens, P., Ueberle, M., & Behr, M. (2008). *Sozialkapital: Grundlagen für Gesundheit und Unternehmenserfolg* [Social capital: Basis for health and business success]. Springer.

Bakker, A. B. (2011). An evidence-based model of work engagement. *Current Directions in Psychological Science, 20*(4), 265–269.

Binnewies, C., & Sonnentag, S. (2013). The application of diary methods to examine workers' daily recovery during off-job time. In A. S. Bakker & K. Daniels (Eds.), *A day in the life of a happy worker* (pp. 72–84). Psychology Press.

Bradburn, N. (1969). *The structure of psychological well-being*. Aldine.

Brandt, J. (2010). *Struktur der Teamqualität. Analyse der Zusammenhänge zwischen Prozessen und Emergent States in Teams mit dem Teamqualitäts-Fragebogen TQF* [Structure of team quality: Analysis of the relationship between processes and emergent states in teams]. Südwestdeutscher Verlag für Hochschulschriften.

Brodsky, S. L. (1988). The psychology of adjustment and well-being. Holt, Rinehart and Winston.

Buchegger, C. (2014). *The effect of the stress-recovery state on the regeneration process – A study in a health resort* [Conference presentation]. AOW Plattform meeting, University of Vienna, Austria.

Bühner, M. (2010). *Einführung in die Test- und Fragebogenkonstruktion* [Introduction into test and questionnaire construction]. Pearson Studium.

Carver, C. S. (2011). Coping. In R. J. Contrada & A. Baum (Eds.), *The handbook of stress science: Biology, psychology, and health* (pp. 221–229). Springer.

Chandola, T., Britton, A., Brunner, E., Hemingway, H., Malik, M., Kumari, M., Badrick, E., Kivimaki, M., & Marmot, M. (2008). Work stress and coronary heart disease: What are the mechanisms? *European Heart Journal, 29*, 640–648.

Cohen, S. (1988). Psychological models of social support in the etiology of physical disease. *Health Psychology*, 7, 269–297.

Cohen, S. (2004). Social relationships and health. *American Psychologist, 59*(8), 676–684.

Collatz, J. (2002). Forschungsergebnisse zur Qualität und Effektivität von Mütter- und Mutter-Kind-Maßnahmen [Research findings to quality and effectiveness of mothers and mother-child measures]. In J. Collatz, S. Sperlich, & S. Arnhold-Kerri (Eds.), *II. Wissenschaftliches Symposium: Brauchen Mütter rehabilitative Maßnahmen?* (pp. 44–62). Verlag für Wissenschaft und Bildung.

Cooper, C. L. (Ed.). (2000). *Theories of stress*. Oxford University Press.

Debus, G. (1981). Das Konzept der reaktiven Anspannungssteigerung [The concept of reactive increase of actvation]. In L. Tent (Ed.), *Erkennen, Wollen, Handeln* (pp. 233–252). Hogrefe.

Deinzer, R., & Schuller, N. (1998). Dynamics of stress-related decrease of salivary immunoglobulin A (sIgA): Relationship to symptoms of the common cold and studying behavior. *Behavioral Medicine, 24*(1), 27–27.

DeLongis, A., Folkman, S., & Lazarus, R. S. (1988). The impact of daily stress on health and mood: Psychological and social resources as mediators. *Journal of Personality and Social Psychology, 54*(3), 486–495.

Düker, H. (1963). Über reaktive Anspannungssteigerung [On reactive increase of activation]. *Zeitschrift für experimentelle und angewandte Psychologie, 10*, 46–73.

Dweck, C. S. (2006). *Mindset: The new psychology of success*. Random House.

Dweck, C. S. (2012). *Mindset: How you can fulfil your potential*. Constable & Robinson Limited.

Eime, R. M., Young, J. A., Harvey, J. T., Charity, M. J., & Payne, W. R. (2013). A systematic review of the psychological and social benefits of participation in sport for adults: Informing development of a conceptual model of health through sport. *International Journal of Behavioral Nutrition and Physical Activity, 10*, 135–149.

Emmons, R. A. (1986). Personal strivings: An approach to personality and subjective well-being. *Journal of Personality and Social Psychology, 51*, 1058–1068.

Emmons, R. A., & Diener, E. (1985). Factors predicting satisfaction judgments: A comparative examination. *Social Indicators Research, 16*, 157–167.

Erdmann, G., & Janke, W. (1981). *Mehrdimensionale körperliche Symptomliste* [Multidimensional physical symptom list; Unpublished questionnaire]. TU of Berlin/University of Würzburg, Germany.

Erdmann, G., & Janke, W. (2010). *Stressverarbeitungsfragebogen SVF (Handbuch): Stress, Stressverarbeitung und ihre Erfassung durch ein mehrdimensionales Testsystem* [German Coping Inventory SVF (Manual)]. Hogrefe.

Essler, T. (2007). *Entwicklung eines Inventars zur Erfassung von Mobbingverhaltensweisen am Arbeitsplatz* [Development of an inventory to assess work place harassment; Unpublished master's thesis]. University of Graz, Austria.

Folkman, S., & Lazarus, R. S. (1988). *Ways of Coping Questionnaire.* Consulting Psychologists Press.

Frankenhaeuser, M., & Rissler, A. (1970). Effects of punishment on catecholamine release and efficiency of performance. *Psychopharmacologia, 17*, 378–390.

Frese, M., & Zapf, D. (1994). Action as the core of work psychology: A German approach. In H. C. Triandis, M. D. Dunnette, & L. M. Hough (Eds.), *Handbook of industrial and organizational psychology* (Vol. 4, pp. 271–340). Consulting Psychologists Press.

Fukuda, K., Straus, S. E., Hickie, I., Sharpe, M. C., Dobbins, J. G., & Komaroff, A. (1994). The chronic fatigue syndrome: A comprehensive approach to its definition and study. *American College of Physicians, 121*(12), 953–959.

Gaisbachgrabner, K. (2014). *Empirische Untersuchungen zu langen Arbeitszeiten und dem Hypothalamus-Hypophysen-Schilddrüsen-System im Mehrebenenansatz* [Empirical studies on the effects of long working hours on the hypothalamus-pituitary-thyroid-system; Unpublished doctoral dissertation]. University of Graz, Austria.

Gappmaier, E. (2007). *Konflikte und Mobbing unter Berücksichtigung der Aspekte Erholung und Beanspruchung älterer ArbeitnehmerInnen* [Conflicts and mobbing with respect to recovery and stress of aging workers; Unpublished master's thesis]. University of Graz, Austria.

Gerber, M., Schilling, R., Colledge, F., Ludyga, S., Pühse, U., & Brand, S. (2020). More than a simple pastime? The potential of physical activity to moderate the relationship between occupational stress and burnout symptoms. *International Journal of Stress Management, 27*(1), 53–64.

Gloria, C. T., Faulk, K. E., & Steinhardt, M. A. (2013). Positive affectivity predicts successful and unsuccessful adaptation to stress. *Motivation and Emotion, 37*(1), 185–193.

Goettlicher, K. (2014). *Burnout, self-regulation, stress, recovery and job characteristics at work: Modelling the relationship via structural equation model and latent growth curve methodology* [Unpublished doctoral dissertation]. University of Graz, Austria.

Golderberg, D., & Williams, P. (1988). *A user's guide to the General Health Questionnaire.* NFER-Nelson.

Gray, J. A. (1976). 'The behavioural inhibition system: A possible substrate for anxiety'. In M. P. Feldman & A. M. Broadhurst (Eds.), *Theoretical and experimental bases of behaviour modification* (pp. 3–41). Wiley.

Gray, J. A. (1982). *The neuropsychology of anxiety: An enquiry into the functions of the septo-hippocampal system.* Oxford University Press.

Grote, V. (2010). *Schlaferholung und Herzratenvariabilität als Indikatoren für Wohlbefinden und Gesundheit: Ergebnisse zur aktuellen Schlaferholung im Kontext von Schlafdauer, Schlafdefizit, Beanspruchung, Wohlbefinden und kardial-vegetativen Regulationskennwerten der Herzratenvariabilität bei nicht schlafgestörten Erwachsenen* [Sleep recovery and heart rate variability as indicators of well-being and health: Results on current sleep recovery in the context of sleep duration, sleep deficit, stress, well-being and cardio-vegetative regulation parameters of heart rate variability in non-sleep-disordered adults; Unpublished doctoral dissertation]. University of Graz, Austria.

Hacker, W., & Sachse, P. (2014). *Allgemeine Arbeitspsychologie. Psychische Regulation von Tätigkeiten* [General work psychology. Psychic regulation of activities]. Hogrefe.

Hancock, P. A. (2008). *Performance under stress*. Ashgate.

Hellbrück, J., & Fischer, M. (1999). *Umweltpsychologie. Ein Lehrbuch* [Environmental Psychology: A textbook]. Hogrefe.

Hellhammer, D. H., Stone, A. A., Hellhammer, J., & Broderick, J. (2010). Measuring stress. In G. F. Koob, M. Le Moal, & R. F. Thompson (Eds.), *Encyclopedia of behavioral neuroscience* (pp. 186–191). Academic Press.

Henry, J. P., & Stephens, P. M. (1977). *Stress, health, and the social environment. A sociobiological approach to medicine*. Springer.

Hobfoll, S. E. (1989). Conservation of resources: A new attempt at conceptualizing stress. *American Psychologist, 44*(3), 513–524.

Hobfoll, S. E., Halbesleben, J., Neveu, J.-P., & Westman, M. (2018). Conservation of resources in the organizational context: The reality of resources and their consequences. *Annual Review of Organizational Psychology and Organizational Behavior, 5*, 103–128.

Hockey, G. R. J. (2013). *The psychology of fatigue: Work, effort and control*. University Press.

Hollnagel, E., Braithwaite, J., & Wears, R. L. (2013). *Resilient health care*. Ashgate.

Holm, J. E., & Holroyd, K. A. (1992). The Daily Hassles Scale (revised): Does it measure stress or symptoms? *Behavioral Assessment, 14*, 465–482.

Holmes, T. H., & Rahe, R. H. (1967). The social readjustment rating scale. *Journal of Psychosomatic Research, 11*(2), 213–221.

Hüppe, M., & Uhlig, T. (1992). Zur Intensität und Spezifität von Motiven im Freizeitsport [On the intensity and specificity of motives in recreational sports]. *Schweizerische Zeitschrift für Psychologie, 51*, 177–190.

Isen, A. M. (1970). Success, failure, attention and reactions to others: The warm glow of success. *Journal of Personality and Social Psychology, 15*, 294–301.

Janke, W. (1976). Psychophysische Grundlagen des Verhaltens [Psychophysic fundamentals of behaviour]. In M. von Kerekjarto (Ed.), *Medizinische Psychologie* (pp. 1–101). Springer.

Janke, W., & Debus, G. (1978). *Die Eigenschaftswörterliste (EWL). Handanweisung* [Adjective Checklist. Manual]. Hogrefe.

Janke, W., & Erdmann, G. (2002). *SVF 78. Eine Kurzform des Stressverarbeitungsfragebogens SVF 120. Manual* [SVF 78. Short version of the Stress Coping Questionnaire. Manual]. Hogrefe.

Janke, W., & Wolffgramm, J. (1995). Biopsychologie von Streß und emotionalen Reaktionen: Ansätze interdisziplinärer Kooperation von Psychologie, Biologie und Medizin [Biopsychology of stress and emotional reactions: Starting points of an interdisciplinary cooperation of psychology, biology, and medicine]. In G. Debus, G. Erdmann, & K. W. Kallus (Eds.), *Biospsychologie von Streß und emotionalen Reaktionen* (pp. 293–349). Hogrefe.

Kallus, K. W. (1989). Effects of initial state on psychophysiological stress reactions: Experimental evidence. In M. Weiner, I. Florin, R. Murison, & D. Hellhammer (Eds.), *Frontiers of stress research: Neuronal control of bodily function. Basic and clinical aspects* (Vol. 3, pp. 379–382). Huber.

Kallus, K. W. (1992). *Beanspruchung und Ausgangszustand* [Stress and initial state]. PVU.

Kallus, K. W. (1994). Belastung im Alltag – Regeneration beim Sport [Workload in everyday life – Regeneration by sports]. In T. Uhlig (Ed.), *Gesundheitssport im Verein. Bericht über den DTB-Kongress 10.-12.11.1994 in Schwäbisch Gmünd Band 2* (pp. 165–168). Karl Hoffmann.

Kallus, K. W. (1995). *Der Erholungs-Belastungs-Fragebogen* [The Recovery-Stress Questionnaire]. Swets & Zeitlinger.

Kallus, K. W. (2002). Impact of recovery in different areas of application. In M. Kellmann (Ed.), *Enhancing recovery: Preventing underperformance in athletes* (pp. 283–300). Human Kinetics.

Kallus, K. W. (2016). *Erstellung von Fragebogen* [Construction of questionnaires]. Facultas.

Kallus, K. W., & Brandt, J. (2011). *Databank on recovery-stress state and team quality*. Institut für Begleitforschung Würzburg/Graz, Germany/Austria.

Kallus, K. W., & Erdmann, G. (1994). Zur Wechselbeziehung zwischen Ausgangszustand, Belastung und Erholung [The interrelations of inital state, stress, and recovery]. In R. Wieland-Eckelmann, H. Allmer, J. Otto, & K. W. Kallus (Eds.), *Arbeit und Erholung. Studien zur Aktivierung, Belastung und zum Arbeits-Erholungszyklus* (pp. 46–67). PVU.

Kallus, K. W., & Krauth, J. (1995). Nichtparametrische Verfahren zum Nachweis emotionaler Reaktionen [Non-parametric methods for the provement of emotional reactions]. In G. Debus, G. Erdmann, & K. W. Kallus (Eds.), *Biopsychologie von Stress und emotionalen Reaktionen* (pp. 23–43). Hogrefe.

Kallus, K. W., & Uhlig, T. (2001). Erholungsforschung: Neue Perspektiven zum Verständnis von Stress [Recovery research: New perspectives in understanding stress]. In R. K. Silbereisen & R. M. Reitzle (Eds.), *Psychologie 2000 – Bericht über den 42. Kongress der Deutschen Gesellschaft für Psychologie in Jena 2000* (pp. 364–379). Pabst Science Publishers.

Karabinski, T., Haun, V. C., Nübold, A., Wendsche, J., & Wegge, J. (2021). Interventions for improving psychological detachment from work: A meta-analysis. *Journal of Occupational Health Psychology, 26*(3), 224–242.

Karasek, R. A. (1979). Job demands, job decision latitude and mental strain: Implications for job redesign. *Administrative Science Quarterly, 24*, 285–308.

Kellmann, M. (2002). Psychological assessment of underrecovery. In M. Kellmann (Ed.), *Enhancing recovery: Preventing underperformance in athletes* (pp. 37–55). Human Kinetics.

Kellmann, M., & Beckmann, J. (Eds.). (2022). *Recovery and well-being in sport and exercise*. Routledge.

Kellmann, M., & Beckmann, J. (Eds.). (2024). *Fostering recovery and well-being in a healthy lifestyle: Psychological, somatic, and organizational prevention approaches*. Routledge.

Kellmann, M., Bertollo, M., Bosquet, L., Brink, M., Coutts, A. J., Duffield, R., Erlacher, D., Halson, S. L., Hecksteden, A., Heidari, J., Kallus, K. W., Meeusen, R., Mujika, I., Robazza, C., Skorski, S., Venter, R., & Beckmann, J. (2018). Recovery and performance in sport: Consensus statement. *International Journal of Sports Physiology and Performance, 13*, 240–245.

Kellmann, M., Jakowski, S., & Beckmann, J. (Eds.). (2023). *The importance of recovery for physical and mental health: Negotiating the effects of underrecovery*. Routledge.

Kellmann, M., Pelka, M., & Beckmann, J. (2024). Psychological relaxation techniques to enhance recovery in sports. In M. Kellmann & J. Beckmann (Eds.), *Fostering recovery and well-being in a healthy lifestyle: Psychological, somatic, and organizational prevention approaches* (pp. 117–130). Routledge.

Ketttä, G., & Hassmén, P. (1998). Overtraining and recovery. *Sports Medicine, 26*, 1–16.

Kogler, B. (2007). *Beanspruchung und Erholung bei älteren Arbeitnehmerinnen* [Stress and recovery in aging workers; Unpublished master's thesis]. University of Graz, Austria.

Kolodej, C., Reiter, M., & Kallus, K. W. (2013). Inventar zur Erhebung resilienten Verhaltens im Arbeitskontext (REVERA) [Inventory of resilient behaviour at the work place]. *Wirtschaftspsychologie, 15*(2–3), 16–25.

Kolodej, C., Voutsinas, A., Jimènez, P., & Kallus, K. W. (2005). Inventar zur Messung des Eskalationsgrades von Konflikten in der Arbeitswelt [Inventory to assess conflict-escalation in the workplace]. *Wirtschaftspsychologie, 4*, 19–28.

Kraxner, M. (2002). *Erholungs-Beanspruchungszustand und oxidativer Stress* [Recovery-stress state and oxidativ stress; Unpublished doctoral dissertation]. University of Graz, Austria.

Kryter, K. D. (1970). *The effects of nose on man*. Academic Press.

Kuiper, N. A., Martin, R. A., & Olinger, L. J. (1993). Coping humour, stress, and cognitive appraisals. *Canadian Journal of Behavioural Science, 25*, 81–96.

Lakey, B., & Orehek, E. (2011). Relational regulation theory: A new approach to explain the link between perceived social support and mental health. *Psychological Review, 118*, 482–495.

Lazarus, R. S. (1966). *Psychological stress and the coping process*. McGraw-Hill.

Lazarus, R. S. (1991). *Emotion and adaptation*. Oxford University Press.

Lazarus, R. S. (1993). Coping theory and research: Past, present, and future. *Psychosomatic Medicine, 55*, 234–247.

Lazarus, R. S. (1999). *Stress and emotion. A new synthesis*. Free Association Books.

Lazarus, R. S., & Launier, R. (1978). Stress-related transactions between person and environment. In L. A. Pervon & M. Lewis (Eds.), *Perspectives in interactional psychology* (pp. 287–327). Plenum.

Leiter, M. P., & Harvie, P. (1998). Conditions for staff acceptance of organizational change: Burnout as a mediating construct. *Anxiety, Stress & Coping, 11*, 1–25.

Lernbeiss, S. (2008). *Validierung des Erholungs-Belastungs-Fragebogens für den arbeitsspezifischen Bereich (EBF-Work)* [Validation of the Recovery-Stress Questionnaire for the work area (RESTQ-Work); Unpublished master's thesis]. University of Graz, Austria.

Lienert, G. A. (1969). *Testaufbau und Testanalyse* [Development and analysis of tests]. Beltz.

Lienert, G. A., & Raatz, U. (1994). *Testaufbau und Testanalyse* [Development and analysis of tests]. PVU.

Lord, F. M., & Novick, M. R. (1968). *Statistical theories of mental test scores*. Addison-Wesley.

Maslach, C., & Leiter, M. P. (1997). *The truth about burnout*. Jossey-Bass.

McClelland, D. (1988). *Human motivation*. Cambridge University Press.

McEwen, B. S. (1998). Stress, adaption and disease. Allostasis and allostatic load. *Annals of the New York Academy of Sciences, 840*, 33–44.

McNair, D. M., Lorr, M., & Droppleman, L. F. (1971/1992). *Manual for the Profile of Mood States*. Educational and Industrial Testing Services.

Meijman, T. F., & Mulder, G. (1998). Psychological aspects of workload. In P. J. D. Drenth & H. Thierry (Eds.), *Handbook of work and organizational psychology. Work psychology* (pp. 5–33). Psychology.

Moosbrugger, H. (1982). Dimensionalitätsuntersuchungen von FPI-Skalen mit dem Klassischen Latent-Additiven Testmodell (KLA-Modell) [Dimensionality studies of FPI-scales with the classical latent-additive test model (CLA-model)]. *Zeitschrift für Differentielle und Diagnostische Psychologie, 3*, 241–264.

Neufeld, R. W. J. (1999). Dynamic differentials of stress and coping. *Psychological Review, 106*, 385–397.

Noor, N., Urits, I., Degueure, A., Rando, L., Kata, V., Cornett, E. M., Kaye, A. D., Imani, F., Narimani-Zamanabadi, M., Varrassi, G., & Viswanath, O. (2021). A comprehensive update of the current understanding of Chronic Fatigue Syndrome. *Anesthesiology and Pain Medicine, 11*(3), e113629. https://doi.org/10.5812/aapm.113629

Ostendorf, F., & Angleitner, A. (2004). *NEO-Persönlichkeitsinventar nach Costa und McCrae. Revidierte Fassung (NEO-PI-R)* [NEO Personality Inventory according to Costa and McCrae. Revised version (NEO-PI-R)]. Hogrefe.

Parker, S. L., Sonnentag, S., Jimmieson, N. L., & Newton, C. J. (2020). Relaxation during the evening and next-morning energy: The role of hassles, uplifts, and heart rate variability during work. *Journal of Occupational Health Psychology, 25*(2), 83–98.

Pinel, J. P. (2013). *Biopsychology*. Pearson.

Pines, A. (1993). Burnout: An existential perspective. In W. B. Schaufeli, D. Maslach, & T. Marek (Eds.), *Professional burnout: Research developments in theory and research* (pp. 386–402). Taylor & Francis.

Prather, A. A., Bogdan, R., & Hariri, A. R. (2013). Impact of sleep quality on amygdala reactivity, negative affect, and perceived stress. *Psychosomatic Medicine, 75*(4), 350–358.

Rau, R. (2006). Learning opportunities at work as predictor for recovery and health. *European Journal of Work and Organizational Psychology, 15*(2), 158–180.

Rau, R., & Richter, P. (1996). Psychophysiological analysis of strain in real life work situations. In J. Fahrenberg & M. Myrtek (Eds.), *Ambulatory assessment. Computer-assisted psychological and psychophysiological methods in monitoring and field studies* (pp. 271–285). Hogrefe & Huber.

Rauscher, M. (2007). *Arbeitsfähigkeit älterer ArbeitnehmerInnen und Arbeitsloser unter Berücksichtigung der Beanspruchung und Erholung, den Stressverarbeitungsweisen und der Hoffnungslosigkeit* [Workability of aging workers and unemployed with respect to stress and recovery; Unpublished master's thesis]. University of Graz, Austria.

Renzland, J., & Eberspächer, H. (1988). *Regeneration im Sport* [Regeneration in sports]. bps.

Roe, R. A. (2014). Test validity from a temporal perspective. Incorporating time in validation research. *European Journal of Work & Organizational Psychology, 23*(5), 754–768.

Rüger, U., Blomert, A. F., & Förster, W. (1990). *Coping. Theoretische Konzepte, Forschungsansätze, Messinstrumente zur Krankheitsbewältigung* [Coping. Theoretical concepts, research approaches, measuring tools in coping with the disease]. Vandenhoeck & Ruprecht.

Salmon, P. (2001). Effects of physical exercise on anxiety, depression, and sensitivity to stress: A unifying theory. *Clinical Psychology Review, 21*, 33–61.

Schaufeli, W. B., & Bakker, A. B. (2004). Job demands, job resources, and their relationship with burnout and engagement. *Journal of Organizational Behavior, 25*, 293–315.

Schönpflug, W. (1983). Coping efficiency and situational demands. In G. R. J. Hockey (Ed.), *Stress and fatigue in human performance* (pp. 299–330). Wiley.

Schönpflug, W. (1987). Beanspruchung und Belastung bei der Arbeit – Konzepte und Theorien [Strain and stress during work – concepts and theories]. In U. Kleinbeck & J. Rutenfranz (Eds.), *Arbeitspsychologie. Enzyklopädie der Psychologie* (Part III/1, pp. 131–184). Hogrefe.

Schulz, P., & Schlotz, W. (2002). Das Trierer Inventar zur Erfassung von chronischem Stress (TICS) [The Trier Inventory to assess chronic stress (TICS)]. *ErgoMed, 26*(4), 118–119.

Schulz, P., Schlotz, W., & Becker, P. (2004). *TICS – Trierer Inventar zum chronischen Stress* [TICS – Trier Inventory of Chronic Stress]. Hogrefe.

Schuster, J. (2007). *Weiterbildungspartizipation älterer ArbeitnehmerInnen im Zusammenhang mit Leistungsfähigkeit und Leistungsmotivation: Eine Untersuchung bei Pflegepersonal* [Participation in continuing education with aging workers with respect to achievement potential and performance motivation: A study on patient care personnel; Unpublished master's thesis]. University of Graz, Austria.

Seligman, M. (1979). *Erlernte Hilflosigkeit* [Learned helplessness]. Urban und Schwarzenberg.

Seligman, M., & Csikszentmihalyi, M. (2000). Positive psychology: An introduction. *American Psychologist, 55*, 5–14.

Selye, H. (1981). Geschichte und Grundzüge des Stresskonzepts [History and ground concept of the stress concept]. In J. R. Nitsch (Ed.), *Stress – Theorien, Untersuchungen, Maßnahmen* (pp. 163–187). Huber.

Siegrist, J. (1996). Adverse health effects of high effort – Low reward conditions at work. *Journal of Occupational Health Psychology, 1*, 27–43.

Smolders, K. C. H. J., de Kort, Y. A. W., & Cluitmans, P. J. M. (2012). A higher illuminance induces alertness even during office hours: Findings on subjective measures, task performance and heart rate measures. *Physiology and Behavior, 107*, 7–16.

Sonnentag, S. (2018). The recovery paradox: Portraying the complex interplay between job stressors, lack of recovery, and poor well-being. *Research in Organizational Behavior, 38*, 169–185.

Sonnentag, S., Cheng, B. H., & Parker, S. L. (2022). Recovery from work: Advancing the field toward the future. *Annual Review of Organizational Psychology and Organizational Behavior, 9*, 33–60.

Sonnentag, S., & Fritz, C. (2007). The Recovery Experience Questionnaire: Development and validation of a measure for assessing recuperation and unwinding from work. *Journal of Occupational Health Psychology, 12*(3), 204–221.

Sonnentag, S., & Fritz, C. (2015). Recovery from job stress: The stressor-detachment model as an integrative framework. *Journal of Organizational Behavior, 36*(Suppl. 1), S72–S103.

Sonnentag, S., & Zijlstra, F. R. H. (2006). Job characteristics and off-job activities as predictors of need for recovery, well-being, and fatigue. *Journal of Applied Psychology, 91*(2), 330–350.

Spielberger, C. D., Gorsuch, R. L., & Lushene, R. E. (1970). *Manual for the State-Trait Anxiety Inventory*. Consulting Psychologists Press.

Steinacker, J. M., Kellmann, M., Böhm, B. O., Liu, Y., Opitz-Gress, A., Kallus, K. W., Lehmann, M., Altenburg, D., & Lormes, W. (1999). Clinical findings and parameters of stress and regeneration in rowers before World Championships. In M. Lehmann, C. Foster, U. Gastmann, H. Keizer, & J. M. Steinacker (Eds.), *Overload, fatigue, performance incompetence, and regeneration in sport* (pp. 71–80). Plenum.

Stelzhammer, J. (2008). *Sozialkapital in Organisationen: Entwicklung und Validierung des Social Capital Questionnaires* [Social capital in organisations: Development and validation of the Social Capital Questionnaires; Unpublished diploma thesis]. University of Graz, Austria.

Steptoe, A., Hamer, M., & Chida, Y. (2007). The effects of acute psychological stress on circulating inflammatory factors in humans: A review and meta-analysis. *Brain, Behavior, and Immunity, 21*(7), 901–912.

Streit, B. (2008). *Kardiovaskuläre Veränderungen und die Rolle der antizipativen Verhaltenssteuerung in simulierten kritischen Flugsituationen* [Cariovascular changes and the role of anticipatory behavior control in simulated critical flight situations; Unpublished master's thesis]. University of Graz, Austria.

Strohmaier, A. (2008). *Erholung, Belastung und Stressverarbeitung älterer und jüngerer FahrerInnen im öffentlichen Personennahverkehr* [Recovery, stress and coping of older and younger public transportation operators; Unpublished master's thesis]. University of Graz, Austria.

Tuomi, K., Ilmarinen, J., Jahkola, A., Katajarinne, L., & Tulkki, A. (1998). *Work ability index*. Finnish Institute of Occupational Health.

van Veldhoven, M., & Broersen, S. (2003). Measurement quality and validity of the "need for recovery scale". *Occupational and Environmental Medicine, 60*, 3–9.

van Veldhoven, M., & Meijman, T. (1994). *Het meten van psychosociale arbeidsbelasting met een vragenlijst: De Vragenlijst Beleving en Beoordeling van de Arbeid (VVBA)* [Measurement of psychosocial job demands with a questionnaire: The questionnaire experience and evaluation of work (VBBA)]. NIA.

von Holst, D. (1998). The concept of stress and its relevance for animal behavior. *Advances in the Study of Behavior, 27*, 1–131.

Wagner, G. (2000). *Die Latent-State-Trait-Eigenschaften des Erholungs-Belastungs-Fragebogens* [The latent-state-trait concept of the Recovery-Stress Questionnaire; Unpublished diploma thesis]. University of Graz, Austria.

Weick, K. E., & Sutcliffe, K. (2001). *Managing the unexpected: Assuring high performance in an age of complexity*. Jossey Bass.

Werner, E. E. (1971). *The children of Kauai: A longitudinal study from the prenatal period to age ten*. University of Hawaii Press.

Wiegelmann, M., Völker, J., & Sonnentag, S. (2023). Sleep has many faces: The interplay of sleep and work in predicting employees' energetic state over the course of the day. *Journal of Occupational Health Psychology, 28*(1), 52–63.

Wieland-Eckelmann, R., & Baggen, R. (1994). Beanspruchung und Erholung im Arbeits-Erholungs-Zyklus [Stress and recovery in the work-recovery-cycle]. In R. Wieland-Eckelmann, H. Allmer, K. W. Kallus, & J. Otto (Eds.), *Erholungsforschung* (pp. 102–154). PVU.

Windisch, P. (2008). *Durchführung und Evaluation eines Team-Ressource-Management-Trainings bei SchülerInnen* [Implementation and evaluation of team-resource management training with pupils; Unpublished master's thesis]. University of Graz, Austria.

Wittmann, W. W. (1988). Multivariate reliability theory. Principles of symmetry and successful validation strategies. In J. R. Nesselroade & R. B. Cattell (Eds.), *Handbook of multivariate experimental psychology* (pp. 505–560). Plenum Press.

Wolf, A., Wolf, F., & Susa, M. (2008). Burnout und chronic fatigue-syndrome (CFS). *Journal of Preventive Medicine, 4*(1), 170–180.

Zijlstra, F. R., Cropley, M., & Rydstedt, L. W. (2014). From recovery to regulation: An attempt to reconceptualize 'recovery from work'. *Stress and Health, 30*(3), 244–252.

3 Recovery-Stress Questionnaire for Athletes

Michael Kellmann and K. Wolfgang Kallus

Scope and application

The Recovery-Stress Questionnaire for Athletes (RESTQ-Sport) was developed to measure the frequency of current stress symptoms along with the frequency of recovery-associated activities and states in athletes. The RESTQ-Sport is based on the basic module, RESTQ-Basic-48 (Kallus, this volume, Chapter 2), and therefore, was not developed from scratch to serve the needs in sport (Jeffries et al., 2020) but the sport-specific scales were added to serve that purpose. However, at the time of development in the mid-1990 of the last century, the RESTQ-Sport was as closest as it could be to assess stress and recovery in sport.

The current recovery-stress state depends on preceding stress and recovery activities. Through the simultaneous assessment of stress and recovery, a differentiated picture of the current recovery-stress state can be provided. The specific characteristics of the RESTQ-Sport are that it allows systematic and direct measurement of appraised events, states, and activities regarding their frequency, while simultaneously considering stress and recovery processes (Kellmann & Beckmann, 2022, 2024; Kellmann et al., 2018, 2023). Furthermore, it differentiates non-specific and sport-specific areas of recovery and stress. By recording recovery and stress at the same time, the RESTQ-Sport closes a theoretically as well as practically important gap, illustrated by the review *Overtraining and Recovery* by Kenttä and Hassmén (1998). In the last century, the authors characterize the RESTQ-Sport as one of the few questionnaires that "attempts to address the full complexities of stress and recovery" (Kenttä & Hassmén, 1998, p. 12). Furthermore, the RESTQ-Sport is recommended as an important tool to monitor training and for diagnostics in the applied field (Carfagno & Hendrix, 2014; Halson, 2014; Kellmann, 2010; Kellmann et al., 2018; Meeusen et al., 2013; Nederhof, Zwerver, et al., 2008; Saw et al., 2016).

With 19 scales, the RESTQ-Sport assesses potentially stressful and restful events and their subjective consequences during *the past (3) days/nights*. Without essential changes in the internal consistency of the scales, the time frame can be extended

Kellmann, M., & Kallus, K. W. (2025). The Recovery-Stress Questionnaire for Athletes. In M. Kellmann & K. W. Kallus (Eds.), *The Recovery-Stress Questionnaires: A User Manual* (pp. 76–136). Routledge.

DOI: 10.4324/9781032643380-3

up to two weeks, depending on the research question (Kellmann & Kallus, this volume, Chapter 1). The appraisal of the recovery-stress state is a result of a quantitative assessment of the frequency of stress and recovery activities in the *past (3) days/nights*. The questionnaire considers subjectively appraised events and states. Basing the method on the concepts of overload and stress is well founded, in that there is a transactional relationship between conditions and actively appraising persons. The RESTQ-Sport endeavors to represent the recovery-stress state in temporary states, including physical, emotional, and behavioural aspects, with certain persistence (Bradburn, 1969).

The RESTQ-Sport-76 is based on the basic module, RESTQ-Basic-48 consisting of seven stress scales and five recovery scales. Scales 1 through 7 consider social-emotional stress, in general (whether temporary or stable), performance(-related) stress, and physical aspects of stress. Scales 8 through 12 consider temporary or stable non-specific recovery activities (for details of the basic module see Kallus, this volume, Chapter 2).

Seven sport-specific areas assess additional aspects of stress (scales 13 through 15) and recovery (scales 16 through 19). Table 3.1 provides an overview of the RESTQ-Sport specific scales. The sport-specific scale *Disturbed Breaks* is sensitive to deficiencies of recovery and interrupted recovery during periods of rest

Table 3.1 Sport-specific scales of the Recovery-Stress Questionnaire for Athletes.

Number	*Scale* *Summary*
13	***Disturbed Breaks*** This scale deals with recovery deficits, interrupted recovery, and situational aspects that come in the way during periods of rest (e.g., teammates, coaches).
14	***Emotional Exhaustion*** High scores are reached by athletes who feel burned out and want to quit their sport.
15	***Injury*** High scores signal an acute injury or vulnerability to injuries.
16	***Being in Shape*** Athletes with high scores describe themselves as fit, physically efficient, and vital.
17	***Personal Accomplishment*** High scores are reached by athletes who feel integrated in their team, communicate well with their teammates, and enjoy their sport.
18	***Self-Efficacy*** This scale is characterized by how convinced the athlete is that he/she has trained well and is optimally prepared.
19	***Self-Regulation*** The uses of mental skills for athletes to prepare, push, motivate, and set goals for themselves are assessed by this scale.

(e.g., halftimes, time-outs), both of which can impair subsequent performance. *Emotional Exhaustion* (based on Maslach's Burnout Inventory, MBI; Maslach & Jackson, 1986) is characterized by wanting to give up or lack of persistence. This relates to any disappointments in the context of sport that might lead to quit the sport. Injury consists of any statements dealing with injuries, vulnerability to injuries, and an impairment of physical strength. *Being in Shape* assesses subjective feelings about performance ability and competence, one's perceived fitness, and vitality. *Personal Accomplishment* primarily asks about appreciation and empathy within the team and the realization of personal goals in sport. This area is also related to the MBI. *Self-Efficacy* measures the level of expectation and competence regarding an optimal performance preparation in practice. *Self-Regulation* refers to the use of psychological skills training when preparing for performance (e.g., goal setting, mental training, motivation).

In this manual, two versions of the RESTQ-Sport are available. The RESTQ-Sport-76 comprises 76 statements (items) plus an introductory item (warm-up item), which is not included in the scoring. Each scale of the RESTQ-Sport-76 consists of four items; a reduced version with 36 items and six general and six sport-specific scales with three items each (RESTQ-Sport-36) is also available. In prior manuals (Kellmann & Kallus, 2001, 2016) the RESTQ-Sport-52 (52 items, 19 scales) was also introduced. All forms of the RESTQ-Sport refer in their standard version to a time frame of the *past (3) days/nights*.

Since the German (Kellmann & Kallus, 2000), the English (Kellmann & Kallus, 2001, 2016), and the Portuguese (Kellmann et al., 2009) manuals were published the RESTQ-Sport was regularly used in applied practice and research. Already in the year 2006, Ziemainz et al. described the RESTQ-Sport to be the most frequently used questionnaire in German Sport Psychology. Worldwide the RESTQ-Sport is often part of the toolbox of sport psychologists working in private practice, in National Training Centers, and at Institutes of Sports. The RESTQ-Sport can be used well between 14 and 88 years.

Facets of stress and recovery in sports: Theory of the sport-specific scales

In sport, the connection between the current recovery-stress state and competition or training achievement is obvious, and physical and mental recovery has received increasing attention in research and practice (Hausswirth & Mujika, 2013; Kellmann & Beckmann, 2022, 2024; Kellmann et al., 2018, 2023). To avoid overtraining and to optimize performance, physiological and psychological recovery should be programmed as an integral component of training (Meeusen & De Pauw, 2022). Rowbottom et al. (1998) pointed out that "too often the recovery element is overlooked as an essential aspect of any training regime" (p. 57). The consequence, underrecovery, can be the result of excessively prolonged and/or intense exercise, stressful competition, or other stressors. However, being underrecovered over a longer period may not necessarily lead to overtraining but leads to progressive fatigue and underperformance (Halson, 2014). Moreover, sufficient recovery during phases of intensive training is needed to prevent athletes from overtraining. Within the training camp, when the extent and intensity of the training are deliberately increased, it is important to monitor the subjective view because if inadequate recovery takes place, psychological and physiological consequences may occur (Kellmann et al., 2018; Meeusen & DePauw, 2022).

These negative effects are also a risk with too strenuous or critical competitive programs. Of course, appropriate training is the prerequisite to improve performance (Coutts et al., 2022; Meeusen et al., 2013), but uncertainty about the extent and content of training will often lead to inappropriate training responses of the athlete and insufficient competition results or overreaching and in the long run to staleness, the burnout syndrome, or the overtraining syndrome (Kellmann et al., 2018). Hoffman et al. (1999) pointed out that peak athletic performance depends on the proper manipulation of training intensity and volume as well as providing for adequate rest and recovery between practice sessions. However, the exact point where training becomes overtraining is difficult to define (Koutedakis et al., 1999). In conclusion, not a reduction of the training load is proposed, but sometimes training load needs to be individualized to achieve the best performance development (Halson, 2014). For a conscious integration of recovery phases in the competition and training cycles, it is desirable to train athletes in close cooperation among coaches, sport physicians, and sport psychologists, thus utilizing the available medical, psychological, and performance data on an interdisciplinary basis.

Until the RESTQ-Sport was published in 2001, research of training monitoring, overtraining and/or underrecovery dealt mainly with the Profile of Mood States (POMS; McNair et al., 1971/1992) and Borg's Rating of Perceived Exertion (RPE; Borg, 1998). Recently the Acute Recovery and Stress Scale (ARSS) and Short Recovery and Stress Scale (SRSS) have been developed by Kellmann and Kölling (2019, 2020) to assess the current recovery-stress state of an athlete at an emotional, mental, physical, and overall level. In contrast to the RESTQ-Sport, the ARSS and the SRSS asses the current recovery-stress state 'right now' based on adjectives [see also the German Adjective Check List EWL (Janke & Debus, 1978) which has been used to validate the early versions of the RESTQ].

Snyder (1998) reported that the changes in the ratio of RPE and blood lactate were found to be a reliable predictor of overreaching/overtraining. Foster (1998) reported a simple modification of the RPE in which the athletes were asked to rate the global intensity of the entire training (also labelled as session-RPE). Twenty-five athletes (mostly speed skaters) recorded their training using a method that integrates the exercise session RPE and the duration (including warm-up, cool-down, and recovery intervals) of the training session. It was observed that a high percentage of illness could be accounted for when individual athletes exceeded individually identifiable training thresholds mostly related to the strain of training.

Using the POMS, a self-rating instrument for the assessment of mood (*Tension, Depression, Anger, Vigor, Fatigue, Confusion*), Morgan et al. (1987) reported mood changes in swimmers during the season. Early in the season, swimmers displayed the iceberg profile (Lochbaum et al., 2021; Morgan & Costill, 1996), a profile indicative of positive mental health that is associated with successful athletic performance characterized by high vigor. During overtraining, mood disturbances significantly increased and were accompanied by a profile reflecting diminished mental health. After the training intensity was significantly reduced, the swimmers again exhibited the original iceberg profile. The existence of a dose-response relationship was demonstrated between training volume and mood disturbances (Mujika et al., 2004). Increases in training volume go along with corresponding elevations in mood disturbance (e.g., more anger, depression, tension, fatigue, and less vigor and well-being). Mood improvements occur if training volume is reduced (Collette et al., 2018; Hanin, 2014; Pelka et al., 2018). Morgan and colleagues (1987) recommend that the symptoms associated with overtraining and staleness should be monitored continuously during athletic training, so that training volumes can be adjusted as soon as negative symptoms begin to appear.

Since recovery can be characterized not merely as a lack of stress (Kellmann & Kallus, this volume, Chapter 1), but also as a pro-active individualized process to re-establish psychological and physiological resources (Kellmann, 2002a; Kellmann et al., 2018), the POMS, which is the most frequently used measure, may be insufficient to explore recovery processes. The POMS was initially developed as an economical method of identifying and assessing transient, fluctuating affective states (McNair et al., 1971/1992). Consequently, the POMS only vaguely reflect recovery processes. A more detailed assessment of these processes is needed for systematic development of training plans that combine intensive training and recovery in the form of dynamic, intensive processes. The RESTQ-Sport assesses mood-oriented stress- and recovery-associated activities using items such as … *I was angry with someone* or … *I had a good time with my friends*. In other words, the RESTQ-Sport basically asks the question, *what happened in the past (3) days/nights?* and provides a differentiated picture of the current recovery-stress state based on twelve non-specific and seven sport-specific scales. This demonstrates how it differs from the POMS, which only assesses the current mood state and therefore shows no specific starting points for intervention. In addition, general and/or sport-specific activities can also be considered a cause and a mediator for mood states, which is supported by the considerable correlations between the RESTQ-Sport and the POMS (Gnacinski et al., 2021; Kellmann et al., 2001; Reynoso-Sánchez et al., 2021).

The sport-specific scales of the RESTQ-Sport cover relevant aspects as they directly and indirectly influence and/or reflect recovery processes. For example, the break serves as a phase for psychological (e.g., mental, emotional) and physiological regeneration during competition for athletes and for their interaction with coaches and advisors (Kellmann & Weidig, 2010; Raya-Castellano et al., 2023). In athletic activity, it is often shown that the athletes are given more information than they can digest during the recovery phase. According to Mason et al. (2020), the amount of feedback provided to players is of particular importance because of the detrimental impact of cognitive overload on physical performance (Smith et al., 2015) and decision-making (Smith et al., 2016). Many coaches are unaware of the meaning of the recovery phase and are not conscious of its correlation with the recovery process. This can result in insufficient or disturbed recovery such as interrupted recovery or an irregular recovery pattern. Insufficient recovery can be the result of too short breaks with an absence of optimal recovery. Nevertheless, inadequate recovery can result, if the requirements of adequate recovery are present, but the athlete is disturbed through other means (i.e., emotional discussions between coach and athlete, noise). Therefore, the coach's behaviour plays a central role in the structure of recovery between stress situations (Kellmann & Weidig, 2010). In laboratory experiments, Kallus and Krauth (1995) indicated that during the regeneration phase, there is a considerable increase in the amount of sensitivity toward disturbances, annoyances, and irritations. Therefore, slight interruptions in the normal situation during the break may have great effects on an athlete's performance and judgment of the situation (Pelka et al., 2017). The recovery phase does not just compensate for exhaustion; it is also a significant preventive measure for stress situations (Kellmann, 2002b).

For many years, burnout has become meaningful in stress research, and it is agreed on that burnout is a reaction to chronic stress (DiFiori et al., 2014; Raedeke, 2014). According to Maslach and Jackson (1986), the burnout syndrome is apparent through emotional exhaustion, depersonalization, and lack of personal accomplishment. This does not only have a negative effect on performance but it also amounts to an increase in the dropout rate of the practiced activities. After research on burnout was carried out in the social professions, it was expanded to other professional groups. Next to teachers (Heidari et al., 2021; Kellmann & Heidari, 2020), coaches were the center of attention in burnout research focusing on the recovery-stress state (Altfeld & Kellmann, 2013, 2015; Altfeld et al., 2015; Kellmann et al., 2015; Schaffran et al., 2016, 2019, 2020). Burnout has been shown to influence athletes (Goodger et al., 2007; Gustafsson et al., 2017; Pires & Ugrinowitsch, 2021; Woods et al., in press). Moreover, with an increase in the degree of burnout, the athlete's performance declines and becomes inconsistent (Cohn, 1990; Smith, 1986).

There is not only a connection between the degree of burnout and decreases in performance but also with increases in dropout. The effect is amplified by overtraining, routine, monotony, boredom, and a lack of diversity (Goodger et al., 2007). Kellmann (2002a) argues that burnout is caused by a lack of recovery, so-called underrecovery, over a longer period of time. Neither psychological nor physiological recovery is possible during an intensive season with a high amount of training during the off-season. According to Henschen (1993), if burnout occurs, the only useful measure is to give the athlete a long recovery phase or a temporary reduction in athletic activities. This can prevent the athlete having to end his/her athletic career. Therefore, the coach/advisor must be sensitive to the athlete's psychological and/or physical recovery demands and contribute to the maintenance of an optimal recovery-stress state.

Another important aspect of the RESTQ-Sport deals with self-efficacy. The concept of self-efficacy is closely related to Bandura (1977). He proved that a person's actions are influenced by the person's expectations of their effectiveness. A person's positive and/or negative expectations of an action determine the duration of the action and the stress intensity (if the action is initiated in a stress situation). The influence of intensity on efficacy expectations depends on how high a person's demands are and how much the person is convinced of an action's effectiveness.

Motivated actions are separated into a cognitive representation of a chain of events (situation-action-outcome-consequences) in which the single elements are closely bound with each other through certain expectations (Short, 2014): outcome-consequence-expectation (instrumentality), situation-action-expectation (expected competence), action-outcome-expectation (expected consequence). The expected consequence means that, according to the person's evaluation, a certain action results in a certain outcome. The expected competence is a person's conviction of being able to use behaviour that results in a certain outcome (see *Vroom's Model of Motivation*, 1964). The expected competence is also the subjective evaluation of the action's availability and is combined with the expected consequence of the action's execution. Accordingly, the expected consequence is not relevant without the expected competence. Therefore, not only the knowledge of correct forms of movement is necessary to carry out an action successfully but also the subjective conviction that these motions can be carried out successfully in any relevant situation. Additionally, the instrumentality decides if the outcome is meaningful for higher goals; for example, winning a competition that does not bring a financial reward or points for the ranking list has less instrumentality for a professional athlete.

Self-efficacy has a positive influence on an athlete's performance (Feltz et al., 2008; LaForge-MacKenzie & Sullivan, 2014). The straightforwardness and verification of these results largely correlate with the theoretical fundamentals of this concept. McAuley (1985) reported that the increase in self-efficacy accompanies a reduction in fear, which can also increase the athlete's well-being. Feltz and Riessinger (1990) proved that self-efficacy depends on one's own experience (86%), whereas the information on environmental conditions plays a secondary role. Thus, it is not the information about environmental conditions (i.e., the athletic opponent) that leads to a change in expected competence, but the athlete's expectations, which are based on the athlete's own experience. This aspect is covered by the scale *Self-Efficacy*. Closely related to self-efficacy and a kind of prerequisite is the competence of an athlete in self-regulation. Methods of self-regulation are essential components of mental training approaches (Mayer & Hermann, 2011) and to optimize performance in training and competition (Beckmann, 2023).

Versions, scoring, and reference values of the RESTQ-Sport

This section summarizes the versions, scoring, and reference values of the RESTQ-Sport. Table 3.2 gives an overview of the RESTQ-Sport versions, scales, and numbers of items for each scale.

The RESTQ-Sport-76 (48 non-specific and 28 sport-specific items) is the product of continuous development over more than a decade (for details see

Table 3.2 Scales, number of items for the sport-specific RESTQ-versions.

RESTQ-Sport scales	*76*	*36*
1 General Stress	4	3
2 Emotional Stress	4	—
3 Social Stress	4	3
4 Conflicts/Pressure[a]	4	—
5 Fatigue	4	3
6 Lack of Energy	4	—
7 Physical Complaints	4	—
8 Success	4	—
9 Social Recovery	4	3
10 Physical Recovery	4	—
11 General Well-being	4	3
12 Sleep Quality	4	3
13 Disturbed Breaks	4	3
14 Emotional Exhaustion	4	3
15 Injury	4	3
16 Being in Shape	4	3
17 Personal Accomplishment	4	3
18 Self-Efficacy	4	3
19 Self-Regulation	4	—

[a] In 2014 the item … *I felt I had to perform well in front of others* was exchanged by … *I had to do something I did not like to do.*

Kellmann & Kallus, 2000, 2001). The items were lined up randomly and attached to the general RESTQ (RESTQ-Basic; Kallus, this volume, Chapter 2). It is important to note that in 2014 the item … *I felt I had to perform well in front of others* was exchanged by … *I had to do something I did not like to do.* This was due to various analysis of psychometric properties and this modification is further elaborated by Kallus (this volume, Chapter 2).

To avoid a misunderstanding as to whether the sport-specific items are related to practice or to competition, a general directive was provided in the instructions: *The statements related to performance should refer to performance during competition as well as during practice.*

The initial selection and development of the sport-specific scales was based on research in sport psychology and the results of reliability analysis by Kellmann (1991). During the analysis of the various items of the basic RESTQ, it became obvious, for example, that the conceptualization of *Physical Complaints* and

Physical Recovery seemed too general for athletes. These scales measure physical complaints and recovery for the general population, but not for athletes, where more sport-specific questions are needed; however, for the performance ability of an athlete, physical fitness is a key factor. If the physical conditions are not optimally set up or injuries occur, the quality of performance is limited. Therefore, the scales *Injury* and *Being in Shape* were constructed to reflect the physical fitness of an athlete. *Injury* consists of any statements dealing with injuries, vulnerability to injuries, and an impairment of physical strength. *Being in Shape* assesses subjective feelings about performance ability and competence, one's perceived fitness, and vitality.

As Kallus and Kellmann (2000) pointed out, burnout is an important factor in sports. Based on the MBI, the most important aspects of the *Emotional Exhaustion* and *Personal Accomplishment* scales were included in the RESTQ-Sport. Fender (1989) has stated that the MBI can be used to assess burnout in athletes. Based on the frequency-based format of the MBI, selected items were adapted to the RESTQ-Sport item format. *Emotional Exhaustion* is characterized by the component of wanting to give up or lack of persistence (Maslach & Jackson, 1986). This relates to any disappointments in the context of sport that might lead to quit the sport. *Personal Accomplishment* primarily asks about appreciation and empathy within the team and the realization of personal goals in sports.

Scales focusing on sport psychological components are *Self-Efficacy* and *Self-Regulation*. These components become more important during long training camps and when a competition arises. *Self-Efficacy* (Bandura, 1977) measures the level of expectation and competence regarding an optimal performance preparation in practice. *Self-Regulation* refers to the use of psychological skills training when preparing for performance (e.g., goal setting, mental training, motivation; Beckmann, 2023; Jones & Turner, 2014).

Recovery in training and competition takes place during breaks; however, the subjective view of recovery of an athlete is more important than coaches' perspective – and both can differ. *Disturbed Breaks* is sensitive to deficiencies of recovery and interrupted recovery during periods of rest (e.g., halftimes, time-outs), both of which can impair subsequent performance.

RESTQ-Sport-36

The RESTQ-Sport-76 was revised to address concerns about length and considering the findings from Confirmatory Factor Analysis (CFA; Kellmann & Kawabata, 2016). Problems always arise, when the modular structure is of minor relevance (Davis et al., 2007). During the modification, seven scales (*Emotional Stress*, *Conflicts/Pressure*, *Lack of Energy*, *Physical Complaints*, *Success*, *Physical Recovery*, and *Self-Regulation*) were removed from the questionnaire on theoretical, empirical, and practical grounds. While the removal of full scales is rather unusual it was due to the development of the RESTQ-Sport. To retain the modular system of the RESTQ, at least partly, Kellmann and Kallus (2001) have accepted that some of the basic RESTQ scales were rather weak for the sport-specific context.

Furthermore, to facilitate the reduction of scale length, one item was removed from each of the remaining twelve scales based upon the size of standardized factor loadings in CFA, as well as the expected size of cross-loadings indicated by the Lagrange Multiplier Test. The revised RESTQ-Sport-76 (referred to RESTQ-Sport-36 hereafter) consists of twelve scales (three items per scale) that are equally balanced between four sections of *Overall Stress*, *Overall Recovery*, *Sport-specific Stress*, and *Sport-specific Recovery*.

Instruction

The questionnaire is supplied with a cover sheet that gives detailed instructions on how to answer the questionnaire, including an example. This makes it possible to complete the questionnaire without the help of a third person. In addition, the cover sheet contains the directive that the statements related to performance should refer to performance during competition, as well as during training or practice. The cover sheet should be read thoroughly before starting the questionnaire.

Participants are asked to fill out the RESTQ-Sport without taking any long breaks. While completing the questionnaire, they should be undisturbed, and it is important that each person fills out the questionnaire individually. Depending on the version, it takes between six and twelve minutes to answer the questionnaire the first time. After the test has been taken repeatedly, the completion time is reduced.

Item format of the RESTQ-Sport

The RESTQ-Sport assesses potentially stressful events and their consequences, along with the frequency of recovery-associated activities and their effects *in the past (3) days/nights*. The items of the RESTQ-Sport identify activities or conditions in the form of incomplete sentences. Together with the standard time frame given at the top of the page (*In the past (3) days/nights*), each item forms a statement. A Likert-type scale is used with values ranging from 0 (*never*) to 6 (*always*) indicating how often the respondent participated in various activities during *the past (3) days/nights* (Table 3.3). As with the basic RESTQ, the sport-specific version includes a warm-up item that is not included in the analysis.

Scoring

The scale values are calculated by taking the mean of the item values (checked numbers; rounded off to two decimal points). The formation of the mean is

Table 3.3 Sample item, standard time frame, and answer mode of the RESTQ-Sport.

In the past (3) days/nights							
... I felt vulnerable to injuries							
	0	1	2	3	4	5	6
	never	seldom	sometimes	often	more often	very often	always

appropriate because of the different number of questions in the various versions of the RESTQ-Sport. In case of missing data, the mean should only be calculated when at least 50% of the items of each scale have been answered. In the *Sleep Quality* scale, the items for disturbed sleep first have to be inverted (6 minus item value=raw item score; e.g., 6 → 0; 5 → 1; 4 → 2; 3=3; 2 → 4; 1 → 5; 0 → 6). Scoring sheets are available for manual scoring. Additionally, the data can be represented graphically in a *recovery-stress profile.*

The mean of each scale can range from 0 – 6. High scores in the stress-associated activity scales reflect high subjective stress, whereas high scores in the recovery-oriented scales reflect plenty of recovery activities.

RESTQ-Sport-76

- The scales in the area of stress can be summarized in an *Overall Stress*-oriented score (mean of scales 1–7).
- Correspondingly, a total mean for recovery can be formed from the scales in an *Overall Recovery*-related score (mean of scales 8–12).
- The same procedure applies for the *Sport-specific Stress* (mean of scales 13–15) and *Sport-specific Recovery* areas (mean of scales 16–19).
- The overall and sport-specific stress and recovery scores can be combined to calculate global *Total Stress* and *Total Recovery* scores, respectively. However, this procedure is only recommended for group comparisons.

RESTQ-Sport-36

- The scales in the area of stress (*General Stress, Social Stress, Fatigue*) can be summarized in an *Overall Stress*-oriented score (mean of scales 1–3).
- Correspondingly, a total mean for recovery (*Social Recovery, General Well-being, Sleep Quality*) can be formed from the scales in an *Overall Recovery*-related score (mean of scales 4–6).
- The same procedure applies for the *Sport-specific Stress* (*Disturbed Breaks, Emotional Exhaustion, Injury*; mean of scales 7–9) and *Sport-specific Recovery* areas (*Being in Shape, Personal Accomplishment, Self-Efficacy*; mean of scales 10–12).
- The overall and sport-specific stress and recovery scores can be combined to calculate global *Total Stress* and *Total Recovery* scores, respectively. However, this procedure is only recommended for group comparisons.

Kellmann and Kallus (this volume, Chapter 1, p. 2) state that:

> *stress and recovery should not be combined to a single value, as they constitute two conceptually independent dimensions as far as the frequency in the past days/nights is concerned.* The relationship between the scales for recovery and stress is neither linear nor symmetrical. ***Consequently, the calculation of one overall single score of all stress and recovery scales does not make sense and is strongly prohibited.***

Reference values

The RESTQ-Sport is constructed in accordance with the *Classical Test Theory* (*Classical-Latent-Additive Model*; Moosbrugger, 1982). Therefore, an interpretation of the scale mean as an absolute value is not possible. Hence, the interpretation of the RESTQ-Sport profile should refer to either a reference group of the athlete, to intraindividual changes over time, or to the mean and variability of single samples found in the Online Appendix A.B1. Moreover, it is important to check if the RESTQ-Sport version corresponds to the chosen time frame and the moment of testing of the respective comparison group.

Prior manuals of the RESTQ-Sport (Kellmann & Kallus, 2000, 2001) provided reference values which should not be considered as norms. The recovery-stress state varies during training camps, cycles of competitions, working weeks of a year, different phases of life, and because of specific stress and recovery activities. Therefore, the provided means constitute a general situation-unspecific foundation and should be interpreted as a reference value rather than as a norm. Despite the circumstances mentioned above, the accumulated empirical results show overall central tendencies in the scales, which are change-sensitive but seem to be typical under 'normal conditions', thus we decided to calculate large sample reference values. For the pooled English (ES1/ES2) and German Samples (GS1/GS2) reference values were calculated which can serve as a kind of norms (Online Appendix A.B1 and A.B2).

However, in these pooled samples only the first measurement of the data collection was considered. Therefore, the data included in the analysis represent either a) the only measurement of the data collection, or b) the first data collection within a training camp. Consequently, the means of the reference values do not represent scores during a high training load/intensity phase. However, it needs to be noticed that the provided scores for the pooled English (ES1/ES2) sample are somewhat higher compared to the German ones. We cannot provide an explanation if this is due to samples, assessment points, training phases, or other reasons.

In addition to statistical calculation of reference values, a new approach in providing guidance for the users was added. Coaches, sport medicine specialists, training scientists, and sports psychologists from around the world were contacted that had experience in working with the RESTQ-Sport to receive additional reference values by experts. The experts were asked: What do you think are the still tolerable/bearable values for the following situations?

> C) *Maximum values before an important competition/tournament* in case of questions regarding stress and respectively the minimum values in case of questions regarding recovery.
>
> S) *Maximum values for an 8-week seasonal peak of healthy top-class athletes* (e.g., the period where championship, cup and international competitions must be managed at the same time) in case of questions regarding stress and respectively the minimum values in case of questions regarding recovery.

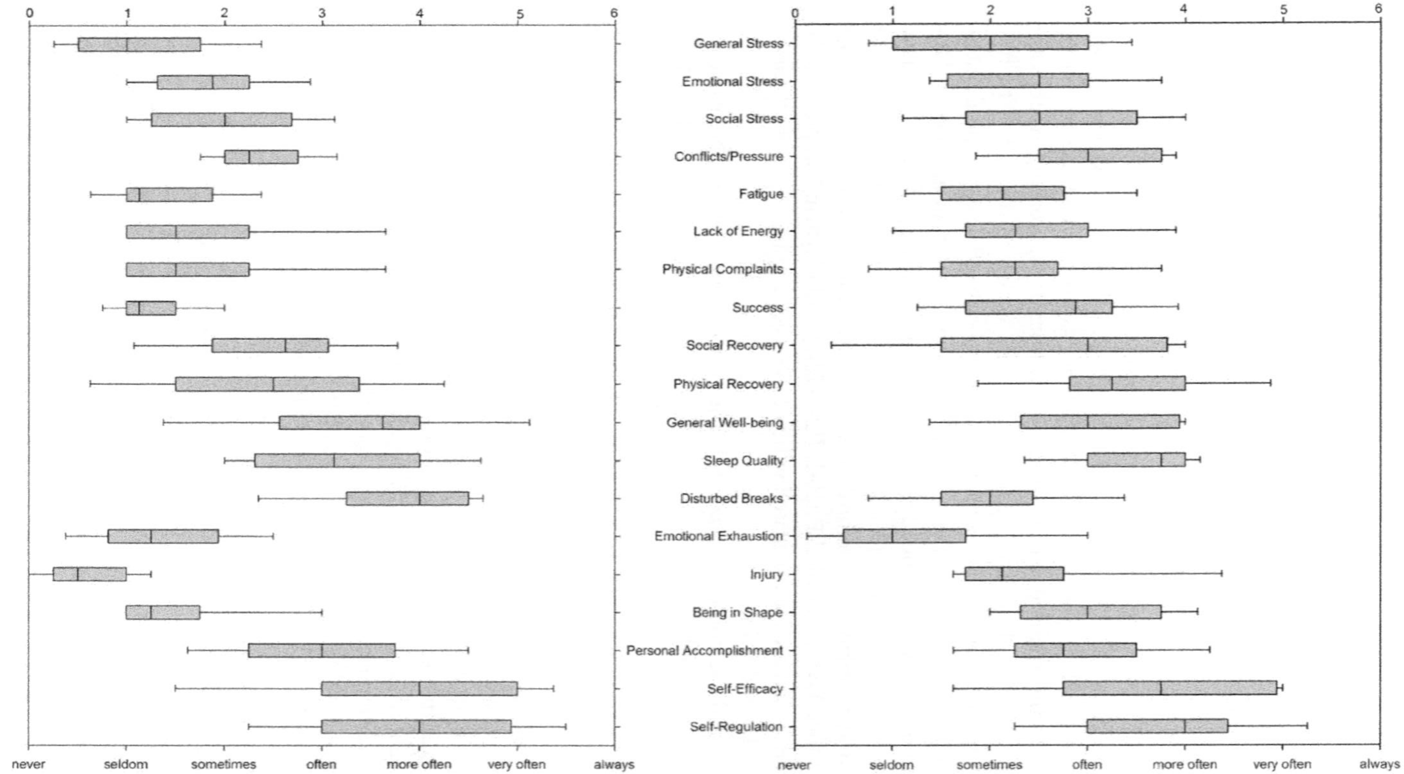

Figure 3.1 Box-plots of the German expert-rating on the RESTQ-Sport scales for *Maximum values before an important competition/tournament athletes* (left) and *Maximum values for an eight-week seasonal peak of healthy top-class athletes* (right).

Note: The box shows us the middle values of a variable (25th and 75th percentile; median), while the whiskers stretch to the greatest and lowest value of that variable.

Twenty-four German[1] (Figure 3.1) and twenty-two international experts[2] (Online Appendix A.B3a and A.B3b) completed the RESTQ-Sport items; scale means were calculated and Box-Plots were used to display the results.

The rather large windows which are depicted in Figure 3.1 call for more research in this area. However, the large windows can be due to the method and the instruction, but it can also be an indication that different coaches/experts consider very different values of stress and recovery as tolerable for their athletes. Of course, different values must be expected for well-paid high-performance professionals and adolescent amateurs. Possibly different values for different sports and different levels must be anticipated. In addition, the recovery-stress balance over time might be an interesting question as this has been a matter of professional training camps.

Reliability

The construction of the RESTQ-Sport was an iterative process that took more than a decade and involved numerous athletic research samples (for details, see Kellmann & Kallus, 2000, 2001). The development of the English and German versions of the RESTQ-Sport was an almost parallel development for both languages.

Samples

Based on the research samples shown in Table 3.4, test statistics as well as reliability and validities were calculated for this manual. In preparation for the analysis, the authors contacted researchers worldwide who have used the RESTQ-Sport and pooled the various sub-samples to the English (ES1, ES2) and German (GS1) samples.

The researchers who provided the data reported that all studies were conducted with the relevant institutions' ethical approval and in accordance with their standards of ethical conduct (e.g., informed consent). By checking each athlete's age, gender, and sport, it was verified that data for individual athletes were only included once across all the samples. Sample GS2 were elite German athletes participating in an online data assessment within the research project: *Optimization of Training and Competition: Management of Regeneration in Elite Sports*. Some data from the German Junior National Rowing Teams (R1–R5) and a Canadian sample (C1) have also been included into the analysis. Table 3.4 gives an overview of the research samples and the variations of the RESTQ-Sport employed. Furthermore, the publication by Gnacinski et al. (2021) is explicitly referred to when discussing analysis of the RESTQ-Sport-36.

Table 3.4 Research samples used to test validity and reliability of the RESTQ-Sport.

	ES1	*ES2*	*GS1*	*GS2*	*C1*
Author/ year	Kellmann and Kawabata (2016)	Kellmann and Kawabata (2016)	Kellmann et al. (2015)	Kellmann et al. (2015)	Kellmann et al. (1999)
Sample size	$N=734$	$N=458$	$N=820$	$N=597$	$N=88$
Gender distribution	Male = 382 Female = 350 ni = 2	Male = 350 Female = 108	Male = 507 Female = 313	Male = 300 Female = 295 ni = 2	Male = 35 Female = 51 ni = 2
Sports	Various sports	Various sports	Various sports	Various sports	Various sports
Age	$M=20.06$ $SD=3.97$	$M=27.95$ $SD=11.01$	$M=18.58$ $SD=4.31$	$M=20.87$ $SD=7.79$	$M=23.68$ $SD=3.78$ $R=18-38$
RESTQ-version	RESTQ-Sport-76	RESTQ-Sport-76	RESTQ-Sport-76	RESTQ-Sport-76	RESTQ-Sport
Time frame	3 days/nights	3 days/nights	3 days/nights	3 days/nights	3 days/nights
Measurements	1	1	1	1	1
Instruments	RESTQ-Sport	RESTQ-Sport	RESTQ-Sport	RESTQ-Sport	RESTQ-Sport, POMS, SCI
Country	USA, Canada	Australia, New Zealand	Germany	Germany	Canada
Special features	Pooled sample	Pooled sample	Pooled sample	Elite athletes	

(*Continued*)

Table 3.4 (Continued)

	R1	*R2*	*R3*	*R4*	*R5*
Author/ year	Kellmann et al. (1995)	Kellmann et al. (1996)	Kellmann et al. (1997)	Kellmann et al. (1998)	Kellmann et al. (2000)
Sample size	$N = 42$	$N = 45$	$N = 62$	$N = 58$	$N = 58$
Gender distribution	Male = 28 Female = 14	Male = 22 Female = 23	Male = 37 Female = 25	Male = 33 Female = 25	Male = 33 Female = 25
Sports	JNT-Rowing	JNT-Rowing	JNT-Rowing	JNT-Rowing	JNT-Rowing
Age	$M = 17.45$ $SD = 0.71$ $R = 16 - 18$	$M = 17.24$ $SD = 0.74$ $R = 15 - 18$	$M = 17.15$ $SD = 0.85$ $R = 15 - 18$	$M = 17.1$ $SD = 0.72$ $R = 16 - 18$	$M = 17.1$ $SD = 0.72$ $R = 16 - 18$
RESTQ-version	RESTQ-Sport-80	RESTQ-Sport-80	RESTQ-Sport-80	RESTQ-Sport-76	RESTQ-Sport-76
Time frame	3 days/nights	3 days/nights	3 days/nights	3 days/nights	3 days/nights
Measurements	5	5	5	9	9
Instruments	RESTQ-Sport, MPSL	RESTQ-Sport	RESTQ-Sports, VCQ, POMS	RESTQ-Sport	RESTQ-Sport
Country	Germany	Germany	Germany	Germany	Germany
Special features	Sportmedical data, Performance data	Sportmedical data, Performance data	Sportmedical data, Performance data	Sportmedical data, Performance data	Sportmedical data, Performance data

Note: N = Sample size; M = Mean; SD = Standard deviation; ni = no information; JNT = Junior National Team; POMS = Profile of Mood States; VCQ = Volitional Component Questionnaire; MPSL = Multidimensional Physical Symptom List; SCI = German Stress Coping Inventory; RESTQ-Sport = Recovery-Stress Questionnaire for Athletes.

Classical reliability measures

The basic part of the RESTQ-Sport is based on the RESTQ-Basic-48 (Kallus, this volume, Chapter 2). Kallus introduced this version in the RESTQ manual using 48 items and pointed out that it is sufficiently reliable and valid.

Homogeneity

For most of the RESTQ-Sport-76 scales, an overview of the reliability coefficients (Table 3.5a) shows good to satisfactory estimations of the accuracy of measurement based on the homogeneity of the scales. In contrast to other scales, *Personal Accomplishment* shows fluctuations in the internal consistencies over the displayed samples.

Consistent with earlier findings, the internal consistencies of the *Conflicts/Pressure* and *Success* scales turned out to be slightly below Cronbach's $\alpha = .70$ (Table 3.5a), and depending on the sample, the interpretation for those scales is limited. The meaning of the general formulated dimension, such as … *I finished important tasks,* is different for athletes compared to non-athletes. Also, the item … *I had some good ideas* from the *Success* scale is mostly irrelevant for athletes during daily practice because they must follow the instructions of the coach. 'Good ideas' are not important in daily practice. A similar situation exists for *Conflicts/Pressure* (i.e., … *I worried about unresolved problems*; … *I felt under pressure*), where the relevance differs depending on the time of assessment. The statements have a different meaning when the RESTQ-Sport is completed after the selection trials for the national team compared to midway during training camp. The importance of *Conflicts/Pressure* increases when the World Championships approach, which is usually reflected by a clear increase of Cronbach's α. It must be noted that *Personal Accomplishment* includes two items in the RESTQ-Sport-76 referring to teammates. Since most of the participants in the English sample ES1 came from individual sports, the term teammate may be used differently. In German samples, the Cronbach's α is higher if athletes from team sports are involved. In general, with large samples, either an analysis of the internal consistency is recommended before interpretation or the *Conflicts/Pressure*, *Success*, or *Personal Accomplishment* scales should be interpreted cautiously.

The satisfactory but not outstanding internal consistencies for *Physical Complaints* indicate that this scale may not be sufficiently sensitive for athletes. This interpretation is supported by the high Cronbach's α for the physically oriented sport-specific fitness scales, *Being in Shape* and *Injury*. Obviously, these items assess the athletes' situations more sensitively and are more relevant to daily practice than the global formulations for non-athletes.

Table 3.5a Estimation of reliability (Cronbach's α) for the RESTQ-Sport for English (ES1, ES2) and German (GS1, GS2, R1-3) samples.

	Cronbach's α					
Samples	*ES1*	*ES2*	*GS1*	*GS2*	*R1-3*	*R1-3*
	N = 734	*N = 458*	*N = 820*	*N = 597*	*N = 149*	*N = 149*
RESTQ-Sport scales					*1. time*	*2. time*
1 General Stress	.86	.87	.82	.86	.75	.76
2 Emotional Stress	.78	.80	.74	.81	.66	.71
3 Social Stress	.87	.85	.82	.86	.80	.85
4 Conflicts/Pressure	.69	.69	.60	.57	.55	.68
5 Fatigue	.79	.79	.78	.79	.71	.78
6 Lack of Energy	.73	.70	.75	.77	.58	.72
7 Physical Complaints	.70	.69	.72	.72	.71	.71
8 Success	.68	.74	.61	.61	.53	.67
9 Social Recovery	.80	.75	.80	.84	.76	.80
10 Physical Recovery	.75	.77	.80	.82	.77	.85
11 General Well-being	.89	.85	.85	.90	.84	.84
12 Sleep Quality	.81	.76	.80	.83	.81	.83
13 Disturbed Breaks	.81	.80	.77	.78	.65	.79
14 Emotional Exhaustion	.82	.78	.76	.77	.65	.71
15 Injury	.77	.80	.77	.81	.73	.78
16 Being in Shape	.84	.85	.84	.85	.80	.88
17 Personal Accomplishment	.62	.74	.73	.76	.67	.80
18 Self-Efficacy	.86	.83	.84	.84	.84	.89
19 Self-Regulation	.82	.79	.84	.82	.81	.83

Table 3.5a contains the changes in homogeneity of the RESTQ-Sport for the pooled samples (R1–3) of the German Junior National Rowing Team from 1995 to 1997. For the first measurement, the Cronbach's α are lower compared to the second measurement. As a rule, internal consistency increases with the familiarity with the instrument. Consequently, an introductory measurement

is recommended for the applied use, as well as for research questions with repeated measurements, so that athletes get to know the RESTQ-Sport. This finding applies not only to the RESTQ-Sport but also to questionnaires, in general ('Socrates-effect'; Jagodzinski et al., 1987). This fundamental problem of changes in the internal consistencies of questionnaire studies receives little attention and is rarely considered in research designs. In repeated measurement studies, changes can be assumed to occur in the responses of the participants. For example, with performance tests, it is a standard procedure to have an introductory test because of the training effect in repeated measurements (Debus & Janke, 1978).

For most of the RESTQ-Sport-36 scales, an overview of the reliability coefficients (Table 3.5b) shows good to satisfactory estimations of the accuracy of measurement based on the homogeneity of the scales. As mentioned above, *Personal Accomplishment* shows fluctuations in the internal consistencies over the displayed samples.

In an independent study with American athletes, Gnacinski et al. (2021) demonstrated acceptable levels of reliability (omega coefficients) for all scales except *Personal Accomplishment* (both CFA and ESEM procedures) and *Being*

Table 3.5b Estimation of reliability (Cronbach's α) for the RESTQ-Sport-36 for English ES1, ES2) and estimation of reliability (Omega coefficients ω) by Gnacinski et al. (2021).

Samples	*ES1*	*ES2*	*Gnacinski et al. (2021)*	
	N = 734	*N = 458*	*N = 494*	*N = 494*
RESTQ-Sport scales	*Cronbach's α*		*CFA ω*	*ESEM ω*
1 General Stress	.85	.85	.85	.80
2 Social Stress	.88	.85	.88	.88
3 Fatigue	.83	.78	.84	.85
4 Social Recovery	.72	.67	.79	.78
5 General Well-being	.89	.87	.78	.78
6 Sleep Quality	.75	.69	.79	.78
7 Disturbed Breaks	.80	.79	.79	.72
8 Emotional Exhaustion	.80	.74	.90	.71
9 Injury	.78	.79	.79	.80
10 Being in Shape	.82	.81	.80	.54
11 Personal Accomplishment	.60	.73	.67	.67
12 Self-Efficacy	.83	.80	.83	.71

in Shape (ESEM procedure only). While *Personal Accomplishment* low reliability scores may be explained by the two items (out of three) related to teammates in a sample which consists of 45% of individual sport athletes (in which the word teammates may has a different connotation), the reason for the low level of reliability for *Being in Shape* in the ESEM ω remains open.

Test-retest reliability

Kallus (1995) has shown that the test-retest reliability of all basic stress and recovery scales is quite high after 24 hours for an instrument that records variable states. This is also true for scales that only showed a satisfactory internal consistency, as in the case of *Physical Complaints* and *Physical Recovery*. The consistently high short-term stability, however, clearly shows the reliability of the procedure. The test-retest reliability always lies clearly above $r = .79$, which implies that intraindividual differences in the recovery-stress states can be well reproduced (Kallus, this volume, Chapter 2). Moreover, the high test-retest reliability shows that the results of the RESTQ are stable concerning short-term functional fluctuations and minor short-term changes in the recovery-stress state.

Table 3.6 displays the test-retest reliability of the RESTQ-Sport after two, three, ten, 14, 21, 28, and 36 days for the German sample R5.

Test-retest reliabilities were calculated for seven measurements, and those that best demonstrate the changes over time are listed in Table 3.6. These results replicate the findings of Kellmann (1991), who stated that the test-retest reliability declines over longer time periods corresponding with the measurement intent of the RESTQ-Sport.

Psychometrics of international versions

Up to now, the RESTQ-Sport has been translated into different languages and has been used in various settings. The manual has been published in German (Kellmann & Kallus, 2000), English (Kellmann & Kallus, 2001, 2016), and Portuguese (Kellmann et al., 2009). In copyright agreement with Kellmann and Kallus a Dutch (Nederhof, Brink, et al., 2008), Spanish (González-Boto et al., 2008), Estonian (Mäestu et al., 2006), and Danish (Elbe et al., 2016) version have been developed. While for the Dutch (Nederhof, Brink, et al., 2008) and Spanish (González-Boto et al., 2008) versions publications are available dealing with the psychometrics and the development of the RESTQ-Sport, others have included the psychometrics as a side information within an article (Mäestu et al., 2006).[3]

Table 3.7 contains the reliability scores for different languages supporting the picture displayed earlier for the English and German version. Cronbach's α of *Conflicts/Pressure* and *Success* across different samples/languages do not meet the

Table 3.6 Test-retest reliability of the RESTQ-Sport referring to the past (3) days/nights in various time spans for the German sample R5 (N=58).

	Time between the intervals of testing						
RESTQ-Sport scales	*2 days*	*3 days*	*10 days*	*14 days*	*21 days*	*28 days*	*36 days*
1 General Stress	.71	.72	.44	.41	.32	.41	.33
2 Emotional Stress	.78	.53	.46	.48	.31	.41	.33
3 Social Stress	.69	.68	.39	.45	.21	.40	.21
4 Conflicts/Pressure	.78	.52	.66	.78	.36	.33	.38
5 Fatigue	.63	.75	.61	.39	.38	.48	.39
6 Lack of Energy	.66	.78	.45	.45	.54	.36	.45
7 Physical Complaints	.61	.65	.57	.58	.40	.37	.40
8 Success	.85	.79	.82	.82	.50	.42	.31
9 Social Recovery	.87	.74	.88	.76	.19	.50	.43
10 Physical Recovery	.81	.78	.71	.62	.59	.43	.42
11 General Well-being	.86	.57	.79	.72	.39	.35	.39
12 Sleep Quality	.74	.66	.83	.44	.53	.47	.43
13 Disturbed Breaks	.63	.74	.66	.22	.34	.40	.29
14 Emotional Exhaustion	.69	.78	.64	.44	.48	.49	.43
15 Injury	.68	.61	.84	.53	.53	.58	.37
16 Being in Shape	.80	.87	.81	.69	.55	.56	.48
17 Personal Accomplishment	.81	.74	.88	.78	.55	.36	.35
18 Self-Efficacy	.81	.71	.82	.66	.75	.43	.43
19 Self-Regulation	.81	.75	.83	.75	.55	.37	.41

.70 criteria. *Personal Accomplishment* and *Physical Complaints* also show variability across samples/languages indicating that depending on the language these scales should be interpreted cautiously.

However, the present manual and the download options via the Routledge Resource Centre allow bringing together all different versions into one compact hub (for details, see Kellmann & Kallus, this volume, Preface).

Table 3.7 Estimation of reliability (Cronbach's α) for the RESTQ-Sport for Dutch (Nederhof, Brink, et al., 2008), Spanish (Gonzales-Boto et al., 2008), and Estonian (Mäestu et al., 2006) samples.

	Cronbach's α				
Languages	*Estonian*	*Spanish*	*Portuguese*	*Dutch*	*Dutch*
	N = 158	*N = 194*	*N = 134*	*N = 123*	*N = 90*
RESTQ-Sport scales				*1. time*	*2. time*
1 General Stress	.91	.85	.79	.84	.84
2 Emotional Stress	.91	.75	.79	.77	.77
3 Social Stress	.95	.79	.80	.75	.72
4 Conflicts/Pressure	.72	.67	.61	.62	.73
5 Fatigue	.75	.77	.76	.78	.79
6 Lack of Energy	.81	.70	.70	.60	.70
7 Physical Complaints	.74	.66	.77	.58	.53
8 Success	.77	.63	.58	.56	.59
9 Social Recovery	.93	.63	.82	.74	.84
10 Physical Recovery	.78	.71	.75	.64	.70
11 General Well-being	.91	.91	.81	.87	.89
12 Sleep Quality	.83	.82	.70	.83	.80
13 Disturbed Breaks	.81	.67	.77	.73	.83
14 Emotional Exhaustion	.87	.77	.76	.67	.72
15 Injury	.73	.54	.70	.73	.74
16 Being in Shape	.93	.88	.85	.85	.84
17 Personal Accomplishment	.87	.63	.64	.63	.69
18 Self-Efficacy	.86	.73	.70	.76	.80
19 Self-Regulation	.78	.78	.81	.56	.71

Construct validity

Construct validity has been studied with respect to the intercorrelations of scales, the factorial structure, linear structure modelling, and the stability of the intercorrelations across different samples. Relationships to mood states, volitional components, and other criteria are covered in the section on criterion validity.

Scale intercorrelations

The height of the scale intercorrelations proved to be only partially stable across different samples; however, the fundamental correlation pattern is almost unchanged across all samples with respect to stress and recovery areas.

Both, the stress and the recovery scales correlate positively with each area, but they have a negative relationship with the scales of the other areas. This pattern is mainly stable in the comparison between different samples (Table 3.8a and b), genders (Table 3.8c), and levels of familiarity with the instrument (Online Appendix A.B4).

The possible moderating variables, gender, and familiarity do not seem to influence the relationship between the scales. The height of the correlations does not necessarily increase with experience in completing the questionnaire (Online Appendix A.B4, first vs. second measurement). In addition, no pattern-oriented differences of the correlations can be detected for females or for males.

Latent structure measurement models

Measurement models for the scales of the RESTQ-Sport are reported for the 76-item version only. The model is based on the German sample GS2.

As can be expected based on the item-total correlations and the internal consistency from *Classical Test Theory*, most of the scales (except *Emotional Exhaustion*, *Being in Shape*, and *Sleep Quality*) from the basic and sport-specific scales show a good model fit on at least two of the fit indices (Kellmann & Kallus, this volume, Chapter 2). Figure 3.2 represents the model for *Self-Regulation*, which fits well without any modifications.

The model shows similar loading for all items. All fit indices exceed the limits for a satisfactory model fit. Table 3.9 gives an overview over the fit indices of the RESTQ-Sport scales and the opportunities for improvement, when correlated errors of measurement (i.e., specific variance in two items) are allowed. For most of the scales the initial model can be kept, as at least two of the fit indices indicate an acceptable initial model.

For the scale *Emotional Exhaustion*, it is necessary to allow a correlation of item 63 … *I felt emotionally drained from performance* with item 54 … *I felt burned out by my sport* and/or with item 76 … *I felt frustrated by my sport*. Note that item 63 is the only one in the scale, which has no reference to 'my sport'.

Table 3.8a Intercorrelations of the RESTQ-Sport scales for the samples ES1 ($N=734$) and ES2 ($N=458$).

	Upper data matrix: E1																		
RESTQ-Sport scales	*1*	*2*	*3*	*4*	*5*	*6*	*7*	*8*	*9*	*10*	*11*	*12*	*13*	*14*	*15*	*16*	*17*	*18*	*19*
1 General Stress		**.79**	**.74**	.59	.54	.62	.67	−.21	−.32	−.47	−.58	−.47	.54	.67	.41	−.35	−.33	−.36	−.19
2 Emotional Stress	**.78**		**.81**	.60	.53	.61	.63	−.17	−.30	−.41	−.53	−.47	.49	.63	.36	−.31	−.32	−.33	−.17
3 Social Stress	**.75**	**.80**		.50	.47	.54	.55	−.12	−.22	−.33	−.47	−.39	.44	.56	.30	−.23	−.32	−.27	−.11
4 Conflicts/Pressure	.58	.63	.52		.54	.51	.52	−.01	−.13	−.36	−.33	−.47	.49	.53	.36	−.17	−.17	−.18	−.03
5 Fatigue	.48	.51	.46	.52		.48	.69	−.06	−.15	−.40	−.33	−.52	.61	.53	.48	−.29	−.15	−.18	−.01
6 Lack of Energy	.64	.67	.58	.56	.51		.58	−.28	−.20	−.42	−.34	−.42	.47	.51	.38	−.34	−.26	−.30	−.20
7 Physical Complaints	.62	.61	.58	.50	.56	.58		−.19	−.28	−.50	−.46	−.51	.58	.58	.55	−.43	−.25	−.35	−.14
8 Success	−.05	.01	.01	.10	.12	−.08	.00		.48	.56	.49	.20	−.14	−.17	−.08	.56	.49	.51	.45
9 Social Recovery	−.26	−.20	−.18	−.14	−.12	−.10	−.19	.42		.51	**.72**	.24	−.15	−.22	−.09	.51	.46	.49	.40
10 Physical Recovery	−.30	−.29	−.22	−.25	−.19	−.25	−.32	.58	.50		**.70**	.50	−.36	−.35	−.27	**.75**	.51	.64	.45
11 General Well-being	−.41	−.39	−.34	−.27	−.19	−.24	−.33	.53	.65	**.79**		.46	−.31	−.42	−.17	.62	.55	.58	.45
12 Sleep Quality	−.32	−.34	−.26	−.36	−.41	−.28	−.28	.20	.27	.41	.42		−.47	−.39	−.30	.36	.30	.29	.20

(Continued)

Table 3.8a (Continued)

RESTQ-Sport scales	*1*	*2*	*3*	*4*	*5*	*6*	*7*	*8*	*9*	*10*	*11*	*12*	*13*	*14*	*15*	*16*	*17*	*18*	*19*
13 Disturbed Breaks	.54	.55	.54	.53	.54	.53	.53	.16	−.10	−.13	−.16	−.36		.60	.50	−.28	−.21	−.22	−.05
14 Emotional Exhaustion	.64	.59	.55	.55	.36	.57	.55	−.04	−.10	−.23	−.27	−.27	.57		.46	−.33	−.28	−.32	−.10
15 Injury	.39	.42	.40	.46	.38	.42	.57	.05	−.08	−.19	−.18	−.16	.53	.53		−.30	−.09	−.15	−.02
16 Being in Shape	−.19	−.15	−.13	−.09	−.11	−.17	−.23	.56	.36	**.73**	.63	.31	−.09	−.16	−.18		.52	**.75**	.62
17 Personal Accomplishment	−.03	−.01	−.01	.02	.02	−.04	−.01	.56	.31	.50	.43	.21	.08	.02	.12	.57		.60	.58
18 Self-Efficacy	−.26	−.21	−.20	−.15	−.15	−.26	−.20	.50	.34	.61	.55	.33	−.12	−.18	−.08	**.74**	.59		.69
19 Self-Regulation	−.10	−.04	−.04	.06	.02	−.12	−.04	.40	.21	.34	.28	.13	.01	−.02	.12	.53	.54	.67	
										Lower data matrix: E2									

Note: $r \geq .70$ are bolded.

Table 3.8b Intercorrelations of the RESTQ-Sport scales for the samples GS1 ($N=820$) and GS2 ($N=597$).

	Upper data matrix: G1																		
RESTQ-Sport scales	*1*	*2*	*3*	*4*	*5*	*6*	*7*	*8*	*9*	*10*	*11*	*12*	*13*	*14*	*15*	*16*	*17*	*18*	*19*
1 General Stress		**.71**	.57	.49	.47	.59	.52	−.08	−.32	−.52	−.55	−.47	.46	**.71**	.36	−.48	−.35	−.43	−.41
2 Emotional Stress	**.79**		**.74**	.48	.38	.52	.46	−.02	−.25	−.45	−.49	−.44	.38	.53	.33	−.38	−.31	−.32	−.30
3 Social Stress	.66	**.78**		.38	.29	.46	.35	.00	−.18	−.32	−.32	−.32	.34	.43	.27	−.28	−.26	−.18	−.24
4 Conflicts/Pressure	.58	.59	.53		.38	.29	.40	.24	−.13	−.25	−.26	−.34	.30	.45	.30	−.22	−.01	−.16	−.06
5 Fatigue	.47	.38	.35	.44		.36	.58	.05	−.17	−.46	−.27	−.43	.53	.47	.47	−.49	−.10	−.21	−.23
6 Lack of Energy	.60	.57	.51	.45	.50		.40	−.04	−.16	−.38	−.32	−.32	.44	.45	.25	−.36	−.28	−.34	−.40
7 Physical Complaints	.62	.53	.44	.49	.56	.52		.02	−.12	−.53	−.33	−.45	.44	.47	.64	−.51	−.14	−.28	−.23
8 Success	−.06	.01	.10	.22	.12	−.03	−.05		.21	.30	.32	.08	.00	−.08	.00	.29	.30	.29	.28
9 Social Recovery	−.34	−.30	−.18	−.15	−.11	−.20	−.19	.27		.40	.62	.29	−.18	−.22	−.05	.38	.30	.29	.33
10 Physical Recovery	−.55	−.41	−.29	−.31	−.45	−.42	−.63	.31	.43		.68	.59	−.43	−.44	−.33	**.81**	.45	.60	.56
11 General Well-being	−.62	−.57	−.41	−.31	−.27	−.39	−.42	.34	.66	.69		.51	−.28	−.43	−.14	.63	.46	.56	.52
12 Sleep Quality	−.53	−.49	−.45	−.37	−.51	−.38	−.52	.13	.30	.55	.53		−.43	−.38	−.29	.58	.31	.40	.38

(*Continued*)

Table 3.8b (Continued)

RESTQ-Sport scales	*1*	*2*	*3*	*4*	*5*	*6*	*7*	*8*	*9*	*10*	*11*	*12*	*13*	*14*	*15*	*16*	*17*	*18*	*19*
13 Disturbed Breaks	.55	.51	.48	.50	.61	.47	.59	.16	−.16	−.42	−.32	−.54		.50	.42	−.51	−.19	−.29	−.34
14 Emotional Exhaustion	.64	.53	.47	.47	.48	.47	.54	−.03	−.26	−.47	−.45	−.46	.59		.42	−.46	−.27	−.37	−.36
15 Injury	.27	.27	.20	.35	.37	.26	.62	.03	−.03	−.38	−.14	−.27	.47	.40		−.40	−.05	−.10	−.10
16 Being in Shape	−.50	−.37	−.25	−.30	−.48	−.40	−.62	.27	.36	**.85**	.61	.54	−.47	−.50	−.44		.48	.65	.64
17 Personal Accomplishment	−.25	−.20	−.13	.04	−.03	−.18	−.14	.42	.32	.35	.41	.18	−.03	−.21	.01	.38		.52	.57
18 Self-Efficacy	−.46	−.35	−.20	−.18	−.21	−.36	−.37	.35	.32	.60	.58	.38	−.22	−.38	−.14	.63	.55		**.73**
19 Self-Regulation	−.44	−.30	−.20	−.08	−.23	−.35	−.34	.33	.34	.55	.54	.31	−.24	−.38	−.09	.58	.58	**.75**	

Lower data matrix: G2

Note: $r \geq .70$ are bolded.

Table 3.8c Intercorrelations of the RESTQ-Sport scales for females ($n = 350$) and males ($n = 382$) for the sample ES1.

	Upper data matrix: E1 (female)																		
RESTQ-Sport scales	*1*	*2*	*3*	*4*	*5*	*6*	*7*	*8*	*9*	*10*	*11*	*12*	*13*	*14*	*15*	*16*	*17*	*18*	*19*
1 General Stress		**.80**	**.76**	.58	.54	.61	.67	−.26	−.37	−.47	−.56	−.46	.46	.65	.44	−.34	−.39	−.35	−.20
2 Emotional Stress	**.79**		**.81**	.61	.49	.62	.63	−.24	−.35	−.43	−.53	−.47	.39	.64	.33	−.30	−.39	−.36	−.19
3 Social Stress	**.72**	**.80**		.51	.39	.52	.55	−.20	−.31	−.35	−.49	−.37	.39	.55	.27	−.20	−.40	−.31	−.14
4 Conflicts/Pressure	.59	.59	.48		.51	.53	.52	−.15	−.22	−.39	−.36	−.43	.40	.57	.29	−.18	−.29	−.25	−.07
5 Fatigue	.54	.55	.52	.56		.51	.68	−.12	−.13	−.38	−.29	−.46	.57	.53	.53	−.27	−.16	−.16	−.03
6 Lack of Energy	.62	.58	.54	.48	.45		.61	−.33	−.24	−.38	−.31	−.38	.45	.49	.42	−.30	−.27	−.28	−.21
7 Physical Complaints	.66	.62	.54	.52	.69	.55		−.25	−.33	−.49	−.46	−.49	.54	.62	.60	−.40	−.28	−.28	−.10
8 Success	−.17	−.12	−.05	.11	−.01	−.23	−.14		.53	.62	.52	.33	−.20	−.18	−.15	.62	.49	.54	.48
9 Social Recovery	−.29	−.25	−.15	−.05	−.17	−.15	−.23	.43		.54	**.75**	.31	−.20	−.23	−.06	.57	.52	.55	.46
10 Physical Recovery	−.47	−.40	−.32	−.32	−.41	−.45	−.50	.50	.49		**.71**	.50	−.35	−.36	−.25	**.75**	.57	.61	.45
11 General Well-being	−.60	−.54	−.45	−.29	−.37	−.36	−.46	.47	.69	.69		.47	−.29	−.40	−.15	.68	.62	.62	.51
12 Sleep Quality	−.47	−.45	−.39	−.50	−.56	−.44	−.50	.10	.18	.51	.44		−.40	−.37	−.28	.39	.37	.36	.27

(Continued)

Table 3.8c (Continued)

RESTQ-Sport scales	*1*	*2*	*3*	*4*	*5*	*6*	*7*	*8*	*9*	*10*	*11*	*12*	*13*	*14*	*15*	*16*	*17*	*18*	*19*
13 Disturbed Breaks	.59	.55	.45	.56	.64	.46	.60	−.09	−.11	−.37	−.32	−.50		.53	.49	−.27	−.25	−.24	−.09
14 Emotional Exhaustion	.69	.63	.58	.51	.53	.51	.57	−.18	−.21	−.37	−.44	−.41	.66		.52	−.31	−.31	−.31	−.09
15 Injury	.37	.38	.32	.42	.45	.33	.51	−.03	−.10	−.30	−.18	−.31	.50	.40		−.26	−.05	−.09	.04
16 Being in Shape	−.36	−.31	−.25	−.17	−.31	−.38	−.47	.50	.45	**.74**	.57	.34	−.28	−.36	−.33		.53	**.72**	.62
17 Personal Accomplishment	−.27	−.25	−.23	−.05	−.14	−.23	−.20	.50	.41	.47	.48	.21	−.16	−.26	−.13	.50		.65	.58
18 Self-Efficacy	−.36	−.31	−.24	−.12	−.19	−.32	−.40	.49	.45	.66	.55	.23	−.20	−.35	−.21	**.78**	.55		.74
19 Self-Regulation	−.18	−.16	−.09	.01	.00	−.18	−.18	.43	.35	.46	.40	.14	−.02	−.11	−.06	.62	.58	.66	
								Lower data matrix: E1 (male)											

Note: $r \geq .70$ are bolded.

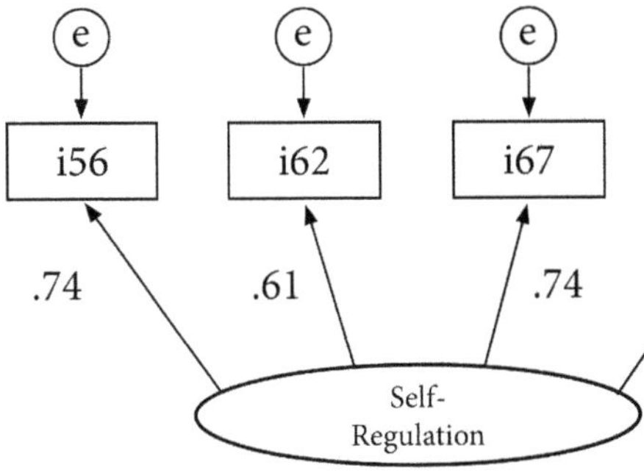

Figure 3.2 Measurement model for *Self-Regulation* (GFI = .99, AGFI = .96, CFI = .99, RMSEA = .07; e = error term, i56 = item 56).

Table 3.9 Fit indices and proposed specific correlations for the RESTQ-Sport scales.

RESTQ-Sport scales		*GFI*	*AGFI*	*CFI*	*RMSEA*	*Modification*
13 Disturbed Breaks	Model Modification	1.00 —	.99 —	1.00 —	.12 —	No modification
14 Emotional Exhaustion	Model Modification	.97 1.00	.85 1.00	.91 1.00	.18 .00	(Item 54 ↔ 63, 63 ↔ 76)
15 Injury	Model Modification	1.00 —	1.00 —	1.00 —	.00 —	No modification
16 Being in Shape	Model Modification	.98 1.00	.89 1.00	.97 1.00	.15 .00	(Item 53 ↔ 69, 53 ↔ 61)
17 Personal Accomp-lishment	Model Modification	.99 —	.97 —	.99 —	.06 —	No modification
18 Self-Efficacy	Model Modification	.98 1.00	.90 1.00	.98 1.00	.13 .00	(Item 52 ↔ 59, 53 ↔ 61)
19 Self-Regulation	Model Modification	.99 —	.96 —	.99 —	.07 —	No modification

Thus, the specificity of item 63 can be attributed to the specific formulation. The same argument applies for item 53 … *I recovered well physically* of the scale *Being in Shape*, which is the only process-oriented item. However, for *Being in Shape* and *Self-Efficacy* all indices except RMSEA indicate a satisfactory fit of the simple measurement model, which can be accepted well without further modification.

Measurement models for the RESTQ-Sport indicate a good model fit for the scales, except for *Emotional Exhaustion*, which might require special attention in the linear structural models.

Factorial structure of the scales

Since factor analysis has established itself as a classic instrument for describing the inter-correlational structure, one example result will be displayed briefly. More results of factor analysis are reported by Kellmann and Kallus (2001). Regarding the modular construction of the RESTQ-Sport, the factor analysis was performed separately for the basic and the sport-specific parts. Scales of sample ES1 were factor analyzed via Principal Component Analysis followed by a Varimax rotation. After the stop criterion (Eigenvalue < 1; Kaiser), two factors could be extracted for the basic as well as for the sport-specific parts of the RESTQ-Sport (Tables 3.10a and b).

The results confirm the two-factor solution pointed out by Kallus (this volume, Chapter 2). The factor analysis suggests one stress-related and one recovery-related factor (Table 3.10a). However, *Sleep Quality* loads negatively (a = −.60) on the stress-related factor. Moderate negative loading also holds for some recovery scales in the stress-related factor. The basic stress-related factor explains approximately 42% of the variance; the recovery-related factor 24%. Kellmann and Kallus (2001) also reported sample-dependent-explained variance; for example, in one sample, the recovery-related factor explains 13% of the variance; in another sample, it is 27%. In general, it can be concluded that the two-factor solution clearly separates the basic scales of the RESTQ-Sport into one stress-related and one recovery-related factor.

For the sport-specific scales, a two-factor solution can also be clearly separated into one stress- and one recovery-related factor (Table 3.10b). The sport-specific stress factor (*Disturbed Breaks*, *Emotional Exhaustion*, *Injury*) explains about 41% of the variance; the recovery factor (*Being in Shape*, *Personal Accomplishment*, *Self-Efficacy*, *Self-Regulation*) explains approximately 30%. For the interpretation of the %-values for the basic and sport-specific scales, it is important to note that stress and recovery factors are based on different numbers of scales.

Table 3.10a Two-factor-solution (with a > .25) for the basic scales of the RESTQ-Sport for the samples ES1 (N=734).

RESTQ-Sport scales	*Factor 1*	*Factor 2*	h^2
1 General Stress	.83	−.28	.77
2 Emotional Stress	.85		.76
3 Social Stress	.80		.65
4 Conflicts/Pressure	.78		.61
5 Fatigue	.76		.59
6 Lack of Energy	.72		.56
7 Physical Complaints	.78		.67
8 Success		.81	.65
9 Social Recovery		.82	.69
10 Physical Recovery	−.39	.75	.71
11 General Well-being	−.39	.80	.80
12 Sleep Quality	−.60	.31	.45
Eigenvalue	6.04	1.86	
Variance in %	41.87	23.80	

Structural modelling

RESTQ-Sport-76

The results from Exploratory Factor Analysis and the basic pattern of intercorrelations which turned out to be stable across different populations, different versions, and different translations led to the hypothesis that the two-dimensional structure with a latent variable for the stress and a recovery dimension of the RESTQ-Sport can well be modelled in a structural model of linear equations with a good model fit. The structural model for the scales of the RESTQ-Sport used the scales as 'manifest variables' (Kallus, this volume, Chapter 2), as the solutions for the scales resulted in acceptable measurement models. A model with two latent variables representing the dimensions 'stress' and 'recovery' fits the data very well, as expected from former Exploratory Factor Analysis.

Figure 3.3 shows that a model with one sport-specific recovery factor and a sport-specific stress factor with two sub-dimensions gives a good representation of the variance. The separation of a sport-specific stress and a sport-specific recovery factor, which emerges from the correlational structure and the Exploratory Factor Analysis, can be strengthened by the linear structural models. At

Table 3.10b Two-factor-solution (with a > .25) for the sport-specific scales of the RESTQ-Sport for the sample ES1 (N=734).

RESTQ-Sport scales	*Factor 1*	*Factor 2*	h^2
13 Disturbed Breaks		.84	.72
14 Emotional Exhaustion		.81	.69
15 Injury		.80	.63
16 Being in Shape	.81	−.29	.74
17 Personal Accomplishment	.78		.62
18 Self-Efficacy	.89		.82
19 Self-Regulation	.88		.78
Eigenvalue	3.29	1.70	
Variance in %	41.05	30.29	

the same time, only a low negative correlation between the latent variables of recovery and stress appears on the specific level of the RESTQ-Sport, which contrasts high correlation on the high aggregation level of the RESTQ-Basic. Between the dimensions and the option of the two sub-dimensions within the stress domain should be commented upon. For the structural model, the two sub-dimensions of stress can be omitted without losing the model fit. Thus, the overall stress score can well be interpreted. The model strongly supports the separation of the stress and the recovery dimensions.

However, Figure 3.3 shows that low specific correlations between *Injury* from the *Sport-specific Stress* dimension and two scales of the *Sport-specific Recovery* dimensions should be included to obtain the very good model fit. While the negative correlation of scale 15 *Injury* with scale 16 *Being in Shape* can be attributed to the physical component in both scales, the correlation to scale 19 *Self-Regulation* might be due to the fact that injury requires increased self-regulation on a functional level. Note that *Physical Complaints* had also to be modelled with a specific covariance for the RESTQ-Basic.

The most interesting common model for the specific scales of the RESTQ-Sport and the RESTQ-Basic did not result in an acceptable fit for the linear structural models. More than 60 modifications were needed until a model with acceptable fit indices emerged. This might be due to the very different levels of abstraction in the basic and the specific part of the RESTQ-Sport. While the simple correlations indicate high validity with respect to the bivariate correlations, the latent variables cannot be directly related in a simple way. Problems with variables of different generality-specificity have repeatedly been discussed. The nonreciprocal relationship of global high-level variables and specific low-level variables is partly due to incomplete part-whole relations. It can also

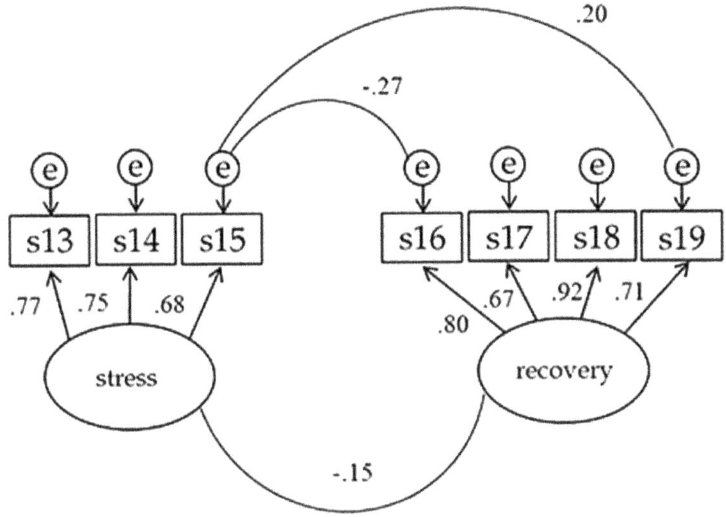

Figure 3.3 Structural model of the RESTQ-Sport scales (GFI = .97, AGFI = .91, CFI = .97, RMSEA = .08).
Note: s13: *Disturbed Breaks*, s14: *Emotional Exhaustion*, s15: *Injury*, s16: *Being in Shape*, s17: *Personal Accomplishment*, s18: *Self-Efficacy*, s19: *Self-Regulation*.

be viewed from the perspective of the 'Bandwidth-Fidelity-Dilemma' in Differential Psychology and personnel selection (Briley & Tucker-Drob, 2012; Cheng et al., 2008; Cronbach & Gleser, 1965). All in all, this might be another argument in favor of the modular concept of the RESTQ-Sport.

RESTQ-Sport-36

Gnacinski et al. (2021) tested structural complexity using Confirmatory Factor Analysis (CFA) procedures. Model 1 in Figure 3.4 represents the first-order factor structure, with 36 items loading on twelve latent variables. Model 2 represents the structure described in Model 1 with the addition of the four second-order general and sport-specific latent variables. Model 3 represented the structure described in Model 2 with the addition of the two third-order *Total Stress* and *Total Recovery* latent variables.

Exploratory Structural Equation Modeling (ESEM) is also applied to Model 1 to account for cross-loading between elements and to provide flexibility in presenting a complex measurement model such as RESTQ-Sport-36. As part of the ESEM process, target rotation (orthogonal) was used. Fit quality is compared across all tested models to assess cost effectiveness. To determine sub-range reliability, McDonald's omega was calculated using parameters from both, the first-order CFA model and the ESEM model. An Omega ratio above .70 was considered acceptable by Gnacinski et al. (2021). Missing data were considered to be completely random missing data and were treated with a maximum

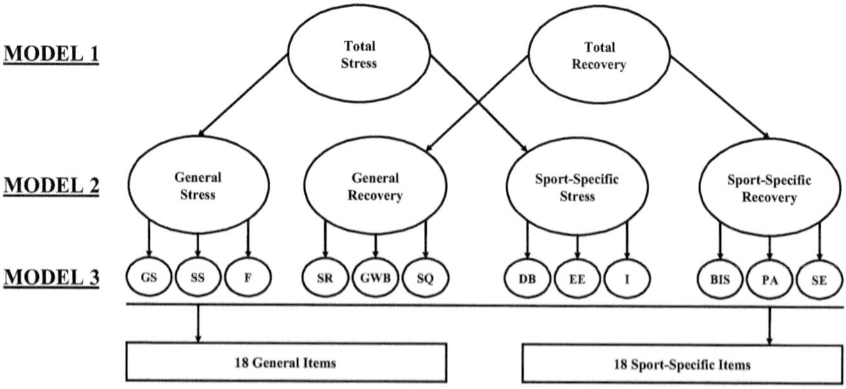

Figure 3.4 Hypothesized models tested by Gnacinski et al. (2021, p. 4).
Note: GS: *General Stress*, SS: *Social Stress*, F: *Fatigue*, SR: *Social Recovery*, GWB: *General Well-being*, SQ: *Sleep Quality*, DB: *Disturbed Breaks*, EE: *Emotional Exhaustion*, I: *Injury*, BIS: *Being in Shape*, PA: *Personal Accomplishment*, SE: *Self-Efficacy. Covariance between latent variables is not depicted. The term Model may be misleading, the authors of this chapter would prefer the term Level.*

likelihood estimate of complete information for incomplete data (Enders & Bandalos, 2001; Kline, 2011).

Gnacinski et al. (2021) analyzed the covariance matrix using maximum likelihood estimation. To define units within Model 1, the unstandardized loading of one item from each first-order latent variable was constrained to 1.0. For Models 2 and 3, a standardization approach was used where the variance of a common factor was constrained to 1.0. To assess model fit, chi-squared test of fit, residual-based indices [i.e., Root Mean Square Error of Approximation (RMSEA), Standardized Root Mean Square Residual (SRMR)] and incremental fit indices [i.e., Comparative Fit Index (CFI), Tucker-Lewis Index (TLI)] were calculated and reported. All calculated model fit indices were collectively evaluated considering previous literature on model fit determination (Hu & Bentler, 1999; Marsh et al., 2004).

Parsimony of the measurement model was observed in Model 1 [$\chi^2_{(528)} = 1129.941$, $p < .001$; SRMR = .050; CFI = .929], indicating that the first-order 12-factor structure is the best-fitting model of the three models tested. No support was observed for the fit of any hierarchical model. This finding was further supported by the ESEM model test [$\chi^2_{(264)} = 575.424$, $p < .001$; SRMR = .013; CFI = .963], which showed improvements in the SRMR and CFI parameters beyond those observed in the CFA procedure for Model 1.

Interestingly, the structure of the RESTQ-Sport was replicated with the short version, RESTQ-Sport-36. In addition, the failure of replicating the second-order model calls for caution in calculating total scores for the RESTQ-Sport-36 based on the analysis by Gnacinski et al. (2021).

Convergent and discriminant validity

The recovery-stress state could be validated against a broad range of criteria, which cover psychological measures such as mood state, classical criteria such as performance, and biological state indicators.

Correlations with actual condition/state

The expected relationships between the actual state and the RESTQ-Sport have been empirically verified, which supports the validity of the RESTQ-Sport. For the RESTQ-Sport, the link to the actual psychophysical state has been covered by the correlation with the Multidimensional Physical Symptom List (MPSL; Erdmann & Janke, 1981), the POMS and the State-Trait-Anxiety Inventory (STAI; Spielberger et al., 1970). The MPSL measures various physiological processes and complaints. Based on these items, the participants should rate how they currently feel. The MPSL *General Physical Oversensitivity* scale highly correlates with the physically oriented RESTQ-Sport scales (Online Appendix A.B5). Positive correlations with *Physical Complaints* and *Injury* as well as negative relationships with *Physical Recovery* and *Being in Shape* occur. The highest correlations with *Stressed Respiration* are shown for *General Stress*, *Emotional Stress*, *Lack of Energy*, *Physical Complaints*, and the sport-specific stress-related scales, *Disturbed Breaks*, *Emotional Exhaustion*, and *Injury*.

The original English version of the POMS is a 65-item Likert-format questionnaire with intensity scales ranging from 1 (*not at all*) to 4 (*extremely*). The POMS provides a measure of general mood disturbances and six mood states (*Tension*, *Depression*, *Anger*, *Vigor*, *Fatigue*, *Confusion*). To match the results of the RESTQ-Sport and the POMS, the time frame in the heading of the POMS was changed to *in the past (3) days/nights* based on the suggestion by McNair et al. (1971/1992). Although the RESTQ-Sport and the POMS apply different types of scales – frequency vs. intensity (Diener & Emmons, 1984) – analysis revealed close and theoretically expected correlation patterns which are matching results in German (Kellmann et al., 2001), American (Gnacinski et al., 2021), Dutch (Nederhof, Brink, et al., 2008), Portuguese (Kellmann et al., 2009), and Mexican (Reynoso-Sánchez et al., 2021) samples. *Tension*, *Depression*, *Anger*, *Fatigue*, and *Confusion* negatively correlate with recovery-related scales, whereas for *Vigor*, a positive relationship occurs (Table 3.11a). The stress-related RESTQ-Sport scales show a positive interrelation with *Tension*, *Depression*, *Anger*, *Fatigue*, and *Confusion* but a negative interrelation with *Vigor*. Interestingly, for *Vigor*, the correlation with the recovery-related scales is higher compared to the stress-related scales.

The same pattern (Table 3.11b) was found by Gnacinski et al. (2021) correlating the RESTQ-Sport-36 and the Brief-POMS (30 items; time frame in the heading of the POMS: *the past week*). In addition to these data, Kellmann (2002c)

Table 3.11a Correlation between the RESTQ-Sport-76 and the POMS for the Canadian sample C1 ($n = 65$).

	Scales of the Profile of Mood States					
RESTQ-Sport scales	*Tension*	*Depression*	*Anger*	*Vigor*	*Fatigue*	*Confusion*
1 General Stress	**.70**	**.74**	**.73**	−.19	.45	**.72**
2 Emotional Stress	**.75**	.61	.65	−.34	.51	.64
3 Social Stress	**.75**	.69	**.75**	−.34	.50	**.71**
4 Conflicts/Pressure	.68	.55	.46	−.30	.45	.67
5 Fatigue	.40	.34	.28	−.20	.50	.33
6 Lack of Energy	.59	.45	.43	−.38	.57	.69
7 Physical Complaints	.42	.48	.46	−.29	.55	.38
8 Success	−.14	−.16	−.13	.37	−.09	−.19
9 Social Recovery	−.32	−.33	−.17	.44	−.28	−.24
10 Physical Recovery	−.57	−.42	−.43	.49	−.50	−.46
11 General Well-being	−.62	−.47	−.46	.60	−.52	−.51
12 Sleep Quality	−.67	−.45	−.49	.45	−.58	−.56
13 Disturbed Breaks	.51	.38	.40	−.28	.42	.45
14 Emotional Exhaustion	.50	.58	.50	−.31	.42	.56
15 Injury	.38	.43	.35	−.23	.56	.39
16 Being in Shape	−.38	−.34	−.25	.61	−.49	−.34
17 Personal Accomplishment	−.25	−.22	−.13	.29	−.18	−.12
18 Self-Efficacy	−.34	−.40	−.22	.40	−.27	−.36
19 Self-Regulation	−.10	−.10	−.13	.43	−.20	−.05

Note: $r \geq .70$ are bolded.

reported the parallel changes over time of some RESTQ-Sport and POMS scales over the testing period, which also suggests that both questionnaires seem to be sensitive to events in the life of athletes that affect the recovery-stress state and mood, respectively. Furthermore, Nederhof, Brink, et al. (2008) showed similar changes of the POMS and RESTQ-Sport profiles for an athlete classified as nonfunctional overreached (NFO), an athlete recovering from NFO, and a healthy control athlete.

A clear pattern was also found for the recovery and stress-related scales and anxiety measured by the STAI. A positive correlation was found between stress

Table 3.11b Correlation between the RESTQ-Sport-36 and the Brief-POMS for an American sample ($n = 304$; Gnacinski et al., 2021).

	Scales of the Profile of Mood States					
RESTQ-Sport scales	*Tension*	*Depression*	*Anger*	*Vigor*	*Fatigue*	*Confusion*
1 General Stress	**.70**	**.78**	.64	−.44	.61	.62
2 Social Stress	.54	.54	**.73**	−.30	.49	.48
3 Fatigue	.47	.40	.30	−.26	.62	.38
4 Social Recovery	−.36	−.40	−.34	.46	−.40	−.28
5 General Well-being	−.49	−.56	−.52	.56	−.42	−.46
6 Sleep Quality	−.54	−.44	−.40	.39	−.56	−.45
7 Disturbed Breaks	.35	.27	.25	−.21	.39	.34
8 Emotional Exhaustion	.44	.53	.48	−.31	.50	.41
9 Injury	.29	.19	.19	−.07	.50	.19
10 Being in Shape	−.36	−.33	−.33	.50	−.46	−.38
11 Personal Accomplishment	−.31	−.29	−.38	.40	−.19	−.32
12 Self-Efficacy	−.36	−.35	−.32	.43	−.40	−.42

Note: $r \geq .70$ are bolded.

and anxiety and a negative correlation between anxiety and recovery (Online Appendix A.B6).

Relationships to motivational components

The Volitional Component Questionnaire (VCQ; Kuhl & Fuhrmann, 1998) measures individual differences in volitional or self-regulatory abilities. Generally, this questionnaire can measure how susceptible individuals are, for example, to becoming alienated from their own preferences. The correlation between the current state of stress and different motivational components is shown in Online Appendix A.B7. From the original 32 VCQ scales, 12 were chosen as relevant for the current results pertaining to athletics. At first sight, the correlations follow the POMS-RESTQ pattern, which has already been described. Negative correlations exist with the basic and sport-specific areas of stress and the positive components of volitional control. These positive components positively correlate with the recovery areas. The negative components of volitional control show the opposite.

On closer look, it becomes apparent that the relationships between the basic and sport-specific areas of recovery and the positive components of volitional control are considerably higher than in the area of stress. The correlations between the *Positive Self-Motivation, Emotion Control, Self-Relaxation, Initiative,* and *Volitional Self-Efficacy* scales and the RESTQ-Sport *Physical Recovery, Being in Shape, Self-Efficacy,* and *Self-Regulation* scales are almost all above $r > .40$. The relations with the *General Stress, Sleep Quality,* and *Personal Accomplishment* areas are somewhat lower and not quite as consistent. The negative components of volitional control show another pattern. The *Susceptibility to Intrusions, Alienation, Rumination,* and *Passive Avoidance* scales correlate beyond $r > .40$ with the RESTQ-Sport *General Stress* scale. *Susceptibility to Intrusions* also correlates beyond $r > .40$ with the RESTQ-Sport *Emotional Stress, Social Stress, Conflicts/Pressure,* and *Lack of Energy* scales.

Recovery-stress state patterns

Frequencies of stress and recovery have repeatedly been proven to independent dimensions (Kallus, this volume, Chapter 2). Two overall scores can be developed from the positive correlations within the stress and recovery scales. To get a closer look at the empirical distribution of the possible recovery-stress state patterns, the group is divided at the median of the recovery and stress area and the parts are compared with each other. In the analysis of the four recovery-stress state patterns (*I. low stress – low recovery, II. high stress – low recovery, III. low stress – high recovery, IV. high stress – high recovery*), a consistent distribution pattern has been found across different samples (Table 3.12).

Table 3.12 Empirical distribution of recovery-stress state patterns for English (ES1, ES2) and German (GS1, GS2, R4) samples.

Recovery-stress state pattern	***ES1*** *n = 674*	***ES2*** *n = 443*	***GS1*** *n = 799*	***GS2*** *n = 566*	***R4*** N = 58	*Mean*
I. Low stress – low recovery	18.2%	20.1%	15.5%	15.4%	24.1%	18.6%
II. High stress – low recovery	32.5%	29.8%	34.3%	35.2%	31.0%	32.6%
III. Low stress – high recovery	34.4%	30.2%	35.3%	35.3%	29.3%	32.9%
IV. High stress – high recovery	14.8%	19.9%	14.9%	14.1%	15.6%	15.9%

The recovery-stress patterns *II. high stress – low recovery* and *III. low stress – high recovery* each represent about one-third of the empirical distribution. The other third is shared by the patterns *I. low stress – low recovery* and *IV. high stress – high recovery*. As shown in Table 3.12, the exact distribution of the four types varies slightly within the different analysis samples, although it remains remarkably constant.

For 76 German athletes, Kellmann and Kallus (2001) utilized a two-factor Multivariate Analysis of Variance to show the differences in the habitual components of volitional control between the recovery-stress state patterns. The 2 × 2 analysis did not show significant interactions, but only the main effects of recovery and stress. The main effect for recovery is highly significant for the habitual components of volitional control [$F_{(12,61)} = 5.53$; $p < .001$], and the main effect for stress is also significant [$F_{(12,61)} = 2.13$; $p < .05$]. For the factor stress, the univariate follow-up tests for the scales *Procrastination* and *Self-Discipline* are relevant. These scales are not significant in the follow-up tests for recovery, as the scales *Susceptibility to Intrusions* and *Alienation*. All other VCQ scales reach a minimum significance level of $p < .05$. The analyses show that the difference between most motivational components of the VCQ can be reduced to the factor recovery. The scales *Procrastination, Susceptibility to Intrusions, Alienation*, and *Self-Discipline* do not fit into this pattern (Beckmann & Kellmann, 2004).

Changes in the recovery-stress state

The recovery-stress state is dependent on current activities regarding stress and recovery. Although the recovery-stress state is stable in the face of temporary functional fluctuations, it is affected by activities in the daily life of individuals. For example, vacations or training load changes influence the recovery-stress state quite a bit.

Effects of vacation

In a repeated measurement study, Kellmann et al. (1998) found significant improvement of the recovery-stress state in American female swimmers (NCAA Division I) after a four-day Thanksgiving break. Twenty-one athletes (age $M=19.43$ years; $SD=1.25$) completed the RESTQ-Sport and the POMS (McNair et al., 1971/1992) throughout the season. The swimmers were instructed to complete the questionnaires 48 hours before each intercollegiate competition. The first competition took place six days prior to the four-day Thanksgiving break. The second took place two days after the holidays. The analysis with paired *t*-tests showed a dramatic improvement in the recovery-stress state after the four-day vacation (Figure 3.5). The general stress level diminished and recovery increased over the vacation break, especially *Physical Recovery*, *General*

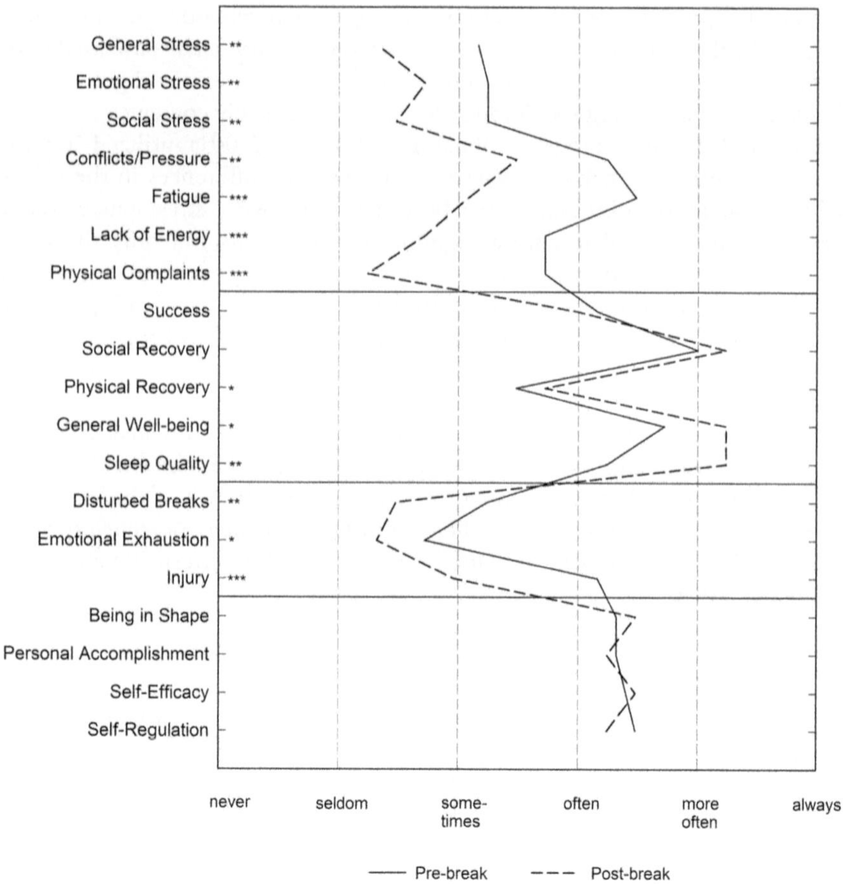

Figure 3.5 Recovery-stress states of American female swimmers before and after the Thanksgiving vacation (p-value: *: $.05 \geq p > .01$; **: $.01 \geq p > .001$; ***: $p \leq .001$).

Well-being, and *Sleep Quality*. Matching those changes, the sport-specific scales *Injury*, *Emotional Exhaustion*, and *Disturbed Breaks* decreased.

This result is not surprising, since taking a break is the purpose of a vacation; however, it is also important to look at individual situations. Athletes who had to travel a long distance to get home could not profit from the break as much as swimmers who lived near the university. For some, Thanksgiving vacation was a time to rest and enjoy a slower pace of life. For others, it was characterized by higher emotional intensity associated with activities involving family, friends, and significant others. Although such activities may represent a change in the normal training regimen, they may not be less emotionally stressful.

For a detailed analysis, the individual interpretation of the RESTQ-Sport is useful, because it gives the support staff (e.g., coach, sport psychologist) a clear picture of the athlete's recovery-stress state. The study highlights that recovery should not only be understood as an integral part of training but should also be recognized in activities apart from sport that affect the athlete's recovery-stress state.

Effects within a training camp

The RESTQ-Sport has been used in various sports (e.g., triathlon, swimming, soccer, rugby) and nations (e.g., Australia, Brazil, Canada, Germany, Estonia, France) to monitor athletes and the impact of training during the preparation camp for World Championships and Olympic Games (Brink et al., 2010; Coutts et al., 2007; Filaire et al., 2009; Hough et al., 2013; Kellmann & Günther, 2000; Mäestu et al., 2006; Meister et al., 2013). Even during a 105-day ground-based space simulation (Nicolas & Gushin, 2015), the RESTQ-Sport was used to monitor stress and recovery responses of the participants and in experiments simulating microgravity (Nicolas, 2009; Nicolas & Weiss, 2009).

Evaluation of the use of the instrument has found that changes in training volume were reflected by significant changes in RESTQ-Sport scales. In one of the first studies, Kellmann and Günther (2000) investigated changes in stress and recovery in rowers during preparation for the Atlanta Olympic Games in 1996. The results show that a dose-response relationship exists between training volume indicated by the average number of minutes of daily extensive endurance training and the subjective assessment of stress and recovery. High training load is indicated by an elevated level of stress and, at the same time, a decreased level of recovery. Shortly after, a group of Estonian researchers published a series of studies in rowing (Jürimäe et al., 2004; Purge et al., 2004, 2005, 2006) confirming that increases in training volume were reflected in elevated stress and reduced recovery scores measured by the RESTQ-Sport. In addition, the relationship between training load and the RESTQ-Sport has also been examined in soccer (Brink et al., 2013; Coker et al., 2017; Laux et al., 2015; Rollo et al., 2014), Australian Rules Football (Campbell et al., 2020), basketball (di Fronso et al., 2013; Nunes et al., 2014), cycling (Costello et al., 2023; Otter et al., 2016; Wallett et al., 2018), tennis (Filaire et al., 2013; Thiel et al., 2011), triathlon (Barnett et al., 2012; Coutts et al., 2007; Stephenson et al., 2019), kayaking (Garatachea et al., 2011), swimming (Dobson et al., 2020; Elbe et al., 2016; Lima-Borges et al., 2018), judo (Morales et al., 2014), ultra-marathon (Nicolas et al., 2011), rugby (Coutts & Reaburn, 2008; Dubois et al., 2020), volleyball (Berriel et al., 2020; Horta et al., 2019), netball (Russell et al., 2021), Brazilian jiu-jitsu (Campos et al., 2022), and other sports such as ballroom dancing (Blevins et al., 2022; De Wet et al., 2022; Liiv et al., 2013).

Bio-psychological state indicators

As one of the first studies, Steinacker et al. (1999, 2000) reported on the time characteristics of hormones and the course of RESTQ-Sport results during a training camp of rowers. *Physical Complaints*, as reported in the RESTQ-Sport, are highest during the phase of most intensive training, which correlates with increased cortisol and creatine kinase (CK). If *Physical Complaints* decrease cortisol and CK also decline. In the same way, the peak amount of norepinephrine corresponds to *Fatigue*. The authors suggested that multivariable analysis should be used in future research, considering physiological and psychological parameters in different courses of time.

Since these publications appeared various authors have utilized the RESTQ-Sport to determine if a specific training protocol was successful, and/or to monitor the changes of various biological parameters such as cortisol, testosterone, CK, and others (Berriel et al., 2020; Bizjak et al., 2021; Bresciani et al., 2010; dos Santos et al., 2014; Filaire et al., 2013; Horta et al., 2019; Skovgaard et al., 2014).

Injury prediction

Steinacker et al. (1999) noted that during training camp, the reported illnesses reached their peak with the most reported *Physical Complaints*. The sample R2 was analyzed to clarify this correlation and to verify whether, using the RESTQ-Sport, a prediction can be made about an athlete's forthcoming medical examination. The following criteria were valid for the analysis:

- Reported recently sick are those athletes who did not have a doctor's appointment (3) days prior to filling out the RESTQ-Sport. The reason behind this somewhat conservative decision was that persons with acute complaints will express these in the RESTQ-Sport. Therefore, the verification of predicted effects was related to medically inconspicuous athletes.
- All forms of treatment were weighed equally; that means, no differentiation was made between a cold, muscle tension, and other complaints.
- The analysis of reported sickness applies to the day of the survey and the following two days, because the RESTQ-Sport has proven to have high test-retest reliability for the duration of two days, and this time frame is considered to be stable.

Table 3.13 Four-field-table of the acute notifications of sickness and the RESTQ-Sport scales *Injury* at time T4 and *Personal Accomplishment* at time T5.

	Injury				*Personal Accomplishment*		
	Low	*High*	Σ		*Low*	*High*	Σ
New sick reports	1	11	12	New sick reports	11	3	14
Remaining athletes	19	11	30	Remaining athletes	9	18	27
Σ	20	22	42	Σ	20	21	41
χ^2-value: 10.4 *df*: 1 $p = .001$				χ^2-value: 7.55 *df*: 1 $p = .006$			

In the analysis, the group of athletes who recently reported being sick (newly sick) were compared with the remaining athletes. Every RESTQ-Sport scale was divided at the para-median. The evaluation of the accomplishments was organized with a four-field table using a χ^2-test. At the time periods T1, T2, and T3, some scales reached a significant χ^2-value ($p < .05$), whereas at T4 and T5, consistent patterns were present. At time T4, the distribution of the physically oriented scales (*Physical Complaints*, *Physical Recovery*, *Being in Shape*, *Injury*, *Self-Regulation*, and *Self-Efficacy*) had a significant systematic relationship. The athletes who consider themselves to be highly stressed and/or insufficiently recovered will probably go to the doctor within the next two days. This becomes apparent in the distribution of the *Injury* scale, which is shown in Table 3.13.

At time T4, there is still no significant distribution of new sick reports due to change in the *Personal Accomplishment* scale. Just before the World Championships, the distribution of the *Personal Accomplishment* scale changes dramatically. Eleven of the 14 athletes showing low values for *Personal Accomplishment* consulted their team doctor. In the RESTQ-Sport, significant distribution patterns were also present in the general recovery area (*Social Recovery*, *Physical Recovery*, *General Well-being*), and a trend was found for the *General Stress* and *Emotional Stress* scales. The distributions for *Fatigue*, *Self-Efficacy*, and *Self-Regulation* remained stable. A change in the meaning of the physically oriented areas just before competition seems to be portrayed by the distribution patterns, especially their changes in time periods T4 and T5. After a long preparation period, the various aspects of recovery, as well as *Personal Accomplishment*, *Self-Efficacy*, and *Self-Regulation*, become increasingly more important for sickness prediction when the competition gets closer.

Shriee and Hallé (2011) explored the relationship between potential psychological risk factors and injury risk in circus artists. Forty-seven circus artists who wanted to become Cirque du Soleil artists completed the RESTQ-Sport during their first two weeks of training to assess the injury risk ratio (odds ratio). *Injury*, *Emotional Exhaustion*, *Self-Efficacy*, and *Fatigue* were associated with an increase in injury risk (risk ratios between 1.8 and 2.8). Regarding several specific psychological aspects that are considered risk factors for injury, low self-efficacy had the strongest relationship. Shriee and Hallé concluded that most of the strong psychological risk factors for injuries identified in athletes also appear to be risk factors in circus artists. Furthermore, Laux et al. (2015) found in professional football players that the stress-related scales *Fatigue*, *Disturbed Breaks*, and *Injury* and the recovery-related scale *Sleep Quality* significantly predicted injuries in the month after the assessment.

Brink et al. (2012) prospectively monitored sport-specific performance and assessed the recovery-stress balance in overreached (OR) soccer players and controls ($N=94$) over two seasons. Seven players with performance decrement of at least a month were classified as OR. Stress and recovery measures were assessed between overreached group vs. healthy players and at different times within the OR group. An unfavorable total recovery score appeared two months before diagnosis when compared with the reference values of the healthy group established at the start of the season and also over the two seasons. *Emotional Stress*, *Physical Recovery*, *General Well-being*, and *Sleep Quality* were sensitive to OR compared with the average of the healthy group over the two seasons. From those, *Fatigue* and *Being in Shape* demonstrated the largest changes in stress and recovery within the OR players.

Performance criteria

Kellmann and Kallus (1993) presented the option of using the RESTQ-Sport to predict performance prior to competition. To replicate those findings, Kellmann et al. (1996) confirmed a close relationship between the recovery-stress state and performance in competition for the basic stress-oriented and the recovery-related areas, as well as for most single RESTQ-Sport scales (for details see Kellmann & Kallus, 2001). Furthermore, Purge et al. (2005) investigated changes in the perceived recovery-stress state and performance in six highly trained Estonian rowers preparing for major competitions and representing Estonia in double sculls. The performance constantly decreased from World Cup 1 to World Cup 3 as indicated by percent losses for winning boats. The results indicate that the recovery-stress state affects performance of rowers in international competitions. In addition, Kalda et al. (2004) investigated the possible relationship between recovery-stress state and competition results in 21 sprinters and jumpers. They found that the scales were correlated with IAAF points during Indoor Championships Scores for *Fatigue* ($r=-.74$) and *Emotional Stress* ($r=-.79$). Furthermore, competition results from the Outdoor Championships were correlated with scores on the *Physical Complaints* ($r=-.70$) and *General Well-being* ($r=.63$) scales.

Using the RESTQ-Sport as a control variable to determine if the participants were overreached, Dupuy and colleagues (2014) researched the effect of a two-week overload period immediately followed by a one-week taper period on different cognitive processes including executive and nonexecutive functions, and related heart rate variability. They reported a moderate increase in the overall reaction time to the (three) conditions of the Stroop task after the overload period followed by a return to baseline after the taper period. No association between cognitive performance and cardiac parasympathetic control at baseline were observed as well as none between changes in these measures. With a similar approach Nederhof et al. (2007) reported a trend toward psychomotor slowness for the functional overreached athletes compared to the control group after high load training. However, the number of participants and the impact of training were rated to be too low to finalize conclusions at that stage.

Barnett et al. (2010) examined RESTQ-Sport data from an elite female triathlete collected over a 111-day training period to model the relationship between training and self-reported fatigue. The dynamic linear model analysis (West & Harrison, 1997) showed the independent effects of the (3) modes of triathlon training on fatigue, how these can change across time, and the possible influence of other unmeasured variables. In addition, Barnett et al. (2012) reported the relationships of training loads with a performance-related state (*Self-Efficacy*) and the role of potential mediating bio-psycho-social states variables (*Fatigue*, *Lack of Energy*, and *Being in Shape*) in explaining these relationships in an elite triathlete across time. It is important to highlight that the RESTQ-Sport was successfully applied using dynamic linear models in single case studies.

Individual-specific diagnostic case studies

The evaluation based on the RESTQ-Sport scales and, in specific cases, also on the item level provides information about activities where 'room for improvement' is obvious. This information can be used as an active component to modify behaviour in the future. Consequently, since the consultant gets a clear picture of what happened during the preceding days for groups and/or individuals, the RESTQ-Sport is favorable in applied settings. Through the assessment of mood-oriented activities, the results of the RESTQ-Sport reflect a precise situational description of individual and/or group processes.

The following two cases are derived from the 2001 manual of the RESTQ-Sport (Kellmann & Kallus, 2001) which contains more case studies. On the first view the case studies look maybe simplistic, but they should introduce some approaches the RESTQ-Sport can be utilized in applied settings. The main purpose is to identify athletes whose recovery-stress states during training camp do not correspond with the training schedule. Through early intervention, individual training can be adapted to help the athlete dealing with training stress and prevent overtraining. The internal consistencies for some scales bring about some limitations for individual diagnosis based on single scales. Therefore, the complete profile will be considered, and deviation on more than one scale will be used as a screening method for individual problems. Three approaches can be applied for diagnostic purposes:

A. For individual assessment, an 'area of tolerance' is calculated using the mean plus or minus the standard deviation ($M \pm 1$ SD) of the whole team. If more than two scores deviate from this tolerance range, these athletes receive special attention. Since training volume changes throughout training camp, the area of tolerance must be recalculated for each measurement.

B. Individual profiles provide much detailed information about the changes in the recovery-stress state over time.
C. A combination of approaches A and B can also be applied.

In general, it should be noted that low scores in the stress-related areas and high scores in the recovery-related areas are 'positively' labeled, and vice versa. However, in this context, terms such as good/bad or positive/negative do not exist. It must always be kept in mind that the RESTQ-Sport profile reflects just one short period in a person's life, which may change drastically within a few days.

Case 1: Rower A

Description and diagnosis: The first RESTQ-Sport assessment took place three days after the beginning of the training camp. Compared to the group, rower A seemed to be similarly stressed because her scores were in the area of tolerance ($M \pm 1$ *SD*) except for the *Fatigue* scale; however, her recovery-stress state revealed low scores in the *Physical Recovery* and *Sleep Quality* scales (Figure 3.6). In combination with the *Fatigue* scale, it could be concluded that she was experiencing a lack of sleep.

Intervention: After consultation with the head coach, the coach of the boat contacted the rower and found a simple cause for her sleep deficit. She was sleeping in a bed that was in very bad shape, and she had trouble falling asleep at night and during the recovery times after lunch. After acquiring a board and putting it under the mattress, she slept better. Control measurements showed an improvement in *Physical Recovery*, a decrease in *Fatigue*, and clearly better scores in *Sleep Quality* despite a higher training load. The solution is not always that simple but is often easier than expected. In this case, the athlete did not talk to the coach at all about what bothered her but revealed the current situation in the RESTQ-Sport.

Case 2: Rowers B and C

Description and diagnosis: Two rowers (B and C) were in the same boat, had the same coach, and consequently also had the same training load during training camp. After a day and a half off from practice, which was part of the training schedule, completely different developments were detected for both athletes (Figure 3.7). For rower B, stress decreased and recovery increased as expected. No large changes occurred for rower C in the stress-related scales, but the scores of the recovery-related fields dropped significantly after the day and a half off.

Intervention: Based on the results, the coach talked to the athletes about possible causes for the decrease in the recovery scales. One consequence was that

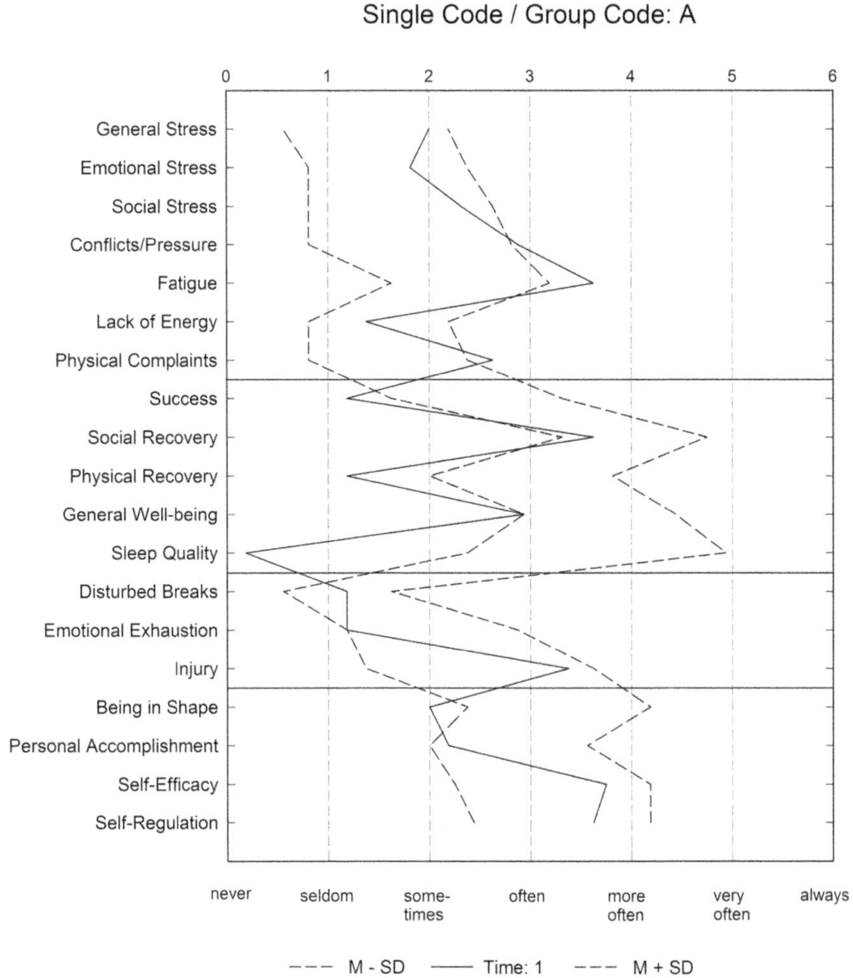

Figure 3.6 RESTQ-Sport profile for female rower A and the area of tolerance for the total group (between the broken lines) for the first point of time in the survey (time: 1).

the training had to be adapted for rower C (i.e., the number of rounds reduced in the weightlifting portion). Knowing that a training reduction for just one person creates an awkward situation, all team members were informed that for the next few days the weightlifting training would be individually adapted, meaning that some athletes would train more than others.

Application areas of the RESTQ-Sport

In the past years, some questions occurred when to use which version of the RESTQ-Sport. The dilemma is typical for using the possible shortest version to

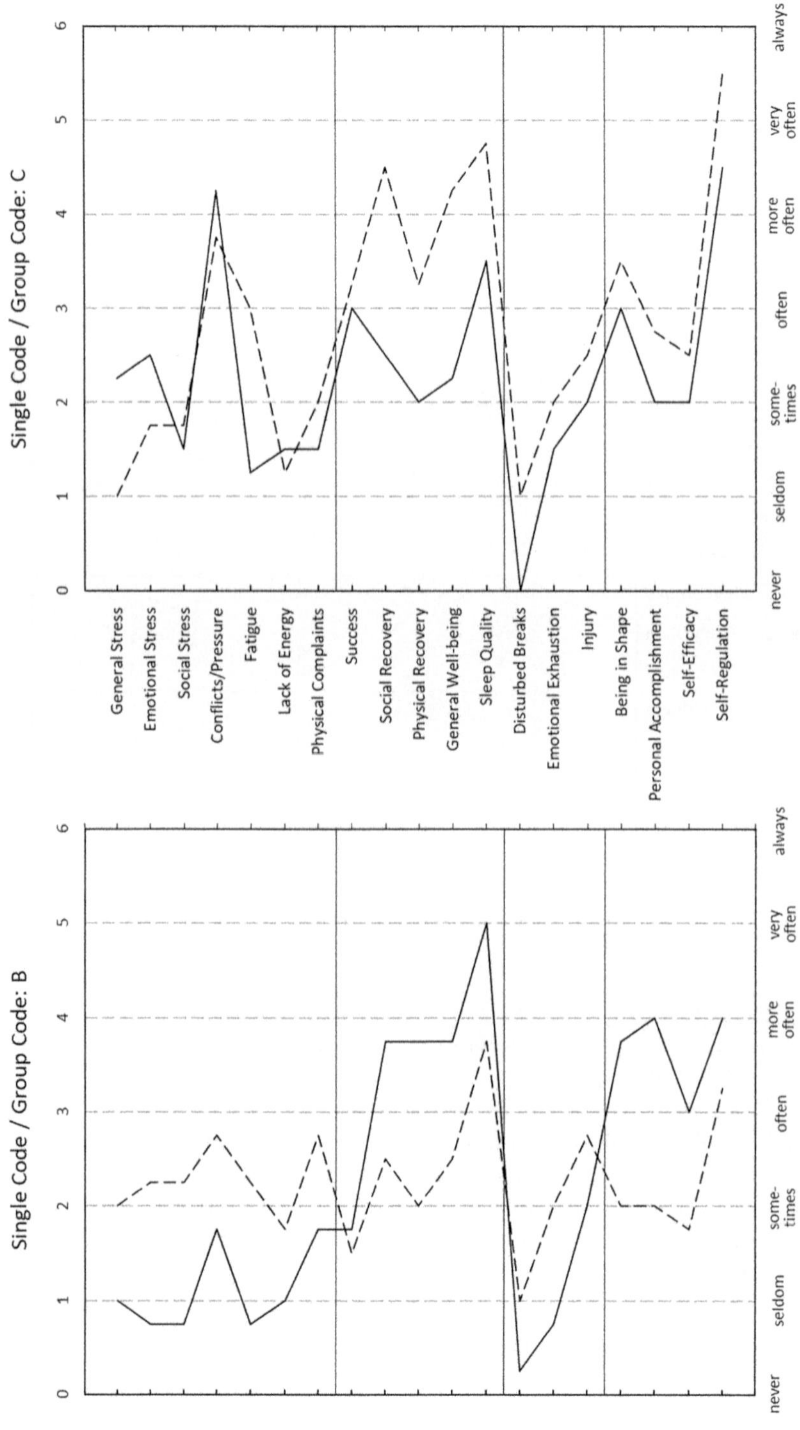

Figure 3.7 Recovery-stress state for rower B and C at T4 (broken line) and T5 (solid line).

Table 3.14 Overview of usability for the RESTQ-Sport versions.

RESTQ-Sport version	*76*	*36*
Individual Diagnostic	x	—
Broad Overview	x	—
Group Diagnostic	x	x
Monitoring	x	x
Collapsed Scores	x	x

increase the commitment of athletes or participants in a study with a maximum information outcome (Saw et al., 2017). Here, strong guidance is provided when to use which version of the RESTQ-Sport (Table 3.14).

In general, the RESTQ-Sport-76 *must be used* whenever an *individual diagnostic* is the aim of the assessment; meaning the individual RESTQ-Sport profile will be used for diagnostic purposes or for an intervention. However, this is not always the case as in many research studies the RESTQ-Sport is used to monitor training processes or as an independent variable to group athletes into a category. Sometimes also only the four main areas of the RESTQ-Sport (*Overall Stress*, *Overall Recovery*, *Sport-specific Stress*, *Sport-specific Recovery*) are used for analyses or the detailed information in the general scales is not the focus of interest. In response to concerns about the RESTQ-Sport being too long, the RESTQ-Sport-36 was developed to make a more user-friendly version of the questionnaire available. The use of the RESTQ-Sport-36 is reasonable when a screening of a group of athletes or research questions with group comparisons is in the focus. Screening in larger samples when monitoring is not a central use of the RESTQ-Sport but might be useful in non-top athletes.

However, the catch is that researchers and sport psychologists must carefully consider all options of their assessment in advance to choose the right version of the RESTQ-Sport. If you are not sure what exactly you may use the data for, it is highly recommended to use the RESTQ-Sport-76 since it leaves all options open.

Summary of the RESTQ-Sport features

- Top performances are only achieved by athletes who can recover fast during competition and deal optimally with the changes between stress, recovery, and upcoming stress.
- The RESTQ-Sport shows specific starting points for intervention.
- The RESTQ-Sport includes a precise subjective appraisal of events in the assessment and an accurate focus on the frequency of behaviour.
- The RESTQ-Sport provides a differentiated picture of the current recovery-stress state for athletes based on twelve non-specific and seven sport-specific scales.

- Depending on the purpose, two forms of the RESTQ-Sport are available.
- The RESTQ-Sport has proven to be reliable and valid.
- The results of the RESTQ-Sport are stable in the face of short-term functionary fluctuations and short-term changes in recovery-stress state.
- All-factor analysis clearly suggests one stress-related and one recovery-related factor for the general as well as for the sport-specific parts of the RESTQ-Sport.
- The RESTQ-Sport also makes it possible to observe individuals and/or groups over the course of a season, during training camps, as well as over many years.
- The recovery-stress state reflects the training load and corresponding changes with training volume existing between hormone levels and RESTQ-Sport results.

Notes

1 We like to thank S. Altfeld, J. Beckmann, P. Born, R. Collette, S. Eickel, A. Ferrauti, A. Frytz, K. Hottenrott, M. Kasch, J. Ohlert, P. Pfannkoch, M. Pfeiffer, C. Raeder, A. Richter, K. Schulze, J. Steinacker, O. Stoll, G. Treff, T. Wiewelhove, and J. Wöhrmann and other researchers for providing the German expert rating.

2 We like to thank M. Bertollo, M. Brink, T. Clark, R. Corban, B. De Cuyper, K. Dieffenbach, A.-M. Elbe, E. Filho, S. di Fronso, P. Haberl, T. Hamill, V. Heynen, A. Kable, D. King, M. Nicolas, F. Nakamura, R. Simola and other researchers for providing the English expert rating.

3 In addition to the official copyright holders some other translations have been published without contacting Kellmann and Kallus. For example, Chatelier (2003) or Martinent et al. (2014) have not received the official copyright for the French version from Kellmann or Kallus. A similar case occurred for an Italian version and some other languages. We are pointing this out because sometimes authors just translate an instrument without contacting the authors. Besides breaching the copyright this may lead to difficulties in the development and interpretation; we are aware of cross-cultural differences which have an impact on the translation. For example, developing the Portuguese (in Brazil) version, we have experienced that a direct translation of terms (without considering the content with the specific cultural background) leads to an unreliable translation.

References

Altfeld, S., & Kellmann, M. (2013). Burnout bei Trainern: Ein Review [Burnout in coaches: A review]. *Zeitschrift für Sportpsychologie, 20*, 47–58.

Altfeld, S., & Kellmann, M. (2015). Are German coaches highly exhausted? A study of differences in personal and environmental factors. *International Journal of Sports Science & Coaching, 10*, 637–654.

Altfeld, S., Mallett, C., & Kellmann, M. (2015). Coaches' burnout, stress, and recovery over a season: A longitudinal study. *International Sport Coaching Journal, 2*, 137–151.

Bandura, A. (1977). Self-efficacy: Toward a unifying theory of behavioral change. *Psychological Review, 84*, 191–215.

Barnett, A., Cerin, E., Reaburn, P., & Hooper, S. (2010). The effects of training on performance and performance-related states in individual elite athletes: A dynamic approach. *Journal of Sports Sciences, 28*(10), 1117–1126.

Barnett, A., Cerin, E., Reaburn, P., & Hooper, S. (2012). Identifying mediators of training effects on performance-related psychobiosocial states: A single-case observational study in an elite female triathlete. *Psychology of Sport and Exercise, 13*, 541–549.

Beckmann, J. (2023). Self-regulation of recovery. In M. Kellmann, S. Jakowski, & J. Beckmann (Eds.), *The importance of recovery for physical and mental health: Negotiating the effects of underrecovery* (pp. 53–69). Routledge.

Beckmann, J., & Kellmann, M. (2004). Self-regulation and recovery: Approaching an understanding of the process of recovery from stress. *Psychological Reports, 95*, 1135–1153.

Berriel, G. P., Costa, R. R., da Silva, E. S., Schons, P., de Vargas, G. D., Peyré-Tartaruga, L. A., & Kruel, L. F. M. (2020). Stress and recovery perception, creatine kinase levels, and performance parameters of male volleyball athletes in a preseason for a Championship. *Sports Medicine – Open, 6*(1), 26. https://doi.org/10.1186/s40798-020-00255-w

Bizjak, D. A., Treff, G., Zügel, M., Schumann, U., Winkert, K., Schneider, M., Abendroth, D., & Steinacker, J. M. (2021). Differences in immune response during competition and preparation phase in elite rowers. *Frontiers in Physiology, 12*, 803863. https://doi.org/10.3389/fphys.2021.803863

Blevins, P., Moyle, G., Erskine, S., & Hopper, L. (2022). Mindfulness, recovery-stress balance, and well-being among university dance students. *Research in Dance Education, 23*(1), 142–155.

Borg, G. (1998). *Borg's Perceived Exertion and Pain Rating Scales*. Human Kinetics.

Bradburn, N. M. (1969). *The structure of physiological well-being.* Aldine.

Bresciani, G., Cuevas, M. J., Garatachea, N., Molinero, O., Almar, M., de Paz, J. A., Márquez, S., & González-Gallego, J. (2010). Monitoring biological and psychological measures during an entire season in male handball players. *European Journal of Sport Science, 6*, 377–384.

Briley, D. A., & Tucker-Drob, E. M. (2012). Broad bandwidth or high fidelity? Evidence from the structure of genetic and environmental effects on the facets of the five factor model. *Behavior Genetics, 42*(5), 746–763.

Brink, M. S., Visscher, C., Arends, S., Zwerver, J., Post, W., & Lemmink, K. (2010). Monitoring stress and recovery: New insights for the prevention of injuries and illnesses in elite youth soccer players. *British Journal of Sport Medicine, 44*, 809–815.

Brink, M. S., Visscher, C., Coutts, A., & Lemmink, K. (2012). Changes in perceived stress and recovery in overreached young elite soccer players. *Scandinavian Journal of Medicine & Science in Sports, 22*, 285–292.

Brink, M. S., Visscher, C., Schmikli, S. L., Nederhof, E., & Lemmink, K. (2013). Is an elevated submaximal heart rate associated with psychomotor slowness in young elite soccer players? *European Journal of Sport Science, 13*, 207–214.

Campbell, P. G., Stewart, I. B., Sirotic, A. C., & Minett, G. M. (2020). The effect of overreaching on neuromuscular performance and wellness responses in Australian Rules Football Athletes. *Journal of Strength and Conditioning Research, 34*(6), 1530–1538.

Campos, F., Molina Correa, J. C., Canevari, V. C. M., Branco, B. H. M., Andreato, L. V., & de Paula Ramos, S. (2022). Monitoring internal training load, stress-recovery responses, and immune-endocrine parameters in Brazilian jiu-jitsu training. *Journal of Strength and Conditioning Research, 36*(3), 723–731.

Carfagno, D. G., & Hendrix, J. C. (2014). Overtraining syndrome in the athlete: Current clinical practice. *Current Sports Medicine Reports, 13*, 45–51.

Chatelier, S. (2003). *Validation française du RESTQ-Sport à partir de la méthodologie de validation de Vallerand* [French validation of the RESTQ-Sport based on Vallerand's validation methodology]. Mémoire de Maîtrisé STAPS.

Cheng, Y., Wang, W., & Ho, Y. H. (2008). Multidimensional Rasch analysis of a psychological test with multiple subtests: A statistical solution for the bandwidth-fidelity dilemma. *Educational and Psychological Measurement, 69*(3), 369–388.

Cohn, P. (1990). An explanatory study of sources of stress and athlete burnout in youth golf. *The Sport Psychologist, 4*, 95–106.

Coker, N. A., Wells, A. J., Ake, K. M., Griffin, D. L., Rossi, S. J., & McMillan, J. L. (2017). Relationship between running performance and recovery-stress state in Collegiate soccer players. *Journal of Strength and Conditioning Research, 31*(8), 2131–2140.

Collette, R., Kellmann, M., Ferrauti, A., Meyer, T., & Pfeiffer, M. (2018). Relation between training load and recovery-stress state in highperformance swimming. *Frontiers in Physiology, 9*, 845. https://doi.org/10.3389/fphys.2018.00845

Costello, S. E., Rossiter, J. R. W., Howatson, G., Bell, P. G., O'Neill, B. V., van Someren, K., & Haskell-Ramsay, C. F. (2023). Effect of intensified training on cognitive function, psychological state & performance in trained cyclists. *European Journal of Sport Science, 23*(7), 1334–1344.

Coutts, A. J., Crowcroft, S., & Kempton, T. (2022). Developing athlete monitoring systems: Theoretical basis and practical applications. In M. Kellmann & J. Beckmann (Eds.), *Recovery and well-being in sport and exercise* (pp. 17–31). Routledge.

Coutts, A. J., & Reaburn, P. R. J. (2008). Monitoring changes in stress and recovery during overreaching in rugby league players. *Perceptual and Motor Skills*, 106, 904–916.

Coutts, A. J., Wallace, L. K., & Slattery, K. M. (2007). Monitoring changes in performance, physiology, biochemistry, and psychology during overreaching and recovery in triathletes. *International Journal of Sports Medicine, 28*(2), 125–134.

Cronbach, L. J., & Gleser, G. C. (1965). *Psychological tests and personnel decisions*. University of Illinois Press.

Davis, H. IV., Orzeck, T., & Keelan, P. (2007). Psychometric item evaluations of the Recovery-Stress Questionnaire for Athletes. *Psychology of Sport and Exercise, 8*, 917–938.

De Wet, J. S., Africa, E., & Venter, R. (2022). Recovery-stress states of professional ballet dancers during different phases of a ballet season. *Journal of Dance Medicine & Science, 26*(1), 8–15.

Debus, G., & Janke, W. (1978). Psychologische Aspekte der Psychopharmakotherapie [Psychological aspects of psychopharmaca therapy]. In L. J. Pongratz (Ed.), *Handbuch der Psychologie* (Vol. 8, pp. 2161–2227). Hogrefe.

di Fronso, S., Nakamura, F. Y., Bortoli, L., Robazza, C., & Bertollo, M. (2013). Stress/recovery balance in basketball amateur players: Differences by gender and preparation phases. *International Journal of Sports Physiology and Performance, 8*, 618–622.

Diener, E., & Emmons, R. (1984). The interpedendence of positive and negative affect. *Journal of Personality and Social Psychology, 47*, 105–117.

DiFiori, J. P., Benjamin, H. J., Brenner, J., Gregory, A., Jayanthi, N., Landry, G. L., & Luke, A. (2014). Overuse injuries and burnout in youth sports: A position statement from the American Medical Society for Sports Medicine. *Clinical Journal of Sport Medicine, 24*, 3–20.

Dobson, J., Harris, B., Claytor, A., Stroud, L., Berg, L., & Chrysosferidis, P. (2020). Selected cardiovascular and psychological changes throughout a competitive season in collegiate female swimmers. *Journal of Strength and Conditioning Research, 34*(11), 3062–3069.

dos Santos, P. B., Kuczynski, K. M., Machado, T. A., Osiecki, A. C.V., & Stefanello, J. M. F. (2014). Psychophysiological stress in under-17 soccer players. *Journal of Exercise Physiology Online, 17*(2), 67–80.

Dubois, R., Lyons, M., Paillard, T., Maurelli, O., & Prioux, J. (2020). Influence of weekly workload on physical, biochemical and psychological characteristics in professional Rugby Union players over a competitive season. *Journal of Strength and Conditioning Research, 34*(2), 527–545.

Dupuy, O., Lussier, M., Fraser, S., Bherer, L., Audiffren, M., & Bosquet, L. (2014). Effect of overreaching on cognitive performance and related cardiac autonomic control. *Scandinavian Journal of Medicine & Science in Sports, 24*, 234–242.

Elbe, A. M., Rasmussen, C. P., Nielsen, G., & Nordsborg, N. B. (2016). High intensity and reduced volume training attenuates stress and recovery levels in elite swimmers. *European Journal of Sport Science, 16*(3), 344–349.

Enders, C. K., & Bandalos, D. L. (2001). The relative performance of full information maximum likelihood estimation for missing data in structural equation models. *Structural Equation Modeling, 8*, 430–457.

Erdmann, G., & Janke, W. (1981). *Mehrdimensionale körperliche Symptomliste* [Multidimensional physical symptom list; Unpublished questionnaire]. TU of Berlin/University of Würzburg, Germany.

Feltz, D. L., Chow, G. M., & Helper, T. J. (2008). Path analysis of self-efficacy and diving performance revisited. *Journal of Sport & Exercise Psychology*, 30, 401–411.

Feltz, D. L., & Riessinger, C. A. (1990). Effects on in vivo emotive imagery and performance feedback on self-efficacy and muscular endurance. *Journal of Sport & Exercise Psychology*, 12, 132–143.

Fender, L. (1989). Athlete burnout: Potential for research and intervention strategies. *The Sport Psychologist, 3*, 63–71.

Filaire, E., Ferreira, J. P., Oliveira, M., & Massart, A. (2013). Diurnal patterns of salivary alpha-amylase and cortisol secretion in female adolescent tennis players after 16 weeks of training. *Psychoneuroendocrinology, 38*, 1122–1132.

Filaire, E., Rouveix, M., & Duclos, M. (2009). Training and 24-hr urinary catecholamine excretion. *International Journal of Sports Medicine, 30*(1), 33–39.

Foster, C. (1998). Monitoring training in athletes with reference to overtraining syndrome. *Medicine and Science in Sports and Exercise, 30*, 1164–1168.

Garatachea, N., García-López, D., José Cuevas, M., Almar, M., Molinero, O., Márquez, S., & González-Gallego, J. (2011). Biological and psychological monitoring of training status during an entire season in top kayakers. *Journal of Sports Medicine and Physical Fitness, 51*, 339–346.

Gnacinski, S. L., Meyer, B. B., & Wahl, C. A. (2021). Psychometric properties of the RESTQ-Sport-36 in a collegiate student-athlete population. *Frontiers in Psychology, 12*, 671919. https://doi.org/10.3389/fpsyg.2021.671919

González-Boto, R., Salguero, A., Tuero, C., Márquez, S., & Kellmann, M. (2008). Spanish adaptation and analysis by structural equation modelling of an instrument for monitoring overtraining: The Recovery-Stress Questionnaire (RESTQ-Sport). *Social Behavior and Personality, 36*(5), 635–650.

Goodger, K., Gorely, T., Lavallee, D., & Harwood, C. (2007). Burnout in sport: A systematic review. *The Sport Psychologist, 21*, 127–151.

Gustafsson, H., DeFreese, J. D., & Madigan, D. J. (2017). Athlete burnout: Review and recommendations. *Current Opinion in Psychology, 16*, 109–113.

Halson, S. L. (2014). Monitoring training load to understand fatigue in athletes. *Sport Medicine, 44*(Suppl. 2), S139–S147.

Hanin, Y. L. (2014). Self-regulation. In R. C. Eklund & G. Tenenbaum (Eds.), *Encyclopedia of sport and exercise psychology* (Vol. 1, pp. 361–366). Sage.

Hausswirth, C., & Mujika, I. (2013). *Recovery for performance in sport*. Human Kinetics.

Heidari, J., Burton, N., McCuaig, L., & Kellmann, M. (2021). "I never thought it would be that bad" – Increasing teachers' awareness of psychological well-being through recovery-stress monitoring and individualised feedback. *WORK: A Journal of Prevention, Assessment & Rehabilitation, 69*(4), 1217–1227.

Henschen, K. (1993). Athletic staleness and burnout: Diagnosis, prevention, and treatment. In J. Williams (Ed.), *Applied sport psychology* (pp. 328–337). Mayfield Publishing Company.

Hoffman, J. R., Epstein, S., Yarom, Y., Zigel, L., & Einbinder, M. (1999). Hormonal and biochemical changes in elite basketball players during a 4-week training camp. *Journal of Strength Condition Research, 13*, 280–285.

Horta, T. A. G., Bara Filho, M. G., Coimbra, D. R., Miranda, R., & Werneck, F. Z. (2019). Training load, physical performance, biochemical markers, and psychological stress during a short preparatory period in Brazilian elite male volleyball players. *Journal of Strength and Conditioning Research, 33*(12), 3392–3399.

Hough, J., Corney, R., Kouris, A., & Gleeson, M. (2013). Salivary cortisol and testosterone responses to high-intensity cycling before and after an 11-day intensified training period. *Journal of Sports Sciences, 31*, 1614–1623.

Hu, L., & Bentler, P. M. (1999). Cutoff criteria for fit indexes in covariance structure analysis: Conventional criteria versus new alternatives. *Structural Equation Modeling, 6*, 1–55.

Jagodzinski, W., Kühnel, S. M., & Schmidt, P. (1987). Is there a 'Socratic effect' in nonexperimental panel studies? *Sociological Methods & Research, 15*, 259–302.

Janke, W., & Debus, G. (1978). *Die Eigenschaftswörterliste (EWL). Handanweisung* [Adjective Checklist. Manual]. Hogrefe.

Jeffries, A. C., Wallace, L., Coutts, A. J., McLaren, S. J., McCall, A., & Impellizzeri, F. M. (2020). Athlete-reported outcome measures for monitoring training responses: A systematic review of risk of bias and measurement property quality according to the COSMIN guidelines. *International Journal of Sports Physiology and Performance, 15*(9), 1203–1215.

Jones, M. V., & Turner, M. J. (2014). Self-regulation. In R. C. Eklund & G. Tenenbaum (Eds.), *Encyclopedia of sport and exercise psychology* (Vol. 2, pp. 653–656). Sage.

Jürimäe, J., Mäestu, J., Purge, P., & Jürimäe, T. (2004). Changes in stress and recovery after heavy training in rowers. *Journal of Science and Medicine in Sport, 7*, 334–339.

Kalda, J., Jürimäe, T., & Jürimäe, J. (2004). Relationships between recovery-stress state and performance in sprinters and jumpers. *Perceptual and Motor Skills, 99*(1), 12–16.

Kallus, K. W. (1995). *Der Erholungs-Belastungs-Fragebogen* [The Recovery-Stress Questionnaire]. Swets & Zeitlinger.

Kallus, K. W., & Kellmann, M. (2000). Burnout in athletes and coaches. In Y. L. Hanin (Ed.), *Emotions in sport* (pp. 209–230). Human Kinetics.

Kallus, K. W., & Krauth, J. (1995). Nichtparametrische Verfahren zum Nachweis emotionaler Reaktionen [Non-parametric methods for the provement of emotional reactions]. In G. Debus, G. Erdmann, & K. W. Kallus (Eds.), *Biopsychologie von Stress und emotionalen Reaktionen* (pp. 23–43). Hogrefe.

Kellmann, M. (1991). *Die Abbildung des Beanspruchungszustandes durch den Erholungs-Belastungs-Fragebogen: Untersuchungen zur Leistungsprädiktion im Sport* [The assessment of the recovery-stress state by the Recovery-Stress Questionnaire: Studies dealing with performance prediction in sports; Unpublished diploma thesis]. University of Würzburg, Germany.

Kellmann, M. (2002a). Underrecovery and overtraining: Different concepts – Similar impact? In M. Kellmann (Ed.), *Enhancing recovery: Preventing underperformance in athletes* (pp. 3–24). Human Kinetics.

Kellmann, M. (Ed.). (2002b). *Enhancing recovery: Preventing underperformance in athletes.* Human Kinetics.

Kellmann, M. (2002c). Psychological assessment of underrecovery. In M. Kellmann (Ed.), *Enhancing recovery: Preventing underperformance in athletes* (pp. 37–55). Human Kinetics.

Kellmann, M. (2010). Preventing overtraining in athletes in high-intensity sports and stress/recovery monitoring. *Scandinavian Journal of Medicine & Science in Sports, 20*(Suppl. 2), 95–102.

Kellmann, M., Altenburg, D., Lormes, W., & Steinacker, J. M. (2001). Assessing stress and recovery during preparation for the World Championships in rowing. The Sport Psychologist, 15, 151–167.

Kellmann, M., & Beckmann, J. (Eds.). (2022). *Recovery and well-being in sport and exercise.* Routledge.

Kellmann, M., & Beckmann, J. (Eds.). (2024). *Fostering recovery and well-being in a healthy lifestyle: Psychological, somatic, and organizational prevention approaches.* Routledge.

Kellmann, M., Bertollo, M., Bosquet, L., Brink, M., Coutts, A. J., Duffield, R., Erlacher, D., Halson, S. L., Hecksteden, A., Heidari, J., Kallus, K. W., Meeusen, R., Mujika, I., Robazza, C., Skorski, S., Venter, R., & Beckmann, J. (2018). Recovery and performance in sport: Consensus statement. *International Journal of Sports Physiology and Performance,* 13, 240–245.

Kellmann, M., & Günther, K.-D. (2000). Changes in stress and recovery in elite rowers during preparation for the Olympic Games. *Medicine and Science in Sport and Exercise,* 32, 676–683.

Kellmann, M., & Heidari, J. (2020). Changes in the perception of stress and recovery in German secondary school teachers. *Teacher Development,* 24, 242–257.

Kellmann, M., Jakowski, S., & Beckmann, J. (Eds.). (2023). *The importance of recovery for physical and mental health: Negotiating the effects of underrecovery.* Routledge.

Kellmann, M., Johnson, M. S., & Wrisberg, C. A. (1998). Auswirkungen der Erholungs-Beanspruchungs-Bilanz auf die Wettkampfleistung von amerikanischen Schwimmerinnen [The effects that the recovery-stress state has on the performance of American female swimmers]. In D. Teipel, R. Kemper, & D. Heinemann (Eds.), *Sportpsychologische Diagnostik, Prognostik und Intervention* (pp. 123–126). bps.

Kellmann, M., & Kallus, K. W. (1993). The Recovery-Stress Questionnaire: A potential tool to predict performance in sports. In J. R. Nitsch & R. Seiler (Eds.), *Movement and sport: Psychological foundations and effects* (Vol. 1, pp. 242–247). Academia.

Kellmann, M., & Kallus, K. W. (2000). Der *Erholungs-Belastungs-Fragebogen für Sportler: Manual* [The Recovery-Stress Questionnaire for Athletes: Manual]. Swets Test Services.

Kellmann, M., & Kallus, K. W. (2001). The *Recovery-Stress-Questionnaire for Athletes: Manual.* Human Kinetics.

Kellmann, M., & Kallus, K. W. (2016). Recovery-Stress Questionnaire for Athletes. In K. W. Kallus & M. Kellmann (Eds.), *The Recovery-Stress Questionnaires: User manual* (pp. 86–131). Pearson.

Kellmann, M., Kallus, K. W., & Kurz, H. (1996). Performance prediction by the Recovery-Stress Questionnaire. *Journal of Applied Sport Psychology, 8*(Suppl.), S22.

Kellmann, M., Kallus, K. W., Samulski, D., Costa, L., & Simola, R. (2009). *Questionário de Estress e Recuperação para Atletas* [The Recovery-Stress Questionnaire for Athletes]. Imprensa Universitaria.

Kellmann, M., & Kawabata, M. (2016). *Confirmatory factor analysis of the Recovery-Stress Questionnaire for Athletes: Evaluation and refinement* [Unpublished report]. Ruhr University Bochum, Germany.

Kellmann, M., & Kölling, S. (2019). *Recovery and stress in sport: A manual for testing and assessment*. Routledge.

Kellmann, M., & Kölling, S. (2020). *Das Akutmaß und die Kurzskala zur Erfassung von Erholung und Beanspruchung für Erwachsene und Kinder/Jugendliche* [The Acute Measure and the Short Scale of Recovery and Stress for adults and children/adolescents]. Sportverlag Strauß.

Kellmann, M., & Weidig, T. (2010). *Der Pausenverhaltensfragebogen (PVF) – Manual* [The Rest-Period Questionnaire – Manual]. Sportverlag Strauß.

Licensed Kenttä, G., & Hassmén, P. (1998). Overtraining and recovery. *Sports Medicine, 26*, 1–16.

Kline, R. (2011). *Principles and practice of structural equation modeling* (3rd ed.). Guilford Press.

Koutedakis, Y., Myszkewycz, L., Soulas, D., Papapostolou, V., Sullivan, I., & Sharp, N. C. C. (1999). The effects of rest and subsequent training on selected physiological parameters in professional female classical dancers. *International Journal of Sports Medicine, 20*, 379–383.

Kuhl, J., & Fuhrmann, A. (1998). Decomposing self-regulation and self-control: The Volitional Components Inventory. In J. Heckhausen & C. Dweck (Eds.), *Life span perspectives on motivation and control* (pp. 15–49). Cambridge University Press.

LaForge-MacKenzie, K., & Sullivan, P. J. (2014). A comparison of the self-efficacy-performance relationship between continuous and non-continuous sport conditions. *Journal of Applied Sport Psychology, 26*, 363–376.

Laux, P., Krumm, B., Diers, M., & Flor, H. (2015). Recovery-stress balance and injury risk in professional football players: A prospective study. *Journal of Sports Sciences, 33*(20), 2140–2148.

Liiv, H., Jurimae, T., Klonova, A., & Cicchella, A. (2013). Performance and recovery: Stress profiles in professional ballroom dancers. *Medical Problems of Performing Artists, 28*(2), 65–69.

Lima-Borges, D. S., Martinez, P. F., Vanderlei, L. C. M., Barbosa, F. S. S., & Oliveira-Junior, S. A. (2018). Autonomic modulations of heart rate variability are associated with sports injury incidence in sprint swimmers. *The Physician and Sportsmedicine, 46*(3), 374–384.

Lochbaum, M., Zanatta, T., Kirschling, D., & May, E. (2021). The Profile of Mood States and athletic performance: A meta-analysis of published studies. *European Journal of Investigation in Health, Psychology and Education, 11*(1), 50–70.

Mäestu, J., Jürimäe, J., Kreegipou, K., & Jürimäe, T. (2006). Changes in perceived stress and recovery during heavy training in highly trained rowers. *The Sport Psychologist, 20*, 24–39.

Marsh, H. W., Hau, K.-T., & Wen, Z. (2004). In search of golden rules: Comment on hypothesis-testing approaches to setting cutoff values for fit indexes and dangers in overgeneralizing Hu and Bentler's (1999) findings. *Structural Equation Modeling, 11*, 320–341.

Martinent, G., Decret, J. C., Isoard-Gautheur, S., Filaire, E., & Ferrand, C. (2014). Evaluations of the psychometric properties of the Recovery-Stress Questionnaire for Athletes among a sample of young French table tennis players. *Psychological Reports, 114*, 326–340.

Maslach, C., & Jackson, S. E. (1986). *Maslach Burnout Inventory*. Consulting Psychologists Press.

Mason, R. J., Farrow, D., & Hattie, J. A. C. (2020). An analysis of in-game feedback provided by coaches in an Australian Football League competition. *Physical Education and Sport Pedagogy*, *25*(5), 464–477.

Mayer, J., & Hermann, H.-D. (2011). *Mentales Training* [Mental training]. Springer.

McAuley, E. (1985). Modeling and self-efficacy: A test of Bandura's model. *Journal of Sport Psychology*, 7, 28–295.

McNair, D., Lorr, M., & Droppleman, L. F. (1971/1992). *Profile of Mood States manual.* Educational and Industrial Testing Service.

Meeusen, R., & De Pauw, K. (2022). Overtraining – What do we know? In M. Kellmann & J. Beckmann (Eds.), *Recovery and well-being in sport and exercise* (pp. 51–62). Routledge.

Meeusen, R., Duclos, M., Foster, C., Fry, A., Glesson, M., Nieman, D., Raglin, J., Rietjens, G., Steinacker, J. M., Urhausen, A., European College of Sport Science, & American College of Sports Medicine. (2013). Prevention, diagnosis and treatment of the overtraining syndrome: Joint consensus statement of the European College of Sport Science (ECSS) and the American College of Sport Medicine (ACSM). *Medicine & Science in Sports & Exercise*, *45*, 186–205.

Meister, S., Faude, O., Ammann, T., Schnittker, R., & Meyer, T. (2013). Indicators for high physical strain and overload in elite football players. *Scandinavian Journal of Medicine & Science in Sports, 23*(2), 156–163.

Moosbrugger, H. (1982). Dimensionalitätsuntersuchungen von FPI-Skalen mit dem Klassischen Latent-Additiven Testmodell (KLA-Modell) [Dimensionality studies of FPI-scales with the classical latent-additive test model (CLA-model)]. *Zeitschrift für Differentielle und Diagnostische Psychologie*, *3*, 241–264.

Morales, J., Alamo, J. M., García-Massó, X., Buscà, B., López, J. L., Serra-Añó, P., & González, L. M. (2014). The use of heart rate variability in monitoring stress and recovery in judo athletes. *Journal of Strength and Conditioning Research*, *28*, 1896–1905.

Morgan, W. P., Brown, D. R., Raglin, J. S., O'Conner, P. J., & Ellickson, K. A. (1987). Psychological monitoring of overtraining and staleness. *British Journal of Sport Medicine, 21*, 107–114.

Morgan, W. P., & Costill, D. L. (1996). Selected psychological characteristics and health behaviors of aging marathon runners: A longitudinal study. *International Journal of Sport Medicine, 17*, 305–312.

Mujika, I., Padilla, S., Pyne, D., & Busso, T. (2004). Physiological changes associated with the pre-event taper in athletes. *Sports Medicine*, *34*(13), 891–927.

Nederhof, E., Brink, M. S., & Lemmink, K. (2008). Reliability and validity of the Dutch Recovery-Stress Questionnaire for Athletes. *International Journal of Sport Psychology*, *39*, 301–311.

Nederhof, E., Lemmink, K. A. P. M., Zwerver, J., & Mulder, T. (2007). The effect of high load training on reaction time in cyclists. *International Journal of Sports Medicine*, *28*, 595–601.

Nederhof, E., Zwerver, J., Brink, M. S., Meeusen, R., & Lemmink, K. (2008). Different diagnostic tools in nonfunctional overreaching. *International Journal of Sports Medicine*, *29*, 590–597.

Nicolas, M. (2009). Personality, social support and affective states during simulated microgravity in healthy women. *Advances in Space Research*, *44*, 1470–1478.

Nicolas, M., Banizette, M., & Millet, G. Y. (2011). Stress and recovery states after a 24h ultra-marathon race: A one-month follow-up study. *Psychology of Sport and Exercise, 12*, 368–374.

Nicolas, M., & Gushin, V. (2015). Stress and recovery responses during a 105-day ground-based space simulation. *Stress and Health, 31*(5), 403–410.

Nicolas, M., & Weiss, K. (2009). Stress and recovery assessment during simulated microgravity: Effects of exercise during a long-term head-down tilt bed rest in women. *Journal of Environmental Psychology, 29*, 522–528.

Nunes, J. A., Moreira, A., Crewther, B. T., Nosaka, K., Viveiros, L., & Aoki, M. S. (2014). Monitoring training load, recovery-stress state, immune-endocrine responses and physical performance in elite female basketball players during a periodized training program. *Journal of Strength and Conditioning Research, 28*, 2973–2980.

Otter, R. T., Brink, M. S., van der Does, H. T., & Lemmink, K. A. (2016). Monitoring perceived stress and recovery in relation to cycling in female athletes. *International Journal of Sports Medicine, 37*(1), 12–18.

Pelka, M., Ferrauti, A., Meyer, T., Pfeiffer, M., & Kellmann, M. (2017). How does a short, interrupted recovery break affect performance and how is it assessed? A study on acute effects. *International Journal of Sports Physiology and Performance, 12*(Suppl. 2), S2114–S2121.

Pelka, M., Schneider, P., & Kellmann, M. (2018). Development of pre- and post-match morning recovery-stress states during in-season weeks in elite youth football. *Science and Medicine in Football, 2*, 127–132.

Pires, D. A., & Ugrinowitsch, H. (2021). Burnout and coping perceptions of volleyball players throughout an annual sport season. *Journal of Human Kinetics, 79*, 249–257.

Purge, P., Jürimäe, J., & Jürimäe, T. (2004). Body composition, physical performance and psychological factors contributing to 2000M sculling in elite rowers. *Journal of Human Movement Studies, 47*(5), 367–378.

Purge, P., Jürimäe, J., & Jürimäe, T. (2005). Changes in recovery-stress state and performance in elite rowers during preparation for major competitions. *Perceptual and Motor Skills, 101*, 375–381.

Purge, P., Jürimäe, J., & Jürimäe, T. (2006). Hormonal and psychological adaptation in elite male rowers during prolonged training. *Journal of Sports Sciences, 24*(10), 1075–1082.

Raedeke, T. (2014). Burnout. In R. C. Eklund & G. Tenenbaum (Eds.), *Encyclopedia of sport and exercise psychology* (Vol. 1, pp. 94–98). Sage.

Raya-Castellano, P. E., Reeves, M. J., Cárdenas-Vélez, D., Fradua, L., & McRobert, A. P. (2023). The half-time talk: A mixed-method examination of youth-elite football coaches' behaviours and team-management strategies. *International Journal of Sports Science & Coaching, 18*(3), 655–667.

Reynoso-Sánchez, L. F., Pérez-Verduzco, G., Celestino-Sánchez, M. Á., López-Walle, J. M., Zamarripa, J., Rangel-Colmenero, B. R., Muñoz-Helú, H., & Hernández-Cruz, G. (2021). Competitive recovery-stress and mood states in Mexican youth athletes. *Frontiers in Psychology, 11*, 627828. https://doi.org/10.3389/fpsyg.2020.627828

Rollo, I., Impellizzeri, F. M., Zago, M., & Iaia, F. M. (2014). Effects of one versus two games a week on physical and subjective scores of sub-elite soccer players. *International Journal of Sports Physiology and Performance, 9*, 425–431.

Rowbottom, D. G., Keast, D., & Morton, A. R. (1998). Monitoring and preventing of overreaching and overtraining in endurance athletes. In R. B. Kreider, A. C. Fry, & M. L. O'Toole (Eds.), *Overtraining in sport* (pp. 47–66). Human Kinetics.

Russell, S., Simpson, M. J., Evans, A. G., Coulter, T. J., & Kelly, V. G. (2021). Physiological and perceptual recovery-stress responses to an elite netball tournament. *International Journal of Sports Physiology and Performance, 16*(10), 1462–1471.

Saw, A. E., Kellmann, M., Main, L. C., & Gastin, P. B. (2017). Athlete self-report measures in research and practice: Considerations for the discerning reader and fastidious practitioner. *International Journal of Sports Physiology and Performance, 12*(Suppl. 2), S2127–S2135.

Saw, A. E., Main, L. C., & Gastin, P. B. (2016). Monitoring the athlete training response: Subjective self-reported measures trump commonly used objective measures: A systematic review. *British Journal of Sports Medicine, 50*(5), 281–291.

Schaffran, P., Altfeld, S., & Kellmann, M. (2016). Burnout in sport coaches: A review of correlates, measurement and intervention. *Deutsche Zeitschrift für Sportmedizin, 67*, 121–126.

Schaffran, P., Kleinert, J., Altfeld, S., Zepp, C., Kallus, K. W., & Kellmann, M. (2019). Early risk detection of burnout: Development of the Burnout Prevention Questionnaire for Coaches. *Frontiers in Psychology, 10*, 714. https://doi.org/10.3389/fpsyg.2019.00714

Schaffran, P., Kleinert, J., Altfeld, S., Zepp, C., Kallus, K. W., & Kellmann, M. (2020). Response commentary: Early risk detection of burnout: Development of the Burnout Prevention Questionnaire for Coaches. *Frontiers in Psychology, 11*, 545159. https://doi.org/10.3389/fpsyg.2020.545159

Short, S. (2014). Self-efficacy. In R. C. Eklund & G. Tenenbaum (Eds.), *Encyclopedia of sport and exercise psychology* (Vol. 2, pp. 636–638). Sage.

Shriee, I., & Hallé, M. (2011). Psychological predictors of injuries in circus artists: An exploratory study. *British Journal of Sport Medicine, 45*, 433–436.

Skovgaard, C., Christensen, P. M., Larsen, S., Andersen, T. R., Thomassen, M., & Bangsbo, J. (2014). Concurrent speed endurance and resistance training improves performance, running economy, and muscle NHE1 in moderately trained runners. *Journal of Applied Physiology, 117*(10), 1097–1109.

Smith, R. E. (1986). Toward a cognitive-affective model of athletic burnout. *Journal of Sport Psychology, 8*, 36–50.

Smith, M. R., Marcora, S. M., & Coutts, A. J. (2015). Mental fatigue impairs intermittent running performance. *Medicine and Science in Sports and Exercise, 47*(8), 1682–1690.

Smith, M. R., Zeuwts, L., Lenoir, M., Hens, N., De Jong, L. M., & Coutts, A. J. (2016). Mental fatigue impairs soccer-specific decision-making skill. *Journal of Sports Sciences, 34*(14), 1297–1304.

Snyder, A. C. (1998). Overtraining and glycogen depletion hypothesis. *Medicine and Science in Sport and Exercise*, 7, 1146–1150.

Spielberger, C. D., Gorsuch, R. L., & Lushene, R. E. (1970). *Manual for the State-Trait Anxiety Inventory (STAI)*. Consulting Psychologist Press.

Steinacker, J. M., Lormes, W., Kellmann, M., Liu, Y., Reisnecker, S., Opitz-Gress, A., Baller, B., Gunther, K., Petersen, K. G., Kallus, K. W., Lehmann, M., & Altenburg, D. (2000). Training of junior rowers before World Championships. Effects on performance, mood state and selected hormonal and metabolic responses. *Journal of Sports Medicine and Physical Fitness, 40*, 327–335.

Steinacker, J. M., Kellmann, M., Bohm, B. O., Liu, Y., Opitz-Gress, A., Kallus, K. W., Lehmann, M., Altenburg, D., & Lormes, W. (1999). Clinical findings and parameters of stress and regeneration in rowers before World Championships. In M. Lehmann, C. Foster, U. Gastmann, H. Keizer, & J. M. Steinacker (Eds.), Overload, fatigue, *performance incompetence, and regeneration in sport* (pp. 71–80). Plenum.

Stephenson, B. T., Leicht, C. A., Tolfrey, K., & Goosey-Tolfrey, V. L. (2019). A multifactorial assessment of elite paratriathletes' response to 2 weeks of intensified training. *International Journal of Sports Physiology and Performance, 14*(7), 911–917.

Thiel, C., Vogt, L., Bürklein, M., Rosenhagen, A., Hübscher, M., & Banzer, W. (2011). Functional overreaching during preparation training of elite tennis professionals. *Journal of Human Kinetics, 28*, 79–89.

Vroom, V. H. (1964). *Work and motivation*. Wiley.

Wallett, A. M., Woods, A. L., Versey, N., Garvican-Lewis, L. A., Welvaert, M., & Thompson, K. G. (2018). Effect of intensified endurance training on pacing and performance in 4000-m cycling time trials. *International Journal of Sports Physiology and Performance, 13*(6), 735–741.

West, M., & Harrison, J. (1997). *Bayesian forecasting and dynamic models*. Springer.

Woods, S., Dunne, S., Gallagher, P., & McNicholl, A. (in press). A systematic review of the factors associated with athlete burnout in team sports. *International Review of Sport and Exercise Psychology*. https://doi.org/10.1080/1750984X.2022.2148225

Ziemainz, H., Neumann, G., Rasche, F., & Stemmler, M. (2006). Zum Einsatz sportpsychologischer Diagnostik in der Praxis des Leistungssports: Eine Befragung der Sportpsychologen der BISp-Sportpsychologie Expertendatenbank [The application of psychological assessment methods in sport psychology: A survey of sport psychologists in the BISp sport psychology expert database]. *Zeitschrift für Sportpsychologie, 13*(2), 53–59.

4 Recovery-Stress Questionnaire for Coaches

Michael Kellmann, K. Wolfgang Kallus, and Sebastian Altfeld

Scope and application

The Recovery-Stress Questionnaire for Coaches is an instrument that systematically assesses the recovery-stress state of a coach. The recovery-stress state indicates the extent to which the coach is physically and/or mentally stressed, and whether the coach is capable of using individual strategies for recovery. Through the simultaneous assessment of stress and recovery, a differentiated picture of the current recovery-stress state can be provided.

The questionnaire can be applied in almost all work fields of sports coaches. The RESTQ-Coach pictures the recovery-stress state of full-time, part-time, and voluntary coaches. This instrument is useful for all kind of sports and provides important information to prevent critical coaches' health situations (Altfeld & Kellmann, 2014a).

The RESTQ-Coach expands the RESTQ-Basic-48 (12 scales; Kallus, this volume, Chapter 2) by adding 28 additional items related to two coach-specific stress scales (*Disturbed Breaks*, *Emotional Exhaustion*), and five coach-specific recovery scales (*Personal Accomplishment*, *Being in Shape*, *Motivation as a Coach*, *Success as a Coach*, *Self-Efficacy*). Four overall and specific scores (*Overall Stress*, *Overall Recovery*, *Coach-specific Stress*, *Coach-specific Recovery*) can be created by summing the scores of the scales and calculating mean values. In summary, the RESTQ-Coach consisted of 76 items; 19 scales with four items (plus one warm-up item) measuring the frequency of current stress along with the frequency of recovery-associated activities in the *past (7) days/nights* (note: earlier versions used a time frame of 2–3 weeks and 3 days/nights).

The coach answers retrospectively on a Likert-type scale with values ranging from 0 (*never*) to 6 (*always*). Thereby, high scores in the stress-associated scales reflect intense subjective stress, whereas high scores in the recovery-oriented scales display frequent recovery activities.

Kellmann, M., Kallus, K. W., & Altfeld, S. (2025). Recovery-Stress Questionnaire for Coaches. In M. Kellmann & K. W. Kallus (Eds.), *The Recovery-Stress Questionnaires: A User Manual* (pp. 137–170). Routledge.

DOI: 10.4324/9781032643380-4

The scales *Overall Stress* and *Overall Recovery* are equivalent to the scales of the RESTQ-Basic; Kallus, this volume, Chapter 2). The *Coach-specific Stress* and *Coach-specific Recovery* scores additionally assess aspects of the special work profile of coaches (Table 4.1).

The coach-specific scale *Disturbed Breaks* is sensitive to deficiencies of recovery and interrupted recovery during periods of rest (e.g., leisure time). *Emotional Exhaustion* is characterized by the arising feeling of frustration and lack of energy caused by the coaching job. *Personal Accomplishment* displays the coach's feeling of being empathetic regarding the coached athletes. With *Being in Shape* the RESTQ-Coach measures the frequency of activities providing effort to the personal fitness of the coach. Additionally, the individual preparation and creativity of the coach is monitored by the scale *Motivation as a Coach*. The RESTQ-Coach assesses the frequency of successful events as a coach by the scale *Success as a Coach*. The scale *Self-Efficacy* is characterized by the level of expectation and competence regarding an optimal coaching performance during practice and competition. The RESTQ-Coach can be used well between 14 and 88 years.

Table 4.1 Coach-specific scales of the Recovery-Stress Questionnaire for Coaches.

Number	*Scale* *Summary*
13	***Disturbed Breaks*** This scale deals with recovery deficits, interrupted recovery, and situational aspects that come in the way during periods of rest (e.g., athletes, family members).
14	***Emotional Exhaustion*** High scores are reached by coaches who feel burned out and want to quit their sport.
15	***Personal Accomplishment*** High scores are reached by coaches who communicate well with their athletes, perceive themselves as empathy, and enjoy their sport.
16	***Being in Shape*** Coaches with high scores describe themselves as fit, physically efficient, and vital.
17	***Motivation as a Coach*** High scores are reached by coaches who feel motivated for practice and the work with athletes.
18	***Success as a Coach*** This scale deals with the frequency of successful events as coach.
19	***Self-Efficacy*** This scale is characterized by how convinced the coach is that he/she has well prepared the athletes for competitions.

Facets of stress and recovery in coaches: Theory of the coach-specific scales

Coaches are a critical component in the sport system having significant impact on athlete's performance and career (Chan & Mallett, 2011; Cook et al., 2021; Davis et al., 2018; Nichol et al., 2019). In addition to research examining coaching style and coaching behaviour (Carpentier & Mageau, 2013; Cook et al., 2021; Ekstrand et al., 2018), prior research has examined the relationship between personal well-being of coaches, optimal coaching performances, and prevention of unhealthy states in athletes (Altfeld & Kellmann, 2013a; Bentzen et al., 2020; Olusoga et al., 2019). In a vocation in which the workers are typically judged by performance outcomes, coaches' well-being might be endangered by a range of potential stressors, including emotional and physical demands (Bentzen et al., 2020; Mallett, 2010; Pinheiro et al., 2021). Thus, coaches need to deal adequately with public pressure to perform, time, and resource constraints and competing demands. Nonetheless, they need to manage their own emotional/physical state using self-regulation strategies and personal recovery means to perform at their optimal level (Hassmén et al., 2019; Kallus & Kellmann, 2000; Thelwell et al., 2008). Accordingly, an arising imbalance between stress and recovery of the coaches might also affect athlete performance in the coach-athlete-performance relationship (Bentzen et al., 2017; Davis et al., 2018; Gearity & Murray, 2011; Lundkvist et al., 2012; Olusoga et al., 2010; Thelwell et al., 2017).

In contrast to many jobs, coaches have long, non-traditional, and irregular working times (e.g., morning and night practice, weekends) and extensive travel (Potts et al., 2023; Simpson et al., in press). Balk et al. (2019) stress in their findings that due to the day structure and organizational stressors, coaches experience difficulties to detach from work impacting the personal state of recovery. According to the authors, this seems to have a negative impact on the personal and the athletes' well-being. Even on the weekend they cannot calm down like most of the working people because during the season there are usually competitions and matches. Kellmann et al. (2016) as well as Altfeld et al. (2015) supported these statements by the results that coaches in their studies increasingly showed insufficient recovery over the course of a season. Regarding this, Weigelt and colleagues (2019) found out that working people who cannot refrain from their work experience increased feeling of exhaustion and burnout. Additionally, because of the non-traditional working times, Dixon and Bruening (2007) reported that coaches often experienced private conflicts which affected the recovery process and the personal well-being. In a study examining the stressors of full-time, part-time, and voluntary coaches, participants reported most frequently that they are stressed by conflicts with athletes, their social environment (e.g., family), or with management in their workplace (Altfeld & Kellmann, 2014b). Consequently, the RESTQ-Coach assesses the frequency of disturbed breaks of the coach to display the arising of stressors during personal leisure time.

Furthermore, coaches must cope with challenging demands in consideration of the length of a competitive season (Burke, 2006). The combination of high and often unrealistic expectations by others (e.g., media, fans, administration), high job demands, and workload can reinforce the pressure increasing the risk of feeling highly exhausted and of burning out (Altfeld & Kellmann, 2013b; Pinheiro et al., 2021; Potts et al., 2023). Burnout describes a state of mental and physical exhaustion, which is maintained by accompanied maladaptive motivational processes and the generation of dysfunctional attitudes and behaviors toward the job (Schaufeli & Enzmann, 1998). Schaufeli et al. (2001) claim that emotional exhaustion can be considered as the key symptom of burnout. Therefore, the RESTQ-Coach measures the arising feeling of emotional exhaustion of the coach.

Because of the time demands, Balk et al. (2019) underlined that coaches often forget or are not able to take time for themselves to recover from the stress of their job. This phenomenon is comparable to the situation in many occupations in which employees invest high amounts of time to meet the challenging demands of their work life at the expense of their own leisure time (Dall'Ora et al., 2020; Kyvik, 2013; Todd & Binns, 2013; Vandevala et al., 2017). Regarding this, previous research supported the positive impact of exercise on the personal well-being and the value as a crucial recovery strategy (Anderson & Durstine, 2019; Mandolesi et al., 2018). Consequently, with the scale *Being in Shape* the RESTQ-Coach displays the frequency of activities providing effort to the personal fitness of the coach.

Another important aspect of the RESTQ-Coach deals with the self-efficacy of the coach. As Bandura (1977) suggested, the development of resilient self-efficacy in athletes is influenced by the coaching style and efficacy of the coach. According to Bandura, the coaches' actions are influenced by the individual expectations of their effectiveness. Feltz et al. (1999) defined coaching efficacy as the extent to which the coach believes having the capacity to affect the learning and performance of the supervised athletes. They proposed that coaching efficacy is influenced by one's past performance and experience. Thus, coaching experience, coaching preparation, previous success, and failure might influence the coach's perception of the own self-efficacy. Therefore, the RESTQ-Coach assesses the frequency of success as a coach, personal accomplishment, motivation as a coach, and the self-efficacy as a coach.

Versions and scoring

The RESTQ-Coach was developed to assess the coach's temporary state of stress and recovery quantitatively (Kallus, 1995). The temporary state of stress is a result of the coach's preceding stress levels and at the same time the preceding recovery activities.

In Table 4.2, the versions of the RESTQ-Coach are displayed. The first version of the RESTQ-Coach consisted of twelve scales of the RESTQ-Basic-48 (Kallus, this volume, Chapter 2) and seven additional coach-specific scales (*Emotional Exhaustion*, *Personal Accomplishment*, *Being in Shape*, *Motivation as a*

Table 4.2 Scales, number of items, time frame, year of development for the coach-specific RESTQ versions.

RESTQ-Coach scales	*1995*	*2009*	*2014*	*2014*
1 General Stress	4	4	4	2
2 Emotional Stress	4	4	4	2
3 Social Stress	4	4	4	2
4 Conflicts/Pressure[1]	4	4	4	2
5 Fatigue	4	4	4	2
6 Lack of Energy	4	4	4	2
7 Physical Complaints	4	4	4	2
8 Success	4	4	4	2
9 Social Recovery	4	4	4	2
10 Physical Recovery	4	4	4	2
11 General Well-being	4	4	4	2
12 Sleep Quality	4	4	4	2
13 Disturbed Breaks	—	4	4	4
14 Emotional Exhaustion	6	4	4	4
15 Personal Accomplishment	6	4	4	4
16 Being in Shape	6	4	4	4
17 Motivation as a Coach	6	4	4	4
18 Success as a Coach	6	4	4	4
19 Self-Efficacy	6	4	4	4
20 Self-Regulation	6	—	—	—
Sum items	90	76	76	52
Time frame	2–3 weeks	3 days/ nights	7 days/ nights	7 days/ nights

Coach, *Success as a Coach*, *Self-Efficacy*, *Self-Regulation*) with 42 items. The first RESTQ-Coach version assessed possible stressful events and their consequences as well as recovery of coaches in the past 2–3 weeks.

The second version in 2009 consisted of 77 items and 19 scales, respectively, with four items each (plus one warm-up item). In comparison to the first version, the further development included the reduction of the amount of items. Based on coaches' work profile analysis, the authors constructed the scale *Disturbed Breaks* with four items to measure recovery deficits, interrupted recovery, and situational aspects that come in the way during periods of rest of the coach.

Additionally, the scale *Self-Regulation* was omitted because of marginal relevance. Finally, all coach-specific items ordered in the same way as the RESTQ-Sport version with 76 and 52 items (Kellmann & Kallus, this volume, Chapter 3). The assessed time frame was changed to the *past (3) days/nights*.

The scale values are calculated by taking the mean of the item values (checked numbers; rounded off to two decimal points). In the case of missing data, the mean should only be calculated when at least 50% of the items of each scale have been answered. In the *Sleep Quality* scale, the items for disturbed sleep first have to be inverted (6 minus item value = raw item score; e.g., 6 → 0; 5 → 1; 4 → 2; 3 = 3; 2 → 4; 1 → 5; 0 → 6). Scoring sheets are available for manual scoring. Additionally, the data can be represented graphically in a *recovery-stress profile*.

The mean of each scale can range from 0 – 6. High scores in the stress-associated activity scales reflect high subjective stress, whereas high scores in the recovery-oriented scales reflect plenty of recovery activities.

The current version of the RESTQ-Coach included the adaptation of the scale *Conflicts/Pressure* (Table 4.2 and Kallus, this volume, Chapter 2). Moreover, the standard time frame of the current version was changed to the *past (7) days/nights* which allows the comparison of scores with the Recovery-Stress Questionnaire for Work (Jiménez et al., this volume, Chapter 5) which might be relevant especially for full-time coaches.

The RESTQ-Coach-76 (48 non-specific and 28 sport-specific items) and the RESTQ-Coach-52 (24 non-specific and 28 sport-specific items) are available. The main difference between both is that the RESTQ-Coach-52 consists of two items only for each basic RESTQ scales, allowing a limited interpretation of these scores compared to the RESTQ-Coach-76.

In addition to the information provided by Kallus (this volume, Chapter 2), the following guidelines must be pointed out:

- The scales in the area of stress can be summarized in the scale *Overall Stress* (mean of scales 1–7).
- Correspondingly, the *Overall Recovery* scale can be formed from the recovery scales (mean of scales 8–12).
- The same procedure applies for the *Coach-specific Stress* (mean of scales 13–14) and *Coach-specific Recovery* (mean of scales 16–19).
- The basic and coach-specific stress and recovery scales can be combined to calculate *Total Stress* and *Total Recovery* scores, respectively. However, this procedure is only recommended for group comparisons.

Kallus (1995) as well as Kellmann and Kallus (this volume, Chapter 1, p. 2) state that:

> *stress and recovery should not be combined to a single value, as they constitute two conceptually independent dimensions as far as the frequency in the past days/nights is concerned. The relationship between the scales for recovery and stress is neither linear nor symmetrical.* ***Consequently, the calculation of one overall single score of all stress and recovery scales does not make sense and is strongly prohibited.***

Table 4.3 German (GC) and English samples (EC) used to test validity and reliability.

	GC1	*GC2*	*GC3.1*	*GC3.2*	*GC3.3*
Sample size	$N=195$	$N=123$	$N=722$	$N=126$	$N=99$
Gender distribution	Male = 175 Female = 20	Male = 101 Female = 22	Male = 591 Female = 131	Male = 97 Female = 29	Male = 76 Female = 23
Sport	Various team and individual sports	Various team and individual sports	Various team and individual sports	Various team and individual sports	Various team and individual sports
Employment situation	Full-time, part-time	Full-time, part-time, voluntary	Full-time, part-time, voluntary	Full-time, part-time, voluntary	Full-time, part-time, voluntary
Age	$M=41.45$ $SD=10.24$	$M=30.11$ $SD=10.56$	$M=36.98$ $SD=12.00$	$M=38.61$ $SD=12.60$	$M=36.86$ $SD=11.84$
Time frame	2–3 weeks	3 days/nights	3 days/nights	3 days/nights	3 days/nights
Measurements	1	1	1	1	1
Instruments	RESTQ-Coach	RESTQ-Coach, MBI-C, CBQ	RESTQ-Coach, MBI-C	RESTQ-Coach, MBI-C	RESTQ-Coach, MBI-C
Special features			Longitudinal study with 3 measurements		
Related publications	Kallus et al. (1996)	Altfeld and Kellmann (2014a)	Altfeld and Kellmann (2014b, 2015), Altfeld et al. (2015)		

(*Continued*)

Table 4.3 (Continued)

	GC4	EC1
Sample size	*N* = *309*	*N* = *133*
Gender distribution	Male = 268 Female = 41	Male = 83 Female = 50
Sport	Various team and individual sports	Various team and individual sports
Employment situation	Full-time, part-time, voluntary	Full-time, part-time, voluntary
Age	*M* = 40.65 *SD* = 12.60	*M* = 40.07 *SD* = 10.58
Time frame	7 days/nights	3 days/nights
Measurements	1	1
Instruments	RESTQ-Coach, MBI-C, POMS	RESTQ-Coach

Note: N = Sample size; *M* = Mean; *SD* = Standard deviation;
MBI-C = Maslach Burnout Inventory for Coaches;
CBQ = Coach Burnout Questionnaire; POMS = Profile of Mood States.

Reference values

Online Appendix A.C1–A.C3 provides reference values from sample GC3.1 (N=722), GC4 (N=309), EC1 (N=91), and EC2 (N=82) for both genders. However, computation of deviations from the 'norms' should be based on overall scores.

Reliability

Samples

Based on the research samples shown in Table 4.3, test statistics as well as reliability and validity were calculated. There are two different groups of samples, German (GC1–GC4) and English coaches (EC1, EC2). The sample GC3 represents a longitudinal study with three measurements and is divided in three sub-samples for the analysis.

Classical reliability measures

The overview of the reliability coefficients (Table 4.4) shows good to satisfactory estimations of Cronbach's α over different samples and time frames. For almost all scales of the RESTQ-Coach, the internal consistencies were consistent over the single examinations. Along with the reduction of the time frame from the *past 2 to 3 weeks* (GC1) to the *past (3) days/nights* (GC3.1), there was an increase of Cronbach's α for most of the scales, but specifically for *Success* and *Motivation as a Coach*. The increase of the time frame from three to seven days for the final version of the RESTQ-Coach [*past (7) days/nights*] did not lead to a decrease of reliability but showed satisfactory results. Content wise the decision was based on the Recovery-Stress Questionnaire for Work (Jiménez et al., this volume, Chapter 5) which has a time frame of seven days/nights. Since both RESTQ versions include the work environment, it is reasonable to apply the same time frame.

The internal consistencies of *Conflicts/Pressure* were consistently below Cronbach's α=.70. These results might be explained by the fact that on the one hand, the scale is consisting of two constructs. Thus, the scale is assessing the frequency of experienced conflicts as well as the frequency of individual experienced situations of pressure. On the other hand, the relevance of this scale differs depending on the time of assessment. The statements (i.e., … *I felt I had to perform well in front of others; … I felt under pressure*) have a different meaning when the RESTQ-Coach is completed after the final of the playoffs or during the pre-season. Consequently, the interpretations of this scale need to be considered with caution but are useful for the deeper understanding. Furthermore, in 2014 the item … *I felt I had to perform well in front of others* was exchanged by … *I had to do something I did not like to do* (sample GC4, Kallus, this volume, Chapter 2).

Table 4.4 Estimation of reliability (Cronbach's α).

Samples *RESTQ-Coach scales*	*GC1* *N=175*	*GC3.1* *N=722*	*GC3.2* *N=126*	*GC3.3* *N=99*	*GC4*[2] *N=309*	*EC1* *N=133*	*EC2*[3] *N=82*
1 General Stress	.84	.88	.90	.82	.85	.86	.83
2 Emotional Stress	.74	.79	.83	.77	.81	.73	.86
3 Social Stress	.86	.86	.89	.87	.84	.88	.88
4 Conflicts/Pressure	.54	.62	.58	.48	.67	.56	.74
5 Fatigue	.77	.84	.88	.86	.83	.79	.84
6 Lack of Energy	.74	.81	.88	.81	.83	.55	.76
7 Physical Complaints	.70	.81	.80	.88	.81	.73	.69
8 Success	.67	.72	.76	.71	.72	.81	.69
9 Social Recovery	.84	.84	.82	.84	.86	.80	.82
10 Physical Recovery	.82	.83	.87	.89	.81	.74	.68
11 General Well-being	.87	.89	.90	.92	.92	.87	.90
12 Sleep Quality	.85	.83	.84	.81	.87	.71	.69
13 Disturbed Breaks	—	.81	.83	.85	.81	.66	.69
14 Emotional Exhaustion	.76	.83	.88	.83	.81	.87	.82
15 Personal Accomplishment	.74	.80	.83	.81	.83	.83	.73
16 Being in Shape	.81	.87	.91	.87	.86	.90	.85
17 Motivation as a Coach	.47	.78	.80	.85	.84	.67	.74
18 Success as a Coach	.79	.76	.79	.78	.78	.76	.72
19 Self-Efficacy	.81	.85	.87	.89	.78	.89	.86

Table 4.5 displays the test-retest reliability of the RESTQ-Coach after 12 and 24 weeks for the German sample GC3.3.

Test-retest reliabilities were calculated for three measurements. The results show consistent satisfactory correlations for the two-time frames which are rather stable and higher than the short-term stabilities for the basic module (Kallus, this volume, Chapter 2) and the RESTQ-Sport (Kellmann & Kallus, this volume, Chapter 3).

Table 4.5 Test-retest reliability of the RESTQ-Coach referring to the past (3) days/nights in two-time spans for the German sample GC 3.3 (N=99).

RESTQ-Coach scales	*12 Weeks*	*24 Weeks*
1 General Stress	.59	.46
2 Emotional Stress	.51	.50
3 Social Stress	.51	.49
4 Conflicts/Pressure	.47	.49
5 Fatigue	.67	.68
6 Lack of Energy	.66	.67
7 Physical Complaints	.63	.54
8 Success	.58	.69
9 Social Recovery	.52	.56
10 Physical Recovery	.64	.61
11 General Well-being	.49	.58
12 Sleep Quality	.49	.57
13 Disturbed Breaks	.69	.68
14 Emotional Exhaustion	.67	.52
15 Personal Accomplishment	.70	.72
16 Being in Shape	.73	.64
17 Motivation as a Coach	.73	.78
18 Success as a Coach	.49	.57
19 Self-Efficacy	.64	.77

Construct validity

Construct validity has been studied with respect to the intercorrelations of scales, the factorial structure, linear structure modelling, and the stability of the intercorrelations across different samples. Relationships to mood states and burnout are covered in the section on criterion validity.

Scale intercorrelations

The fundamental correlation pattern is almost unchanged across all samples with respect to stress and recovery areas. Both the stress and the recovery scales correlate positively with the scales of the related areas, but they have a negative relationship with the scales of the opposite areas. This pattern is mainly stable in the comparison between different samples [Tables 4.6a–4.6c; Online Appendix A.C4 and time frames (3) vs. (7) days/nights].

Latent structure measurement models

Measurement models for the scales of the RESTQ-Coach are reported for the long version only. The model is based on the German sample GC4 as it represents the standard time frame. As can be expected based on the item-total correlations and the internal consistency from *Classical Test Theory* all scales show a good model fit in three out of four fit indices. Figure 4.1 represents the model for scale 15 *Personal Accomplishment* as an example, which fits well without any modifications. The model shows similar loading for three of the items while item 62 has a slightly reduced contribution to the scale.

For all scales the initial model can be kept, as at least three of the fit indices indicate an acceptable initial model. Table 4.7 indicates options for improvement with a RMSEA above .08 for *Emotional Exhaustion* and *Being in Shape*, which parallels the results with the RESTQ-Sport. In addition, *Motivation as a Coach* and *Success as a Coach* indicate options for improvement, which are not necessary and result in an overfitting. Thus, measurement models for the RESTQ-Coach indicate a good model fit for all coach-specific scales.

Factor analysis

The factor analysis were performed separately for the basic and the sport-specific parts regarding the modular construction of the RESTQ-Sport. Scale values of sample GC3.1 and GC4 were factor analyzed via Principal Component Analysis followed by a Varimax rotation. After the stop criterion (Eigenvalue < 1; Kaiser), two factors could be extracted for the basic as well as for the coach-specific parts of the RESTQ-Coach (Tables 4.8a–d).

For the basic scales of the RESTQ-Coach, the results confirm the two-factor solution published by Kallus (1995). All factor analysis suggest one stress-related and one recovery-related factor. Side loadings of recovery scales on the stress factors appear in both samples. However, it can be concluded that the two-factor solution clearly separates the basic scales of the RESTQ-Coach into one stress-related and one recovery-related factor. The basic stress-related factor explains approximately 51%–56% of the variance. The recovery-related factor ranges between 11% and 14%.

For the coach-specific part of the RESTQ-Coach, analysis clearly separate the coach-specific scales into one stress-related and one recovery-related factor. The coach-specific stress factor (*Disturbed Breaks*, *Emotional Exhaustion*) explains about 24%–26% of the variance; the recovery factor (*Personal Accomplishment*, *Being in Shape*, *Motivation as a Coach*, *Success as a Coach*, *Self-Efficacy*) explains approximately 50%. Note that *Being in Shape* could be an inverted stress scale ('not being in shape'). In summary, the coach-specific recovery-related factor

Table 4.6a Intercorrelations of the RESTQ-Coach scales for the samples GC2 (*N*=123) and GC3.1 (*N*=722) (time frame *in the past (3) days/nights*).

	Upper data matrix: GC2																		
RESTQ-Coach scales	*1*	*2*	*3*	*4*	*5*	*6*	*7*	*8*	*9*	*10*	*11*	*12*	*13*	*14*	*15*	*16*	*17*	*18*	*19*
1 General Stress		**.75**	**.70**	.53	.59	.42	.64	−.03	−.36	−.53	−.52	−.56	.59	.64	.03	−.49	−.12	.03	−.15
2 Emotional Stress	**.77**		**.78**	.49	.48	.43	.55	−.11	−.35	−.52	−.49	−.53	.52	.51	−.07	−.50	−.13	.03	−.18
3 Social Stress	.68	**.76**		.46	.45	.43	.49	.04	−.26	−.36	−.35	−.47	.56	.55	−.04	−.39	−.10	.01	−.17
4 Conflicts/Pressure	.57	.58	.53		.49	.35	.47	.19	−.17	−.35	−.18	−.39	.52	.35	.09	−.31	.10	.21	−.02
5 Fatigue	.57	.55	.47	.49		.42	.64	.01	−.27	−.55	−.36	−.55	.66	.37	.03	−.50	.03	.14	.00
6 Lack of Energy	.62	.59	.49	.47	.55		.35	−.10	−.17	−.38	−.26	−.33	.36	.42	−.07	−.35	−.08	−.06	−.20
7 Physical Complaints	.62	.58	.48	.43	.59	.56		−.01	−.26	−.59	−.39	−.63	.62	.42	−.03	−.54	−.05	.07	−.05
8 Success	−.14	−.09	−.02	.15	−.01	−.20	−.15		.18	.41	.33	.15	.06	−.05	.32	.34	.29	.37	.33
9 Social Recovery	−.32	−.33	−.24	−.20	−.26	−.20	−.25	.23		.46	.69	.36	−.26	−.25	.04	.43	.00	−.05	.15
10 Physical Recovery	−.55	−.52	−.41	−.37	−.53	−.48	−.63	.37	.50		.67	.59	−.46	−.39	.24	**.86**	.22	.16	.31
11 General Well-being	−.55	−.54	−.37	−.31	−.36	−.41	−.42	.45	.67	**.73**		.48	−.30	−.34	.30	.63	.24	.15	.34
12 Sleep Quality	−.56	−.53	−.41	−.39	−.61	−.53	−.56	.21	.34	.62	.54		−.51	−.47	.02	.55	.04	−.10	.07

(*Continued*)

Table 4.6a (Continued)

RESTQ-Coach scales	*1*	*2*	*3*	*4*	*5*	*6*	*7*	*8*	*9*	*10*	*11*	*12*	*13*	*14*	*15*	*16*	*17*	*18*	*19*
13 Disturbed Breaks	.56	.54	.53	.45	.62	.49	.49	.02	−.35	−.47	−.39	−.53		.53	.06	−.50	.02	.10	−.06
14 Emotional Exhaustion	.67	.57	.55	.42	.54	.50	.48	−.09	**−.28**	−.44	−.43	−.50	.62		−.01	−.37	−.12	.05	−.17
15 Personal Accomplishment	−.15	−.14	−.09	.03	−.08	−.20	−.15	.49	.19	.37	.37	.19	−.03	−.13		.24	**.74**	.69	**.75**
16 Being in Shape	−.51	−.48	−.38	−.31	−.56	−.48	−.61	.40	.47	**.84**	**.70**	.62	−.50	−.42	.44		.14	.15	.28
17 Motivation as a Coach	−.22	−.15	−.09	.01	−.16	−.29	−.18	.45	.18	.37	.38	.24	−.12	−.18	.67	.43		.59	**.79**
18 Success as a Coach	−.13	−.10	−.04	.08	−.09	−.15	−.13	.51	.14	.29	.31	.17	−.03	−.08	.63	.36	.62		.60
19 Self-Efficacy	−.27	−.21	−.13	−.05	−.19	−.26	−.20	.46	.18	.37	.37	.24	−.14	−.26	**.71**	.43	**.76**	**.70**	
								Lower data matrix: GC3.1											

Note: $r \geq .70$ are bolded.

Table 4.6b Intercorrelations of the RESTQ-Coach scales for the sample GC4 (N= 309; time frame *in the past (7) days/nights*) and sample EC1 (N= 133; time frame *in the past (3) days/nights*).

	Upper data matrix: G4																		
RESTQ-Coach scales	*1*	*2*	*3*	*4*	*5*	*6*	*7*	*8*	*9*	*10*	*11*	*12*	*13*	*14*	*15*	*16*	*17*	*18*	*19*
1 General Stress		**.83**	.69	.60	.58	.66	.67	−.10	−.42	−.66	−.64	−.60	.55	.63	−.15	−.55	−.14	−.13	.11
2 Emotional Stress	**.78**		**.76**	.61	.56	.65	.64	−.09	−.43	−.67	−.64	−.61	.54	.55	−.18	−.57	−.09	−.13	**.83**
3 Social Stress	**.72**	**.78**		.55	.42	.48	.48	−.06	−.29	−.56	−.51	−.49	.50	.50	−.13	−.49	−.07	−.11	.69
4 Conflicts/Pressure	.47	.40	.37		.48	.57	.43	.20	−.33	−.47	−.45	−.47	.52	.38	.06	−.38	.11	.07	.60
5 Fatigue	.50	.55	.46	.47		.62	.61	−.03	−.40	−.60	−.46	−.62	.64	.48	−.02	−.57	−.10	−.02	.58
6 Lack of Energy	.55	.59	.47	.31	.52		.62	−.20	−.31	−.59	−.48	−.52	.62	.50	−.21	−.56	−.22	−.17	.66
7 Physical Complaints	.62	.60	.52	.42	**.72**	.64		−.07	−.32	−.67	−.46	−.59	.52	.47	−.04	−.64	−.06	−.03	.67
8 Success	−.27	−.26	−.24	.18	−.15	−.34	−.23		.20	.26	.33	.19	−.06	−.16	.54	.26	.45	.49	−.10
9 Social Recovery	−.32	−.37	−.26	−.23	−.32	−.13	−.21	.31		.57	**.71**	.50	−.36	−.30	.20	.46	.13	.15	−.42
10 Physical Recovery	−.45	−.52	−.38	−.30	−.53	−.49	−.54	.57	.53		**.77**	.67	−.55	−.46	.25	**.82**	.18	.21	−.66
11 General Well-being	−.61	−.65	−.59	−.34	−.54	−.46	−.53	.53	.68	**.77**		.64	−.44	−.42	.32	.69	.24	.28	−.64
12 Sleep Quality	−.38	−.40	−.34	−.25	−.38	−.28	−.30	.27	.32	.43	.51		−.55	−.48	.22	.61	.13	.17	−.60

(Continued)

Table 4.6b (Continued)

RESTQ-Coach scales	*1*	*2*	*3*	*4*	*5*	*6*	*7*	*8*	*9*	*10*	*11*	*12*	*13*	*14*	*15*	*16*	*17*	*18*	*19*
13 Disturbed Breaks	.47	.44	.43	.47	.41	.47	.52	−.21	−.24	−.37	−.38	−.26		.58	.02	−.54	−.05	.05	.55
14 Emotional Exhaustion	.54	.52	.50	.39	.37	.38	.46	−.25	−.33	−.43	−.49	−.16	.64		−.23	−.44	−.25	−.11	.63
15 Personal Accomplishment	−.24	−.24	−.23	.05	−.05	−.27	−.26	.65	.21	.48	.40	.21	−.27	−.36		.30	**.75**	**.78**	−.15
16 Being in Shape	−.36	−.43	−.31	−.17	−.41	−.52	−.53	.56	.44	**.83**	.68	.29	−.36	−.37	.54		.27	.27	−.55
17 Motivation as a Coach	−.25	−.32	−.21	.05	−.18	−.24	−.23	.64	.28	.53	.45	.22	−.29	−.27	**.73**	.58		.67	−.14
18 Success as a Coach	−.26	−.31	−.19	.07	−.09	−.35	−.29	.65	.24	.49	.40	.25	−.22	−.21	**.81**	.55	**.77**		−.13
19 Self-Efficacy	−.25	−.26	−.22	.07	−.09	−.28	−.26	.65	.17	.52	.38	.26	−.21	−.21	**.82**	.55	**.73**	**.84**	
									Lower data matrix: EC1										

Note: $r \geq .70$ are bolded.

Table 4.6c Intercorrelations of the RESTQ-Coach scales for male ($n = 268$) and female ($n = 41$) coaches of the samples GC4 (time frame *in the past (7) days/nights*).

	Upper data matrix: GC4 (male)																		
RESTQ-Coach scales	*1*	*2*	*3*	*4*	*5*	*6*	*7*	*8*	*9*	*10*	*11*	*12*	*13*	*14*	*15*	*16*	*17*	*18*	*19*
1 General Stress		**.84**	**.71**	.58	.57	.64	.67	−.07	−.40	−.65	−.62	−.57	.55	.63	−.15	−.55	−.13	−.11	−.09
2 Emotional Stress	**.81**		**.78**	.60	.55	.65	.64	−.07	−.40	−.67	−.64	−.60	.54	.55	−.18	−.57	−.09	−.12	−.08
3 Social Stress	.57	**.70**		.56	.45	.51	.51	−.07	−.28	−.58	−.52	−.53	.53	.52	−.13	−.51	−.07	−.11	−.11
4 Conflicts/Pressure	**.71**	**.72**	.50		.46	.58	.42	.22	−.30	−.45	−.43	−.46	.53	.37	.05	−.38	.09	.07	.06
5 Fatigue	.65	.64	.25	.58		.61	.61	.02	−.36	−.58	−.42	−.59	.61	.46	−.02	−.55	−.08	−.02	−.03
6 Lack of Energy	**.75**	.67	.37	.54	**.73**		.62	−.15	−.27	−.58	−.45	−.51	.63	.51	−.20	−.55	−.17	−.13	−.15
7 Physical Complaints	.64	.68	.36	.59	.67	.61		−.05	−.30	−.66	−.44	−.57	.50	.47	−.04	−.65	−.07	−.02	−.03
8 Success	−.23	−.22	−.03	.10	−.30	−.43	−.13		.19	.24	.32	.15	−.02	−.12	.51	.22	.38	.48	.41
9 Social Recovery	−.58	−.66	−.38	−.46	−.67	−.50	−.48	.30		.52	.68	.49	−.30	−.25	.20	.42	.13	.17	.14
10 Physical Recovery	−.69	**−.72**	−.45	−.58	**−.73**	−.65	**−.75**	.34	**.78**		**.75**	.66	−.50	−.44	.26	**.81**	.18	.23	.23
11 General Well-being	**−.75**	**−.76**	−.44	−.56	−.68	−.66	−.59	.39	**.86**	**.89**		.61	−.40	−.40	.33	.66	.24	.30	.26
12 Sleep Quality	**−.73**	**−.70**	−.29	−.57	**−.83**	−.56	−.68	.43	.62	**.78**	**.78**		−.52	−.43	.22	.60	.12	.18	.16

(*Continued*)

Table 4.6c (Continued)

RESTQ-Coach scales	*1*	*2*	*3*	*4*	*5*	*6*	*7*	*8*	*9*	*10*	*11*	*12*	*13*	*14*	*15*	*16*	*17*	*18*	*19*
13 Disturbed Breaks	.59	.63	.34	.49	**.80**	.64	**.70**	−.25	−.64	**−.75**	−.64	**−.71**		.60	.02	−.51	−.05	.04	−.03
14 Emotional Exhaustion	.63	.60	.37	.45	.59	.49	.51	−.38	−.52	−.54	−.54	**−.70**	.51		−.21	−.43	−.24	−.09	−.21
15 Personal Accomplishment	−.15	−.18	−.09	.15	−.03	−.24	−.02	.69	.22	.20	.23	.20	.01	−.32		.31	**.76**	**.79**	**.79**
16 Being in Shape	−.60	−.62	−.36	−.34	−.68	−.65	−.69	.48	**.72**	**.90**	**.84**	.69	**−.71**	−.47	.28		.27	.30	.27
17 Motivation as a Coach	−.12	−.10	−.06	.19	−.18	−.39	.04	**.75**	.15	.18	.22	.18	−.05	−.31	**.75**	.32		.68	**.79**
18 Success as a Coach	−.21	−.22	−.13	.06	−.04	−.34	−.09	.52	.04	.09	.15	.13	.11	−.25	**.71**	.16	.65		**.70**
19 Self-Efficacy	−.19	−.22	−.14	.02	−.06	−.26	−.08	.62	.18	.22	.22	.27	.00	−.42	**.85**	.24	**.72**	**.75**	
										Lower data matrix: GC4 (female)									

Note: $r \geq .70$ are bolded.

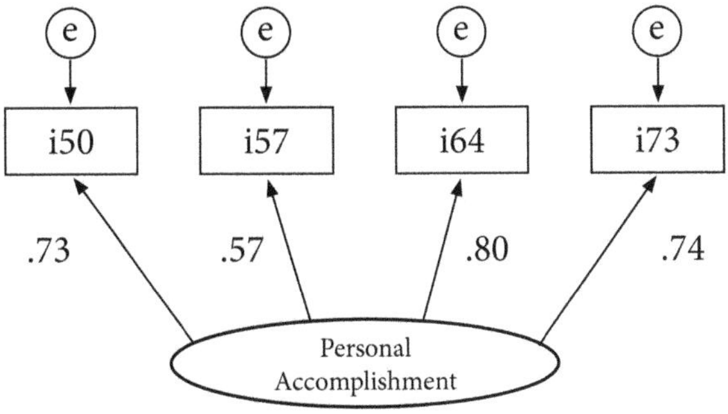

Figure 4.1 Measurement model for *Personal Accomplishment* (GFI = .99, AGFI = .95, CFI = .99, RMSEA = .09; e = error term, i50 = item 50).

Table 4.7 Fit indices and proposed specific correlations for the RESTQ-Coach scales.

RESTQ-Coach scales		*GFI*	*AGFI*	*CFI*	*RMSEA*	*Modification*
13 Disturbed Breaks	Model	1.00	1.00	1.00	.00	No modification
	Modification	—	—	—	—	
14 Emotional Exhaustion	Model	.97	.85	.97	.17	(Item 64 ↔ 79)
	Modification	1.00	1.00	1.00	.00	
15 Personal Accomplishment	Model	.99	.95	.99	.08	No modification
	Modification	—	—	—	—	
16 Being in Shape	Model	.98	.90	.98	.14	(Item 59 ↔ 68)
	Modification	1.00	.98	1.00	.05	
17 Motivation as a Coach	Model	.97	.87	.95	.17	(Item 52 ↔ 74,
	Modification	1.00	1.00	1.00	.00	58 ↔ 74)
18 Success as a Coach	Model	.97	.87	.96	.16	(Item 53 ↔ 69)
	Modification	1.00	.99	1.00	.02	
19 Self-Efficacy	Model	1.00	.99	1.00	.04	No modification
	Modification	—	—	—	—	

explains a higher amount of variance. However, for the interpretation of the %-values for the basic and coach-specific scales, it is important to note that stress and recovery factors are based on different numbers of scales.

Structural modelling

As the intercorrelations of the RESTQ-Coach reproduced the basic pattern of RESTQ-Basic and the RESTQ-Sport a two-dimensional structure with a latent variable for the stress dimension and a latent variable for recovery dimension was modelled with a structural linear equations model. The structural model for the scales of the RESTQ-Coach was based on the scales as 'manifest variables' (Kallus, this volume, Chapter 2), as the solutions for the scales resulted in well acceptable measurement models. A model with two latent variables representing

Table 4.8a Two-factor-solution (with a > .25) for the basic scales of the RESTQ-Coach for the sample GC3.1 (*N*=722).

RESTQ-Coach scales	*Factor 1*	*Factor 2*	h^2
1 General Stress	.82	−.28	.75
2 Emotional Stress	.84		.75
3 Social Stress	.79		.62
4 Conflicts/Pressure	.78		.61
5 Fatigue	.75		.59
6 Lack of Energy	.70		.56
7 Physical Complaints	.70	−.30	.59
8 Success		.76	.60
9 Social Recovery		.69	.52
10 Physical Recovery	−.52	.69	.75
11 General Well-being	−.38	.81	.80
12 Sleep Quality	−.61	.45	.58
Eigenvalue	6.07	1.64	
Variance in %	50.59	13.67	

Table 4.8b Two-Factor-Solution (with a > .25) for the coach-specific scales of the RESTQ-Coach for the sample GC3.1 (*N*=722).

RESTQ-Coach scales	*Factor 1*	*Factor 2*	h^2
13 Disturbed Breaks		.90	.81
14 Emotional Exhaustion		.85	.73
15 Personal Accomplishment	.86		.75
16 Being in Shape	.45	−.66	.64
17 Motivation as a Coach	.86		.75
18 Success as a Coach	.85		.72
19 Self-Efficacy	.88		.82
Eigenvalue	3.51	1.70	
Variance in %	50.14	24.31	

Table 4.8c Two-Factor-Solution (with a > .25) for the basic scales of the RESTQ-Coach for the sample GC4 (N=309).

RESTQ-Coach scales	*Factor 1*	*Factor 2*	h^2
1 General Stress	.86		.78
2 Emotional Stress	.87		.79
3 Social Stress	.77		.60
4 Conflicts/Pressure	.81		.66
5 Fatigue	.71	−.26	.57
6 Lack of Energy	.74		.61
7 Physical Complaints	.72		.58
8 Success	.18	.84	.73
9 Social Recovery	−.41	.62	.55
10 Physical Recovery	−.70	.54	.78
11 General Well-being	−.57	.67	.78
12 Sleep Quality	−.66	.45	.64
Eigenvalue	6.70	1.37	
Variance in %	55.85	11.39	

Table 4.8d Two-Factor-Solution (with a > .25) for the coach-specific scales of the RESTQ-Coach for the sample GC4 (N=309).

RESTQ-Coach scales	*Factor 1*	*Factor 2*	h^2
13 Disturbed Breaks		.89	.81
14 Emotional Exhaustion		.81	.67
15 Personal Accomplishment	.92		.86
16 Being in Shape	.25	−.76	.64
17 Motivation as a Coach	.87		.78
18 Success as a Coach	.88		.77
19 Self-Efficacy	.90		.83
Eigenvalue	3.51	1.86	
Variance in %	50.07	26.53	

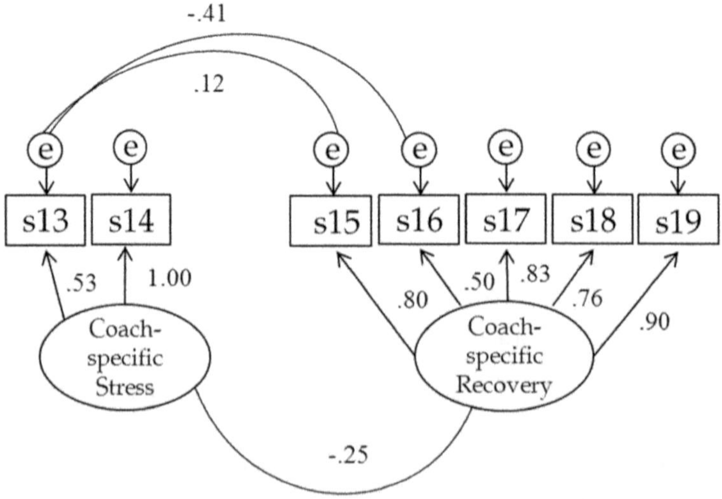

Figure 4.2 Structural model of the RESTQ-Coach scales (GFI = .95, AGFI = .87, CFI = .95, RMSEA = .13).

Note: s13: Disturbed Breaks, s14: Emotional Exhaustion, s15: Personal Accomplishment, s16: Being in Shape, s17: Motivation as a Coach, s18: Success as a Coach, s19: Self-Efficacy.

the dimensions 'stress' and 'recovery' fits the data satisfactorily, as expected from former Exploratory Factor Analysis. Figure 4.2 shows that the model with one recovery factor and a stress factor with two scales gives a good representation of the covariance structure after allowing two specific correlations. Both stem from the stress dimension (scale 13 *Disturbed Breaks*) and show specific correlations with the recovery scale 15 *Personal Accomplishment* and scale 16 *Being in Shape.*

The low positive correlation between scale 13 *Disturbed Breaks* and scale 15 *Personal Accomplishment* might reflect specific item content, as items in the scale *Personal Accomplishment* refer to effective dealing with athletes' emotional problems, which might interfere with breaks. In addition, the rather high negative specific correlation between scale 13 *Disturbed Breaks* and scale 16 *Being in Shape* again makes sense. This specific correlation indicates the breaks play a specific role for coaches, which is not covered by the global scores of *Coach-specific Stress* and *Coach-specific Recovery*. However, *Coach-specific Stress* and *Coach-specific Recovery* show a weak negative correlation, which supports the view that stress and recovery should be treated as separate concepts.

No easy linear common model for the specific scales of the RESTQ-Coach and the RESTQ-Basic could be found based on the scales. More than 60 modifications were needed until a model with acceptable fit indices emerged, which is a result comparable to the analysis conducted for the RESTQ-Sport (Kellmann & Kallus, this volume, Chapter 3). This might be due to the very different levels of abstraction in the basic and the specific part of the RESTQ. While the simple correlations indicate high validity with respect to the bivariate variables, the latent variables cannot be directly related in a simple way. Problems with variables of different generality-specificity have repeatedly discussed as this is another side of the coin of the so-called 'Bandwidth-Fidelity-Dilemma' in Differential Psychology and personnel selection (Briley & Tucker-Drob, 2012; Cheng et al., 2008; Cronbach & Gleser, 1965). All in all, this might be another argument in favor of the modular concept of the RESTQ-Coach. However, this problem might be the reason why some researchers criticized the modular structure as it is not a most easy and economic measurement approach, but a technique, which allows drawing back on a broad range of validities and permits theoretically based approaches for interventions.

Convergent validity

Convergent validity has been estimated by correlating the RESTQ-Coach with instruments measuring related constructs (e.g., burnout, mood).

The recovery-stress state of coaches is theoretically related to the Freudenberger (1974) and Maslach (1976) described burnout symptoms, emotional exhaustion, and depersonalization (Altfeld & Kellmann, 2013b; Kellmann, 2002). Accordingly, the RESTQ-Coach showed expected relationships to the burnout measurements Maslach Burnout Inventory (MBI; Maslach & Jackson, 1986), which was adapted to coaches by Altfeld and Kellmann (2014a). Moreover, analysis also examined expected relationship to the Coach Burnout Questionnaire (CBQ; Harris, 2005; Harris & Ostrow, 2008) and the Profile Mood States (POMS; McNair et al., 1971/1992). The correlations are displayed in Tables 4.9 and 4.10.

The results show expected satisfactory correlations of the RESTQ-Coach scales with the scales of the MBI-C, CBQ, and POMS. The RESTQ-Coach scales measuring the basic stress and the coach-specific stress are positively correlated with the burnout dimension *Emotional Exhaustion* of the MBI-C. Moreover, similar medium to high relationships were examined for the scale *Emotional Exhaustion* of the CBQ. High and moderate correlations were found for the POMS's dimensions.

For the scales measuring basic recovery and coach-specific recovery negative correlations were expected for *Emotional Exhaustion* of the MBI-C and the CBQ. Moreover, positive relationships were examined regarding the *Personal Accomplishment* of the MBI-C and the *Vigor* of the POMS.

Individual-specific diagnostic case studies

Case 1: Tennis coach

Description: A 31-year-old full-time tennis coach was in the preparation period for the next season, when he completed the RESTQ-Coach. The coach worked with athletes performing on national highest and international level. During the diagnostic session, he reported that he worked 48 hours per week as a coach. That affects his relationship to his wife. Moreover, he described that he and his family are dependent on the income of his job.

The RESTQ-Coach profile shows that the coach felt often stressed and exhausted over the past seven days. His stress scores *Social Stress*, *Conflicts/*

Table 4.9 Correlation of the RESTQ-Coach scales with the MBI-C and CBQ for the sample GC2 ($N=123$) and GC3.1 ($N=722$).

	MBI-C EE		*MBI-C DP*		*MBI-C PA*		*CBQ EE*	*CBQ SP*	*CBQ RA*
RESTQ-Coach scales	*GC2*	*GC3.1*	*GC2*	*GC3.1*	*GC2*	*GC3.1*	*GC2*	*GC2*	*GC2*
1 General Stress	.41	.51	.16	.34	−.09	−.09	.52	.36	.29
2 Emotional Stress	.41	.46	.25	.36	−.12	−.12	.42	.29	.34
3 Social Stress	.44	.42	.31	.37	−.16	−.16	.43	.33	.29
4 Conflicts/Pressure	.26	.40	.06	.33	−.08	−.08	.23	.25	.18
5 Fatigue	.41	.61	.05	.32	−.13	−.13	.30	.25	.19
6 Lack of Energy	.45	.45	.23	.35	−.05	−.05	.35	.33	.30
7 Physical Complaints	.28	.45	−.07	.24	−.00	−.00	.35	.18	**.82**
8 Success	−.15	−.07	−.02	−.05	−.06	−.06	−.04	.03	−.32
9 Social Recovery	−.25	−.37	−.15	−.16	.06	.06	−.26	−.17	−.20
10 Physical Recovery	−.43	−.49	−.08	−.25	.12	.12	−.38	−.20	−.44
11 General Well-being	−.31	−.42	−.16	−.20	.04	.04	−.37	−.13	−.29
12 Sleep Quality	−.34	−.48	−.15	−.26	.04	.04	−.36	−.25	−.15
13 Disturbed Breaks	.44	.59	−.09	.32	−.06	−.06	.49	.38	.31
14 Emotional Exhaustion	.53	.62	.40	.42	−.15	−.15	.59	.49	.41
15 Personal Accomplishment	−.06	−.09	−.02	−.15	.26	.26	.04	−.12	−.41
16 Being in Shape	−.44	−.50	−.13	−.24	.12	.12	−.43	−.20	−.45
17 Motivation as a Coach	−.09	−.18	−.03	−.10	.26	.26	.02	−.26	−.43
18 Success as a Coach	−.07	−.08	.03	−.04	.11	.11	−.07	−.09	−.38
19 Self-Efficacy	−.17	−.20	−.07	−.14	.27	.27	−.07	−.25	−.57

Note: $r \geq .70$ are bolded; MBI-C = Maslach Burnout Inventory for Coaches; CBQ = Coach Burnout Questionnaire; EE = *Emotional Exhaustion*, DP = *Depersonalization*, PA = *Personal Accomplishment*, SP = *Sport Devaluation*, RA = *Reduced Sense of Accomplishment*.

Table 4.10 Correlation of the RESTQ-Coach scales with the MBI-C and POMS for the sample GC4 ($N = 309$).

RESTQ-Coach scales	*MBI-C* *EE*	*MBI-C* *DP*	*MBI-C* *PA*	*POMS* *Depression*	*POMS* *Fatigue*	*POMS* *Vigor*	*POMS* *Anger*
1 General Stress	.46	.34	−.21	**.71**	.66	−.57	.67
2 Emotional Stress	.47	.38	−.13	.68	.66	−.53	**.76**
3 Social Stress	.42	.33	−.11	.55	.51	−.38	**.75**
4 Conflicts/Pressure	.32	.19	.05	.42	.43	−.27	.48
5 Fatigue	.57	.30	−.06	.40	**.73**	−.50	.42
6 Lack of Energy	.51	.38	−.18	.52	.69	−.54	.56
7 Physical Complaints	.49	.29	−.11	.49	.67	−.50	.48
8 Success	−.28	−.18	.38	−.22	−.19	.38	−.19
9 Social Recovery	−.35	−.21	.13	−.35	−.45	.43	−.38
10 Physical Recovery	−.55	−.36	.22	−.51	−.69	.67	−.59
11 General Well-being	−.44	−.25	.32	−.58	−.58	.66	−.62
12 Sleep Quality	−.52	−.33	.20	−.53	−.61	.52	−.55
13 Disturbed Breaks	.55	.36	.00	.40	.64	−.43	.47
14 Emotional Exhaustion	.57	.43	−.26	.58	.58	−.49	.54
15 Personal Accomplishment	−.25	−.30	.57	−.27	−.21	.36	−.27
16 Being in Shape	−.55	−.32	.24	−.46	**−.72**	.65	−.59
17 Motivation as a Coach	−.26	−.28	.48	−.21	−.25	.37	−.19
18 Success as a Coach	−.22	−.27	.49	−.28	−.17	.33	−.22
19 Self-Efficacy	−.25	−.26	.49	−.19	−.19	.32	−.19

Note: $r \geq .70$ are bolded; MBI-C = Maslach Burnout Inventory for Coaches; POMS = Profile of Mood States; EE = *Emotional Exhaustion*, DP = *Depersonalization*, PA = *Personal Accomplishment*.

Pressure, *Fatigue*, *Disturbed Breaks*, and *Emotional Exhaustion* were unfavorable (Figure 4.3). Additionally, his recovery scores *Social Recovery*, *General Well-being*, and *Being in Shape* seem to be critically low. In combination with his given information, the coach seemed to have less time with his family because of his amount of working hours. Moreover, due to the time amount the coach showed a lack of work out for his personal well-being. However, the coach showed good scores for his personal coaching motivation, *Self-Efficacy* and *Personal Accomplishment*. In conclusion, although the coach felt exhausted and stressed, he still perceived himself as motivated and successful in working with athletes.

Intervention: The coach needed to have more leisure time for himself and his family to refill his personal energy storage, increase his fitness level, and to

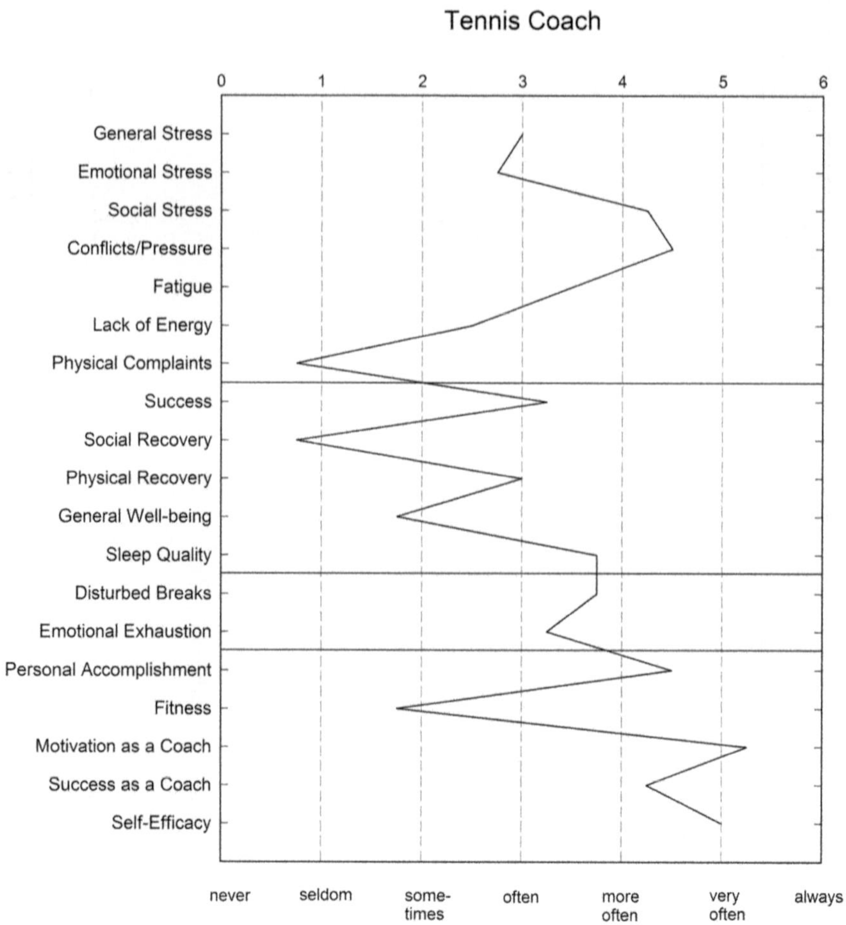

Figure 4.3 Recovery-stress state for a full-time tennis coach.

prevent a critical stress level. Time management skills supported him restructuring his daily routines and tasks to create new spaces of time. Moreover, it was helpful to create fixed time frames for responding e-mails and phone calls. The coach reported that his leisure time was constantly interrupted by incoming calls and other disturbances affecting his recovery process. These interventions had a positive impact on his RESTQ-Coach profile and his personal life situation.

Case 2: Basketball coach

Description: The assessment of the recovery-stress profile of a male part-time basketball coach took place in the middle of the competitive season. Besides his coaching, he studied at the university and worked in several jobs. The coach reported that the amount of tasks stressed him and that he felt very exhausted. Moreover, he reported that the management of his club tried to have influence on his roster and that there were several conflicts regarding administrative issues. The coach additionally underlined that he was not able to satisfactorily coach his athletes during practice and competitions due to his energy level and the conflicts with the management.

The profile displays critical scores for almost all stress and recovery scales of the coach (Figure 4.4). Regarding the profile, the coach shows high deficits in recovery and high stress level. According to his report, he seems to have a lot of stressful events during the past week. Moreover, recovery rarely took place what seem to have negative impact on his well-being and coaching performance. Over a longer period without intervention, critical health states (e.g., burnout) could arise.

Intervention: The coach needed to change crucial points in his personal life. He had to quit one of his jobs beside coaching and university to create more leisure time for recovering. Moreover, the coach learned a relaxation technique (progressive muscle relaxation) to increase his recovery level during the day and to treat his problems falling asleep. By constructive conversations and the support by other coaches the conflicts with the management could be solved what had a positive impact on his recovery-stress balance.

Case 3: Gymnastic coach

Description: The female gymnastic coach was 40 years old at the start of the recovery-stress monitoring. The full-time coach daily worked with several high-performance athletes over an entire season. The RESTQ-Coach was applied on three measurements (t1–t3) during the season (Figure 4.5).

The RESTQ-Coach profile pictures the increase of stress scores and increase of recovery scores over the season. Compared to t1, which displays the recovery-stress state in the preparation period, the stress scales *General Stress*, *Emotional Stress*, *Social Stress*, *Conflicts/Pressure*, and *Emotional Exhaustion*

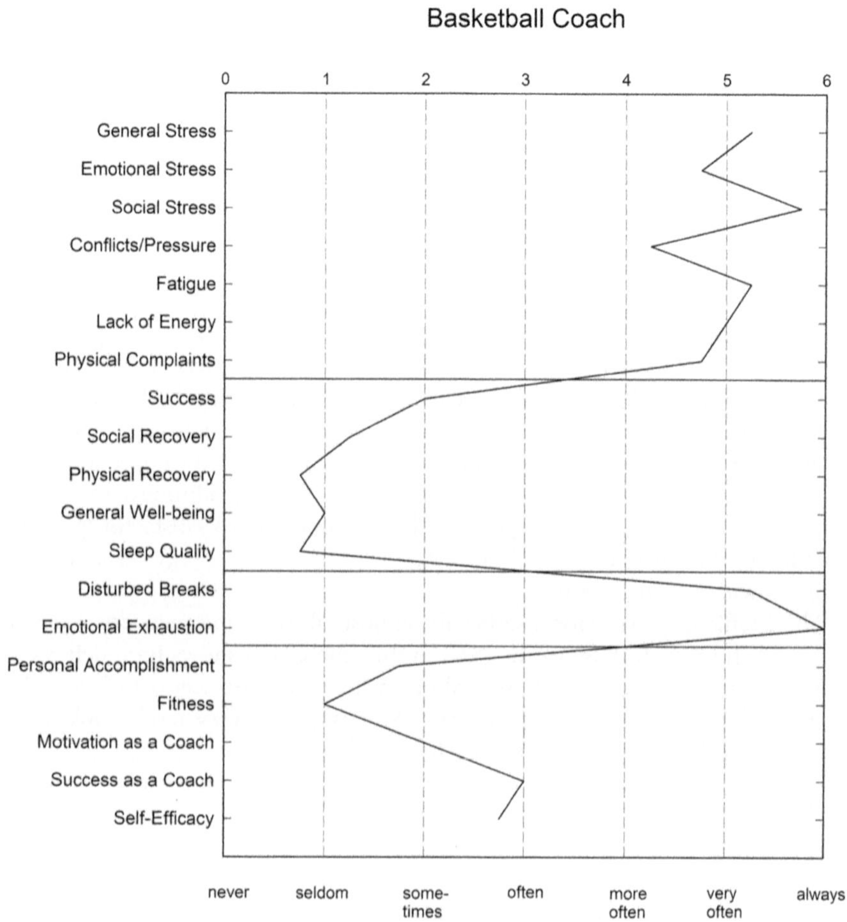

Figure 4.4 Recovery-stress state for a part-time basketball coach.

show higher scores in the end of the season (t3). Moreover, the recovery scales *Success* and *Social Recovery* decreased over the season. Interesting are the low scores of *Success as a Coach*. Furthermore, *Being in Shape*, *Physical Recovery*, *General Well-being*, and *Sleep Quality* evidently decreased from t1 to the other measurements.

Intervention: After presenting the results to the coach, she reported about the unsuccessful season of her athletes and that she tried to move in on this situation by investing more time into practice. Obviously, the higher amount of invested practice hours and video analysis had an impact on the coach's recovery routines. Time for own work out had run out and she felt increasingly unwell.

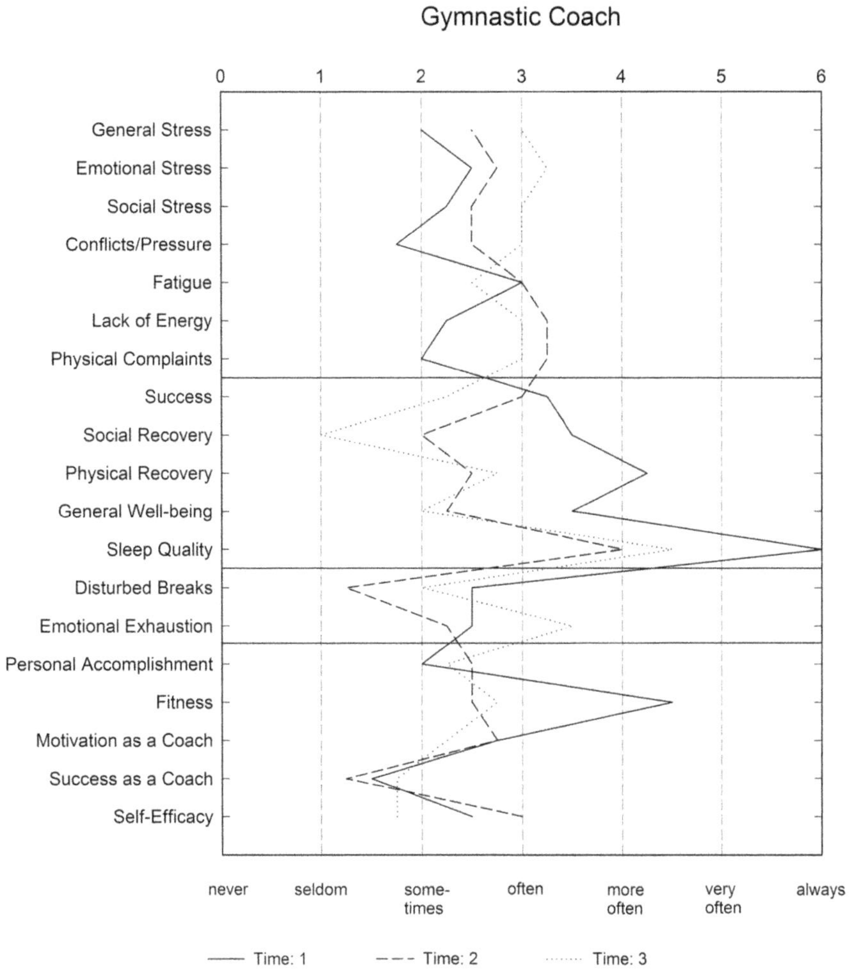

Figure 4.5 Recovery-stress state for a full-time gymnastic coach for three measurements.

Application of the Recovery-Stress Questionnaire for Coaches

The RESTQ-Coach can be applied in almost all work fields and levels of sports coaches. As the instrument is validated for full-time, part-time, and voluntary coaches, the questionnaire can be used to picture the recovery-stress state over an entire season for all kinds of coaches.

The RESTQ-Coach is a useful tool for diagnostic purposes, planning interventions, and research. Accordingly, the questionnaire might be helpful to monitor the recovery-stress state of coaches during exhausting time frames in the season. The use of the questionnaire is recommended during the final period (e.g., playoffs) or during a tournament (e.g., World Cup) to secure the optimal

Table 4.11 Overview of usability for the RESTQ-Coach versions.

RESTQ-Coach version	*76*	*52*
Individual Diagnostic	x	–
Broad Overview	x	x
Group Diagnostic	x	x
Monitoring	x	x
Collapsed Scores	x	x

performance level of the coaches. In this manner, potential stressors and insufficient recovery states could be detected to plan matching interventions.

The RESTQ-Coach represents a validated instrument which could be easily applied to studies dealing with coaches' burnout, stress, or other performance and health-related constructs (Gáspár & Szabó, 2019; Pinheiro et al., 2021). Schaffran and colleagues used the RESTQ-Coach for the validation of the Burnout Prevention Questionnaire for Coaches (Schaffran et al., 2019). For the analysis, the profiles could be used as well as the four main areas of the RESTQ-Coach (*Overall Stress, Overall Recovery, Coach-specific Stress, Coach-specific Recovery*). However, in cases to secure the economics of an examination, the RESTQ-Coach-52 is an appropriate version to enhance the acceptability which is needed for longitudinal designs (Table 4.11).

However, it is important that researchers and sport psychologists must carefully consider all options of their assessment in advance to choose the right version of the RESTQ-Coach. If you are not sure what exactly you may use the data for, it is highly recommended to use the RESTQ-Coach-76 since it leaves all options open.

Summary of the RESTQ-Coach features

- As an instrument that systematically assesses the recovery-stress state of sport coaches in almost all work fields, the RESTQ-Coach is useful for research. Moreover, it might be used in the applied field to prevent critical coaches' health situations.
- The RESTQ-Coach-52 is an appropriate version to enhance the acceptability and to secure the economics of examinations in research designs (e.g., longitudinal studies).
- The RESTQ-Coach showed good to satisfactory estimations of Cronbach's α over different samples and time frames.
- The RESTQ-Coach showed expected relationships to instruments assessing the related constructs burnout and mood.
- Factor analysis confirmed the structure of the general and the coach-specific scales of the RESTQ-Coach. For parts, one stress-related and one recovery-related factor was examined which clearly separates stress and recovery.

Notes

1 In 2014 the item … *I felt I had to perform well in front of others* was exchanged by … *I had to do something I did not like to do.*
2 In this sample the exchanged item … *I had to do something I did not like to do* was used.
3 In this sample the exchanged item … *I had to do something I did not like to do* was used. Also the time frame of the *past (7) days/nights* was applied.

References

Altfeld, S., & Kellmann, M. (2013a). Burnout bei Trainern: Ein Review [Burnout in coaches: A review]. *Zeitschrift für Sportpsychologie, 20*, 47–58.

Altfeld, S., & Kellmann, M. (2013b). Burnout of coaches. In B. Doolittle (Ed.), *Psychology of burnout: New research* (pp. 193–210). Nova Science Publishers.

Altfeld, S., & Kellmann, M. (2014a). Erfassung von Burnout bei Trainern: Validität und Reliabilität von drei Burnoutfragebögen [Measurement of coaches' burnout: Reliability and validity of three burnout questionnaires]. *Deutsche Zeitschrift für Sportmedizin, 65*, 43–49.

Altfeld, S., & Kellmann, M. (2014b). Analyse der Beanspruchungs- und Erholungsbilanz deutscher Trainer [Analyses of the stress-recovery balance of German coaches]. *Zeitschrift für Sportpsychologie, 21*, 137–148.

Altfeld, S., & Kellmann, M. (2015). Are German coaches highly exhausted? A study of differences in personal and environmental factors in relation to emotional exhaustion. *International Journal of Sports Science and Coaching, 10*(4), 637–654.

Altfeld, S., Mallett, C. J., & Kellmann, M. (2015). Coaches' burnout, stress, and recovery over a season: A longitudinal study. *International Sport Coaching Journal, 2*(2), 137–151.

Anderson, E., & Durstine, J. L. (2019). Physical activity, exercise, and chronic diseases: A brief review. *Sports Medicine and Health Science, 1*(1), 3–10.

Balk, Y. A., de Jonge, J., Geurts, S. A., & Oerlemans, W. G. (2019). Antecedents and consequences of perceived autonomy support in elite sport: A diary study linking coaches' off-job recovery and athletes' performance satisfaction. *Psychology of Sport and Exercise, 44*, 26–34.

Bandura, A. (1977). Self-efficacy: Toward a unifying theory of behavioral change. *Psychological Review, 84*, 191–215.

Bentzen, M., Kentta, G., Richter, A., & Lemyre, P. N. (2020). Impact of job insecurity on psychological well-and ill-being among high performance coaches. *International Journal of Environmental Research and Public Health, 17*(19), 6939. https://doi.org/10.3390/ijerph17196939

Bentzen, M., Lemyre, N., & Kentta, G. (2017). A comparison of high-performance football coaches experiencing high-versus low-burnout symptoms across a season of play: Quality of motivation and recovery matters. *International Sport Coaching Journal, 4*(2), 133–146.

Briley, D. A., & Tucker-Drob, E. M. (2012). Broad bandwidth or high fidelity? Evidence from the structure of genetic and environmental effects on the facets of the five factor model. *Behavior Genetics, 42*(5), 746–763.

Burke, K. (2006). Using sport psychology to improve basketball performance. In J. Dosil (Ed.), *The sport psychologist's handbook. A guide for sport-specific performance enhancement* (pp. 121–137). John Wiley & Sons.

Carpentier, J., & Mageau, G. A. (2013). When change-oriented feedback enhances motivation, well-being and performance: A look at autonomy-supportive feedback in sport. *Psychology of Sport and Exercise, 14*, 423–435.

Chan, J. T., & Mallett, C. J. (2011). The value of emotional intelligence for high performance coaching. *International Journal of Sports Science and Coaching, 6*, 315–328.

Cheng, Y., Wang, W., & Ho, Y. H. (2008). Multidimensional Rasch analysis of a psychological test with multiple subtests: A statistical solution for the bandwidth-fidelity dilemma. *Educational and Psychological Measurement, 69*(3), 369–388.

Cook, G. M., Fletcher, D., & Carroll, C. (2021). Psychosocial functioning of Olympic coaches and its perceived effect on athlete performance: A systematic review. *International Review of Sport and Exercise Psychology, 14*(1), 278–311.

Cronbach, L. J., & Gleser, G. C. (1965). *Psychological tests and personnel decisions*. University of Illinois Press.

Dall'Ora, C., Ball, J., Reinius, M., & Griffiths, P. (2020). Burnout in nursing: A theoretical review. *Human Resources for Health, 18*, 41. https://doi.org/10.1186/s12960-020-00469-9

Davis, L., Appleby, R., Davis, P., Wetherell, M., & Gustafsson, H. (2018). The role of coach-athlete relationship quality in team sport athletes' psychophysiological exhaustion: Implications for physical and cognitive performance. *Journal of Sports Sciences, 36*(17), 1985–1992.

Dixon, M. A., & Bruening, J. E. (2007). Work-family conflict in coaching I: A top-down perspective. *Journal of Sport Management, 21*, 377–406.

Ekstrand, J., Lundqvist, D., Lagerbäck, L., Vouillamoz, M., Papadimitiou, N., & Karlsson, J. (2018). Is there a correlation between coaches' leadership styles and injuries in elite football teams? A study of 36 elite teams in 17 countries. *British Journal of Sports Medicine, 52*(8), 527–531.

Feltz, D. L., Chase, M. A., Moritz, S. E., & Sullivan, P. J. (1999). A conceptual model of coaching efficacy: Preliminary investigation and instrument development. *Journal of Educational Psychology, 91*, 675–776.

Freudenberger, H. (1974). Staff burnout. *Journal of Social Issues, 30*, 159–165.

Gáspár, Z., & Szabó, A. (2019). Burnout in football coaching. In E. Konter, J. Beckmann, & T. Loughead (Eds.), *Football psychology: From theory to practice* (pp. 150–162). Routledge.

Gearity, B. T., & Murray, M. A. (2011). Athletes' experiences of the psychological effects of poor coaching. *Psychology of Sport and Exercise, 12*, 213–221.

Harris, B. (2005). *Coach and athlete burnout: The role of coaches' decision-making style*. West Virginia University, Morgantown, USA.

Harris, B., & Ostrow, A. (2008). Coach and athlete burnout: The role of coaches' decision-making style. In S. R. Bakere (Ed.), *Hot topics in sports and athletics* (pp. 143–157). Nova Science Publishers.

Hassmén, P., Herttä, G., Hjälm, S., Lundkvist, E., & Gustafsson, H. (2019). Burnout symptoms and recovery processes in eight elite soccer coaches over 10 years. *International Journal of Sports Science and Coaching, 14*(4), 431–443.

Kallus, K. W. (1995). *Der Erholungs-Belastungs-Fragebogen* [The Recovery-Stress Questionnaire]. Swets & Zeitlinger.

Kallus, K. W., & Kellmann, M. (2000). Burnout in athletes and coaches. In Y. L. Hanin (Ed.), *Emotions in sport* (pp. 209–230). Human Kinetics.

Kallus, K. W., Kellmann, M., Eberspächer, H., & Hermann, H.-D. (1996). Beanspruchung, Erholung und Streßbewältigung von Trainern im Leistungssport [Stress, recovery and coping of performance coaches]. *Psychologie und Sport, 3*, 115–126.

Kellmann, M. (2002). Psychological assessment of underrecovery: Preventing underperformance in athletes. In M. Kellmann (Ed.), *Enhancing recovery: Preventing underperformance in athletes* (pp. 37–55). Human Kinetics.

Kellmann, M., Altfeld, S., & Mallett, C. (2016). Recovery-stress imbalance in Australian football league coaches: A pilot longitudinal study. *International Journal of Sport and Exercise Psychology, 14*, 240–249.

Kyvik, S. (2013). Academic workload and working time: Retrospective perceptions versus time-series data. *Higher Education Quarterly, 67*, 2–14.

Lundkvist, E., Gustafsson, H., Hjälm, S., & Hassmén, P. (2012). An interpretative phenomenological analysis of burnout and recovery in elite soccer coaches. *Qualitative Research in Sport and Exercise, 4*, 400–419.

Mallett, C. (2010). Becoming a high-performance coach: Pathways and communites. In J. Lyle & C. Cushion (Eds.), *Sports coaching: Professionalism and practice* (pp. 119–134). Churchill Livingstone.

Mandolesi, L., Polverino, A., Montuori, S., Foti, F., Ferraioli, G., Sorrentino, P., & Sorrentino, G. (2018). Effects of physical exercise on cognitive functioning and wellbeing: Biological and psychological benefits. *Frontiers in Psychology, 9*, 509. https://doi.org/10.3389/fpsyg.2018.00509

Maslach, C. (1976). Burned-out. *Human Behavior, 5*, 16–22.

Maslach, C., & Jackson, S. (1986). *Maslach Burnout Inventory manual*. Consulting Psychologist Press.

McNair, D., Lorr, M., & Droppleman, L. F. (1971/1992). *Profile of Mood States manual*. Educational and Industrial Testing Service.

Nichol, A. J., Hall, E. T., Vickery, W., & Hayes, P. R. (2019). Examining the relationships between coaching practice and athlete "outcomes": A systematic review and critical realist critique. *International Sport Coaching Journal, 6*(1), 13–29.

Olusoga, P., Bentzen, M., & Kentta, G. (2019). Coach burnout: A scoping review. *International Sport Coaching Journal, 6*(1), 42–62.

Olusoga, P., Butt, J., Maynard, I., & Hays, K. (2010). Stress and coping: A study of world class coaches. *Journal of Applied Sport Psychology, 22*, 274–293.

Pinheiro, G., de Mello, M. T., dos Santos, F. G., Vieira, L. F., & da Costa, V. T. (2021). Analysis of stress level and recovery of formative football coaches: Case studies. *Retos, 41*, 345–353.

Potts, A. J., Didymus, F. F., & Kaiseler, M. (2023). Psychological stress and psychological well-being among sports coaches: A meta-synthesis of the qualitative research evidence. *International Review of Sport and Exercise Psychology, 16*, 554-583.

Schaffran, P., Kleinert, J., Altfeld, S., Zepp, C., Kallus, K. W., & Kellmann, M. (2019). Early risk detection of burnout: Development of the Burnout Prevention Questionnaire for Coaches. *Frontiers in Psychology, 10*, 714. https://doi.org/10.3389/fpsyg.2019.00714

Schaufeli, W., Bakker, A. B., Hoogduin, K., Schaap, C., & Kladler, A. (2001). On the clinical validity of the Maslach Burnout Inventory and the burnout measure. *Psychology and Health, 16*, 565–582.

Schaufeli, W., & Enzmann, D. (1998). *The burnout companion to study and practice: A critical analysis*. Taylor & Francis.

Simpson, R. A., Didymus, F. F., & Williams, T. L. (in press). Organizational stress and well-being in competitive sport: A systematic review. *International Review of Sport and Exercise Psychology*. https://doi.org/10.1080/1750984X.2021.1975305

Thelwell, R. C., Wagstaff, C. R., Chapman, M. T., & Kenttä, G. (2017). Examining coaches' perceptions of how their stress influences the coach-athlete relationship. *Journal of Sports Sciences, 35*(19), 1928–1939.

Thelwell, R., Weston, J. V., Greenless, I. A., & Hutchings, N. (2008). Stressors of elite sports: A coach perspective. *Journal of Sport Sciences*, *26*, 905–918.

Todd, P., & Binns, J. (2013). Work-life balance: Is it now a problem for management? *Gender, Work & Organization*, *20*, 219–231.

Vandevala, T., Pavey, L., Chelidoni, O., Chang, N. F., Creagh-Brown, B., & Cox, A. (2017). Psychological rumination and recovery from work in intensive care professionals: Associations with stress, burnout, depression and health. *Journal of Intensive Care*, *5*, 16. https://doi.org/10.1186/s40560-017-0209-0

Weigelt, O., Gierer, P., & Syrek, C. J. (2019). My mind is working overtime – Towards an integrative perspective of psychological detachment, work-related rumination, and work reflection. *International Journal of Environmental Research and Public Health*, *16*(16), 2987. https://doi.org/10.3390/ijerph16162987

5 Recovery-Stress Questionnaire for Work

Paulino Jiménez, Anita Bregenzer, and K. Wolfgang Kallus

Scope and application

Assessing stress at the workplace is an important aspect in many organizational projects such as workplace health promotion, incident/accident prevention, and psychosocial risk assessment. Creating a health-promoting workplace by identifying so-called 'risks' is a legal obligation in many European countries (Directive 89/391/EEC; EU Commission, 2008). To reach the goal of healthy workplaces, psychosocial risks and their possible impairing effects on the individual's psychological state must be assessed and managed for every workplace. The assessment of psycho-social risks can be done with different approaches (Leka et al., 2011) and should be done together with an assessment of the employees' psychological conditions.

The employee's stress in the workplace is the most frequently evaluated condition in workplace health promotion projects and during a risk assessment. However, by assessing stress at the workplace as a standalone concept, important aspects like recovery or individual resources are often overlooked. A simultaneous assessment of work-specific stress and recovery is needed to determine the effects of high demands in dependence of the person's individual recovery process, the person's individual resources, as well as workplace resources. This relationship between demands and resources is highlighted in the *Job Demands-Resources Theory* (JD-R; Bakker et al., 2023) where the experience of job demands and of job resources instigate two different processes, a health impairment process and a motivational process. Additionally, job resources can weaken the health-impairing impact of job demands on stress. Thus, an assessment of job resources should be included in a stress assessment tool. As presented by Kellmann and Kallus (this volume, Chapter 1) recovery is a multilevel process in time and this process fills the resources in the end. Therefore, we will use recovery/resources at first as kind of compound.

Jiménez, P., Bregenzer, A., & Kallus, K. W. (2025). Recovery-Stress Questionnaire for Work. In M. Kellmann & K. W. Kallus (Eds.), *The Recovery-Stress Questionnaires: A User Manual* (pp. 171–205). Routledge.

DOI: 10.4324/9781032643380-5

The Recovery-Stress Questionnaire for Work (RESTQ-Work) allows a simultaneous assessment of stress and recovery at the workplace. The RESTQ-Work was specifically developed based on the *Recovery-Stress Balance Model* (Kellmann & Kallus, this volume, Chapter 1). According to this model, negative outcomes of high demands – such as stress – can be reduced by enhancing recovery and getting adequate resources.

In comparison to the other questionnaires in the RESTQ series, the RESTQ-Work specifically includes the aspect of work-resources in its concept. Resources are an important component of work-specific recovery and are thus incorporated in the conceptual part of recovery (Kellmann & Kallus, this volume, Chapter 1). Therefore, when talking about the recovery-stress balance model for work, we include the complex interaction between resources and recovery.

The RESTQ-Work measures the recovery-stress balance at the workplace to receive a detailed profile about stress, recovery, and resources. This can be applied at different levels: individual, group, and organizational level. Measuring demands and resources on these three different levels is in accordance with current standards and norms (as for instance, ISO, 2004) and the Austrian realization (Evers et al., 2012; Österreichisches Normungsinstitut, 2017). In the ISO 10667-2 (2020b), it is defined that procedures or methods in Work Psychology should be categorized in individual, group, and organizational assessment. Each level has a different purpose and different requirements or quality standards. As mentioned before, the RESTQ-Work is based on data from individual persons, which can be analyzed for individual, group as well as organizational purposes. The RESTQ-Work covers the requirements of all levels.

An assessment on the individual, group, and organizational level can be conducted with two different versions (27, and 92 items) and two supplementary versions (8, and 55 items) by interpreting scales and sub-dimensions. The supplementary versions are not available in this publication by Routledge but can be obtained from the first author. The short versions with 8 and 27 items (RESTQ-Work-8, and RESTQ-Work-27) can be used for an assessment of organizational aspects. The RESTQ-Work-8 with eight items is especially useful when conducting a rough assessment of the organization's stress and recovery levels via a smartphone assisted survey. The longer versions of the RESTQ-Work (55, and 92 items) allow both an assessment at the organizational and individual level. With these longer versions, it is also possible to provide comprehensive feedback at both levels. This detailed measurement of stress and recovery on different levels is helpful to develop specific interventions. On the individual level, the interventions should aim to change the individual's experience of stress and the use of recovery strategies. On organizational and group level the results of the RESTQ-Work can be applied to derive practical interventions and prevention activities (e.g., using the feedback in health circles in companies). The RESTQ-Work can be used well between 14 and 88 years.

Facets of stress and recovery in Work and Organizational Psychology: Theory of the work-specific scales

The RESTQ-Work was developed on basis of the Recovery-Stress Questionnaire (RESTQ-Basic; Kallus, this volume, Chapter 2). In addition to the RESTQ-Basic, work-specific items were added to allow a recovery/resources-stress profile specifically for work settings (Jiménez & Kallus, 2005, 2010). Therefore, the work-specific part (RESTQ-Work) has four additional sub-dimensions that can be added to the basic part: 1) *Loss of Meaning/Burnout*, 2) *Leisure/Breaks*, 3) *Psychosocial Recovery*, and 4) *Work-related Recovery*. These four sub-dimensions can be further divided into 14 scales to receive more detailed information about the aspects of work-specific stress and recovery respective resources.

Role of resources in work

We consider *resources* as the *structural basis* in the RESTQ whereas *recovery* and *stress* are seen as the *functional processes* which act on and *use resources*. For the further description of the scales and especially for interpretation of the results of the RESTQ-Work we will use recovery/resources together in many instances as process and outcome often appear together in the *past (7) days/nights.*

The sub-dimensions *Leisure/Breaks*, *Psychosocial Recovery*, and *Work-related Recovery* are in fact measured with the aim of getting insight into the current 'options', that means the person's possibility to use resources at work. This will be explained with example items of the sub-dimensions.

For *Leisure/Breaks* let us look at the item … *I was able to get some rest during my breaks*. In that case, we can see that if a person responds that he/she has these situations 'often' then we can derive that he/she can use strategies for having a good rest which are successful. However, we can see that there are possibilities to get rest, and this means there are resources available for the persons to get rest. From our view we therefore can use the word 'resources'.

In the case of *Psychosocial Recovery* we will see in the item … *I was supported by my colleagues* that she/he had the opportunity of receiving support and that the person also interchanged with their colleagues. This also can be seen as 'resources'.

In the last example for *Work-related Recovery* we will look on the item … *I could use my strengths at work*. If a person was able to tell us that she/he could do that several times in the last week then we conclude that this person is able to use these possibilities, the 'potential', the hidden 'energy', which means resources, at the workplace.

For the interpretation and the derivation of interventions based on the results we therefore can use – at first – recovery (processes) and resources in the same argument. Detailed feedback to individuals or to an organization will have to differentiate between the concepts for sure, which will be shown for the previous example: high values of 'using strengths at work' means for an individual that the person is able to use his/her own competencies. This resource of competency-*usage* leads to a stable recovery level. Feedback to an individual person therefore should reinforce this *strategy*.

When using the RESTQ-Work in a group (team/organization) then the results are aggregated values for that group and these values can be used in an analogous way: high values of 'using strengths at work' mean for an organization that many persons could use the strategy of competency-using which can be seen as a work cultural or at least work environmental aspect in that organization. Feedback to an organization also should encourage the organization to sustain in procedures and structures which support such a 'job-crafting' (Bakker et al., 2023) environment. So, in both levels the resources are important to diagnose and the results are helpful for further interventions. In both cases resources can lead to recovery.

Work-specific sub-dimensions in the RESTQ-Work

Loss of Meaning/Burnout. The sub-dimensions in the RESTQ-Work can be categorized in five scales: *Emotional Exhaustion*, *Loss of Control*, *Loss of Meaning*, *Conflicts with Colleagues*, and *Spillover*. The scale *Emotional Exhaustion* was constructed within the view of Maslach et al. (2001), where next to cynicism and inefficacy, exhaustion is one dimension that is important for developing burnout. The scales *Loss of Control* and *Loss of Meaning* share similarities with the concept of cynicism (Maslach et al., 2001). Experiencing conflicts between colleagues at work (Varhama & Björkqvist, 2004) and experiencing workplace incivility (Jiménez et al., 2018) is strongly correlated with burnout; therefore, the scale *Conflict with Colleagues* is included in this sub-dimension. The last scale, *Spillover*, was added as spillover is also associated with burnout: work-family conflict – especially if work problems spill over to home life – is linked with emotional exhaustion of employees (Bakker et al., 2023; Lambert & Hogan, 2010; Rupert et al., 2009).

Leisure/Breaks. This sub-dimension measures leisure time and the recovery-processes at work. Recovery is related to the leisure time and how it is used. Not all activities in leisure time have a potential for recovery. High-duty activities (e.g., household activities) are negatively related to well-being, whereas social or physical activities have a positive effect (Hahn et al., 2011; Sonnentag, 2001). These aspects are measured with the scales *Undisturbed Leisure Time* and *Leisure*. In addition to leisure time, the RESTQ-Work measures recovery processes during working time. Breaks at work can either be seen as time for regeneration or a bothersome interruption (Jett & George, 2003). The RESTQ-Work measures the quality of breaks with the two scales *Efficient Breaks* and *Undisturbed Breaks*.

Psychosocial Recovery. This sub-dimension provides information for psychosocial recovery and distinguishes between psychosocial recovery for work and those for a non-work-related context. Social support is one of the most effective stress buffers: social support does not directly influence recovery processes; but its potential for positive effects on coping with work demands is high (Otero-López et al., 2008). Halbesleben (2006) showed that work-related social support (support from coworkers or supervisors) is strongly negatively related to exhaustion, because of its direct influence on work demands. Social support from family and friends has a strong negative relationship to the other aspects of burnout – depersonalization and personal accomplishment. Therefore, non-work (*Social Support Friends*) and work-related support (*Social Support Colleagues*) are included in the RESTQ-Work.

Work-related Recovery. Aspects of control at work (e.g., autonomy, participation, opportunity to use skills, independent decision-making options) can help employees dealing with high job demands and thus reduce negative outcomes like chronic stress or burnout (Bakker et al., 2005; Martin et al., 2007; Nahrgang et al., 2011). In the RESTQ-Work, *Work-related Recovery* is measured with the scales *Participation*, *Personal Growth*, and *Action Latitude*. The experience of *Personal Growth* at work depends on the demands of the task related to personal resources (e.g., knowledge, skills, abilities) or the efforts persons have to invest to accomplish this task (Bakker et al., 2023; Hacker, 2003). If the personal resources are high, the work is experienced as stimulating and interesting, which is an important resource at work (Hacker, 2003). *Action Latitude* is based on the model by Karasek and Theorell (1990), where high job demands together with low action latitude exhaust the employee's energy and foster stress at work. High action latitude, however, increases psychological and social well-being (Fernet et al., 2004).

Versions, scoring, and norms

Versions and scoring

Two versions are available for the RESTQ-Work: the RESTQ-Work-27 has 27 items (7 for the basic part and 20 for the work-specific part) and is mainly used as a screening instrument for organizational assessment. The longest version (RESTQ-Work-92) consists of 92 items (48 for the basic part and 44 for the work-specific part) and was specifically created for individual purposes, allowing a detailed diagnosis and feedback for individuals.

The RESTQ-Work-27 can be used very efficiently in workplace health promotion evaluations and in psychosocial risk assessment together with an instrument that measures psychosocial risks.

The supplementary version RESTQ-Work-55 comprises 55 items (24 items for the basic part and 31 for the work-specific part) and allows both individual and organizational assessment. The shortest version (RESTQ-Work-8) has eight items and can be used as a first rough assessment of the organization's stress and recovery levels. This supplementary version is particularly suitable for smartphone-based surveys, as its short length means that it fits well on the small display of a smartphone.

In this manual, two versions of the RESTQ-Work are available: RESTQ-Work-27 and RESTQ-Work-92. The RESTQ-Work-27 is the most optimal and most frequently used version for a short assessment in the organization. The RESTQ-Work-92 can be used most efficiently for individual assessments, coaching and counselling sessions. Information about the RESTQ-Work-8 and RESTQ-Work-55 and the questionnaires are available from the authors on request.

All versions of the RESTQ-Work refer to the *past (7) days/nights* and have a seven-point frequency scale ranging from 0 (*never*) to 6 (*always*). The scale values are calculated by taking the mean of the item values (checked numbers). In the *Undisturbed Leisure Time* scale, first all items have to be inverted. The means for the sub-dimensions are calculated by taking the underlying scales.

Kallus (1995) as well as Kellmann and Kallus (this volume, Chapter 1, p. 2) state that

> *stress and recovery should not be combined to a single value, as they constitute two conceptually independent dimensions as far as the frequency in the past days/nights is concerned.* The relationship between the scales for recovery and stress is neither linear nor symmetrical. ***Consequently, the calculation of one overall single score of all stress and recovery scales does not make sense and is strongly prohibited.***

It is also important to note that all versions are building up on each other, which means that the RESTQ-Work-92 contains the RESTQ-Work-55, the RESTQ-Work-55 can be reduced to the RESTQ-Work-27, and all versions can be reduced to the RESTQ-Work-8. This modularized system allows an easy handling of all versions.

Versions and ISO norm requirements for Work- and Organizational Psychology

Assessment methods in work and organizational settings should be developed based on the requirements stated in the ISO 10667-1 (2020a). As already mentioned, the RESTQ-Work is in accordance with the ISO 10667-2 (2020b), where one should distinguish between assessing stress on organizational, group, and individual level. In addition, the RESTQ-Work allows an assessment on three precision levels (ISO, 2004): level 1 – for accurate measurement purposes; level 2 – for screening purposes; and level 3 – for orientation purposes (Figure 5.1).

The RESTQ-Work-27 should be used to get a first assessment of organizational aspects and can be used for screening and orientation purposes. With the help of screening scores and underlying sub-dimensions, a screening of the organization is possible very quickly. Individual assessment is only possible by using

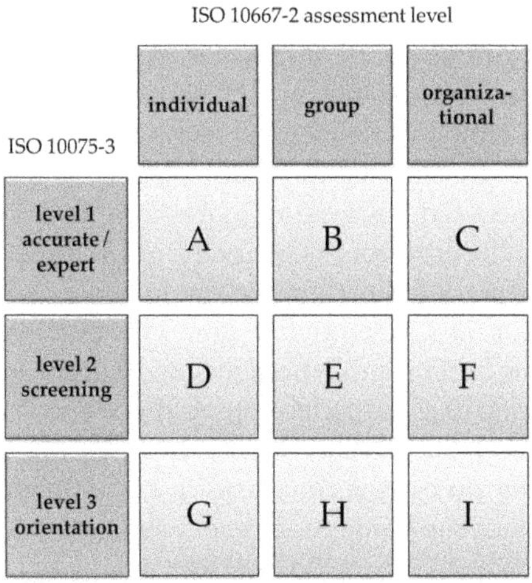

Figure 5.1 Application and assessment possibilities of the RESTQ-Work in line with the ISO 10667-2 (2020b).

Note: A: Screening scores stress/recovery, sub-dimensions, scales. (RESTQ-Work-92)

B: Screening scores stress/recovery, sub-dimensions, scales. (RESTQ-Work-55, 92)

C: Screening scores stress/recovery, sub-dimensions, scales. (RESTQ-Work 55, 92)

D: Screening scores stress/recovery. (RESTQ-Work 27, 55, 92)

E: Screening scores stress/recovery, sub-dimensions. (RESTQ-Work 27, 55, 92)

F: Screening scores stress/recovery, sub-dimensions. (RESTQ-Work 27, 55, 92)

G: Screening scores stress/recovery. (RESTQ-Work 27, 55, 92)

H: Screening scores stress/recovery. (RESTQ-Work 8, 27, 55, 92)

I: Screening scores stress/recovery. (RESTQ-Work 8, 27, 55, 92)

screening scores for stress and recovery. For individual purposes, only the screening scores for recovery and stress can be used. The RESTQ-Work-92 is specifically created for individual purposes. In the RESTQ-Work-92 sub-dimensions and scales can be used to provide comprehensive feedback to individuals about their stress and recovery at work.

Next to the sub-dimensions and scales, screening scores can be used for both organizational and individual assessment. The screening scores for stress and recovery are gained from 27 items (all items of the RESTQ-Work-27) and can be used for a screening of individual and organization as well as for orientation purposes. The screening score for stress consists of seven items from the stress-related sub-dimensions. For the screening score recovery, ten items of the recovery-related sub-dimensions are used. The rationale of the screening scores is outlined shortly. The screening scores were calculated by first obtaining the means for the ten stress-related and 17 recovery-related items, respectively. Then, cut-off-scores, which were obtained by categorizing the norm values into 70%, 15%, and 15%, were extracted for both screening scores. These cut-off-scores can be used to categorize the screening scores into 'traffic lights', where green (G = 70%) refers to a 'healthy' score, orange (O = 15%) means 'caution' and red (R = 15%) shows a 'critical' score. By using the formula of 70%/15%/15%, most of the scores will result in a green traffic light. This overestimation of green results has an important background: the screening scores can be already used on the orientation level (ISO, 2004). Developing the scores in a less sensitive way prevents an overreaction and protects organizations, groups, and individuals from getting a critical result too early. A more sensitive assessment can always be done on the expert level with sub-dimensions and scales.[1]

Reliability

Samples

The following samples were used to calculate reliability and validity for the RESTQ-Work-27 and RESTQ-Work-92 (Table 5.1).

Table 5.1 Sample sizes, demographic data and other information about the samples, GW1, GW2, and EW1.

	GW1	*GW2*	*EW1*
Sample size	*N* = 1219	*N* = 682	*N* = 195
Gender distribution	Male = 35.7% Female = 64.3%	Male = 41.6% Female = 58.4%	Male = 47.2% Female = 52.8%
Industrial Sector	Various sectors	Various sectors	Various sectors
Age	< 31 yrs (32.1%) 31–40 yrs (26.3%) 41–50 yrs (23.5%) 51–60 yrs (16.5%) > 60 yrs (1.6%)	*M* = 42 *SD* = 11.4	< 31 yrs (12.4%) 31–40 yrs (13.3%) 41–50 yrs (18.9%) 51–60 yrs (30.3%) > 60 yrs (25.1%)
Working hours	Full-time = 62.1% Part-time = 32.7% Student job = 5.2%	Full-time = 58% Part-time = 39.4% Student job = 2.6%	Full-time = 66.7% Part-time = 31.3% Student job = 2.1%
RESTQ-version	RESTQ-Work-27	RESTQ-Work-92	RESTQ-Work-92
Time frame	7 days/nights	7 days/nights	7 days/nights
Country	Austria	Austria	United Kingdom

For the RESTQ-Work-27 (GW1), the data was collected with an online-panel. Quota in gender and age were set to obtain a sample that is comparable to the Austrian population, and therefore be seen as representative for the Austrian population. For the RESTQ-Work-92 (GW2), four different research studies in different companies, independently conducted in Austria between 2007 and 2008, were pooled into a large data set.

The data for the English version of the RESTQ-Work-92 (EW1) was also collected with an online-panel – only workers with a job in the United Kingdom were asked to participate in this study. Sample sizes, demographic data, and information about the different data sets are provided in Table 5.1. Means and standard deviations of the scales and sub-dimensions from all samples are depicted in the Online Appendix A.D1–A.D4.

Analysis

For reliability and validity, the main results for the RESTQ-Work-27 (GW1) and RESTQ-Work-92 (GW2, EW1) will be presented. For the latent structure measurement models, the results of the RESTQ-Work-92 (GW2) are displayed. For the structural equation modelling, the results of the RESTQ-Work-27 (GW1) are shown.

Classical reliability measures

To measure the reliability for the sub-dimensions and scales with more than two items, Cronbach's α was calculated.[2] All reliability scores can be found in Table 5.2.

Table 5.2 Reliability scores for the sub-dimensions (dim.) and scales of the RESTQ-Work-27 (GW1), RESTQ-Work-55 (GW2), and RESTQ-Work-92 (GW3, EW1).

		RESTQ-Work-27	*RESTQ-Work-92*			
		GW1	*GW2*		*EW1*	
Sub-dimensions	*RESTQ-Work scales*	*dim.*	*scales*	*dim.*	*scales*	*dim.*
Social-Emotional Stress	1 General Stress	.83	.86	.93	.90	.96
	2 Emotional Stress		.78		.87	
	3 Social Stress		.85		.91	
Performance (-related) Stress	4 Conflicts/Pressure	n/a*	.53	.88	.78	.94
	5 Fatigue		.82		.82	
	6 Lack of Energy		.76		.83	
	7 Physical Complaints		.79		.83	

(*Continued*)

Table 5.2 (Continued)

		RESTQ-Work-27	*RESTQ-Work-92*			
		GW1	*GW2*		*EW1*	
Sub-dimensions	*RESTQ-Work scales*	*dim.*	*scales*	*dim.*	*scales*	*dim.*
Overall Recovery	8 Success	.85	.71	.92	.73	.92
	9 Social Recovery		.84		.83	
	10 Physical Recovery		.83		.79	
	11 General Well-being		.90		.92	
	12 Sleep Quality		.86		.82	
Loss of Meaning/ Burnout	13 Emotional Exhaustion	.92	.79	.90	.87	.93
	14 Loss of Control		.77		.77	
	15 Loss of Meaning		.81		.78	
	16 Conflicts with Colleagues		.80		.87	
	17 Spillover		.78		.80	
Leisure/ Breaks	18 Undisturbed Leisure Time	.90	.81	.90	.83	.85
	19 Efficient Breaks		.84		.79	
	20 Leisure		.86		.86	
	21 Undisturbed Breaks		.84		.74	
Psychosocial Recovery	22 Social Support Friends	.89	.79	.83	.89	.86
	23 Social Support Colleagues		.83		.77	
Work-related Recovery	24 Participation	.90	.76	.88	.79	.89
	25 Personal Growth Factors		.74		.75	
	26 Action Latitude		.75		.61	

Note: * The sub-dimension *Performance(-related) Stress* is not included in the RESTQ-Work-27.

For both samples GW2 and EW1, all scales and sub-dimensions of the RESTQ-Work-92 fulfil the minimum threshold for Cronbach's α of .70, which is at least needed for instruments assessing stress (and recovery) at the workplace (ISO, 2004), with the exception of *Conflicts/Pressure* (GW3) and *Action Latitude* (EW1). However, the scale *Conflicts/Pressure* is shown to have satisfactory reliability coefficients in other studies with other samples (Jiménez & Kallus, 2010). For all sub-dimensions the Cronbach's α is greater than .80 in the RESTQ-Work-27 and RESTQ-Work-92, which indicates very good reliability as stated in the ISO 10075-3 (2004).

Latent structure measurement models

The method of Structural Equation Modelling (SEM) with maximum likelihood method of estimation was used to test the measurement model(s) of each sub-dimension. Although the RESTQ-Work consists of both the basic and work-specific part, only the work-specific part will be statistically analyzed. Further information on the basic part can be found in Kallus (this volume, Chapter 2).

Every sub-dimension (latent variable) was investigated separately according to the underlying structure defined in the RESTQ-Work. This analysis was done on item basis, which means that the items were used as manifest variables that load on their respective scales (first level latent variable) and overlying sub-dimensions (second level latent variable). An overview of χ^2-values, df, p-values and fit indices for all measurement models for sample GW2 can be found in Table 5.3. The single measurement models are described in detail in the next paragraphs.

To test the structure of the sub-dimension *Loss of Meaning/Burnout* on item basis, the corresponding 16 items were taken as manifest variables and assigned to their predefined scales. Finally, the scales load on one final latent factor that represents the overlying sub-dimension, *Loss of Meaning/Burnout*. The fit indices indicate an acceptable fit, with the exception of the RMSEA (Table 5.3). Two

Table 5.3 Overview of χ^2-values, df, p-values and fit indices for the unmodified and modified measurement models on item basis for all sub-dimensions of the RESTQ-Work-92 (GW2).

RESTQ-Work Sub-dimensions	χ^2	*df*	*p*	*AGFI*	*CFI*	*RMSEA*	*Modification*
Loss of Meaning/ Burnout	595.44	99	.001	.87	.90	.09	
Loss of Meaning/ Burnout with two modifications	382.10	97	.001	.91	.94	.07	i59 ↔ i74 i71 ↔ i82
Leisure/Breaks	343.46	51	.001	.89	.94	.09	
Psychosocial Recovery	61.61	8	.001	.92	.97	.10	
Work-related Recovery	236.90	32	.001	.87	.93	.10	
Work-related Recovery with two modifications	158.15	30	.001	.91	.95	.08	i56 ↔ i91 i70 ↔ i73

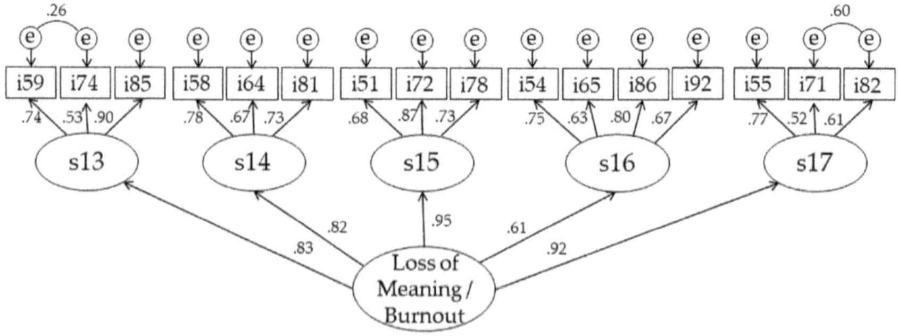

Figure 5.2 Modified model of *Loss of Meaning/Burnout* on item basis with all regression coefficients; all regression coefficients significant with $p < .001$.

Note: s13: *Emotional Exhaustion*, s14: *Loss of Control*, s15: *Loss of Meaning*, s16: *Negative Working Climate*, s17: *Spillover.*

error correlations between measurement errors of indicators were set to modify the model. The first modification is a correlation between the measurement errors of two items from the scale *Emotional Exhaustion* (i59: ... *I felt very exhausted* and i74: ... *I did not feel physically well*). The second modification is a correlation between the measurement errors of two items from the scale *Spillover* (i71: ... *I did not get my work out of my head* and i82: ... *I could not stop thinking about problems of work at home*).

The modified model reached a substantial better fit having the RMSEA below .08 (for requirements, Kellmann & Kallus, this volume, Chapter 1). The model with all regression coefficients can be seen in Figure 5.2.

Analyzing the sub-dimension *Leisure/Breaks* on item basis, twelve items were used as manifest variables and assigned to their corresponding scales. The scales were linked to one major factor which represents the sub-dimension *Leisure/Breaks* (Figure 5.3). The model shows a negative residual variance (also known as 'Haywood-cases') for the latent variable *Efficient Breaks* (s19). In the case of negative residual variance, the residual variance should be set to zero (Chen et al., 2001). Setting the residual variance of *Efficient Breaks* (s19) to zero automatically results in a regression coefficient of 1. Comparing the χ^2-value of the first, unmodified model to the χ^2-value of the model with the fixed residual variance showed a statistically not significant result ($\Delta\chi^2 = .001, \Delta df = 1$). The model shows an acceptable fit with the exception of the RMSEA, which is greater than the acceptable value of .08, but lower than the critical threshold of .10 (Table 5.3). The structure of the model shows very high path coefficients, with the exception of *Undisturbed Leisure Time* (s18). This lower coefficient could be caused by item i66 (... *I had responsibilities in my leisure time*), which also shows a lower path. Another explanation could lie in the scale itself, as this scale is the only scale in the RESTQ-Work that has to be inverted.

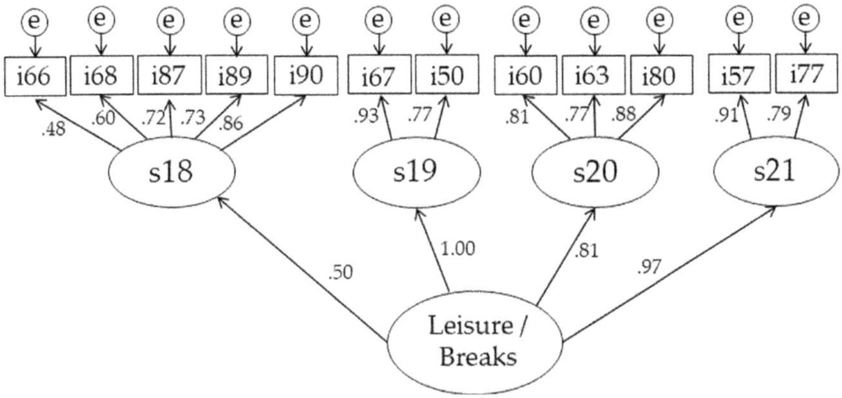

Figure 5.3 Model of *Leisure/Breaks* on item basis with all regression coefficients; all regression coefficients significant with $p < .001$.
Note: s18: *Undisturbed Leisure Time*, s19: *Efficient Breaks*, s20: *Leisure*, s21: *Undisturbed Breaks*.

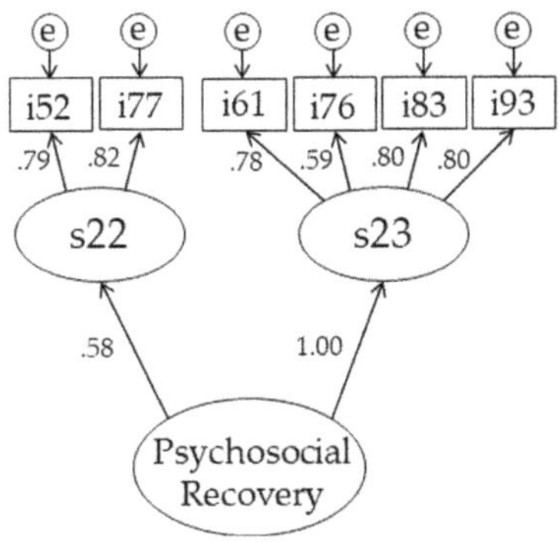

Figure 5.4 Model of *Psychosocial Recovery* on item basis with all regression coefficients; all regression coefficients significant with $p < .001$.
Note: s22: *Social Support Friends*, s23: *Social Support Colleagues*.

To test the structure of the sub-dimension *Psychosocial Recovery* on item basis, six items were taken as manifest variables and assigned to their corresponding scales. These scales load on one final latent factor that represents the overlying sub-dimension, *Psychosocial Recovery*. The model shows a negative residual variance for the latent variable *Social Support Colleagues* (Figure 5.4). As suggested by Chen et al. (2001) the residual variance was fixed to the value zero, automatically resulting in a regression coefficient of 1. Then, the χ^2-value of the first, unmodified model was compared to the model with the fixed residual variance.

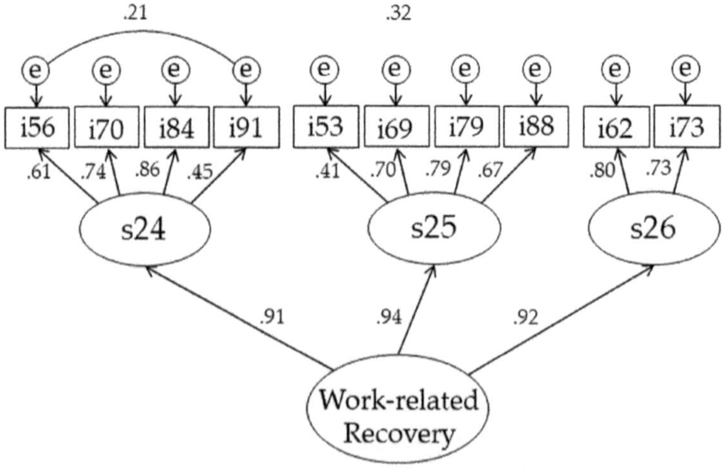

Figure 5.5 Modified model of *Work-related Recovery* on item basis with all regression coefficients; all regression coefficients significant with $p<.001$.
Note: s24: *Participation*, s25: *Personal Growth Factors*, s26: *Action Latitude*.

The result is statistically not significant ($\Delta\chi^2=3113$, $\Delta df=1$). The model shows a good fit with the exception of the RMSEA (Table 5.3). The highest coefficients can be found for items i77 (*... I was supported by my friends*), i83 (*... I experienced cohesion among my colleagues*), and i93 (*... I was supported by my colleagues*).

Analyzing the sub-dimension *Work-related Recovery* on item basis, ten items were used as manifest variables and assigned to their corresponding scales. These scales were linked to one major factor which represents the sub-dimension *Work-related Recovery* (Figure 5.5). Without any modifications to the model, the model reached an acceptable fit with the exception of the RMSEA (Table 5.6). By setting correlations between measurements errors of indicators a good fit can be obtained (Table 5.6). The first modification is a correlation between the measurement errors of two items from the scales *Participation* and *Action Latitude* (i70: *... I could freely express my opinion at work* and i73: *... I could decide myself how I perform my tasks*). The second modification is a correlation between the measurement errors of two items from the scale *Participation* (i56: *... I contributed to important decisions* and i91: *... I got feedback about finalized projects/work*).

Construct validity

Factor analysis

Two-factor analysis using Principal Component Analysis with Varimax rotations were performed, separately for the basic and work-specific part of the RESTQ-Work-92 (Table 5.4).

Table 5.4 Factor loadings for the basic scales of the RESTQ-Work-92 (GW2).

	GW2	
	Factor	
RESTQ-Work scales	*1*	*2*
1 General Stress	.83	
2 Emotional Stress	.80	
3 Social Stress	.74	
4 Conflicts/Pressure	.77	
5 Fatigue	.80	
6 Lack of Energy	.71	
7 Physical Complaints	.71	
8 Success		.80
9 Social Recovery		.73
10 Physical Recovery	−.57	.67
11 General Well-being	−.45	.79
12 Sleep Quality	−.66	.40
Eigenvalue	6.42	1.49
Variance explained in %	53.50	12.40

Note: Factor loadings < .40 are suppressed in this table. Rotation method: Varimax.

In the first step, the factorial structure of the RESTQ-Basic was analyzed. Two factors could be extracted with Eigenvalues of 6.42 (factor 1) and 1.49 (factor 2) explaining 65.83% of total variance [KMO = .90, $\chi^2_{(66)} = 5540.9$, $p < .001$].

One factor is a combination of all scales of the sub-dimensions *Social-Emotional Stress* and *Performance(-related) Stress*. Four scales of the sub-dimension *Overall Recovery* (*Success, Social Recovery, Physical Recovery, General Well-being*) build another factor. *Sleep Quality* shows a different factorial structure as it shares its factor loadings with both factors, having stronger factor loadings on the first, stress-relevant factor. The ambiguous role of *Sleep Quality* is also addressed by Kallus (this volume, Chapter 2).

In the second step, the work-specific scales were analyzed (Table 5.5). As the theoretical structure of the RESTQ-Work suggests four scales, the number of factors to be extracted was set to four in the work-specific part. Analyzing the Eigenvalues of the factorial solutions, three of four values are greater than one, whereas the fourth value is very close to the minimum threshold (.94).

Table 5.5 Factor loadings for the work-specific scales of the RESTQ-Work-92 (GW2).

	GW2			
	Factor			
RESTQ-Work scales	*1*	*2*	*3*	*4*
13 Emotional Exhaustion	−.53	.64		
14 Loss of Control		.74		
15 Loss of Meaning		.72		
16 Conflicts with Colleagues		.75		
17 Spillover		.69		
18 Undisturbed Leisure Time	.69			
19 Efficient Breaks	.81			
20 Leisure	.81			
21 Undisturbed Breaks	.79			
22 Social Support Friends				.79
23 Social Support Colleagues				.73
24 Participation			.85	
25 Personal Growth Factors			.88	
26 Action Latitude			.77	
Eigenvalue	5.57	2.02	1.46	0.94
Variance explained in %	39.80	14.40	10.40	6.70

Note: Factor loadings < .40 are suppressed in this table. Rotation method: Varimax.

The factor model showed four factors with Eigenvalues of 5.57 (factor 1), 2.02 (factor 2), 1.46 (factor 3), and 0.94 (factor 4) explaining 71.3% of total variance [KMO = .85, $\chi^2_{(91)} = 4945.3$, $p < .001$]. One factor is a combination of the five scales of the sub-dimension *Loss of Meaning/Burnout*. Another factor consists of the four scales of the sub-dimension *Leisure/Breaks* and the scale *Emotional Exhaustion*. The two scales of the sub-dimension *Psychosocial Recovery* build a third factor and the three scales of the sub-dimension *Work-related Recovery* load on another factor.[3]

Structural modelling

In the final stage, a Confirmatory Factor Analysis was performed to test the conceptual structure of the RESTQ-Work. The structural models were tested on scale basis with the GW2 data set. An overview of the structural models can be found in Table 5.6, the figures with the specific path coefficients can be obtained by the authors on request.

Table 5.6 Overview of χ^2-values, df, *p*-values and fit indices for the unmodified and modified measurement models on scale basis for all sub-dimensions of the RESTQ-Work-92 (GW2).

RESTQ-Work Sub-dimensions	χ^2	*df*	*p*	*AGFI*	*CFI*	*RMSEA*	*Modification*
Loss of Meaning/Burnout	55.98	5	.001	.91	.96	.12	
Loss of Meaning/Burnout with one modification	30.55	4	.001	.94	.98	.10	s13 ↔ s17
Leisure/Breaks	106.94	2	.001	.65	.93	.28	
Leisure/Breaks with one modification	1.99	1	.157	.99	.99	.04	s18 ↔ s20
Psychosocial Recovery	—	—	—	—	—	—	
Work-related Recovery	7.58	2	.023	.98	.99	.06	

Note: The sub-dimension *Psychosocial Recovery* consists of two scales, therefore a structural modelling calculated with maximum likelihood method of estimation is not reasonable.

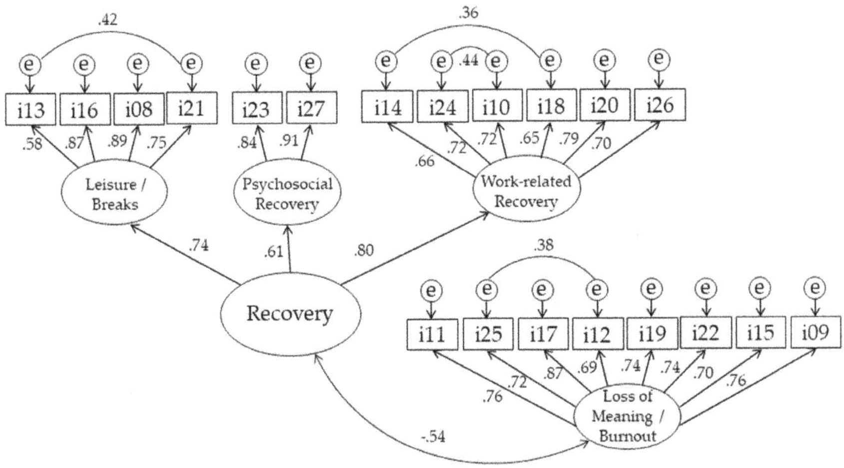

Figure 5.6 Modified model of the RESTQ-Work-27 on item basis with all regression coefficients; all regression coefficients significant with $p < .001$.

Finally, the conceptual model of the RESTQ-Work was tested by using data from the RESTQ-Work-27 data set (GW1). This means that the items are now used as the manifest variables instead of the scales. All sub-dimensions with their underlying items are combined into one main model (Figure 5.6).

Without any modifications the model shows an insufficient fit [$\chi^2_{(166)} = 1652.559$, $p < .001$; AGFI = .81, CFI = .89, RMSEA = .09; Hooper et al., 2008]. Four modifications were set, each of them a correlation between the measurement errors of items. Every correlation indicates the underlying scale. Correlations are as follows: i64 and i18 (… *I was able to make independent decisions* and … *I could decide myself how I perform my tasks*), i13 and i21 (… *I had time for my personal needs* and … *I had the possibility to recover and relax*), i25 and i12 (… *I felt burned out through my work* and … *I felt very exhausted*) as well as i10 and i24 (… *I contributed to important decisions* and … *I had the chance to make suggestions at work*). After these modifications, the model reached an acceptable fit [$\chi^2_{(162)} = 1061.206, p < .01$, AGFI = .88, CFI = .93, RMSEA = .07].

To analyze possible specificities between the scales of RESTQ-Work and RESTQ-Basic, both structural models were combined into one final model. The model shows an insufficient fit and even with additional error correlations between the measurement errors, a good fit is difficult to achieve. Thus, the model was not considered as satisfactory. Modelling stress and recovery/resources in one SEM was found to be close to impossible in other domains of the RESTQ-Work (Wagner-Hartl et al., this volume, Chapter 7).

Convergent and discriminant validity

Analyzing the discriminant validity between stress and recovery, the scales of the RESTQ-Work were intercorrelated (Table 5.7). The four scales of *Leisure/Breaks* and the stress-related scales are negatively related, showing moderate correlations ($r = -.20$ to $-.52$). The correlations between *Psychosocial Recovery* as well as *Work-related Recovery* with the stress-related scales are lower and often fail to reach significance. These results support the assumption that recovery cannot be seen as the opposite of stress and that both aspects can be regarded as separate constructs (Kellmann & Kallus, 2001). The scales related to stress show moderate to high intercorrelations ($r = .35$ to $.65$). High to moderate correlations can be seen between the four scales of the sub-dimension *Leisure/Breaks* ($r = .37$ to $.82$). A moderate correlation can be found when correlating the scales of *Psychosocial Recovery* ($r = .48$) and high correlations occur for the three scales of *Work-related Recovery* ($r = .63$ to $.68$).

Additional results on the RESTQ-Work

The concept of the recovery-stress balance at the workplace is discussed in detail in the publications of Bregenzer et al. (2022), Göttlicher et al. (2011), Jiménez (2012, 2013) as well as Jiménez and Dunkl (2017). Göttlicher et al. (2011) successfully combined volitional competences like self-regulation, self-determination, and self-motivation with the recovery-stress balance at the workplace. Reliability coefficients of older RESTQ-Work versions can be found in Jiménez and Kallus (2010), the concept and factorial structure was tested by Jiménez and Kallus (2005) as well as Langmann (2006).

Furthermore, the recovery-stress balance has been investigated with specific samples like self-employed workers (Jiménez & Kallus, 2011) or older workers

Table 5.7 Intercorrelations of the RESTQ-Work scales for the sample GW2 ($N=682$).

RESTQ-Work scales	*1*	*2*	*3*	*4*	*5*	*6*	*7*	*8*	*9*	*10*	*11*	*12*	*13*	*14*	*15*	*16*	*17*	*18*	*19*	*20*	*21*	*22*	*23*	*24*	*25*
1 General Stress																									
2 Emotional Stress	**.78**																								
3 Social Stress	**.71**	**.78**																							
4 Conflicts/Pressure	.58	.56	.50																						
5 Fatigue	.65	.56	.49	.52																					
6 Lack of Energy	.62	.59	.45	.51	.55																				
7 Physical Complaints	.63	.58	.44	.40	.64	.52																			
8 Success	−.23	−.23	−.11	.07	−.08	−.24	−.15																		
9 Social Recovery	−.39	−.38	−.31	−.27	−.27	−.23	−.30	.33																	
10 Physical Recovery	−.65	−.60	−.46	−.39	−.57	−.50	−.64	.42	.53																
11 General Well-being	−.63	−.61	−.47	−.36	−.41	−.45	−.49	.46	**.70**	**.79**															
12 Sleep Quality	−.62	−.54	−.41	−.44	−.61	−.51	−.64	.21	.39	.64	.57														

(*Continued*)

Table 5.7 (Continued)

RESTQ-Work scales	*1*	*2*	*3*	*4*	*5*	*6*	*7*	*8*	*9*	*10*	*11*	*12*	*13*	*14*	*15*	*16*	*17*	*18*	*19*	*20*	*21*	*22*	*23*	*24*	*25*
13 Emotional Exhaustion	.69	.58	.51	.45	**.73**	.56	**.72**	−.14	−.33	−.62	−.50	−.57													
14 Loss of Control	.55	.50	.49	.36	.41	.46	.36	−.26	−.22	−.38	−.37	−.34	.53												
15 Loss of Meaning	.61	.48	.51	.33	.44	.47	.39	−.28	−.28	−.47	−.45	−.39	.60	.65											
16 Conflicts with Colleagues	.39	.43	.51	.34	.29	.29	.22	−.02	−.09	−.20	−.22	−.23	.35	.49	.44										
17 Spillover	.51	.50	.47	.55	.47	.44	.34	−.05	−.29	−.39	−.37	−.40	.56	.43	.54	.40									
18 Undisturbed Leisure Time	−.37	−.33	−.29	−.37	−.46	−.31	−.33	−.05	.30	.30	.24	.24	−.47	−.29	−.26	−.14	−.37								
19 Efficient Breaks	−.45	−.40	−.35	−.37	−.45	−.35	−.38	.24	.42	.54	.50	.42	−.47	−.33	−.42	−.20	−.38	.37							
20 Leisure	−.52	−.44	−.39	−.41	−.51	−.38	−.41	.24	.57	.63	.59	.47	−.52	−.32	−.39	−.20	−.44	.55	.69						
21 Undisturbed Breaks	−.37	−.32	−.30	−.35	−.39	−.31	−.29	.15	.35	.43	.40	.35	−.41	−.30	−.36	−.21	−.34	.38	**.82**	.65					

(*Continued*)

Table 5.7 (Continued)

RESTQ-Work scales	*1*	*2*	*3*	*4*	*5*	*6*	*7*	*8*	*9*	*10*	*11*	*12*	*13*	*14*	*15*	*16*	*17*	*18*	*19*	*20*	*21*	*22*	*23*	*24*	*25*
22 Social Support Friends	−.25	−.21	−.19	−.11	−.15	−.15	−.17	.25	.44	.32	.38	.21	−.21	−.22	−.25	−.10	−.15	.14	.31	.33	.31				
23 Social Support Colleagues	−.31	−.28	−.30	−.20	−.20	−.17	−.15	.26	.36	.34	.42	.19	−.24	−.34	−.38	−.39	−.30	.14	.38	.40	.39	.48			
24 Participation	−.21	−.17	−.13	.05	−.13	−.16	−.14	.57	.21	.34	.33	.20	−.18	−.41	−.36	−.16	−.07	.02	.32	.25	.26	.29	.47		
25 Personal Growth Factors	−.28	−.21	−.20	.06	−.17	−.19	−.20	.59	.29	.44	.42	.27	−.21	−.35	−.41	−.11	−.02	.02	.36	.32	.28	.26	.40	.68	
26 Action Latitude	−.29	−.22	−.21	−.05	−.16	−.18	−.14	.43	.23	.37	.34	.27	−.19	−.37	−.36	−.28	−.12	.04	.31	.33	.30	.28	.43	.63	.62

Note: $r \geq .70$ are bolded.

(Jiménez et al., 2011). Gaisbachgrabner (2014) compared different samples of employees with long working hours and their individual recovery-stress balance. The findings indicated that workers with 20 hours overtime per week showed a significantly worse recovery-stress balance with very high stress and low recovery.

Also, different language versions have been developed and analyzed: Slovene (Dunkl et al., 2013), Spanish (Krüger, 2014), Croatian/Bosnian/Serbian (Suljagic, 2013), and Romanian (Weiß, 2007), as well as Portuguese and Turkish adaptations.[4]

How to apply the concept of the recovery-stress balance and the RESTQ-Work for practical purposes has been discussed: Lehofer et al. (2011) describe the application of the RESTQ-Work for individual diagnosis, especially for an early detection of burnout-risk. How to apply the RESTQ-Work for organizational, group, and individual diagnosis is stated by Jiménez and Kallus (2012); and the important combination of risk assessment and psychological stress has been published by Jiménez et al. (2014).

The RESTQ-Work can also be used as an evaluation tool for interventions. Dunkl et al. (2012) as well as Jiménez et al. (2013) evaluated the effects of anti-stress seminars. Next to seminars, different shift schedules have been analyzed with the RESTQ-Work regarding health-relevant outcomes (Jiménez, 2010).

Studies on different facets of validity

As the validity of the RESTQ-Basic is discussed by Kallus (this volume, Chapter 2) in the following only the validity results of the work-specific scales of the RESTQ-Work are depicted. Therefore, scale numbers start with 13, as the first twelve scales are not analyzed in this chapter. Validity analysis for the RESTQ-Work-27 is conducted on the sub-dimension level.

Psychophysiological criteria

To analyze the validity of the RESTQ-Work with psychophysiological criteria, the RESTQ-Work scales were correlated with the stress hormone cortisol. For this purpose, a study where 112 persons filled in the RESTQ-Work-92 and delivered their morning cortisol level (salvia) with the help of cotton buds was analyzed. The sample consisted of 50% men and 50% women; the mean age was 40 years ($M = 39.79$; $SD = 13.89$). Most of the participants worked full-time (77.3%), 11.6% worked 26–35 hours/week and 10.7% worked 12–25 hours/week. The correlations between the morning cortisol level and all scales of the RESTQ-Work-92 are non-significant and do not exceed $r = .12$.

Psychological measures

In the next step, the scales and sub-dimensions of the RESTQ-Work were correlated with other psychological questionnaires to test for criterion validity.

The Need for Recovery Scale (NFR; van Veldhoven & Broersen, 2003) measures the necessity for recovery after experiencing exhausting work and can be an (early) indicator for fatigue at work. The NFR was correlated with all scales to calculate criterion validity, but correlations with the recovery-related scales (scales 18–26) also indicate construct validity. For this analysis, 230 persons from the GW2 data set could be used (Table 5.8).

The short form of the General Health Survey (SF-12; Bullinger & Kirchberger, 1998) measures the physiological and mental health status. High scores indicate a better health status; 102 persons from the GW2 data set could be used for this analysis (Table 5.8).

The Work-Ability-Index (WAI; Tuomi et al., 1998) assesses the work ability for physical and mental work demands. A high index of the WAI indicates high work ability. For this analysis, 197 persons from the GW2 data set could be used (Table 5.8).

With the screening version of the Profile Analysis of Job Satisfaction (PAJS-SC; Jiménez, 2008), several aspects of job satisfaction are measured with 16 items and combined into one score of job satisfaction. The correlations were conducted with a sample of 1059 persons from the GW1 data set (Table 5.9).

Table 5.8 Pearson correlations between the RESTQ-Work and the Need for Recovery Scale (NFR), General Health Survey (SF-12), and Work-Ability-Index (WAI) in sample GW2.

RESTQ-Work scales	*NFR*	*SF-12 phys.*	*SF-12 ment.*	*WAI index*
13 Emotional Exhaustion	.64**	−.60**	−.37**	−.52**
14 Loss of Control	.45**	−.20*	−.41**	−.42**
15 Loss of Meaning	.48**	−.29**	−.34**	−.25*
16 Conflicts with Colleagues	.26**	−.17	−.25*	−.21
17 Spillover	.39**	−.22*	−.18	−.30**
18 Undisturbed Leisure Time	−.22*	.34**	.07	.12
19 Efficient Breaks	−.39**	.30**	.28**	.19
20 Leisure	−.38**	.42**	.34**	.17
21 Undisturbed Breaks	−.37**	.29**	.25*	.13
22 Social Support Friends	−.08	.10	−.06	−.09
23 Social Support Colleagues	−.22*	.18	.22*	.02
24 Participation	−.25**	.04	.19	.19
25 Personal Growth Factors	−.26**	.14	.22**	.19
26 Action Latitude	−.21*	.14	.20*	.19

Note: Sample sizes for the questionnaires are as follows, NFR ($N=230$), SF-12 ($N=102$), WAI ($N=197$), PJS ($N=280$), UWES ($N=205$); phys. = physical health; ment. = mental health; p-value: *: $.05 \geq p > .01$; **: $p < .01$.

Table 5.9 Pearson correlations between the RESTQ-Work and the Profile Analysis of Job Satisfaction (PJS), Utrecht Work Engagement Scale (UWES), and questionnaire to assess mental workload (OrgFit).

RESTQ-Work-27 Sub-dimensions	*PJS*	*UWES Vigor*	*UWES Dedication*	*UWES Absorption*	*OrgFit 1*	*OrgFit 2*	*OrgFit 3*	*OrgFit 4*
1 Social-Emotional Stress	−.45**	−.31**	−.20**	−.21**	.39**	.40**	.36**	.44**
2 Overall Recovery	.47**	.42**	.37**	.36**	−.22**	−.39**	−.20**	−.29**
3 Loss of Meaning/ Burnout	−.62**	−.43**	−.37**	−.34**	.46**	.52**	.45**	.55**
4 Leisure/ Breaks	.44**	.38**	.32**	.29**	−.34**	−.41**	−.28**	−.46**
5 Psychosocial Recovery	.39**	.33**	.39**	.35**	−.11**	−.46**	−.20**	−.21**
6 Work-related Recovery	.56**	.60**	.63**	.56**	−.22**	−.52**	−.26**	−.28**

Note: OrgFit 1 = *Work Activities and Tasks*, OrgFit 2 = *Organizational Climate*, OrgFit 3 = *Work Environment*, OrgFit 4 = *Work Flow and Organization*; the sub-dimension *Performance(-related) Stress* is not a part of the RESTQ-Work-27; *p*-value: *: $.05 \geq p > .01$; **: $p < .01$; sample sizes for the questionnaires are as follows, PJS (N = 1059), UWES (N = 411), OrgFit (N = 1219).

The Utrecht Work Engagement Scale (UWES; Schaufeli & Bakker, 2003) measures work engagement with three underlying sub-dimensions: *Vigor, Dedication*, and *Absorption*. The short form with nine items was used in this analysis, where 411 persons from the GW1 data set were used (Table 5.9).

The OrgFit (Jiménez & Dunkl, 2017) assesses mental workload at the workplace in line with international norms (e.g., ISO 10075-1, 2017) with 54 items. The items can be categorized in four dimensions, which reflect four different work characteristics: *Work Activities and Tasks, Organizational Climate, Work Environment*, and *Work Flow and Organization*; 1219 persons from the GW1 data set were used for the analysis (Table 5.9).

The Stress-Coping Inventory (SVF-48; Janke et al., 2002), consists of 48 items which can be categorized in eight scales: *Self-Aggrandizement by Comparison with Others, Distraction, Situation Control, Positive Self-Instructions, Need for Social Support, Escape, Rumination*, and *Resignation*. The first five scales can be combined into the dimension *Positive Coping Strategies* and the last three scales in the dimension *Negative Coping Strategies*. The correlations were conducted with a sample of 197 persons from the GW2 data set (Table 5.10).

Table 5.10 Pearson correlations between the RESTQ-Work and the Stress-Coping Inventory (SVF).

	SVF-scales							
RESTQ-Work scales	*1*	*2*	*3*	*4*	*5*	*6*	*7*	*8*
13 Emotional Exhaustion	−.20**	.06	−.15*	−.23**	.00	.34**	.34**	.40**
14 Loss of Control	−.15*	.03	−.21**	−.23**	−.05	.34**	.29**	.41**
15 Loss of Meaning	−.10	.09	−.22**	−.31**	−.07	.42**	.27**	.43**
16 Conflicts with Colleagues	.13	.14*	−.05	−.15*	−.14*	.20**	.09**	.18**
17 Spillover	−.25**	−.01	−.08	−.16*	.03	.25**	.46**	.33**
18 Undisturbed Leisure Time	.01	.04	−.02	−.07	.00	−.16*	−.19**	−.16
19 Efficient Breaks	.17*	.09	.17*	.20**	.02	−.19**	−.16*	−.21**
20 Leisure	.14*	.16*	.12	.16*	.08	−.26**	−.21**	−.24**
21 Undisturbed Breaks	.08	.03	.14*	.08	.04	−.14*	−.09	−.14*
22 Social Support Friends	−.03	.05	.17*	.16*	.34**	−.21**	−.10	−.24**
23 Social Support Colleagues	.04	−.01	.19**	.20**	.19	−.26**	−.10	−.23**
24 Participation	.27**	−.04	.33**	.26**	.03	−.35**	−.21**	−.35**
25 Personal Growth Factors	.20**	.02	.41**	.34**	.06	−.36**	−.15*	−.36**
26 Action Latitude	.07	−.04	.37**	.33**	.18**	−.31**	.00	−.34**

Note: 1 = *Self-Aggrandizement by Comparison with Others*, 2 = *Distraction*, 3 = *Situation Control*, 4 = *Positive Self-Instructions*, 5 = *Need for Social Support*, 6 = *Escape*, 7 = *Rumination*, 8 = *Resignation*; *p*-value: *: $.05 \geq p > .01$; **: $p < .01$.

Social criteria

To measure social criteria validity, the scales of the RESTQ-Work were correlated with the sub-dimensions of the Health-Promoting Leadership Conditions Questionnaire (HPLC; Jiménez et al., 2017). The HPLC measures the extent of health-promoting leadership conditions from the employees' side of view with seven sub-dimensions: *Health Awareness*, *Low Workload*, *Latitude*, *Reward*, *Community*, *Fairness*, and *Values*. The correlations in Table 5.12 were calculated with the GW1 data set, where 503 persons could be used for this analysis (Table 5.11).

Table 5.11 Pearson correlations between the RESTQ-Work and the Health-Promoting Leadership Conditions (HPLC).

	HPLC-scales						
RESTQ-Work-27 Sub-dimensions	*1*	*2*	*3*	*4*	*5*	*6*	*7*
1 Social-Emotional Stress	−.32**	−.33**	−.35**	−.35**	−.27**	−.33**	−.30**
2 Overall Recovery	.50**	.52**	.53**	.55**	.49**	.52**	.50**
3 Loss of Meaning/Burnout	−.41**	−.43**	−.48**	−.46**	−.37**	−.43**	−.40**
4 Leisure/Breaks	.45**	.55**	.50**	.43**	.42**	.47**	.45**
5 Psychosocial Recovery	.40**	.39**	.44**	.45**	.60**	.45**	.42**
6 Work-related Recovery	.47**	.45**	.61**	.57**	.49**	.53**	.57**

Note: The sub-dimension *Performance(-related) Stress* is not a part of the RESTQ-Work-27; 1 = *Health Awareness*, 2 = *Low Workload*, 3 = *Control*, 4 = *Reward*, 5 = *Community*, 6 = *Fairness*, 7 = *Value-fit*; *p*-value: *: $.05 \geq p > .01$; **: $p < .01$.

Other measures

Additionally, the scales of the RESTQ-Work were correlated with self-reported sickness absence and presentism data (Table 5.12).

The participants of the questionnaire were asked to report their sickness absence days in the last twelve months as well as their presenteeism days (going to work although being sick) in the last twelve months. For this analysis, 989 persons could be used from the GW1 data set.

Individual-specific diagnostic case study

As mentioned earlier, the RESTQ-Work allows a simultaneous, detailed assessment of work-specific stress and recovery on three different levels: organizational, group, and individual level (ISO, 2020b). This can be done with the

Table 5.12 Spearman's Rho correlations between the RESTQ-Work and self-reported sickness absence and presenteeism (sample GW1).

RESTQ-Work-27 Sub-dimensions	*Sickness absence (days)*	*Presentism (days)*
1 Social-Emotional Stress	.11**	.18**
2 Overall Recovery	−.09**	−.13**
3 Loss of Meaning/Burnout	.14**	.17**
4 Leisure/Breaks	−.10**	−.09**
5 Psychosocial Recovery	−.07*	−.03
6 Work-related Recovery	−.10**	−.02

Note: The sub-dimension *Performance(-related) Stress* is not a part of the RESTQ-Work-27; *p*-value: *: $.05 \geq p > .01$; **: $p < .01$.

three different versions (27, 55, and 92 items) and the use of scales, sub-dimensions, and screening scores (Figure 5.1). These values were obtained from various studies and can be used for comparisons with individual and organizational data. Reference values (means and standard deviations) for all versions of the RESTQ-Work can be seen in the Online Appendix A.D1–A.D4. In this chapter, the application for individual purposes is explained. The group and organizational assessment are described in the next chapter.

An individual diagnosis of the recovery-stress balance is possible, especially with the longest version of this instrument – the RESTQ-Work-92. The advantage of the long version is the in-depth examination of the actual working life. With the help of screening scores, sub-dimensions, and scales, the aspects of stress and recovery can be assessed in detail. This distinguishes the RESTQ-Work from other instruments that mostly only allow a rough assessment of the individual state. This detailed assessment in form of an individual profile can be used as a starting point for in-depth consultation and deriving interventions. This way of combining individual profile and feedback conversation has been tried and tested in the practical field and has proven to be successful. In Figure 5.7, an individual profile of person A is shown and compared to the Austrian norm sample. Person A filled-in the RESTQ-Work-92 and therefore individual values are compared to the norm values of the RESTQ-Work-92 (Austrian Norm Sample; depicted in the Online Appendix A.D3).

In the basic part (the upper part of the figure), person A shows higher values in six of seven stress-related scales compared to the Austrian norm sample, especially in *Lack of Energy*, and *Physical Complaints*. Differences can be also found for the recovery-related scales. Compared to the Austrian norm sample, person A has lower values in *Social Recovery*, *Physical Recovery*, *General Well-being*, and *Sleep Quality*.

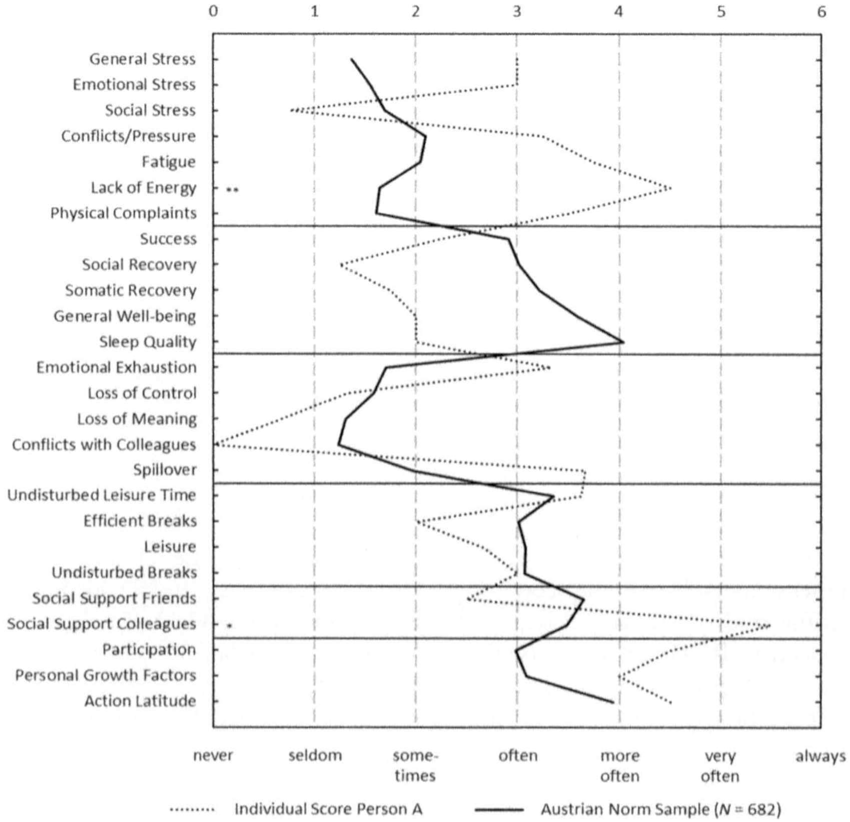

Figure 5.7 Individual recovery-stress profile compared with the Austrian Norm Sample (p-value: *: $.05 \geq p > .01$; **: $p < .01$).

Looking at the scales of the RESTQ-Work, a more detailed insight of stress and recovery at the workplace is obtained. Looking at work-specific stress, person A has lower values in *Loss of Control*, *Loss of Meaning*, and *Conflicts with Colleagues* but states that he/she feels more *Emotional Exhaustion* and experiences more *Spillover*. The recovery-related scales are not conspicuous, with the exception of *Efficient Breaks* and *Social Support Friends* which are lower than in the Austrian norm sample. Worth noting are high values in *Social Support Colleagues*, as well as in *Participation* and *Personal Growth Factors*.

This indicates that person A experiences high organizational resources, as he/she has possibilities to participate and use strengths and competences to accomplish the given tasks. Further, he/she experiences high social support from his/her coworkers. However, person A feels strong emotional exhaustion, and additionally states a lot of work-home spillover, few possibilities to spend his/her breaks in an efficient way and less support from family and friends. These aspects seem to be a crucial point and might be related to person A's higher stress profile. In an additional feedback conversation, this issue can be addressed. As this diagnosis is made with an individual person, the whole assessment process and the feedback must be done by an experienced psychologist (requirements of ISO 10075-3, 2004).

Application of the RESTQ-Work

On the organizational and group level, the RESTQ-Work can be used in typical employee surveys, for example, also in projects for the workplace health promotion; together with other instruments measuring work-specific aspects (e.g., job satisfaction, motivation/demotivation, turnover intention etc.). The results of the RESTQ-Work can be used with results of other organization-diagnostic methods to receive a more in-depth organizational assessment and further specifically derive prevention strategies for employees.

An example of using the RESTQ-Work in an employee survey is depicted in Figure 5.8.

In this example, a profile of company X is shown and compared to the Austrian norm sample. All-in-all 750 employees of company X filled in the RESTQ-Work-27. As the RESTQ-Work-27 allows interpretation on sub-dimension level, the mean values of all 750 employees were calculated for each sub-dimension. It should be mentioned that the sub-dimension *Performance (-related) Stress* is not part of the RESTQ-Work-27 and, therefore, not included in the figure. For a better readability and interpretability of the profile, the two stress-related sub-dimensions are depicted on the upper part, and the four recovery-related sub-dimensions are depicted on the lower part of the figure. The means of the sub-dimensions are compared to the Austrian norm sample for the RESTQ-Work-27. In Figure 5.8, company X shows higher values in both stress-related sub-dimensions (*Social-Emotional Stress* and *Loss of Meaning/Burnout*).

Looking at the recovery-related sub-dimensions, it is possible to interpret the recovery level for company X. The mean values for *Overall Recovery* and *Leisure/Breaks* are not conspicuous, indicating that the employees in company X show a good overall recovery and are able to take sufficient and undisturbed breaks during working-time and are able to spend their leisure time with non-work activities. In addition, the 330 employees in company X stated higher *Psycho-social Recovery* as well as *Work-related Recovery*. This means the employees experience a lot of possibilities for participation, personal growth factors at work and action latitude. In contrary to these valuable resources, the profile figure shows lower values in the sub-dimension *Leisure/Breaks*. This means that the employees experience fewer chances to recover during leisure time and have less opportunities to make health-promoting breaks. This area also points toward a lower work-family balance. These aspects should be considered when deriving organization-specific interventions for company X.

After deriving and implementing interventions, the RESTQ-Work can be used as an evaluation tool to assess work-specific stress and recovery after successfully establishing the intervention at the workplace. This brings us to another

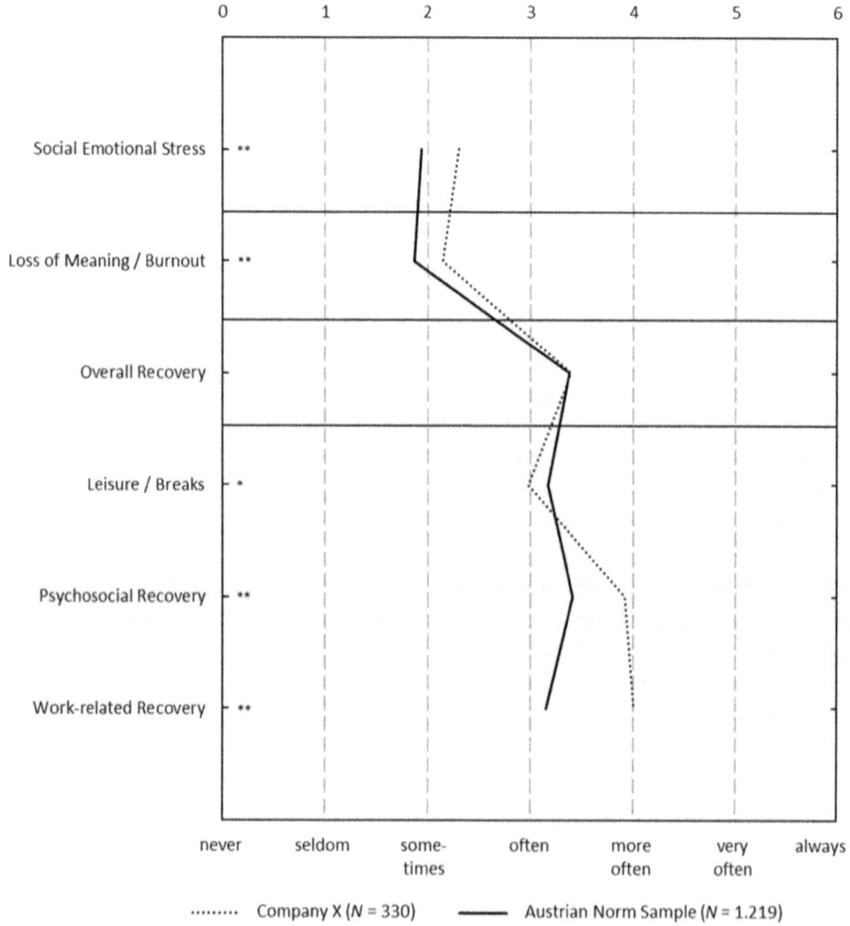

Figure 5.8 Aggregated recovery-stress profile of company X compared with the Austrian Norm Sample (p-value: *: $.05 \geq p > .01$; **: $p < .01$).

important field of application for the RESTQ-Work, as the RESTQ-Work is perfectly suitable for longitudinal designs. Asking about the *past (7) days/nights* the RESTQ-Work measures stress at a current state. This current state can be assessed again at a second measurement point and comparing these two measuring points indicate changes in the individual's recovery-stress balance.

Summary of the RESTQ-Work features

- Application areas of the RESTQ-Work include workplace health promotion evaluations, incident/accident prevention, and individual psychosocial counseling. The RESTQ-Work can be used successfully in psychosocial risk assessment in combination with instruments that measure psychosocial risks.

- The RESTQ-Work measures the recovery-stress balance at the workplace to receive a detailed profile about stress, recovery, and resources at the workplace, based on 12 basic and 14 work-specific scales.
- An assessment on the individual, group, and organizational level (ISO, 2020b) can be conducted with two different versions of the RESTQ-Work (27, and 92 items) and the interpretation of scales and sub-dimensions.
- The RESTQ-Work allows an assessment on three precision levels (ISO, 2004): level 1 – for accurate measurement purposes, level 2 – for screening purposes, and level 3 – for orientation purposes.
- With the results of the RESTQ-Work, specific interventions on individual and organizational level can be developed.
- On the individual level, the interventions can aim to change the individual's experience of stress and recovery strategies.
- On organizational and group level the results of the RESTQ-Work can be used to derive practical intervention and prevention activities.
- The RESTQ-Work has proven to be reliable and valid.
- The results of the latent structure measurement models and the structural equation modeling show acceptable to good fits for each sub-dimension in the RESTQ-Work.

Notes

1 Building the scores and presenting the feedback needs a careful preparation in the organization, especially in the context of risk assessment and workplace health promotion (Jiménez & Kallus, 2010; Jiménez et al., 2014).
2 The formula for Gutmann's Split-Half was used for scales with only two items.
3 In the three-factor-solution, the scales of *Psychosocial Resources* and *Work-related Resources* load on the same factor.
4 The different language versions are available upon request from the authors.

References

Bakker, A. B., Demerouti, E., & Euwema, C. M. (2005). Job resources buffer the impact of job demands on burnout. *Journal of Occupational Health Psychology, 10*(2), 170–180.

Bakker, A. B., Demerouti, E., & Sanz-Vergel, A. (2023). Job demands – Resources theory: Ten years later. *Annual Review of Organizational Psychology and Organizational Behavior, 10*(1), 25–53.

Bregenzer, A., Jiménez, P., & Milfelner, B. (2022). Appreciation at work and the effect on employees' presenteeism. *Work, 73*(1), 109–120.

Bullinger, M., & Kirchberger, I. (1998). *SF-36. Fragebogen zum Gesundheitszustand. Handanweisung* [SF-36. Health status questionnaire. User manual]. Hogrefe.

Chen, F., Bollen, K. A., Paxton, P., Curran, P. J., & Kirby, J. B. (2001). Improper solutions in structural equation models. *Sociological Methods & Research, 29*(4), 468–508.

Dunkl, A., Jiménez, P., Eibel, K., & Šarotar-Žižek, S. (2012, September 19). *Evaluation of three newly developed anti-stress programs in organizations: Results of a pilot study* [Conference session]. 1st Chance4Change International conference, Maribor, Slovenia. https://www.researchgate.net/publication/260024543_Evaluation_of_three_newly_developed_anti-stress_programs_in_organizations_-_results_of_a_pilot_study

Dunkl, A., Jiménez, P., & Šarotar-Žižek, S. (2013, June 19). *Cultural differences of the recovery-stress-balance of Austrian and Slovenian employees* [Conference session]. 2nd Chance4Change International conference, Maribor, Slovenia. https://www.researchgate.net/publication/260024305_Cultural_differences_of_the_recovery-stress-balance_of_Austrian_and_Slovenian_employees

EU Commission. (2008). *Directive 89/391/EEC – OSH "Framework Directive" of 12 June 1989 on the introduction of measures to encourage improvements in the safety and health of workers at work – "Framework Directive"*. Retrieved November 13, 2023 from https://eur-lex.europa.eu/legal-content/EN/ALL/?uri=CELEX:01989L0391-20081211

Evers, A., Muniz, J., Bartram, D., Boben, D., Egeland, J., Fernández-Hermida, J., Frans, Ö., Gintiliené, G., Hagemeister, C., Halama, P., Iliescu, D., Jaworowska, A., Jiménez, P., Manthouli, M., Matesic, K., Schittekatte, M., Sümer, H. C., & Urbánek, T. (2012). Testing practices in the 21st century. Developments and European psychologists' opinions. *European Psychologist*, *17*(4), 300–319.

Fernet, C., Guay, F., & Senécal, C. (2004). Adjusting to job demands: The role of work self-determination and job control in predicting burnout. *Journal of Vocational Behavior*, *65*(1), 39–56.

Gaisbachgrabner, K. (2014). *Empirische Untersuchungen zu langen Arbeitszeiten und dem Hypothalamus-Hypophysen-Schilddrüsen-System im Mehrebenenansatz* [Empirical studies on the effects of long working hours on the hypothalamus-pituitary-thyroid-system; Unpublished doctoral dissertation]. University of Graz, Austria.

Göttlicher, K., Jiménez, P., & Kallus, K. W. (2011, September 9). *Burnout prevention – A structural equation model of stress, recovery and volitional factors among IT professionals* [Conference session]. 7. Tagung der Fachgruppe Arbeits-, Organisations- und Wirtschaftspsychologie der Deutschen Gesellschaft für Psychologie, Rostock, Germany.

Hacker, W. (2003). Action regulation theory: A practical tool for the design of modern work processes? *European Journal of Work and Organizational Psychology*, *12*(2), 105–130.

Hahn, V. C., Binnewies, C., Sonnentag, S., & Mojza, E. J. (2011). Learning how to recover from job stress: Effects of a recovery training program on recovery, recovery-related self-efficacy, and well-being. *Journal of Occupational Health Psychology*, *16*(2), 202–216.

Halbesleben, J. R. B. (2006). Sources of social support and burnout: A meta-analytic test of the conservation of resources model. *The Journal of Applied Psychology*, *91*(5), 1134–1145.

Hooper, D., Coughlan, J., & Mullen, M. R. (2008). Structural equation modelling: Guidelines for determining model fit. *The Electronic Journal of Business Research Methods*, *6*(1), 53–60.

International Organisation for Standardization. (ISO). (2004). *ISO 10075-3. Ergonomic principles related to mental workload part 3: Principles and requirements concerning methods for measuring and assessing mental workload*. Retrieved April 22, 2024 from https://www.iso.org/standard/27571.html

International Organisation for Standardization. (ISO). (2017). *ISO 10075-1: Ergonomic principles related to mental work-load part 1: General terms and definitions*. Retrieved April 22, 2024 from https://www.iso.org/standard/66900.html

International Organisation for Standardization. (ISO). (2020a). *ISO 10667-1. Assessment service delivery – Procedures and methods to assess people in work and organizational settings – Part 1: Requirements for the client*. Retrieved April 22, 2024 from https://www.iso.org/standard/74716.html

International Organisation for Standardization. (ISO). (2020b). *ISO 10667-2. Assessment service delivery – Procedures and methods to assess people in work and organizational settings – Part 2: Requirements for service providers*. Retrieved April 22, 2024 from https://www.iso.org/standard/74717.html

Janke, W., Erdmann, G., & Kallus, K. W. (2002). *SVF-78. Eine Kurzform des Stressverarbeitungsfragebogens SVF-120* [SVF-78. A short version of the Stress-Coping-Inventory SVF-120]. Hogrefe.

Jett, Q. R., & George, J. M. (2003). Work interrupted: A closer look at the role of interruptions in organizational life. *Academy of Management Review*, *28*(3), 494–507.

Jiménez, P. (2008). *PAZ Profilanalyse der Arbeitszufriedenheit. Manual Wiener Testsystem* [Profile analysis of job satisfaction. Test manual in Vienna Test System]. Schuhfried GmbH.

Jiménez, P. (2010). Auswirkungen von Änderungen im Schichtplan auf die Work-Life-Balance der Mitarbeiter [Effects of changes in shift schedules on the employees' work-life balance]. In G. Zülch & P. Stock (Eds.), *Einfluss der Arbeitszeitgestaltung auf die Work-Life-Balance* (pp. 107–133). Karlsruher Institut für Technologie, Institut für Arbeitswissenschaft und Betriebsorganisation, Germany.

Jiménez, P. (2012). Präventionskonzepte zu Burnout aus arbeits- und organisationspsychologischer Sicht [Concepts for prevention of burnout from the view of work- and organizational psychology]. *Spectrum Psychiatrie*, *1*, 36–40.

Jiménez, P. (2013). Arbeits- und organisationspsychologische Aspekte der Burnoutprävention [Occupational and organisational psychological aspects of burnout prevention]. *Psychology of Everyday Activity*, *6*(1), 13–21.

Jiménez, P., Bregenzer, A., Leiter, M. P., & Magley, V. (2018). Psychometric properties of the German version of the workplace incivility scale and the instigated workplace incivility scale. *Swiss Journal of Psychology*, 77(4), 159–172.

Jiménez, P., & Dunkl, A. (2017). Assessment of psychosocial risks and mental stress at work: The development of the instrument OrgFit. *Journal of Ergonomics*, 7(1), 1–6.

Jiménez, P., Dunkl, A., & Eibel, K. (2013). Entwicklung und Evaluierung von Anti-Stress Programmen für den Erhalt bzw. die Verbesserung des Wohlbefindens von ArbeitnehmerInnen [Development and evaluation of anti-stress programmes to maintain and improve the well-being of workers]. In S. Šarotar Žižek, S. Treven, P. Jiménez, & A. Potočnik (Eds.), *Stressabbau als Mittel zur Sicherung des Wohlbefindens* (pp. 113–119). University of Maribor, Slovenia.

Jiménez, P., Dunkl, A., & Kallus, K. W. (2014). Assessing workload, strain and resources in the organization – An integrated perspective. In N. J. A. Andreou, A. Jain, D. Hollis, J. Hassard, & K. Teoh (Eds.), *Looking at the past – Planning for the future: Capitalizing on OHP multidisciplinarity. Book of proceedings* (p. 118). European Academy of Occupational Health Psychology.

Jiménez, P., Eibel, K., Kallus, K. W., & Hoffmann, P. (2011). *Stress and recovery in older workers – Specific effects of age and gender* [Conference session]. 15th Conference of the European Association of Work and Organizational Psychology, Maastricht, Netherlands.

Jiménez, P., & Kallus, K. W. (2005). Stress and recovery of social care professionals: Development of a screening version of the Recovery-Stress Questionnaire for Work. In C. Korunka, P. Hoffmann, & A. Büssing (Eds.), *Change and quality in human service work. Dedicated to the work of André Büssing* (Vol. 4, pp. 311–323). Rainer Hampp Verlag.

Jiménez, P., & Kallus, K. W. (2010). *Analysis of resources and strain at work: The Recovery-Stress Questionnaire for Work (RESTQ-Work). Versions for screening, organizational and individual recovery-strain-analysis* [Conference session]. 27th International Congress of Applied Psychology, Melbourne, Australia.

Jiménez, P., & Kallus, K. W. (2011). *UnternehmerInnen und Burnout – Eine Studie der Universität Graz mit der WK Steiermark* [Entrepreneurs and burnout – A study by the university of Graz with the Styrian chamber of commerce]. In M. Ebner, K. Langthaler, K. Neussl, H. Schützinger, & H. Stadlbauer (Eds.), *Anleitung zum Burnout! oder Wie UnternehmerInnen bei voller Fahrt auftanken* (pp. 201–205). dbv-Verlag.

Jiménez, P., & Kallus, K.W. (2012). *Belastungs-/Beanspruchungs-Ressourcen-Analyse in der Arbeit: Ein Evaluierungsinstrument für die Arbeitswelt. EBF-Work für Screening, Organisationsdiagnose und individuelle Belastungs-Beanspruchungsanalyse* [Stress/strain resource analysis at work: An evaluation tool for the world of work. RESTQ-Work for screening, organizational diagnosis and individual stress/strain analysis; Poster session]. 2. Tagung der AUVA Fokus Mensch im ArbeitnehmerInnenschutz, Wien, Austria.

Jiménez, P., Winkler, B., & Bregenzer, A. (2017). Developing sustainable workplaces with leadership: Feedback about organizational working conditions to support leaders in health-promoting behavior. *Sustainability*, *9*(11), 1944. https://doi.org/10.3390/su9111944

Kallus, K. W. (1995). *Der Erholungs-Belastungs-Fragebogen* [The Recovery-Stress Questionnaire]. Swets & Zeitlinger.

Karasek, R., & Theorell, T. (1990). *Healthy work: Stress, productivity, and the reconstruction of working life*. Basic Books.

Kellmann, M., & Kallus, K.W. (2001). *Recovery-Stress Questionnaire for Athletes: User manual*. Human Kinetics.

Krüger, E. (2014). *Gesundes Führen in unterschiedlichen Kulturen in Europa* [Healthy leadership in different cultures in Europe; Master's thesis]. University of Graz, Austria. https://unipub.uni-graz.at/obvugrhs/download/pdf/239886

Lambert, E. G., & Hogan, N. L. (2010). Work-family conflict and job burnout among correctional staff. *Psychological Reports*, *106*(1), 19–26.

Langmann, A. (2006). *Weiterentwicklung des Erholungs-Belastungsfragebogens für den arbeitsspezifischen Bereich (EBF-Work)* [Further development of the Recovery-Stress Questionnaire for the work-specific area (RESTQ-Work); Unpublished master's thesis]. University of Graz, Austria.

Lehofer, M., Glehr, R., Haring, C., Jiménez, P., Kaspar, S., Lalouschek, W., Marksteiner, J., Musalek, M., Sperner-Unterweger, B., Titscher, G., & Weiss, E. (2011). Burnout und Depression: Ein Leitfaden zur Prävention, Früherkennung und Behandlung [Burnout and depression: A guide to prevention, early diagnosis and treatment]. *Update – Internationale Zeitschrift für Ärztliche Fortbildung*, *21*(9), 1–12.

Leka, S., Jain, A., Cox, T., & Kortum, E. (2011). The development of the European framework for psychosocial risk management: Prima-ef. *Journal of Occupational Health*, *53*(2), 137–143.

Martín, P., Salanova, M., & Peiró, J. M. (2007). Job demands, job resources and individual innovation at work: Going beyond Karasek's model? *Psicothema*, *19*(4), 621–626.

Maslach, C., Schaufeli, W. B., & Leiter, M. P. (2001). Job burnout. *Annual Review of Psychology*, *52*, 397–422.

Nahrgang, J. D., Morgeson, F. P., & Hofmann, D. A. (2011). Safety at work: A meta-analytic investigation of the link between job demands, job resources, burnout, engagement, and safety outcomes. *The Journal of Applied Psychology*, *96*(1), 71–94.

Österreichisches Normungsinstitut. (2017). *ÖNORM D 4000. Anforderungen an Prozesse und Methoden in der Personalauswahl und -entwicklung* [ÖNORM D 4000. Requirements for processes and methods in personnel selection and development].

Otero-López, J., Santiago Marino, M. J., & Bolano, C. C. (2008). An integrating approach to the study of burnout in university professors. *Psicothema*, *20*(4), 766–772.

Rupert, P. A., Stevanovic, P., & Hunley, H. A. (2009). Work-family conflict and burnout among practicing psychologists. *Professional Psychology: Research and Practice*, *40*(1), 54–61.

Schaufeli, W. B., & Bakker, A. B. (2003). *UWES Utrecht Work Engagement Scale: Manual*. Utrecht University, Netherlands.

Sonnentag, S. (2001). Work, recovery activities, and individual well-being: A diary study. *Journal of Occupational Health Psychology*, *6*(3), 196–210.

Suljagic, E. (2013). *Überprüfung der Gütekriterien einer BKS-Version des DSB-WS (Dynamic Sequences of Behavior)* [Checking the quality criteria of a bks version of the dsb-ws (dynamic sequences of behaviour); Master's thesis]. University of Graz, Austria. https://unipub.uni-graz.at/obvugrhs/download/pdf/226640

Tuomi, K., Ilmarinen, J., Jahkola, A., Katajarinne, L., & Tullki, A. (1998). *Work Ability Index*. Finnish Institute of Occupational Health.

van Veldhoven, M., & Broersen, S. (2003). Measurement quality and validity of the "need for recovery scale". *Occupational and Environmental Medicine*, *60*(Suppl. 1), i3–9.

Varhama, L. M., & Björkqvist, K. (2004). Conflicts, workplace bullying and burnout problems among municipal employees. *Psychological Reports*, *94*, 1116–1124.

Weiß, R. (2007). *Erholungs-Belastungs-Fragebogen für den arbeitsspezifischen Bereich (EBF-Work-95/7). Rumänische Version. Testtheoretische* Überprüfung *und Validierung* [Recovery-Stress Questionnaire for Work (RESTQ-Work-95/7). Romanian version. Test-theoretical examination and validation; Unpublished master's thesis]. University of Graz, Austria.

6 Recovery-Stress Questionnaire for Children and Adolescents

Petra Hampel and K. Wolfgang Kallus

Scope and application

Recovery is important in the psychological adjustment to stressful demands among adolescents, which can be measured by the Recovery-Stress Questionnaire for Children and Adolescents (RESTQ-CA). Similar to the RESTQ for adults, this instrument enables the assessment of more stable processes instead of less intense and short accelerating state variations. Thus, unfavorable scores of the recovery-stress balance reflect maladaptive psychological adjustment and suggest that the individual should be allocated to health-promoting interventions or conditions.

The RESTQ-CA is designed for children and adolescents aged from 10 to 14 years and can be filled out in single or group settings. It is a well-defined tool to identify the current recovery-stress balance, and with the determination of change scores it is also possible to evaluate treatment effects.

Facets of stress and recovery among adolescents: Theory of the age-adapted modifications

Previous research has shown that adolescence is characterized by a high increase in stress (Anniko et al., 2019; Hampel, 2007; Seiffge-Krenke, 2000; for a review, see Zimmer-Gembeck & Skinner, 2011). More specifically, adaptation in early and middle adolescence is challenged by an enhancement of developmental tasks as well as normative stressors (Seiffge-Krenke, 2000). Further results have indicated that parent- and school-related stress is perceived more stressful than peer- and romance-related stress among a cross-cultural adolescent sample (Persike & Seiffge-Krenke, 2012). Further studies have demonstrated that interpersonal stressors especially increase during adolescence (Hampel & Petermann, 2006). These interpersonal stressors have been shown to be related strongly with emotional and behavioural problems (for reviews, see Erath & Pettit, 2021; Seiffge-Krenke,

Hampel, P., & Kallus, K. W. (2025). Recovery-Stress Questionnaire for Children and Adolescents. In M. Kellmann & K. W. Kallus (Eds.), *The Recovery-Stress Questionnaires: A User Manual* (pp. 206–225). Routledge.

DOI: 10.4324/9781032643380-6

2011). However, Persike and Seiffge-Krenke (2012) have found that most of the middle and late adolescents coped adaptively with stressors, but maladaptive coping responses accounted for one-fifth of the adolescents' reports. Accordingly, further research has provided some evidence that internal resources, such as coping, self-efficacy, and recovery competence are significant moderators and mediators in the relationship between stressors and psychological adjustment (Anniko et al., 2019; Calvete & Orue, 2012; Calvete et al., 2011; Hampel & Pössel, 2012; Persike & Seiffge-Krenke, 2012; for an overview, see Kellmann & Beckmann, 2022, 2024; Kellmann et al., 2023), which are described briefly below.

Coping

As mentioned by Kellmann and Kallus (this volume, Chapter 1), coping is defined as a set of action-oriented and intrapsychic efforts to manage environmental and internal demands, which are appraised to tax or exceed a person's resources (Lazarus & Launier, 1978). A more current approach describes coping as a subset of broader self-regulatory processes and defines coping as "regulatory efforts that are volitionally and intentionally enacted specifically in response to stress" (Compas et al., 2001, p. 89; Compas et al., 2017). In the past, a dichotomized concept of coping strategies was preferred (Compas et al., 2001, 2017), distinguishing more direct coping modes (i.e., problem-focused, primary control, or approach coping), which consist of strategies directed toward modifying the stressful encounter or individual goals, from more indirect coping efforts (i.e., emotion-focused, secondary control, or avoidance coping). Indirect efforts comprise strategies directed toward regulating stress-related negative emotions. To overcome a confounding of adaptive and maladaptive coping strategies, a three-dimensional concept has been established, in which two adaptive coping styles, such as emotion-focused or support seeking and problem-focused or active coping, are differentiated from a maladaptive coping style (Connor-Smith & Compas, 2002; Hampel & Petermann, 2005; Seiffge-Krenke, 2000). Overall, consistent results were found for internalizing symptoms, which are related to maladaptive (or disengagement) coping strategies such as worrying, resignation, (social) avoidance, and aggression (Hampel & Petermann, 2006; Zammuner, 2019; for a review, see Aldao et al., 2010). In a more current meta-analytic study on coping, emotion regulation, and psychopathology among children and adolescents, this association was replicated, showing a medium effect size (Compas et al., 2017). Finally, this meta-analysis found medium negative associations for emotion regulation with both internalizing and externalizing symptoms.

Although adolescence is characterized by a greater diversity and flexibility in coping abilities (Persike & Seiffge-Krenke, 2012), some results pointed to age-related curvilinear trends of maladaptive coping during early and middle adolescence compared to childhood and late adolescence. Thus, adolescents aged 11–15 years showed higher levels of maladaptive coping strategies, such as resignation, rumination, aggression, avoidance, and lower levels of adaptive strategies like distraction and seeking for social support than primary school children and late adolescents (Hampel, 2007; Hampel & Pössel, 2012; for a review, see Zimmer-Gembeck & Skinner, 2011). Furthermore, a decline in adaptive coping strategies was reported by Vierhaus et al. (2007), who conducted a cohort-sequential design. Finally, a cross-sectional study found decreased adaptive coping strategies (distraction, positive self-instructions, situation control, and social support seeking) in ninth graders compared to fourth graders (Hampel & Petermann, 2017). Regarding gender differences, girls predominantly employ social support and maladaptive coping strategies, such as emotional venting, rumination, resignation, and avoidance (Calvete et al., 2011; Hampel & Petermann, 2005, 2006, 2017). Maladaptive ruminative coping has been shown to be a major risk factor in the development of internalizing problems (Jose & Brown, 2008). Finally, Vierhaus et al. (2007) provided results on increasing age differences in externalizing coping with continuously enhancing scores among boys. Externalizing coping has been found to be associated with externalizing problems in further studies (Calvete & Orue, 2012; Compas et al., 1993). Thus, boys in mid-adolescence are prone to develop externalizing behaviour problems. To summarize, interaction effects of age and gender suggest that girls are high at risk for psychosocial maladjustment during the transition from childhood to early adolescence while boys' vulnerable phase seems to be during the transition from early to late adolescence (Jose & Brown, 2008; Seiffge-Krenke, 2000).

Recovery competence

Although some authors mentioned that the stress process can be explained merely comprehensively by the consideration of the recovery process (Kallus, 2002; Kellmann & Kallus, this volume, Chapter 1; Kellmann & Beckmann, 2022, 2024; Kellmann et al., 2023), effects of the recovery-stress balance on psychological adjustment among adolescents have been neglected in earlier research. As mentioned by Kellmann and Kallus (this volume, Chapter 1), "recovery is described as a stress-regulating factor and health-promoting resource" (Allmer, 1996, p. 76; translation by the authors). Furthermore, Allmer emphasized that an ineffective use and the non-availability of recovery-relevant resources have adverse effects on the adjustment to stressful situations and may impair the health status. Therefore, recovery can be defined as a protective factor in the healthy development. In contrast, if recovery is not employed after dealing with stressful situations, chronic stress effects can be assumed. Studies on athletes have found that a negative recovery-stress balance was associated with lower psychological well-being, motivational state, and performance, but related to psychological and physical strain symptoms (Kallus, 2002). Moreover, higher levels of physical recovery were correlated with higher scores on self-efficacy among adult athletes (Kellmann & Kallus, 2001).

Self-efficacy

Self-efficacy is the central construct of Bandura's (1977) *Social Cognitive Theory* and refers to the individual's expectancy of having the competence to master new or demanding situations. In the current literature, a general concept of perceived self-efficacy is differentiated from domain-specific self-efficacy beliefs. According to Luszczynska et al. (2005, p. 440), general self-efficacy is a basic belief and "reflects to a broad and stable sense of personal competence to deal effectively with a variety of stressful situations". In contrast, the domain-specific construct 'academic self-efficacy' represents the perceived capability to master school-related demands, whereas 'social self-efficacy' consists of beliefs in their capabilities, which are associated with peer relationships (Bandura et al., 1999; Muris, 2002; Satow & Schwarzer, 2003).

Self-efficacy has been shown to be a significant protective factor against the development of internalizing problems in adolescence (Bandura et al., 1999; Muris, 2002). Herman-Stahl and Petersen (1999) have found that self-efficacy beliefs buffer adverse effects of negative life stress on depressive symptoms. Developmental differences suggest an age-related increase in social self-efficacy. A two-year longitudinal study of academic self-efficacy revealed that it levelled off among middle and late adolescents (Satow & Schwarzer, 2003). Regarding gender differences, this study yielded that girls scored lower on social and boys on academic self-efficacy. Luszczynska et al. (2005) found that adolescent girls are prone to develop physical and mental malfunctioning due to their low general self-efficacy, which mediates negative emotions and abolishes the endorsement of adaptive coping strategies. Furthermore, results with significant clinical relevance provided by Pössel et al. (2005) suggest that self-efficacy moderates essentially the effectiveness of prevention programs. These authors found that adolescents with low general self-efficacy improved more from their universal preventive program than students with high self-efficacy.

Scale and item construction

Earlier versions of the RESTQ-CA were developed to adapt the adult version to adolescents. Table 6.1 summarizes the sample characteristics and important aspects of earlier versions, without mentioning the first version of the measure, which was modified for the application in sample GA1 (Amtmann, 2004; Veit, 2004). Thus, three main versions were tested to develop the last version; the RESTQ-CA-40 (Kallus et al., 2005).

All existing versions consist of two parts; first, a basic part with items, which are assessing school-unspecific stress and recovery. Second, school-specific parts, by which school-related aspects in the stress and recovery processes are detected. Related to the seven or five days and nights of the last week, adolescents have to rate their perceived stress and recovery on a seven-point frequency scale (0 = *never*, 6 = *always*).

Samples GA1 and GA2: Characteristics, design, reliability, and validity

Methods

Sample and design. In sample GA1, N = 162 students were included in a school-based intervention study (Amtmann, 2004; Veit, 2004; Table 6.1), which attended the fifth to seventh class level of an intermediate secondary school in rural areas of Graz, Austria. A within-subjects design with three counter-balanced treatment conditions was realized, delivering physical activity combined with relaxation, cognitive-behavioral stress management training, and face-to face coaching. The experimental group consisted of n = 64 and the untreated control group comprised n = 68 adolescents. Questionnaires were filled out by students of the experimental group at six measurement points; before and after each of the three treatment conditions. Assessments of the control group were conducted at the same time.

Additionally, in the cross-sectional pilot study by Missenböck (2003), N = 119 students were included (Table 6.1), which attended a secondary general school in rural areas of Graz, Austria. A three-factorial design was applied; the first factor was represented by the type of school (general vs. sport-specific school),

Table 6.1 Research samples used to test the validity and reliability of the RESTQ-CA.

	GA1	*GA2*	*GA3*	*GA4*
Author/ year	Amtmann (2004) and Veit (2004)	Missenböck (2003)	Kümmel et al. (2008)	Hampel et al. (2009)
Sample size	N = 162	N = 119	N = 202	N = 320
Gender distribution	Male = 84 Female = 87	Male = 62 Female = 57	Male = 112 Female = 90	Male = 160 Female = 160
Sample	Students	Students	Students	Students
Age	M = 13.10 SD = 1.00 R = 11–15	M = 13.03 SD = 1.03 R = 11–15	M = 12.80 SD = 0.66 R = 12–14	M = 11.70 SD = 1.18 R = 10–14
RESTQ-version	RESTQ-CA-39	RESTQ-CA-39	RESTQ-CA-26	RESTQ-CA-40
Time frame	7 days/nights	7 days/nights	5 days/nights	7 days/nights
Measurements	6	1	2	3
Instruments	RESTQ-CA, SCI-CA	RESTQ-CA, SCI-CA	RESTQ-CA, SCI-CA, Self-Efficacy	RESTQ-CA, SCI-CA, Self-Efficacy

Note: N = Sample size; R = Range; M = Mean; SD = Standard deviation; SCI-CA = German Stress Coping Inventory for Children and Adolescents; RESTQ-CA = Recovery-Stress Questionnaire for Children and Adolescents.

the second factor comprised of gender (male vs. female), and the third factor included the class (sixth, seventh, vs. eighth class).

Measures. The RESTQ-CA-39 consisted of 39 items; for the basic part, seven scales represented aspects of stress (*General Stress, Emotional Stress, Social Stress, Conflicts/Pressure, Fatigue, Lack of Energy, Physical Complaints*), five scales assessed aspects of recovery (*Success, Social Recovery, Physical Recovery, General Well-being, Sleep Quality*). Regarding the school-specific part, the scales of *Disturbed Breaks, School-related Emotional Exhaustion*, and *Leisure Stress* measured school-specific stress and scales of *School-related Self-Efficacy* and *Self-Regulation* school-specific recovery. The scale of *General Stress* consisted of three items; all other scales were represented by two items (Table 6.2).

In addition, coping was assessed by the German Stress Coping Inventory for Children and Adolescents (SCI-CA; Hampel & Petermann, 2005). Emotion-focused coping was measured by the scales of *Minimization* and *Distraction/Recreation*; problem-focused coping was represented by *Situation Control, Positive Self-Instructions*, and *Social Support*; finally, maladaptive coping was assessed by *Passive Avoidance, Rumination, Resignation*, and *Aggression*. All coping responses had to be answered in relation to two individually generated common stressors: interpersonal and academic stressors.

Item and scale statistics: Reliability

Item and scale analysis yielded sufficient internal consistencies in most scales of sample GA1 and GA2; Cronbach's α coefficients for scales of stress and recovery varied from .34 to .83 (Table 6.2).

Further results on criterion-oriented validity: Intervention effects

Although statistical intervention effects could not be ascertained for sample GA1, first results pointed to the effectiveness of the face-to-face coaching, particularly in boys of the sixth class.

In summary, sufficient reliability has been shown in general and first hints for the sensitivity to change of the RESTQ-CA-39 could be gained. However, at that time, more data had to be collected for other psychometric measures.

Further results on construct validity: Discriminant validity with respect to coping measures and effects of gender and age

Discriminant validity was approved in general for sample GA2, since scales of the RESTQ-CA did not correlate substantially with scales of the SCI-CA. More specifically, analysis of correlations yielded a single moderate correlation; more school-specific recovery was moderately associated with higher scores on positive self-instructions ($r = .52$).

Table 6.2 Estimation of reliability (Cronbach's α) and number of items for the RESTQ-CA-39 for the samples GA1 and GA2.

Variable (items)	*Cronbach's α* GA1	GA2
General Stress (3i)	.70	.67
Emotional Stress (2i)	.72	.62
Social Stress (2i)	.61	.56
Conflicts (2i)	.55	.49
Fatigue (2i)	.72	.77
Lack of Energy (2i)	.78	.69
Physical Complaints (2i)	.62	.58
Success (2i)	.34	.59
Social Recovery (2i)	.62	.69
Physical Recovery (2i)	.36	.58
General Well-being (2i)	.71	.72
Sleep Quality (2i)	.46	.39
Disturbed Breaks (2i)	.83	.71
School-related Emotional Exhaustion (2i)	.59	.72
Leisure Stress (2i)	.46	.46
School-related Self-Efficacy (2i)	.79	.69
Self-Regulation (2i)	.52	.42

Multivariate analysis of variances (ANOVAs) carried out for three general dimensions and two school-specific dimensions for sample GA2 yielded gender main effects for general stress and recovery. Post-hoc performed univariate ANOVA revealed a gender main effect for *Emotional Stress*, *Physical Recovery*, and *Sleep Quality*, respectively. Girls scored higher on *Emotional Stress* [$F_{(1,107)} = 3.91$, $p = .051, \eta^2 = .035$], but lower on *Physical Recovery* [$F_{(1,107)} = 15.64, p \leq .001, \eta^2 = .128$], and *Sleep Quality* [$F_{(1,107)} = 6.42, p = .013, \eta^2 = .057$].

In summary, sufficient internal consistency and validity have been shown in general, but insufficient internal consistency below $\alpha = .50$ for both samples has been demonstrated for *Sleep Quality* and *Leisure Stress.*

Sample GA3: Sample characteristics, design, reliability, and validity

To collect more data on criterion-oriented validity of the RESTQ-CA, an intervention study was conducted by Kümmel et al. (2008). As schools required decreasing time of assessment, a short form of the RESTQ-CA was designed.

Methods

Sample and design. In total, $N = 202$ students took part in the intervention study by Kümmel et al. (2008; Table 6.1), which attended the seventh or eighth class of a secondary general school in rural areas of Graz, Austria. A three-factorial design was conducted; the first factor was operationalized by the experimental condition (intervention vs. control group), the second factor was represented by gender (male vs. female), and the third factor involved the within-subjects factor with two sample points (pre- vs. post-treatment). The experimental group ($n = 91$) participated at a summer camp with a duration of five days and was compared to an untreated control group ($n = 111$).

Measures. The RESTQ-CA version GA3 consisted of 26 items, assessing general aspects of stress and recovery; six scales represented aspects of stress (*General Stress, Emotional Stress, Social Stress, Fatigue, Lack of Energy, Physical Complaints*) and three scales measured aspects of recovery (*Social Recovery, Physical Recovery, General Well-being*). The scale of *General Stress* consisted of three items; all other scales were represented by two items.

Item and scale statistics: Reliability

Item and scale analysis yielded sufficient internal consistencies; Cronbach's α coefficient for *Overall Stress* (global score for stress) and *Overall Recovery* (global score for recovery) was .84 and .73, respectively. Furthermore, internal consistencies of scales varied from .61 to .72.

Further results on criterion-oriented validity: Intervention effects

Significant time by treatment effects were ascertained by multivariate repeated-measures ANOVA with post-hoc performed univariate ANOVAs; in the intervention group, *Social Recovery* and *General Well-being* were increased after treatment in comparison with baseline. Moreover, at the post-treatment assessment recovery scores in the intervention group were enhanced compared to those in the control group.

In summary, further results on intervention effects supported the criterion-oriented validity. However, internal consistency coefficients about .60 provides support to the assumption that the number of items per scale should be increased. Based on these results, in the consecutive study with sample GA4, the RESTQ-CA was optimized by scales, which were operationalized by four items each.

Reliability and validity of the RESTQ-CA-40

Sample and designs

Psychometric properties of the last version of the RESTQ-CA were investigated within a non-randomized control group study (Hampel et al., 2008, 2009). In total, $N = 320$ students at secondary general schools in rural areas of Graz,

Austria were examined, which attended the fifth to eighth class (Table 6.1). In this study, a four-factorial design with three between-subjects factors and one within-subjects factor was realized. The first factor was operationalized by the experimental condition (intervention vs. control group), the second factor was represented by gender (male vs. female), the third factor was operationalized by the age group (5th/6th vs. 7th/8th class), and the fourth factor comprised three sample points (pre, post, vs. three-month follow-up assessment). The experimental group participated in a stress management training with elements of experiential education (n = 138) and was compared to the untreated control group (n = 182). The experimental treatment was designed as a universal prevention program lasting six weeks and was aimed to improve the internal resources stress management, recovery-stress balance, and self-efficacy.

Internal consistency and construct validity scores were determined at the first sample point and sensitivity to change was examined by time effects, each was aggregated across both experimental conditions. Finally, test-retest-reliability was calculated using data collected from the untreated control group only.

Scores

The RESTQ-CA-40 included four scales measuring stress (*General Stress, Emotional Stress, Social Stress, Fatigue*) and four scales assessing recovery (*Social Recovery, Physical Recovery, General Well-being, Sleep Quality*; Table 6.3).

Regarding the school-specific part, *School-related Emotional Exhaustion* and *School-related Self-Efficacy* were applied. The ten scales were represented by four items each. Online Appendix A.E1 contains an item listing of mean, standard deviation, and corrected item total correlation of the RESTQ-CA for the sample GA4.

As with the adult versions of the RESTQ, the version for children and adolescents includes a warm-up item that is not included in the analysis. A Likert-type scale was used with values ranging from 0 (*never*) to 6 (*always*) indicating how often the respondent participated in various activities in the *past (7) days/nights*. Scoring of the RESTQ-CA-40 was performed as follows; at first, as item 8 ... *my sleep was interrupted easily* was inversely worded, raw scores have to be inverted (6 minus item value = raw item score; e.g., 6 → 0; 5 → 1; 4 → 2; 3 = 3; 2 → 4; 1 → 5; 0 → 6). Afterwards, each response was assigned to raw scores of 0 (*never*) to 6 (*always*), summed up across all items, and divided by four. Thus, range of scales is between 0 and 6. In addition, the scales in the area of stress (*General Stress, Emotional Stress, Social Stress, Fatigue*) can be summarized in an *Overall Stress* scale. Correspondingly, a score for *Overall Recovery* can be formed from the recovery-related scales (*Social Recovery, Physical Recovery, General Well-being, Sleep Quality*). As in the adult versions, high scores in the stress-associated activity scales reflect intense subjective stress and high scores in the recovery-oriented scales represent plenty of recovery activities.

Moreover, coping was assessed by the SCI-CA (Hampel & Petermann, 2005). Incongruent with the original version of the SCI-CA, coping responses had to be answered in relation to interpersonal stressors only. Based on previous studies,

Table 6.3 Scales of the RESTQ-CA-40.

Number	*Scale* *Summary*
1	***General Stress*** Subjects with high values describe themselves as being frequently mentally stressed, depressed, unbalanced, and listless.
2	***Emotional Stress*** Subjects with high values experience mood oriented frequent irritation, aggression, anxieties and restraints or loneliness.
3	***Social Stress*** High values match subjects with frequent arguments, fights, irritation concerning others, being upset, and lack of humor.
4	***Fatigue*** Time pressure in school and life, overfatigue, and lack of sleep characterize this area of stress.
5	***Social Recovery*** High values are reached by frequent pleasurable social contacts and change combined with relaxation and amusement.
6	***Physical Recovery*** Physical recovery, physical well-being, and fitness are characterized in this area.
7	***General Well-being*** Besides frequent good moods and high well-being, general relaxation and being content are also in this scale.
8	***Sleep Quality*** Enough and satisfying sleep, and no sleeping disorders while falling asleep and sleeping through the night characterize recovery sleep.
9	***School-related Emotional Exhaustion*** High scores are reached by adolescents who feel burned out and want to quit their school.
10	***School-related Self-Efficacy*** This scale is characterized by how convinced the adolescent is that he/she has learned well and is optimally prepared.

which found that interpersonal stressors are the most salient stressors for children and adolescents (Clarke, 2006), evaluation of coping responses related to academic stressors was omitted in this study.

Finally, general self-efficacy was assessed by a 10-item scale developed by Schwarzer and Jerusalem (1999) as well as Jerusalem and Mittag (1995). Students were asked to evaluate their self-efficacy on a 4-point Likert scale (1 = *I do not agree*, 4 = *I totally agree*).

Reference values

Online Appendix A.E2 provides reference values from sample GA4 which are split by age and gender due to the large gender-dependent intergroup differences in adolescents. However, computation of deviations from the reference values should be based on overall scores for GA4 ($N = 320$).

Analysis

Descriptive data were used for item and scale statistics. Internal consistency was determined by analysis of reliability, resulting in Cronbach's α coefficients and corrected item-scale correlations [$r_{(i;t-i)}$].

Factorial validity was examined by Principal Component Analysis with Varimax rotation. Extraction of factors was defined by two criteria; the Kaiser-Guttman criterion and inspection of the scree plot. Intercorrelations of scales and associations of the RESTQ-CA-40 were obtained by Pearson-Product-Moment correlations.

Construct validity was determined by age and gender main effects provided by ANOVA; performing three two-way multivariate ANOVAs with post-hoc derived univariate ANOVAs; for general stress, recovery, and the school-specific dimension. To investigate the criterion-oriented validity, sensitivity to change was calculated using three three-way multivariate repeated measures ANOVAs with post-hoc derived univariate repeated measures ANOVAs.

With regard to multiple tests, the alpha level of both sets of multivariate and univariate repeated measures ANOVAs was corrected using the Bonferroni procedure [$p < .05/3$ ($p < .016$)]. To identify dependent and independent mean differences, pairwise comparisons by *t*-Test were conducted with $p < .05$.

Reliability measures: Item and scale statistics

Table 6.4 shows sufficient to good internal consistencies and corrected item-scale correlations for most of the scales. Furthermore, test-retest reliability scores, ranging from $.64 \le r_{tt} \le .87$ indicated sufficient stability. Psychometric properties for both dimensions were also good, but one item of the scale *Sleep Quality* showed an insufficient corrected item-scale correlation [i.e., $r_{(i;t-i)} = .20$]. However, elimination of this item did not change the Cronbach's α coefficient; thus, this item was not excluded from this dimension and scale.

Construct validity of the RESTQ-CA-40

For the RESTQ-CA correlative validities and Exploratory Factor Analysis will be reported. Structural modelling was not applied to the data sets.

Correlative validity: Scale intercorrelations

Table 6.5 presents intercorrelations of all scales of the RESTQ-CA-40, indicating that scales of general stress were strongly interrelated. Likewise, all recovery scales were associated. Nevertheless, sufficient discriminant validity

Table 6.4 Means (*M*), standard deviations (*SD*), mean inter-item correlations (r_{ic}), internal consistencies (Cronbach's α), six-weeks-retest reliabilities (r_{tt}) and variations of corrected item-scale correlations Var [$r_{(i;ti)}$] for scales and dimensions of the RESTQ-CA-40 for GA4 ($N = 320$)[†].

RESTQ-CA scales	*M*	*SD*	$r_{(ic)}$	α	r_{tt}	*Var* ($r_{(i;ti)}$)
1 General Stress	1.11	1.00	.47	.77	.77	.49–.63
2 Emotional Stress	1.26	0.95	.44	.76	.64	.43–.66
3 Social Stress	1.40	1.04	.40	.73	.77	.28–.69
4 Fatigue	1.82	1.41	.52	.81	.82	.59–.72
5 Social Recovery	4.09	1.16	.33	.66	.71	.35–.49
6 Physical Recovery	3.06	1.27	.40	.73	.69	.50–.54
7 General Well-being	4.18	1.18	.50	.80	.82	.57–.64
8 Sleep Quality	3.81	1.34	.32	.66	.75	.28–.38
9 School-related Emotional Exhaustion	1.66	1.37	.51	.80	.87	.54–.70
10 School-related Self-Efficacy	3.08	1.30	.50	.80	.82	.58–.64
Overall Stress	1.40	0.94	.40	.91	.90	.47–.71
Overall Recovery	3.78	0.98	.30	.87	.89	.20–.70

Note: [†] $n_{\text{Retest}} = 182$.

of recovery-related scales was supported by rather moderate correlations. Regarding the school-specific part, both school-specific scales were moderately inversed correlated.

Factorial validity: Factor analysis for scales

Factor analysis was performed to approve the structure of scales, which is described in Table 6.6.

When performing a Principal Component Analysis on all eight scales of the general part, the two-dimensional structure of the RESTQ was replicated. All four scales of stress were assigned to the first factor, which explained 51% of the total variance. All four scales of recovery showed loadings on the second factor, explaining 18% of the total variance. Negative side-loadings resulted for sleep quality on stress, but main loading on the recovery factor was confirmed. More than 50% of the variance ($a_2^2/h^2 = .63$) is explained by recovery, which is substantially more than 37% of the negative side-loading on stress ($a_1^2/h^2 = .37$). Thus, distinct loading of *Sleep Quality* on the recovery factor was supported.

Table 6.5 Scale and dimension intercorrelations of the RESTQ-CA-40 for the sample GA4 ($N = 320$).

RESTQ-CA scales	*1*	*2*	*3*	*4*	*5*	*6*	*7*	*8*	*9*	*10*	*OS*	*OR*
1 General Stress	—											
2 Emotional Stress	**.75**	—										
3 Social Stress	**.70**	**.74**	—									
4 Fatigue	**.61**	**.58**	**.52**	—								
5 Social Recovery	−.16	−.21	−.20	−.09	—							
6 Physical Recovery	−.28	−.34	−.30	−.33	**.40**	—						
7 General Well-being	**−.40**	**−.43**	**−.40**	−.38	**.56**	**.66**	—					
8 Sleep Quality	**−.47**	**−.45**	−.38	**−.45**	.29	**.55**	**.55**	—				
9 School-related Emotional Exhaustion	**.54**	**.54**	**.49**	**.67**	−.05	−.21	−.25	−.35	—			
10 School-related Self-Efficacy	−.13	−.21	−.18	−.17	.27	**.55**	**.51**	.38	−.24	—		
11 Overall Stress	**.88**	**.87**	**.84**	**.83**	−.18	−.37	**−.47**	**−.51**	**.67**	−.20	—	
12 Overall Recovery	**−.42**	**−.45**	**−.41**	**−.40**	**.69**	**.83**	**.87**	**.77**	−.28	**.54**	**−.49**	—

Note: $r \geq .30$ and $< .40$ are underlined, $r \geq .40$ are bolded; OS = *Overall Stress*, OR = *Overall Recovery*.

Table 6.6 Varimax-rotated loading matrix[a] of the Principal Component Analysis for the basic scales of the RESTQ-CA-40 with a ≥ .10 for sample GA4 (N = 320).

RESTQ-CA scales	*F1*	*F2*	h^2	a_1^2/h^2	a_2^2/h^2
1 General Stress	**.88**	−.15	.80	.97	.28
2 Emotional Stress	**.86**	−.21	.79	.94	.06
3 Social Stress	**.83**	−.17	.72	.96	.04
4 Fatigue	**.76**	−.18	.61	.94	.05
5 Social Recovery		**.78**	.60		1.01
6 Physical Recovery	−.22	**.80**	.69	.07	.93
7 General Well-being	<u>−.31</u>	**.83**	.79	.12	.87
8 Sleep Quality	**−.46**	**.60**	.57	.37	.63
Eigenvalue[b]	4.12	1.46			
Variance (%)[b]	51.47	18.23			

Note: [a] Loadings ≥ .30 and < .40 are underlined, loadings ≥ .40 are bolded; [b] Eigenvalue und explanation of variance for the unrotated loading matrix; F = Factor, h^2 = Communality, a^2/h^2 = Variance proportion of the communality.

Convergent and discriminant validity: Correlations with coping and self-efficacy

Discriminant validity of all scales of the RESTQ-CA-40 was approved by low associations to coping and self-efficacy scales (Table 6.7).

Only the stress dimension correlated positively with the scale of *Aggression* and the maladaptive coping style of the SCI-CA. The scale *Physical Complaints* from Hampel and Petermann (2005) was interrelated with the scales of *General Stress*, *Emotional Stress*, and *Fatigue* of the RESTQ-CA-40. Furthermore, this scale was associated with the stress dimension of the RESTQ-CA-40.

Effects of gender and age

A multivariate ANOVA for all four scales of stress revealed a significant gender main effect [$F_{Gender(4,313)} = 3.22, p = .013, \eta^2 = .040$], but other effects were not significant [$F_{Age(4,313)} = 1.12, p = .344, \eta^2 = .014$; $F_{Gender\ x\ Age(4,313)} = 2.18, p = .071, \eta^2 = .027$]. Univariate ANOVAs yielded significant main effects of gender for *General Stress* [$F_{(1,316)} = 6.38, p = .012, \eta^2 = .020$] and *Emotional Stress* [$F_{(1,316)} = 7.88, p = .005, \eta^2 = .024$]. Girls reported more general and emotional stress than boys.

Performing a multivariate ANOVA for all four scales of recovery ascertained a significant gender main effect, but other effects were not significant [$F_{Gender(4,313)} = 5.89, p < .001, \eta^2 = .070$; $F_{Age(4,313)} = .54, p = .703, \eta^2 = .007$; $F_{Gender\ x\ Age(4,313)} = 1.62, p = .170, \eta^2 = .020$]. Post-hoc conducted univariate ANOVAs yielded significant main effects of gender for *Physical Recovery* [$F_{(1,316)} = 8.78, p = .003$,

Table 6.7 Correlations of scales and dimensions of the RESTQ-CA-40 with the SCI-CA, and the scales *General Self-Efficacy* and *Physical Complaints* for sample GA4 ($N = 320$).

RESTQ-CA scales	*1*	*2*	*3*	*4*	*5*	*6*	*7*	*8*	*9*	*10*	*11*	*12*	*13*	*14*
1 General Stress	.02	−.08	−.09	−.23	−.02	.30	.35	.38	**.40**	−.04	−.13	**.48**	−.13	**.61**
2 Emotional Stress	−.09	−.18	−.11	−.27	−.03	.30	.34	.38	**.43**	−.17	−.15	**.48**	−.23	**.55**
3 Social Stress	.00	−.11	−.15	−.23	−.07	.31	.28	.34	**.45**	−.07	−.18	**.46**	−.21	**.48**
4 Fatigue	−.06	−.12	−.09	−.25	−.14	.29	.29	.29	**.45**	−.11	−.19	**.44**	−.19	**.61**
5 Social Recovery	.08	.11	.15	.19	.17	−.10	−.12	−.12	−.07	.11	.21	−.14	.26	−.13
6 Physical Recovery	.21	.21	.24	.38	.15	−.19	−.20	−.25	−.21	.25	.31	−.28	.39	−.29
7 General Well-being	.16	.16	.27	.39	.21	−.25	−.20	−.25	−.30	.19	.35	−.33	.38	−.35
8 Sleep Quality	.10	.14	.12	.32	.10	−.27	−.30	−.26	−.29	.14	.21	−.37	.23	**−.48**
9 School-related Emotional Exhaustion	.03	−.05	−.12	−.25	−.15	.32	.24	.32	**.49**	−.01	−.21	**.45**	−.15	**.45**
10 School-related Self-Efficacy	.10	.13	.26	**.41**	.22	−.14	−.09	−.13	−.24	.14	.36	−.20	**.41**	−.11
11 Overall Stress	−.04	−.14	−.13	−.28	−.09	.35	.36	**.40**	**.51**	−.11	−.19	**.54**	−.22	**.66**
12 Overall Recovery	.17	.19	.24	**.41**	.20	−.26	−.26	−.28	−.28	.22	.34	−.36	**.40**	**−.40**

Note: $r \geq .30$ and $< .40$ are underlined, $r \geq .40$ are bolded; 1 = *Minimization*, 2 = *Distraction/Recreation*, 3 = *Situation Control*, 4 = *Positive Self-Instructions*, 5 = *Social Support*, 6 = *Passive Avoidance*, 7 = *Rumination*, 8 = *Resignation*, 9 = *Aggression*, 10 = *Emotion-focused Coping*, 11 = *Problem-focused Coping*, 12 = *Maladaptive Coping*, 13 = *General Self-Efficacy*, 14 = *Physical Complaints*.

$\eta^2 = .027$] and *Sleep Quality* [$F_{(1,316)} = 4.37, p = .037, \eta^2 = .014$]. Girls scored lower on physical recovery and satisfying sleep than boys.

Finally, carrying out a multivariate ANOVA for the school-specific part, neither main effects nor interaction effects could be ascertained [$F_{Gender(2,315)} = 2.41, p = .092, \eta^2 = .015$; $F_{Age(2,315)} = .40, p = .672, \eta^2 = .003$; $F_{Gender\ x\ Age(2,315)} = 2.98, p = .052, \eta^2 = .019$].

Criterion-oriented validity

A three-way multivariate repeated measures ANOVA for the stress dimension revealed a significant interaction effect of the experimental condition and time [$F_{(8,1236)} = 6.06, p < .001, \eta^2 = .038$; for more detail, see Hampel et al., 2009]. Univariate ANOVAs showed gender by time effects for all four stress-associated scales [*General Stress*: $F_{(2,622)} = 15.34, p < .001, \eta^2 = .047$; *Emotional Stress*: $F_{(2,622)} = 10.27, p < .001, \eta^2 = .032$; *Social Stress*: $F_{(2,622)} = 3.65, p = .029, \eta^2 = .012$; *Fatigue*: $F_{(2,622)} = 16.93, p < .001, \eta^2 = .052$]. Stress scores increased in the control group especially at the three months follow-up assessment compared to baseline. In contrast, stress scores diminished in the experimental group and were significantly lower in the experimental group compared to the controls at the follow-up assessment.

This interaction effect of experimental condition by time was also found in the multivariate repeated measures ANOVA for the recovery dimension [$F_{(8,1240)} = 6.06, p < .001, \eta^2 = .038$]. Univariate repeated measures ANOVAs revealed interaction effects for all four recovery-related scales [*Social Recovery*: $F_{(2,624)} = 12.92, p < .001, \eta^2 = .040$; *Physical Recovery*: $F_{(2,624)} = 10.82, p < .001, \eta^2 = .034$; *General Well-being*: $F_{(2,624)} = 18.67, p < .001, \eta^2 = .056$; *Sleep Quality*: $F_{(2,624)} = 8.59, p < .001, \eta^2 = .027$]. Adolescents in the control group decreased in *General Well-being* and *Social Recovery* at the follow-up assessment in comparison with baseline scores. Contrary, recovery scores were enhanced in the experimental group in the mid-term. Thus, recovery scores of adolescents in the experimental group were substantially higher at the follow-up assessment compared to controls.

Finally, results of a multivariate repeated measures ANOVA for the school-specific dimension also indicated a significant interaction effect of experimental condition by time [$F_{(4,1244)} = 12.25, p < .001, \eta^2 = .038$]. This interaction was found in univariate repeated measures ANOVAs for both scales [*School-related Emotional Exhaustion*: $F_{(2,624)} = 5.07, p = .007, \eta^2 = .016$; *School-related Self-Efficacy*: $F_{(2,624)} = 21.85, p < .001, \eta^2 = .065$]. *School-related Emotional Exhaustion* increased in the control group and was significantly higher in this group in the short- and mid-term compared to the experimental group. *School-related Self-Efficacy* improved in the experimental group and was substantially higher in the short- and mid-term in comparison with controls.

Summary of the results of the RESTQ-CA-40

Item and scale analysis suggested sufficient internal consistencies and retest reliabilities, respectively. Some results were provided for the construct validity of the RESTQ-CA-40. First, item assignment to scales was confirmed by Principal Component Analysis. Second, the eight general scales were assigned distinctively to two dimensions by factor analysis: stress (*General Stress, Emotional Stress, Social Stress, Fatigue*) and recovery (*Social Recovery, Physical Recovery, General Well-being, Sleep Quality*). Third, analysis of correlations showed good discriminant associations of recovery-related scales, but stress-associated scales were strongly interrelated. Furthermore, moderate correlations with coping and general self-efficacy indicated also the construct validity. In addition, construct validity was supported by gender differences, which are in agreement with the literature. Finally, criterion-oriented validity was supported by preliminary results, pointing to the sensitivity to change of the RESTQ-CA-40. Thus, the results suggest that the RESTQ-CA-40 is a reliable and valid self-report measure of recovery and stress among children and adolescents.

References

Aldao, A., Nolen-Hoeksema, S., & Schweizer, S. (2010). Emotion-regulation strategies across psychopathology: A meta-analytic review. *Clinical Psychology Review, 30*(2), 217–237.

Allmer, H. (1996). *Erholung und Gesundheit. Grundlagen, Ergebnisse und Maßnahmen* [Recovery and health. Fundamentals, results, and interventions]. Hogrefe.

Amtmann, E. (2004). *Evaluation eines Stressbewältigungsprogramms für Schülerinnen und Schüler unter besonderer Berücksichtigung der Altersgruppe der 11- bis 15-Jährigen* [Evaluation of a stress management training for students with special consideration in the age group from 11 to 15; Unpublished doctoral dissertation]. University of Graz, Austria.

Anniko, M. K., Boersma, K., & Tillfors, M. (2019). Sources of stress and worry in the development of stress-related mental health problems: A longitudinal investigation from early- to mid-adolescence. *Anxiety, Stress, and Coping, 32*(2), 155–167.

Bandura, A. (1977). Self-efficacy: Toward a unifying theory of behavioral change. *Psychological Review, 84*, 191–215.

Bandura, A., Pastorelli, C., Barbaranelli, C., & Caprara, G.V. (1999). Self-efficacy pathways to childhood depression. *Journal of Personality and Social Psychology, 76*, 258–269.

Calvete, E., Camara, M., Estevez, A., & Villardón, L. (2011). The role of coping with social stressors in the development of depressive symptoms: Gender differences. *Anxiety, Stress and Coping, 24*(4), 387–406.

Calvete, E., & Orue, I. (2012). The role of emotion regulation in the predictive association between social information processing and aggressive behavior in adolescents. *International Journal of Behavioral Development, 36*(5), 338–347.

Clarke, A. T. (2006). Coping with interpersonal stress and psychosocial health among children and adolescents: A meta-analysis. *Journal of Youth and Adolescence, 35*, 11–24.

Compas, B. E., Connor-Smith, J. K., Saltzman, H., Harding Thomsen, A., & Wadsworth, M. E. (2001). Coping with stress during childhood and adolescence: Problems, progress, and potential in theory and research. *Psychological Bulletin, 127*, 87–127.

Compas, B. E., Jaser, S. S., Bettis, A. H., Watson, K. H., Gruhn, M. A., Dunbar, J. P., Williams, E., & Thigpen, J. C. (2017). Coping, emotion regulation, and psychopathology in childhood and adolescence: A meta-analysis and narrative review. *Psychological Bulletin, 143*(9), 939–991.

Compas, B. E., Orosan, P. G., & Grant, K. E. (1993). Adolescent stress and coping: Implications for psychopathology during adolescence. *Journal of Adolescence, 16*, 331–349.

Connor-Smith, J. K., & Compas, B. E. (2002). Vulnerability to social stressors: Coping as a mediator or moderator of sociotropy and symptoms of anxiety and depression. *Cognitive Therapy and Research, 26*, 39–55.

Erath, S. A., & Pettit, G. S. (2021). Coping with relationship stress in adolescence: A decade in review. *Journal of Research on Adolescence, 31*(4), 1047–1067.

Hampel, P. (2007). Brief report: Coping among Austrian children and adolescents. *Journal of Adolescence, 30*, 885–890.

Hampel, P., Kümmel, U., & Meier, M. (2009). Schulbasiertes Stressbewältigungstraining für Jugendliche: Effekte auf den Erholungs-Beanspruchungszustand und die allgemeine Selbstwirksamkeitserwartung [School-based stress management training: Effects on the revovery-strain state and general self-efficacy]. *Zeitschrift für Gesundheitspsychologie, 17*, 1–12.

Hampel, P., Meier, M., & Kümmel, U. (2008). School-based stress management training for adolescents: Longitudinal results from an experimental study. *Journal of Youth and Adolescence, 37*, 1009–1024.

Hampel, P., & Petermann, F. (2005). Age and gender effects on coping in children and adolescents. *Journal of Youth and Adolescence, 34*, 73–83.

Hampel, P., & Petermann, F. (2006). Perceived stress, coping, and adjustment in adolescents. *Journal of Adolescent Health, 38*, 409–415.

Hampel, P., & Petermann, F. (2017). Stressverarbeitung, Lebensqualität und körperliche Beanspruchungssymptome bei Kindern und Jugendlichen [Coping, quality of life, and physical strain among children and adolescents]. *Kindheit und Entwicklung, 26*(1), 58–69.

Hampel, P., & Pössel, P. (2012). Stressverarbeitung und psychische Auffälligkeiten im Jugendalter: Eine 2-Jahres-Längsschnittstudie [Psychological problems and coping among adolescents: A 2-year cohort-sequential study]. *Zeitschrift für Gesundheitspsychologie, 20*, 3–12.

Herman-Stahl, M. A., & Petersen, A. C. (1999). Depressive symptoms during adolescence: Direct and stress-buffering effects of coping, control beliefs, and family relationships. *Journal of Applied Developmental Psychology, 20*, 45–62.

Jerusalem, M., & Mittag, W. (1995). Self-efficacy in stressful life transitions. In A. Bandura (Ed.), *Self-efficacy in changing societies* (pp. 177–201). Cambridge University Press.

Jose, P. E., & Brown, I. (2008). When does the gender differences in rumination begin? Gender and age differences in the use of rumination by adolescents. *Journal of Youth and Adolescence, 37*, 180–192.

Kallus, K. W. (2002). Impact of recovery in different areas of application. In M. Kellmann (Ed.), *Enhancing recovery: Preventing underperformance in athletes* (pp. 283–300). Human Kinetics.

Kallus, K. W., Veit, E., Amtmann, E., Kümmel, U., Meier, M., & Hampel, P. (2005). *Erholungs-Belastungs-Fragebogen für Kinder und Jugendliche (EBF-KJ)* [Recovery-Stress Questionnaire for Children and Adolescents (RESTQ-CA); Unpublished manual]. University of Graz, Austria.

Kellmann, M., & Beckmann, J. (Eds.). (2022). *Recovery and well-being in sport and exercise*. Routledge.

Kellmann, M., & Beckmann, J. (Eds.). (2024). *Fostering recovery and well-being in a healthy lifestyle: Psychological, somatic, and organizational prevention approaches.* Routledge.

Kellmann, M., Jakowski, S., & Beckmann, J. (Eds.). (2023). *The importance of recovery for physical and mental health: Negotiating the effects of underrecovery.* Routledge.

Kellmann, M., & Kallus, K. W. (2001). *The Recovery-Stress-Questionnaire for Athletes: User manual.* Human Kinetics.

Kümmel, U., Hampel, P., & Meier, M. (2008). Einfluss einer erlebnispädagogischen Maßnahme auf Selbstwirksamkeit, Stressverarbeitung und Erholungs-Beanspruchungs-Zustand bei Jugendlichen [Effects of a training with experiential education on self-efficacy, coping, and the revovery-strain state in adolescents]. *Zeitschrift für Pädagogik, 54,* 555–571.

Lazarus, R. S., & Launier, R. (1978). Stress-related transactions between person and environment. In L. A. Pervin & M. Lewis (Eds.), *Perspectives in interactional psychology* (pp. 287–327). Plenum.

Luszczynska, A., Scholz, U., & Schwarzer, R. (2005). The general self-efficacy scale: Muticultural validation studies. *The Journal of Psychology, 139,* 439–457.

Missenböck, U. (2003). *Stressverarbeitung sowie Erholungs- und Belastungsregulation bei Jugendlichen unterschiedlichen Alters, Geschlechts und Schultyps. Eine empirische Studie an Schülerinnen und Schülern einer Sporthauptschule und einer Hauptschule* [Coping and recovery-strain regulation among adolescents of different age, gender, and school type. An empirical study among students of a sports-oriented secondary general school and a secondary general school; Unpublished diploma thesis]. University of Graz, Austria.

Muris, P. (2002). Relationships between self-efficacy and symptoms of anxiety disorders and depression in a normal adolescent sample. *Personality and Individual Differences, 32,* 337–348.

Persike, M., & Seiffge-Krenke, I. (2012). Competence in coping with stress in adolescents from three regions of the world. *Journal of Youth and Adolescence, 41,* 863–879.

Pössel, P., Baldus, C., Horn, A. B., Groen, G., & Hautzinger, M. (2005). Influence of general self-efficacy on the effects of a school-based universal primary prevention program of depressive symptoms: A randomized and controlled follow-up study. *Journal of Child Psychology and Psychiatry, 46,* 982–994.

Satow, L., & Schwarzer, R. (2003). Entwicklung schulischer und sozialer Selbstwirksamkeitserwartung: Eine Analyse individueller Wachstumskurven [Development of perceived self-efficacy in academic and social domains. An analysis of individual growth curves]. *Psychologie in Unterricht und Erziehung, 50,* 168–181.

Schwarzer, R., & Jerusalem, M. (1999). *Skalen zur Erfassung von Lehrer- und Schülermerkmalen. Dokumentation der psychometrischen Verfahren im Rahmen der wissenschaftlichen Begleitung des Modellversuchs Selbstwirksame Schulen* [Scales to assess characteristics of teachers and students. Documentation of the psychometric procedures as part of the scientific monitoring of the Self-Effective Schools pilot project]. Free University of Berlin, Germany.

Seiffge-Krenke, I. (2000). Causal links between stressful events, coping style, and adolescent symptomatology. *Journal of Adolescence, 23,* 675–691.

Seiffge-Krenke, I. (2011). Coping with relationship stressors: A decade review. *Journal of Research on Adolescence, 21*(1), 196–210.

Veit, E. (2004). *Veränderung von Stressverarbeitungsstrategien bei Schülerinnen und Schülern unterschiedlichen Alters* [Changes in coping skills among students with different ages; Unpublished doctoral dissertation]. University of Graz, Austria.

Vierhaus, M., Lohaus, A., & Ball, J. (2007). Developmental changes in coping: Situational and methodological influences. *Anxiety, Stress, and Coping, 20*, 267–282.

Zammuner, V. L. (2019). Adolescents' coping strategies influence their psychosocial well-being. *Current Journal of Applied Science and Technology, 36*(3), 1–17.

Zimmer-Gembeck, M. J., & Skinner, E. A. (2011). The development of coping across childhood and adolescence: An integrative review and critique of research. *International Journal of Behavioral Development, 35*(1), 1–17.

7 The Recovery-Stress Questionnaires

Further applications and overall summary

Verena Wagner-Hartl, K. Wolfgang Kallus, Jens Brandt, Paulino Jiménez, and Michael Kellmann

Overview

The simultaneous assessment of stress and recovery led to a successful application of the RESTQ in the past 40 years since the first congress reports and publications on the instrument were available (Kallus, 1992, 1995). Changes in the recovery-stress state are reflected in the recovery-stress profile of the RESTQ. The overall scores allow a simple reliable screening of the recovery-stress state in different areas of application. The modular structure of the area-specific versions allows for deriving specific conclusions and interventions, and at the same time permits referring results to the broad range of data from the RESTQ-Basic. In this way, the 'Bandwidth-Fidelity Dilemma' (Cheng et al., 2008) is solved with respect to the recovery-stress state. In addition, comparisons with other areas of applications permit a well-founded interpretation of results and maybe foster the transfer of intervention methods from one area of application to another.

This chapter will consolidate common results from the different areas of application and will show that the modular concept of the RESTQ allows drawing a reliable and valid picture of the individual's recovery-stress state. In addition, research on the validity of the RESTQ and results of the different scales of the area-specific versions open up a broad range of unresolved research questions in the field of stressed resources and their restoration, recovery, maintenance, training, and repair. All of these processes profit from the bio-psycho-social view, which characterizes the methodological background of the RESTQ.

This chapter sums up basic features of the RESTQ, adds selected results on other specific applications, and shows on an empirical basis by using results from linear structural modelling that the different versions and fields of application yield truly comparable results. This justifies the idea that the user of the RESTQ will profit from a manual, which summarizes the results from the RESTQ family.

Wagner-Hartl, V., Kallus, K. W., Brandt, J., Jiménez, P., & Kellmann, M. (2025). The Recovery-Stress Questionnaires: Further applications and overall summary. In M. Kellmann & K. W. Kallus (Eds.), *The Recovery-Stress Questionnaires: A User Manual* (pp. 226–253). Routledge.

DOI: 10.4324/9781032643380-7

Interpretation of results

The interpretation of results should primarily be based on the concepts behind the scales, their reliabilities, and their validities, which are outlined in each chapter. *Overall Stress* and *Overall Recovery* resulted in good (above .75) to very good (above .80) values for internal consistencies in data from different areas of application and for versions with different periods of reference (Kallus, this volume, Chapter 2). The same is true for eight out of twelve scales of the RESTQ-Basic and for most of the scales in the area-specific versions as long as the versions with four items per scale are used. The longer versions are recommended for individually oriented approaches with few occasions of measurement. For individual monitoring approaches a combination of long and short versions has proved to be useful with the long version being applied at the beginning, (mid), and end, supplemented by short versions for each monitoring occasion (please see recommendations at the end of the respective chapters). Many scales, even the short versions with two items per scale, show good internal consistencies. However, they should be checked in new samples, if possible. Suitable reference values should be selected from the chapter of relevance.

Especially the scale *Conflicts/Pressure* of the sub-dimension of *Performance (-related) Stress* and the scale *Success* of the recovery-dimension showed repeated problems with internal consistency which led to an item exchange in *Conflicts/Pressure*. Short-term retest data are better (Kallus, this volume, Chapter 2, Table 2.5), which indicates that the problem might be due to missing one-dimensionality of the scales *Conflicts/Pressure* and *Success*. Additional weaknesses for *Fatigue* and for *Sleep Quality* appeared in linear structural equations of measurement models (Kallus, this volume, Chapter 2). These hints on complexities of the scales should be kept in mind when interpreting the profile of the RESTQ-Basic.

High short-term stabilities which decrease over time and high correlations to state measures with low or medium correlations to trait measures show suitable convergent and discriminant validities with respect to temporal stability. This supports the measurement claim of the RESTQ to assess an intermediately stable psychophysical state comparable to mood states.

One of the most important results on construct validity is the unequivocal structure of all versions of the RESTQ with a stress dimension and a recovery dimension. In addition, the expediency of separate analysis on the basic scales and the area-specific scales was supported by the fact that in many instances no simple structural model with appropriate fit indices could be found. The basic structure could be modelled for athletes (with weak model fit) and it fitted even worse for coaches or for the samples of working people.

Structural equation modelling

The following sections will review the results of measurement models for scales, measurement models for sub-dimensions, and structural models for the RESTQ-Basic as well as the attempts to model basic and specific parts of the RESTQ in one model.

Measurement models – Validation with different samples

For each scale of the RESTQ-Basic-48, measurement models were analyzed for the different versions and areas of applications. Items were used as manifest variables, as they represent the measured scores of the different scales of the RESTQ-Basic-48 (Kallus, this volume, Chapter 2). To show how stable the structures of the measurement models of the twelve different scales are (Kallus, this volume, Chapter 2, Table 2.6; sample: GS2), all twelve models were validated with three other samples (GW3, GC3, ES2; Jiménez et al., this volume, Chapter 5; Kallus, this volume, Chapter 2; Kellmann & Kallus, this volume, Chapter 3; Kellmann et al., this volume, Chapter 4). For most samples, the results indicate a good fit of the measurement models (Online Appendix A.F1). The two fit indices GFI and CFI always reach the critical value (Kellmann & Kallus, this volume, Chapter 1). The same applies to other samples, with one exception (score *Social Stress*, sample GW3) for AGFI, which suggests a good fitting of the measurement models modelled on sample GS2 (Kallus, this volume, Chapter 2). However, the situation appears different for the fit index RMSEA. In total, nine times RMSEA did not reach the critical value of RMSEA < .08. Interestingly, five out of nine times the RMSEA failed the critical value validating the measurement model with sample ES2 (scales: *Social Stress*, *Fatigue*, *Physical Complaints*, *Success*, and *General Well-being*). Besides this, RMSEA was too high two times for sample GW3 (*Social Stress*, *General Well-being*) as well as one time for samples GC3 and GS2 (both scores: *Social Recovery*). Nevertheless, it must be stated that measurement models all in all fit well, since the scores are mostly quite near the critical values. In all cases, except one (score *Social Stress*, sample GW3) at least three fit indices GFI, AGFI, and CFI do reach their critical values. In cases where modifications of the initial models are needed, apart from one single exception (*Success* in the English sport sample ES2), improvements of the fit indices occur with small modifications of the models. The results are summarized in detail in Online Appendix A.F1.

Measurement models for sub-dimensions of the RESTQ-Basic – Validation with different samples

For each dimension (*Social-Emotional Stress*, *Performance(-related) Stress*, *Overall Recovery*), measurement models of the RESTQ-Basic-24 were analyzed. Items were used as observed or manifest variables, as they represent the measured scores of the different scales that can be grouped into the different dimensions of the RESTQ-Basic-24. The question arises how stable the structures of the measurement models presented by Kallus (this volume, Chapter 2; sample: GS2) are and if they gain their validity for other samples, too. Therefore, a validation with three other samples (GW3, GC3, ES2, Jiménez et al., this volume, Chapter 5; Kallus, this volume, Chapter 2; Kellmann & Kallus, this volume, Chapter 3; Kellmann et al., this volume, Chapter 4) was performed. The results indicate a good fit of the measurement models for both stress-related dimensions *Social-Emotional Stress* and *Performance(-related) Stress* (Table 7.1).

Table 7.1 Measurement models – validation with other samples.

Dimension	*Sample*	*Fit indices*
Social-Emotional Stress	GS2	GFI = .99, AGFI = .97, CFI = .99, RMSEA = .06
	GW3	GFI = .99, AGFI = .98, CFI = 1.00, RMSEA = .04
	GC3	GFI = .99, AGFI = .96, CFI = .99, RMSEA = .07
	ES2	GFI = .97, AGFI = .91, CFI = .98, RMSEA = .11
Performance(-related)	GS2	GFI = .97, AGFI = .93, CFI = .92, RMSEA = .08
Stress	GW3	GFI = .97, AGFI = .94, CFI = .95, RMSEA = .08
	GC3	GFI = .98, AGFI = .96, CFI = .97, RMSEA = .06
	ES2	GFI = .98, AGFI = .95, CFI = .96, RMSEA = .07

Note: GFI = Goodness of Fit Index, AGFI = Adjusted Goodness of Fit Index, CFI = Comparative Fit Index, RMSEA = Root Mean Square Error of Approximation.

Whereas the measurement models of the two stress-related dimensions can be validated with all three other samples, this does not apply to the measurement model of the dimension *Overall Recovery*. The validation with three different samples results in a good model fit for the sample GC3 (GFI = .96, AGFI = .92, CFI = .95, RMSEA = .08) but in negative error or residual variances, so-called 'Haywood-cases' (Chen et al., 2001) for both samples GW3 and ES2. These improper solutions "indicate something wrong with our model, data, or estimator" (Chen et al., 2001, p. 469). Causes for improper solutions are, for example, sampling fluctuations, model misspecifications, underidentification of the model, empirical underidentification as well as outliers (Bollen, 1987; Rindskopf, 1984; van Driel, 1978). All validation samples were visually inspected for outliers, but the negative error and/or residual variances remained, so new calculations were performed for each sample to gain proper model specifications (Table 7.2). Whereas, for the sample GW3 only one change to the measurement model presented by Kallus (this volume, Chapter 2; set residuum of *Social Recovery* to zero, instead of error variance of item 16 … *I was successful in what I did* to zero) results in an acceptable solution, some more changes have to be realized for the sample ES2. Altogether, two variances of residuals and one error variance have to be set to zero to reach an acceptable model fit. The modifications of correlations of errors, which were also part of the source measurement model (Kallus, this volume, Chapter 2), do not work for sample ES2 (Heywood cases).

As mentioned before, different explanations for the missing fits are possible. For the sample GW3, one potential problem might be caused by the fact that a time frame of seven days/nights is used instead of three days/nights (Kallus, this volume, Chapter 2). Interestingly, both samples (ES2 and GW3) request a modification of the residuum of *Social Recovery,* which indicates that in sports and at work *Social Recovery*, which is linked to social support in a not well-defined way, might need some additional research to check the relation to the other recovery areas.

Table 7.2 Measurement models – dimension *Overall Recovery* – modifications.

Sample	*Modifications*	*Fit indices*
GW3	1. Set the variance of the residuum of *General Well-being* to 0 # 2. Modification results in another negative variance (residuum of *Social Recovery*) → set the variance of this residuum on 0 3. Correlation of errors: item 4 ↔ item 15 # 4. Correlation of errors: item 4 ↔ item 19 # 5. Correlation of errors: item 2 ↔ item 17 #	GFI = .95, AGFI = .91, CFI = .95, RMSEA = .09
ES2	1. Set the variance of the residuum of *General Well-being* to 0 # 2. Modification results in another negative variance (residuum of *Social Recovery*) → set the variance of this residuum on 0 ° 3. Modification results in another negative variance (error of item 27) → set the variance of this item on 0	GFI = .95, AGFI = .91, CFI = .94, RMSEA = .08

Note: # corresponds to modification in the original measurement model, ° corresponds to modification of sample GW3; GFI = Goodness of Fit Index, AGFI = Adjusted Goodness of Fit Index, CFI = Comparative Fit Index, RMSEA = Root Mean Square Error of Approximation.

Comparing the parameter estimates, no matter which sample was analyzed for the measurement model of the dimensions *Social-Emotional Stress* and *Performance(-related) Stress*, all parameters achieve their relations (e.g., relation of the size of parameter estimates of two items of one scale, etc.) with two expected results. First, regarding the measurement model of *Social-Emotional Stress* and its validation with the sample ES2 (Figure 7.1): The size of the error correlation between the items … *I felt down* (i22) and … *I was in a bad mood* (i8) is much smaller than the error correlation between the two items … *I was annoyed* (i37) and … *I was annoyed by others* (i21), while they are almost equal in the original measurement model. This result is not really surprising, since also the intercorrelations presented in Kellmann and Kallus (this volume, Chapter 3, Table 3.8a) suggest that this sample seems to be different.

Second, the validation of the measurement model *Performance-(related) Stress*: Concerning the sample GC3, the parameter estimates of the two items of the scale *Fatigue* are almost equal, whereas in all other samples the parameter estimate of item … *I was tired from work* (i16) is smaller than the one of item … *I was overtired* (i35; Figure 7.2). Also, the parameter estimates of the scales of the dimension *Performance(-related) Stress* do not achieve their expected relation to each other. Whereas the parameter estimate of *Conflicts/Pressure* is always the strongest, the results of all three validation samples suggest that *Physical Complaints* should

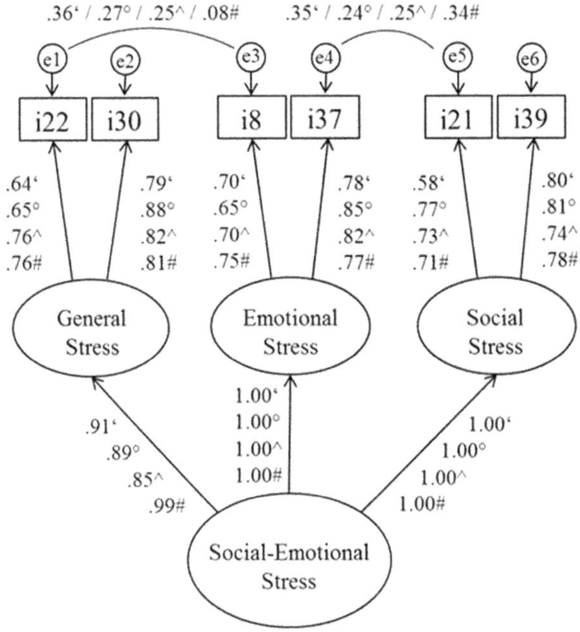

Figure 7.1 Measurement model dimension *Social-Emotional Stress* – comparison of different samples.
Note: ‘ sample GS2; ° sample GW3; ^ sample GC3; # sample ES2.

be seen as a parameter with the lowest β-weight, whilst the result of the source measurement model does not point in this direction (Figure 7.2).

Regarding the dimension *Overall Recovery*, the comparison of the original measurement model (sample GS2) and the validation which achieves a good fit without any new modifications (sample GC3) shows different relations of the three error correlations (Figure 7.3). While the correlation between the items … *I felt physically relaxed* (i9) and … *I had a satisfying sleep* (i27) is the strongest error correlation in both samples, the correlation between the two items … *I laughed* (i6) and … *I was in a good mood* (i34) seems to be stronger for GS2 than for coaches (sample GC3). Although the relations of the parameter estimates of the five scales of the dimension *Overall Recovery* are not quite the same, the strongest as well as the lowest β-weight fit with both samples.

To sum it up, the results of the validation of the measurement models with three different samples suggest that the dimension *Overall Recovery* reacts more strongly on sample-specific differences than the two stress-related sub-dimensions *Social-Emotional Stress* and *Performance(-related) Stress*. Based on additional empirical evidence, this can be interpreted in favor of the area-specific assessment of recovery.

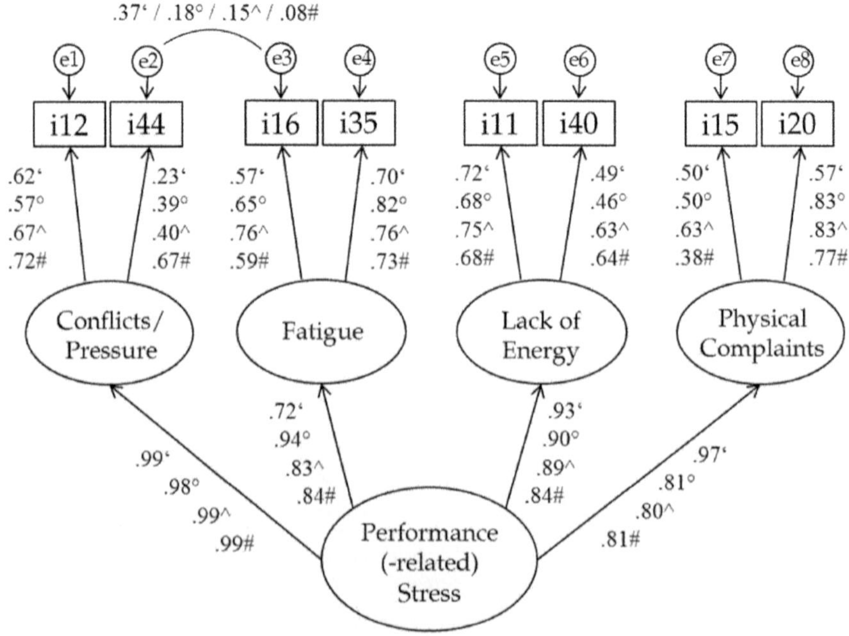

Figure 7.2 Measurement model dimension *Performance(-related) Stress* – comparison of different samples.

Note: ‘ sample GS2; ° sample GW3; ^ sample GC3; # sample ES2.

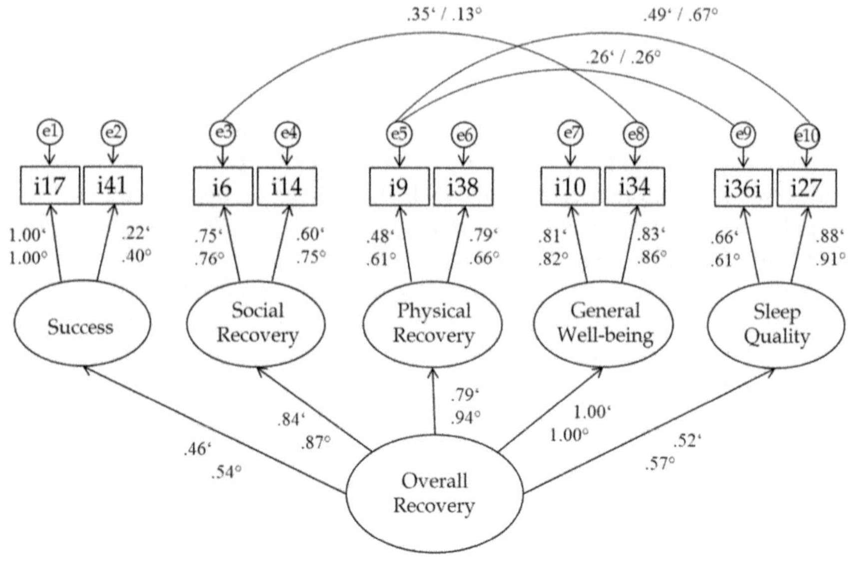

Figure 7.3 Measurement model dimension *Overall Recovery* – comparison of different samples.

Note: ‘ sample GS2; ^ sample GC3.

RESTQ-Basic: Structural equation model – Validation with different samples

The structural equation model of RESTQ-Basic (Kallus, this volume, Chapter 2, Figure 2.5; sample: GS2) was also validated with the three other samples (GW3, GC3, ES2; Jiménez et al., this volume, Chapter 5; Kallus, this volume, Chapter 2; Kellmann & Kallus, this volume, Chapter 3; Kellmann et al., this volume, Chapter 4). The structural equation model fits well into other samples and so, an acceptable model fit can be shown for all three samples (Table 7.3).

The comparison of the parameter estimates shows that all parameters achieve comparable values, no matter which sample was analyzed (Figure 7.4).

Table 7.3 Structural equation models – validation with other samples.

Sample	*Fit indices*
GS2	GFI = .94, AGFI = .89, CFI = .95, RMSEA = .08
GW3	GFI = .94, AGFI = .89, CFI = .96, RMSEA = .09
GC3	GFI = .95, AGFI = .91, CFI = .96, RMSEA = .08
ES2	GFI = .94, AGFI = .89, CFI = .95, RMSEA = .08

Note: GFI = Goodness of Fit Index, AGFI = Adjusted Goodness of Fit Index, CFI = Comparative Fit Index, RMSEA = Root Mean Square Error of Approximation.

A closer look at the parameter estimates reveals that, once again, sample ES2 seems to be a specific one (e.g., correlation between the errors of score *Sleep Quality* ↔ *Physical Complaints*; *Physical Recovery* ↔ *Physical Complaints*; *Overall Recovery* ↔ *Overall Stress*). The sample has similar values but they are overall smaller. This is already reflected in the intercorrelation matrix (Kellmann & Kallus, this volume, Chapter 3, Table 3.8a). For example, the correlations between *Overall Recovery* and *Overall Stress* are much lower than in other samples.

Combined structural equation: RESTQ-Basic and specific modules

The final step is to combine the structural equation models RESTQ-Basic and the different specific parts RESTQ-Sport, RESTQ-Coach, and RESTQ-Work. Every structural equation model was modified before and fits well on its own (Jiménez et al., this volume, Chapter 5; Kallus, this volume, Chapter 2; Kellmann & Kallus, this volume, Chapter 3; Kellmann et al., this volume, Chapter 4) and, therefore, combined models should not need too many additional modifications between them.

While no simple combined model could be obtained, a combined structural equation model of RESTQ-Basic and sport-specific scales of RESTQ-Sport (sample ES2) is shown in Figure 7.5. This model includes significant cross-correlations between *Overall Stress* and *Sport-specific Recovery* and *Overall Recovery*

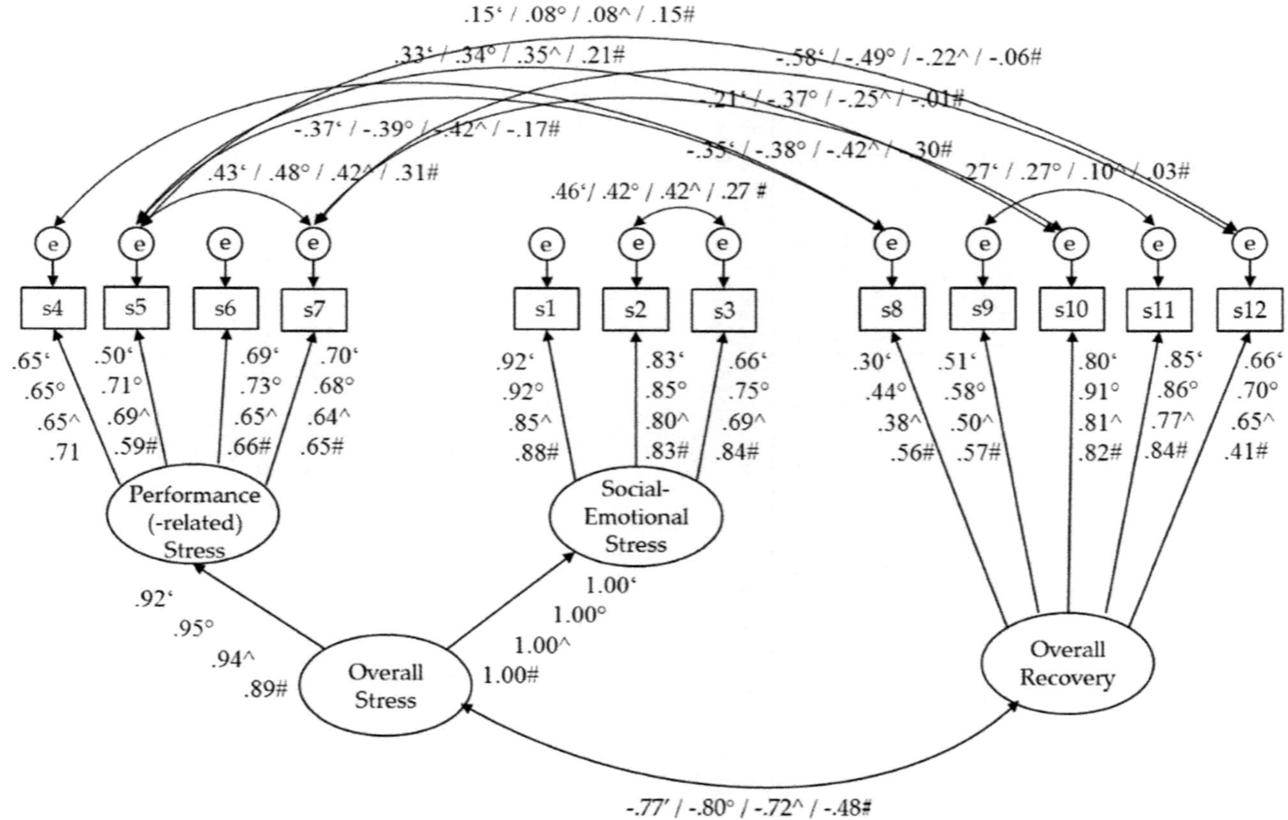

Figure 7.4 Structural equation model – comparison of different samples.
Note: ‘ sample GS2 (Chapter 2); ° sample GW3; ^ sample GC3; # sample ES2; s1: *General Stress*, s2: *Emotional Stress*, s3: *Social Stress*, s4: *Conflicts/Pressure*, s5: *Fatigue*, s6: *Lack of Energy*, s7: *Physical Complaints*, s8: *Success*, s9: *Social Recovery*, s10: *Physical Recovery*, s11: *General Well-being*, s12: *Sleep Quality*.

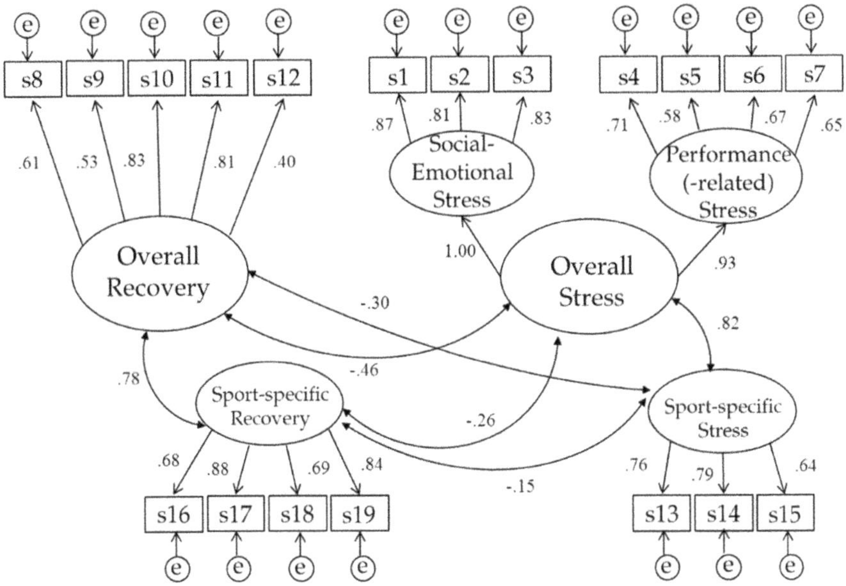

Figure 7.5 Combined structural equation model of RESTQ-Basic and sport-specific scales of RESTQ-Sport.

Note: s1: *General Stress*, s2: *Emotional Stress*, s3: *Social Stress*, s4: *Conflicts/Pressure*, s5: *Fatigue*, s6: *Lack of Energy*, s7: *Physical Complaints*, s8: *Success*, s9: *Social Recovery*, s10: *Physical Recovery*, s11: *General Well-being*, s12: *Sleep Quality*, s13: *Disturbed Breaks*, s14: *Emotional Exhaustion*, s15: *Injury*, s16: *Being in Shape*, s17: *Personal Accomplishment*, s18: *Self-Efficacy*, s19: *Self-Regulation*.

and *Sport-specific Stress*. However, this model does not reach the critical values (Kellmann & Kallus, this volume, Chapter 1) for acceptable fit (GFI = .87, AGFI = .82, CFI = .90, RMSEA = .09). To achieve acceptable fit, four additional modifications were needed (not depicted in Figure 7.5).

The combined structural equation model of RESTQ-Basic and coach-specific scales of RESTQ-Coach (sample GC3) with the same basic structure as depicted in Figure 7.5 fits even worse than the combination of RESTQ-Basic and sport-specific scales of RESTQ-Sport (sample ES2) and, in addition, does not reach the critical values (Kellmann & Kallus, this volume, Chapter 1) for acceptable fit (GFI = .85, AGFI = .79, CFI = .85, RMSEA = .12). Again, modifications between the two models were set to achieve acceptable model fit. The modification process was stopped after ten (additional) modifications between the two models because it did not reach an acceptable fit (GFI = .89, AGFI = .83, CFI = .91, RMSEA = .09). Again, more research is needed to obtain a satisfactory solution for the combined structural equation model of RESTQ-Basic and coach-specific scales of RESTQ-Coach.

Finally, the combined structural equation model of RESTQ-Basic and work-specific scales of RESTQ-Work (sample GW3) was checked. Again, the model showed no acceptable fit (GFI = .79, AGFI = .74, CFI = .85, RMSEA = .10).

More than ten additional modifications were needed to gain acceptable fit. Also in this case, more research is needed to clarify the relation between the specific areas and the unspecific areas. This research might be relevant not only from a methodological point of view but also to explain the structure of a biopsychological concept of recovery, which might be different for specific resources as many modifications of the simple model are needed to obtain a satisfactory solution for the combined structural equation model of RESTQ-Basic and work-specific scales of RESTQ-Work.

Overall, all three combined models (RESTQ-Basic with RESTQ-Sport, RESTQ-Coach, RESTQ-Work) apply that the particular specific stress dimensions are positively related to *Overall Stress* and negatively related to *Overall Recovery* (RESTQ-Basic). At the same time, the particular recovery dimensions are positively related to *Overall Recovery* and negatively related to *Overall Stress*. This is in line with the underlying concept of the RESTQ.

Validity of the RESTQ

The correlation patterns with respect to personality (Kallus, this volume, Chapter 2), motivation, self-efficacy (Jiménez et al., this volume, Chapter 5; Kellmann & Kallus, this volume, Chapter 3; Kellmann et al., this volume, Chapter 4), and habitual coping (Hampel & Kallus, this volume, Chapter 6; Jiménez et al., this volume, Chapter 5; Kallus, this volume, Chapter 2) were moderate but fully consistent with concepts. Especially recovery scales add new perspectives to the established concepts. The same can be concluded for the correlations between RESTQ scales and conceptually related concepts like need for recovery, and burnout (Kellmann et al., this volume, Chapter 4, Table 4.9; Jiménez et al., this volume, Chapter 5, Table 5.8). Convergent validity of the RESTQ with the Trier Inventory of Chronic Stress (TICS; Schulz et al., 2004) is very high and exceeds the values of internal consistency in some instances. This can be due to the close conceptual overlap, the similar item format (frequency scales), and, of course, to a part-whole relationship in time: persons who report stress in the past three or seven days/nights will show increased scores to questions on stress in the past four weeks, which results in higher values for chronic stress. Persons who do not have misbalances in their recovery-stress state in the past days/nights do not have chronic stress by definition. However, TICS yields no data on recovery.

Finally, it has to be pointed out that the specific scale in the different areas of application as well as the general scales of the basic version turned out to be good predictors for a broad range of outcome measures, including performance, and physiological parameters.

In addition to the results mentioned in the previous chapters, Table 7.4 lists published results on psychophysiological stress measures. Interesting new areas of research seem to open up for recovery-stress state and metabolic parameters and their humoral regulation, which is indicated by the results of Baylor and Hackney (2003) with athletes and replicated by Gaisbachgrabner (2014) for

Table 7.4 Examples of published results on psychophysiological stress indicators.

	Version	*N*	*Parameters*
Baylor and Hackney (2003)	RESTQ-Sport-76	21	TSH, fT3, fT4, Leptin
Bresciani et al. (2010)	RESTQ-Sport-76	14	Hematological and Biochemical Factors
Cortis et al. (2010)	RESTQ-Sport-76	8	Oxygen Consumption, Blood Lactate Concentration, Percentage of Hemoglobin Saturation in Muscles
Dupuy et al. (2013)	RESTQ-Sport-76	11	Heart Rate, Heart Rate Variability
Filaire et al. (2013)	RESTQ-Sport-76	12	Alpha-Amylase, Cortisol
Hough et al. (2013)	RESTQ-Sport-76	12	Cortisol, Testosterone
Gaisbachgrabner (2014)	RESTQ-Work-55	203	Thyroidal Dysfunction
Morales et al. (2014)	RESTQ-Sport-76	14	Heart Rate Variability
de Moraes et al. (2019)	RESTQ-Sport-76	20	Serum Catalase, Glutathione Reductase, Superoxide Dismutase Activities, Interleukin 1β, Immunoglobulins
Bizjak et al. (2021)	RESTQ-Sport-76	11	Immune Cell Activation, Cytokines, High-Mobility Group Protein B1, Cell-free DNA, Creatinekinase, Uric Acid, Kynurenine
Campos et al. (2022)	RESTQ-Sport-76	12	Cortisol, Salivary Testosterone, Salivary Immunoglobulin A

blue-collar workers. Note that cortisol is related to *Total Recovery* in the study of Filaire et al. (2013).

Another important feature of the RESTQ is its change-sensitivity, which includes days off work, vacancies, and specific interventions. The high validity with respect to surgical outcome parameters gives additional empirical evidence for the bio-psychological impact of the recovery-stress state, as assessed by the RESTQ. One example is that the RESTQ allows monitoring patients before, during, and after a stay in a clinic or in a rehabilitation center.

Monitoring of recovery-stress states in sports

The area of sports was the first one, in which a systematic monitoring of recovery-stress states was used as information on the effects of training regimes and performance potential (Kellmann et al., 1997, 2001). As in other areas of application the rule 'separate selection and training systematically' should strictly be followed when using the RESTQ as a monitoring tool. The RESTQ helps athletes and coaches to modify the personal and training environment to optimize the training process and helps actively to reduce the risk of overtraining. ***However, you should not use the RESTQ for selection purposes!*** Although the tendency for the results of psychological assessments to affect selection decisions cannot be totally avoided, the practice is unethical and may destroy the relationship of trust between coach and athlete. Furthermore, if a serious, long-lasting unhealthy recovery-stress state is detected, consultation with a trained psychologist or counseling center is highly recommended. This rule should, of course, also be followed in non-sport application areas.

Additional areas of application

The modular structure of the RESTQ allows complementing the RESTQ-Basic with scales from any area, which is relevant for the recovery-stress balance. Examples are: students (Brandt & Kallus, 2023), social capital (Kallus et al., 2009), rehabilitation (Eidenmüller, 2005; Schuster, 1997), clinical settings (Uhlig & Kallus, 2016), and health promotion (Kallus & Brandt, 2015). Two examples will be described in more detail: students as well as clinical settings and health promotion. In each of these areas, empirical data indicate that the RESTQ is able to identify problems in a reliable and valid/trusted way.

RESTQ-Student: Assessing the recovery-stress balance in tertiary education students

As a modularly designed questionnaire, the RESTQ is suitable for domain-specific use. The RESTQ-Work, for example, is a specific version for professionals (Jiménez et al., this volume, Chapter 5). Since there are both similarities and differences between the demands and framework conditions of working life and studying, a version specific to the context of studying was developed on the basis of the RESTQ-Work. With the RESTQ-Student, an instrument is available that enables the detailed assessment of stress and recovery in tertiary education (Brandt & Kallus, 2023). A long version with 60 items has been published (RESTQ-Student-60; Brandt & Kallus, 2023); the short form, the RESTQ-Student-30, with 30 items is included in this manual.

Description of the RESTQ-Student-60

The RESTQ-Student is based on the RESTQ-Work-55 (Jiménez et al., this volume, Chapter 5). Accordingly, the questionnaire, like any specific RESTQ, consists the RESTQ-Basic module (Kallus, this volume, Chapter 2) and a domain-specific module (Kellmann & Kallus, this volume, Chapter 1).

The starting point for the adaptation was that a work activity and a study are two principally similar areas of life, but not all demands and resources relevant in the work context are also relevant in the study context, and a study, in turn, has specific demands and resources. Therefore, it was first examined which elements of the domain-specific part of the RESTQ-Work also play a role in studies and which study-specific aspects should be supplemented. Since work-specific resources, such as latitude for action, are generally less available in studies, the three scales on job-related resources of the work-version, for example, were replaced by four scales for personal resources (e.g., self-affirmation). Here, in turn, personal resources, such as self-efficacy, which are quite important, were omitted if they correspond to the trait approach, since the RESTQ tends to follow the state approach.

As the result, seven of the 14 work-specific RESTQ-Work scales were transferred to the RESTQ-Student, with the term 'work' replaced by 'studies' in the item texts where appropriate. Another eleven scales were newly included in the RESTQ-Student.

Each of the 30 scales (twelve scales from the basic module are included in each version of the RESTQ, seven scales were taken from the domain-specific part of the RESTQ-Work, and eleven scales were newly developed for the study-specific aspects) consists of two items each. The items are related to the period of the last seven days and are answered on a frequency scale with seven grades [from 0 (*never*) to 6 (*always*)]. An example item from the new scale *Overload* is: ... *I had the feeling that I did not meet the requirements of the program.* The scales are assigned to eight sub-dimensions, four of which form the two dimensions stress and recovery. The interpretation takes place – depending on the research question – on the level of the dimensions or on the sub-dimension level.

Stress. Stress is measured with the basic sub-dimensions *Social-Emotional Stress* (*General Stress, Emotional Stress, Social Stress*) and *Performance(-related) Stress* (*Conflicts/Pressure, Fatigue, Lack of Energy, Physical Complaints*) as well as the study-specific sub-dimensions *Experienced Pressure* (*Additional Obligations, Time Pressure, Performance Pressure*), and *Overload* (*Emotional Exhaustion, Loss of Meaning, Overload, Self-doubt*).

Recovery. Recovery is assessed with the basic sub-dimensions *Overall Recovery* (*Success, Social Recovery, Physical* Recovery, *General Well-being, Sleep Quality*) and the study-specific sub-dimensions *Leisure/Breaks* (*Undisturbed Leisure Time, Efficient Breaks, Leisure, Leisure Activities*), *Social Support* (*Social Support by Friends, Social Support by Fellow Students, Appreciation by Others*), and *Personal Resources* (*Resisting Distraction, Overcoming Inner Resistance, Time Management, Self-Affirmation*).

The RESTQ-Student-30[1]

For the short form, RESTQ-Student-30, one of the two items of each scale was selected and thus comprises 30 items. The scale level is therefore omitted, i.e., the eight dimensions are calculated directly from the items. The two dimensions stress and recovery are, in turn, formed from the four associated sub-dimensions.

The following results refer to an unpublished study on stress among university students. This sample comprised $N=164$ participants, of which $n=50$ (30.5%) were male and $n=114$ (69.5%) female. The majority were studying for a Bachelor's degree ($n=112$, 68.3%).

Test-theoretical parameters of RESTQ-Student-30

The mean value of the *Stress* dimension was $M=3.11$ ($SD=1.26$), and the mean value of *Recovery* was $M=2.87$ ($SD=.90$). Cronbach's α of *Stress* had a very good value of .90, and the internal consistency of *Recovery* was good with Cronbach's $\alpha=.77$. The two dimensions were negatively correlated with $r=-.58$ (2-tailed significant at the 1% level). These values differ a little from the validation sample (Brandt & Kallus, 2023), in particular, stress is slightly higher than recovery (see validation sample with $N=281$: *Stress* $M=2.14$, $SD=1.04$, Cronbach's $\alpha=.88$ and *Recovery* $M=3.19$, $SD=.78$, Cronbach's $\alpha=.70$, correlation of *Stress* and *Recovery* $r=-.64$).

Table 7.5 show mean values, standard deviations, intercorrelations, and Cronbach's α of the RESTQ-Student-30 sub-dimensions. In this sample the means of the stress sub-dimensions, with values ranging from 2.81 to 3.55, were slightly higher than those of the recovery sub-dimensions, with values ranging from 2.51 to 3.14. The standard deviations of all sub-dimensions ranged from 1.00 to 1.66. Cronbach's α of all sub-dimensions were above .70, the *Personal Resources* sub-dimension having the lowest value of .72, and *Overload* sub-dimension having the highest value of .90 (Online Appendix A.F2 for findings on means and discriminatory power of the respective items of the sub-dimensions). All sub-dimensions correlated with each other in a medium to high range, with, consistent with the concept, sub-dimensions of stress and recovery correlating positively with each other within the dimension and negatively with sub-dimensions of the other dimension. All correlations were significantly different from zero with $p<.01$.

Construct validity

By using Exploratory Factor Analysis with principal component analysis and Varimax rotation, it was demonstrated that the two dimensions of stress and recovery could be formed on the basis on the eight sub-dimensions. The results in Table 7.6 show that two rotated factors with an Eigenvalue >1 could be identified, which together captured 70.1% of the variance of the eight sub-dimensions.

The results also showed that the Varimax-rotated loadings of the four stress sub-dimensions clearly loaded on the first factor. However, one of the four recovery sub-dimensions had a substantial side loading with −.54 on the first factor (stress) in addition to the high loadings on the second factor (recovery) with .56.

Table 7.7 displays the fit indices of the Confirmatory Factor Analysis. The two-factor model represents the underlying structure of the questionnaire with the two dimensions of stress and recovery as latent variables, to which

Table 7.5 RESTQ-Student-30 sub-dimensions: Number of scales, mean, standard deviations, intercorrelations, Cronbach's α.

	Items	*M*	*SD*	*1*	*2*	*3*	*4*	*5*	*6*	*7*	*8*
1 Social-Emotional Stress	3	2.81	1.31	(.78)							
2 Performance(-related) Stress	4	3.20	1.26	.77**	(.76)						
3 Experienced Pressure	3	3.55	1.45	.59**	.65**	(.76)					
4 Overload	4	2.89	1.66	.74**	.76**	.74**	(.90)				
5 Overall Recovery	5	3.14	1.00	−.46**	−.50**	−.31**	−.44**	(.80)			
6 Leisure/Break	4	2.68	1.26	−.47**	−.52**	−.52**	−.61**	.52**	(.86)		
7 Social Support	3	3.13	1.33	−.32**	−.32**	−.29**	−.31**	.48**	.48**	(.79)	
8 Personal Resources	4	2.51	1.09	−.29**	−.31**	−.29**	−.31**	.59**	.38**	.33**	(.72)

Note: $N = 164$; Cronbach's α in ( ); Items: number of items; ** $p < .01$ (2-tailed); Likert-Scale from 0 to 6.

Table 7.6 Principal Component Analysis followed by a Varimax rotation RESTQ-Student-30.

	F1	*F2*
Social-Emotional Stress	.83	−.23
Performance(-related) Stress	.86	−.26
Experienced Pressure	.83	−.16
Overload	.89	−.24
Overall Recovery	−.29	.81
Leisure/Break	−.54	.56
Social Support	−.18	.71
Personal Resources	−.12	.78
Eigenvalue	3.32	2.29
Explained total variance	41.5%	28.6%

Note: N=164.

Table 7.7 Confirmatory Factor Analysis for RESTQ-Student-30.

	χ^2	*df*	χ^2/df	$p(\chi^2)$	*AIC*	*CFI*	*NFI*	*RMSEA*	*SRMR*
1-Factor model	82.4	19	4.34	.000	116.4	.91	.89	.14	.08
2-Factor model	43.3	18	2.41	.001	79.3	.96	.94	.09	.04

Note: N=164; in the 1-factor model, the covariance between the two factors was fixed at 1. One residual correlation (for residuals of sub-dimensions *Overall Recovery* and *Personal Resources* has been specified); AIC=Akaike weight, CFI=Comparative Fit Index, NFI=Normed Fit Index, RMSEA=Root Mean Square Error of Approximation, SRMR=The Standardized Root Mean Residual.

the corresponding four sub-dimensions are assigned as manifest variables. In the one-factor model, all eight dimensions are combined into only one factor (by fixing the covariance between the two latent variables at 1). As can be seen in Table 7.7, the two-factor model is superior to the one-factor model. The fit indices had better values for the two-factor model and the Akaike weight value was lower for the two-factor model.

Application

Depending on the research question, either the long version with 60 items (Brandt & Kallus, 2023) or the short version with 30 items can be used. For studies in which stress during studies is to be recorded in as much detail as possible, e.g., in order to develop suitable interventions or to evaluate them, the long version should be used and, in addition to stress and recovery, the level of the sub-dimensions should also be considered. For screening surveys, for example, to determine the extent of stress at a university, or for studies with content-related questions – and the use of further questionnaires – the short form with 30 items can be used. Here, only the dimension of stress and recovery should be considered.

Incremental validity in clinical settings and health promotion

Data from applied studies allowed us to validate the RESTQ in clinical settings and in health promotion projects. For the application in clinical settings, a very short version was developed and validated with respect to the incremental validity, which looked promising as the concept of recovery is underrepresented (in comparison to stress and anxiety) in applied psychology. The recovery-stress state as assessed by the RESTQ allowed prediction of surgical outcome indicators such as time of stay in hospital, postoperative pain, and consumption of pain relievers (Uhlig et al., 1999) as well as the risk of postoperative performance decrements (Kiecolt-Glaser et al., 1998). These first indications as well as the increasing number of publications on the role of psychological factors in the perioperative context led to the development of a RESTQ-version, which allows a screening of the recovery-stress related aspects of the preoperative state of patients. Up to the point of developing the RESTQ for the state of patients in the surgical context, anxiety and coping were the dominant psychological constructs and research focused on the incremental validity. Preoperative anxiety and stress-scores of the RESTQ are expected to have a very high correlation. Non-functional coping as assed by the German Stress-Coping Inventory (SVF; Janke et al., 1985, 2002) was studied together with the RESTQ in health promotion projects and in clinical (surgical) projects. Six items were selected to assess dysfunctional coping (Uhlig & Kallus, 2016). Data from pooled health promotion projects (Kallus & Brandt, 2015) included $N = 4527$ persons and showed a Cronbach's $\alpha = .88$ for the dysfunctional coping scale of the SVF. In a large clinical sample ($N = 2669$), Cronbach's $\alpha = .84$ was obtained together with a 24-h retest of $r = .81$ (Uhlig & Kallus, 2016). A path-analysis shows a significant moderation of dysfunctional coping for the relation between stress and recovery (Figure 7.6).

For health promotion projects, the RESTQ-Basic was supplemented by the six dysfunctional coping items. This combination was termed 'Recovery Check'. In these projects, participants received specific feedback on their recovery-stress profiles together with the dysfunctional coping score. The 'Recovery Check'

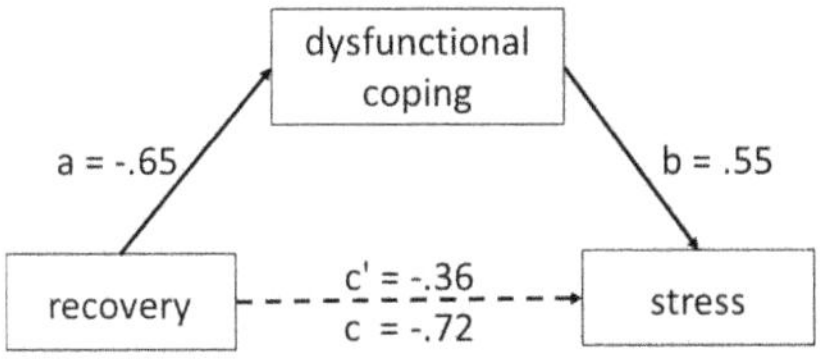

Figure 7.6 Path analysis of recovery and dysfunctional coping in office workers ($N = 4527$). *Note*: a = Effect of recovery on dysfunctional coping, b = Effect of dysfunctional coping on stress, c = Overall effect of recovery on stress, c' = Estimates' the direct effect of recovery on stress.

allows to derive data-based proposals to take measures for a better recovery-stress balance at the workplaces together with task analysis in a large public organization. Due to high impact of the results, the instrument was spread over the whole state-wide organization after a first project in a sub-division.

Even more impact was found for the clinical applications of the RESTQ. For the clinical applications a short version of the RESTQ-Basic was developed, which was supplemented by two items for preoperative anxiety and the dysfunctional coping items mentioned above. This RESTQ version was termed RESTQ-Risco. The RESTQ-Risco is a 14-item questionnaire which describes the psychological state of patients in settings of acute medicine and can be used well between 16 and 88 years.

Facets of stress and recovery in clinical settings

Anxiety and stress are well-known psychological variables which influence perioperative outcome (Cohen et al., 2005; Jamison et al., 1987; Kiecolt-Glaser et al., 1998). These effects are represented in negative affect, higher consumption of analgesics and sedatives after surgery or longer length of stay in hospital (Sime, 1976; Slangen et al., 1993). The data available from isolated concepts like anxiety possibly underestimate the potential influence of psychological factors in perioperative processes. The development of the RESTQ-Risco presents a simple approach for the simultaneous assessment of anxiety, stress, coping, and state of recovery.

As described by Uhlig and Kallus (2016) a typological approach was used to identify patients with an unfavorable psychological state. In addition, a transformation of these variables into a simple and easily applicable risk-score was proposed for screening purposes.

The RESTQ-Risco is a combined 14-item short-form of the following three instruments: the Recovery-Stress Questionnaire (RESTQ-Basic-24; Kallus, 1995), the German Stress-Coping Inventory (Janke et al., 1985, 2002), and the Adjective Checklist (Scaling of Well-being using Categories and Characteristic Words; Janke & Hüppe, 1994). For construction of the RESTQ-Risco, $N=2669$ patients in different hospitals in Germany and Austria participated (Uhlig & Kallus, 2016).

The method of Configuration-Frequency-Analysis (Krauth & Lienert, 1973; Uhlig et al., 1999) was used to build types and categories of patients based on the RESTQ. It turned out that two types of patients were present with high configuration frequencies:

- **Type 1:** High dysfunctional coping style, low recovery and high preoperative anxiety (or stress).
- **Type 2**: Low dysfunctional coping style, high recovery and low preoperative anxiety (or stress).

Patients classified as Type 1 are described as high-risk patients. Patients classified as Type 2 are described as low-risk patients.

To assure the significance of the types mentioned above an additional Interaction-Structure-Analysis was performed which is a special form of the Configuration-Frequency Analysis (Krauth & Lienert, 1973). Highly significant interactions between the components of the types of patients appeared, which indicates that for the labeling of patients in high or low risk a scoring of all three aspects (dysfunctional coping style, recovery, and anxiety) is necessary for the classification of patients. A separation in parts of these aspects is not suitable (for details, see Uhlig & Kallus, 2016).

Reliability measures

In a larger clinical sample internal consistency (Cronbach's α) and retests showed values above $r = .78$ for all components. Good values could be replicated with other samples (Uhlig & Kallus, 2016). For the RESTQ-Risco, the typical information can be transferred to a single score using a discriminant function (Uhlig & Kallus, 2016). With this score, regression models could be used for validation criteria.

Pain

Uhlig and Kallus (2016) indicated that classical clinical scores for operative risks (ASA-score and Goldman-score; Goldman et al., 1977) did not predict postoperative pain in a regression model (Nagelkerkes $R^2 = .001$, $F = 0.346$, $p = .708$). Adding the RESTQ-Risco the model improved the prediction of postoperative pain (Nagelkerkes $R^2 = .062$, $F = 11.002$, $p \leq .001$). Since the determination-coefficient changes significantly through the stepwise analysis, it can be shown that RESTQ-Risco has incremental validity concerning the prediction of postoperative pain. The results could be replicated with a second sample. The first step of regression analysis shows again that a model based only on ASA and Goldman cannot predict postoperative pain (Nagelkerkes $R^2 = .036$, $F = 2.889$, $p = .059$). If the RESTQ-Risco is added, the model predicts postoperative pain (Nagelkerkes $R^2 = .087$, $F = 4.848$, $p = .003$). A similar result was obtained for postoperative nausea. ASA and Goldman alone were not able to predict postoperative nausea (Nagelkerkes $R^2 = .010$, $\chi^2 = 1.175$, $p = .556$). Adding the RESTQ-Risco the model is able to predict postoperative nausea (Nagelkerkes $R^2 = .185$, $\chi^2 = 23.091$, $p < .001$). The predictability significantly increases by the RESTQ-Risco ($\chi^2 = 21.916$, $p < .001$). For the length of hospital stay, ASA and Goldman are able to predict post-operative length of hospital stay. Supplementation of the RESTQ-Risco shows that the predictive validity of the model increases significantly.

Summary of the RESTQ-Risco

Simultaneous information on resources, anxiety, and coping as combined in the RESTQ-Risco allows a prediction of postoperative mood states. Our analyses indicate that RESTQ-Risco is able to increase the predictive validity of ASA and Goldman at least with respect to psychologically mediated outcome variables.

It is not only anxiety or dysfunctional coping or an inadequate state of recovery which may be helpful to explain perioperative stress but also a combination of these concepts. Therefore, the 14-item screening tool was developed. Reliability was demonstrated with high internal consistency. Validation was possible with respect to postoperative complaints and time of stay in intensive care. Grounded in empirical findings and linking psychological risk factors to outcome of surgery, the studies support the utility and validity of the RESTQ-Risco across clinical samples. Although the RESTQ-Risco represents a combination of three well-documented questionnaires with acceptable psychometric properties, the RESTQ-Risco is not just a short version of the underlying instruments but a step in a new direction.

As expected, the RESTQ-Risco better predicts psychological aspects of outcome than the ASA or Goldman score. In addition, the RESTQ-Risco increases the predictive validity of the medical scores. Looking at the length of hospital stay, in particular, the RESTQ-Risco shows an intermediate to strong effect size almost comparable with the effects of age which are well-known predictors in the anesthesiologic literature. For that reason, it might be suitable to explain stress in the perioperative period not only in terms of anxiety but in a more complex framework of a bio-psycho-social approach including resources and recovery processes. Thereby it has to be investigated in future studies whether the significance of these aspects is substantial, too. It is of important clinical relevance to predict serious somatic aspects of outcome. Prediction of postoperative well-being and/or anxiety may be important as well if aspects of the patients' comfort are under discussion. Nevertheless, these concepts leave no answers to the preoperative question of whether a patient's anesthesia has to be managed in a specific way like – in contrast – the medical scores like ASA and Goldman do. In summary, the results of the reported studies show a substantial effect size of the RESTQ-Risco which is somewhat higher compared to other approaches and which probably makes the RESTQ-Risco suitable for an extended prediction of outcome.

The application for individuals or groups

Usually, a test measures characteristics or behaviors of an individual. The scale values are analyzed and the base for interventions for this single person is built. The analysis described in books about test theory normally does not cover the application of tests beyond this individual way (e.g., Kline, 2000 sees the usage of tests in industrial psychology mainly for assessing people).

Using test results of groups, either for a team in a company or a curling team in sports or for a whole division in an organization, allows additional interventions, which is fundamentally different from the individual approach. In team analysis, e.g., the multi-level-analysis is important and the researcher has to decide which level (person, team, organizational unit, or organization) is relevant for the question (Brandt, 2010). In the practical field, this determines also the different phases of data acquisition, the analyses, the preparation of the results, and lastly the derivation of interventions. This is reflected also in the standards for assessing people (ISO 10667-2, 2020b).

If using a test to measure stress and recovery, the most important influential variables should be determined. These key points can be found in the person, but are different when looking at the group level. Especially in the case of the whole family of the RESTQ, the sources for stress and recovery of the *person* are interesting in the first instance. It is intended to derive ways to improve the balance between stress and recovery for that person. In this case, primarily the person with his/her behaviour possibilities is in the focus. Even if the causes of the outer world should be changed, then a person has to do that with his/her own behavior (means), e.g., he/she should talk with the head of the team, etc.

Concerning groups, the task of measuring is more complex. First, there are individual persons, the interaction of the persons within the group, and lastly, the outer world of the group. In the usage of RESTQ-Work, e.g., this is mirrored with dimensions for interactions of the group (e.g., 'colleagues') and the 'outer world' (as we focus on the work place these are e.g., 'friends', 'leisure').

The *field phase for groups* for the RESTQ has to include special aspects above the ones which have to be considered in the individual approach. This means, e.g., the information to the group about anonymity, the data acquisition, the minimum number of people to be aggregated for presenting the results. This problem area is addressed in the norms about testing ISO 10667-1 (ISO, 2020a), ISO 10667-2 (ISO, 2020b), and for employee surveys it is very well described by Borg and Mastrangelo (2008) as well in the standard for risk assessment ISO 45001 (ISO, 2018).

The *analyses of the group level*, therefore, have to be presented in an aggregated form. If it is decided to go into sub-groups, then they have to be large enough to present them [a usual number is eight, the reasons and background are described in Kallus (2016); see also Borg and Mastrangelo (2008)]. The values of the sub-groups can be compared with each other or can be compared with the value of the whole group and/or with a chosen reference group. For group analyses or organizational diagnostics, it is intended to use the results mainly on group level and only as a second target (if ever) for persons individually.

Again, the main purpose is the derivation of *interventions for the group*. The interventions therefore have to be optimized for reaching a good recovery-stress balance. Addressing job resources like possibilities for participation, personal growth factors at work and action latitude allow effective condition-oriented interventions. These group-oriented interventions work primarily on the structure and the procedures of the working place, the conditions and not on behaviour changes of the *single* employee.

For consultancy, one of the important main distinctions in the practical area between the individual usage of a test and using it for a group can be found in a simple word: 'responsibility'. If, e.g., the results of a work group are critical then the managers could attribute this to the individuals of that group, arguing that the employees had too much fun at the weekends and are therefore tired at work. It is important to address the persons who are really 'responsible' and – much more important – have the power to change the *conditions* of the workplace (typically leaders), which leads to a disturbed recovery-stress balance for the group (Jiménez et al., 2017).

Reaching good results for the *intervention phase* means also for the user of the RESTQ to be a good moderator of the process and to help the 'real' responsible persons to change their focus from the personal level to the structures and processes of the team/group/organization as a whole. Especially here, it is very important to prepare the ground for interventions in an interactive mode. That means the results are discussed together with the group and the resulting interventions are derived in a consensual way.

Monitoring problems and change in the recovery-stress state on the group level with organizations recently became a new field of application for the RESTQ. For this purpose, an online instrument called 'Recovery Check' (earlier in this chapter) was implemented which allows monitoring changes in working conditions and the development of risks for chronic stress at the workplace (Institut für Begleitforschung, 2015). This instrument allows identifying fields which tend to overload the workforce. It has been used with more than 3000 persons. Means for the sub-dimensions of the RESTQ-Basic-24 with a time frame of seven days separated for male and female are provided in the Online Appendix A.F3.

Final remarks

A valid picture of the recovery-stress state of an individual or group requires a measurement with the standard version of the RESTQ. The longer versions were developed to obtain a good readability together with an easy unbiased rating. It is recommended to keep the format of the questionnaire and not to transform items to a short list with answers aside, as the item sequence has been systematically developed. The format of the questionnaire was selected to minimize violation of the local stochastic independency of answers. With this format, about seven seconds are needed per item, which means after reading the instruction the RESTQ-Basic-48 will not need more than six minutes to be filled in. A long specific version will be completed in 10–15 minutes. Compliance is normally no problem for the RESTQ. The RESTQ is well accepted in different contexts (e.g., home, work, training camp), and questions are normally interesting for the person, as they mirror part of their life in the past days. Thus, the argument 'the shorter – the better' does not hold, when the individual recovery-stress state is assessed.

However, for screening purposes the shorter version with 24 items for the basic part can be used, which allows an additional first view on the profile.

Formal aspects

A questionnaire like the RESTQ is a system of interrelated items. Items build a fixed compound of questions and answers. This implies that changing items, item format, answer categories, or leaving out items is a strict 'no-go'.

Please be aware that the authors hold the copyright for all languages, except the ones given away. In case you are interested in obtaining permission to translate and validate the *Recovery-Stress Questionnaires* into other languages, please contact the authors for the respective version by e-mail (see Kellmann & Kallus, this volume, Preface). In addition, you must have a background in psychometrics and you need to follow the translation procedure described by Vallerand (1989). Also, the 2018 International Test Commission *Guidelines for Translating and Adapting Tests* #1 to #11 (regarding Pre-Condition Guidelines, Test Development Guidelines, Confirmation Guidelines) must be realized. Also keep in mind that using items, scales or the RESTQ as a whole instrument in the internet or other media by third parties without a written permission is a violation of copyright and will be persecuted.

The RESTQ can be supplemented by project-specific or user-specific scales. For the construction of new scales refer to Kallus (2016) or contact the authors.

Interpretation of results and feedback

The present manual should help the user to interpret the RESTQ profile adequately. Please use your psychological knowledge on the concepts, which are behind the scales and which are outlined in this manual. When users do not have or do not include their psychological knowledge of the concepts in their interpretation of the RESTQ profiles, the risk arises that interpretation may only be based on the naming of scales. This can lead to wrong conclusions and decisions. The RESTQ is a psychological test. The use and interpretation of psychological tests by others than by graduated psychologists is legally prohibited in some states by law on psychological diagnosis and interventions. Thus, the use of the RESTQ at least needs psychological supervision.

Advices and tips for the use of the RESTQ

- Always follow the rule: The questioned person(s) is/are the first instance, which has/have the right to be informed on the results and the right to decide how this information is used. Here again the professional user of the RESTQ has to keep in mind the requirements for service providers (ISO 10667-2, 2020b).

- The data obtained with the RESTQ have to be treated as confidential private personal data and legal as well as ethical principles apply, e.g., the European Data Protection Regulation (European Union, 2016), which applies also for the next two points.
- When data are made anonymous, make sure that this procedure is truly safe.
- When data or results are transferred electronically, make sure to protect them against any unauthorized access.
- The RESTQ is a psychological test and the use of the RESTQ at least needs psychological supervision. Feedback on the results is ideally also provided by a psychologist.
- Especially in sports but also valid for other areas of applications, the RESTQ should not be used for selection purposes (unethical practice)!
- If a serious, long-lasting unhealthy recovery-stress state is detected, consultation with a trained psychologist and/or counseling center is highly recommended.

Use the RESTQ and its versions to help people optimize their resources, enhance recovery, and cope well with any kind of stress effectively.

Note

1 The RESTQ-Student is validated in German only.

References

Baylor, L. S., & Hackney, A. C. (2003). Resting thyroid and leptin hormone changes in women following intense, prolonged exercise training. *European Journal of Applied Physiology*, *88*, 480–484.

Bizjak, D. A., Treff, G., Zügel, M., Schumann, U., Winkert, K., Schneider, M., Abendroth, D., & Steinacker, J. M. (2021). Differences in immune response during competition and preparation phase in elite rowers. *Frontiers in Physiology*, *12*, 803863. https://doi.org/10.3389/fphys.2021.803863

Bollen, K. A. (1987). Outliers and improper solutions: A confirmatory factor analysis example. *Sociological Methods & Research*, *15*, 375–384.

Borg, I., & Mastrangelo, P. M. (2008). *Employee surveys in management: Theories, tools, and practical applications*. Hogrefe.

Brandt, J. (2010). *Struktur der Teamqualität. Analyse der Zusammenhänge zwischen Prozessen und Emergent States in Teams mit dem Teamqualitäts-Fragebogen TQF* [Structure of team quality: Analysis of the relationship between processes and emergent states in teams]. Südwestdeutscher Verlag für Hochschulschriften.

Brandt, J., & Kallus, K. W. (2023). Messung von Stress im Studium. Der Erholungs-Belastungs-Fragebogen für das Studium (EBF-Student) [Measuring student stress. The Recovery Stress Questionnaire for Students (RESTQ-Student)]. *Diagnostica*, *69*(3), 111–120.

Bresciani, G., Cuevas, M. J., Garatachea, N., Molinero, O., Almar, M., de Paz, J. A., Márquez, S., & González-Gallego, J. (2010). Monitoring biological and psychological measures during an entire season in male handball players. *European Journal of Sport Science*, *6*, 377–384.

Campos, F., Molina Correa, J. C., Canevari, V. C. M., Branco, B. H. M., Andreato, L. V., & de Paula Ramos, S. (2022). Monitoring internal training load, stress-recovery responses, and immune-endocrine parameters in Brazilian Jiu-Jitsu training. *Journal of Strength and Conditioning Research, 36*(3), 723–731.

Chen, F., Bollen, K. A., Paxton, P., Curran, P. J., & Kirby, J. B. (2001). Improper solutions in structural equation models. Causes, consequences, and strategies. *Sociological Methods & Research, 29*(4), 468–508.

Cheng, Y., Wang, W., & Ho, Y. H. (2008). Multidimensional Rasch analysis of a psychological test with multiple subtests: A statistical solution for the bandwidth-fidelity dilemma. *Educational and Psychological Measurement, 69*(3), 369–388.

Cohen, L., Fouladi, R. T., & Katz, J. (2005). Preoperative coping strategies and distress predict postoperative pain and morphine consumption in women undergoing abdominal gynaecologic surgery. *Journal of Psychosomatic Research, 58*, 201–209.

Cortis, C., Tessitore, A., D 'Artibale, E., Meeusen, R., & Capranica, L. (2010). Effects of post-exercise recovery interventions on physiological, psychological, and performance parameters. *International Journal of Sports Medicine, 31*, 327–335.

de Moraes, W. M. A. M., de Moura, F. C., da Costa Moraes, T. C., Oliveira de Sousa, L. G., Dos Santos Rosa, T., Schoenfeld, B. J., Machado Maia, F. M., & Prestes, J. (2019). Oxidative stress, inflammation, psychological status, and severity of respiratory infections are negatively affected during the pre-contest period in amateur bodybuilders. *Applied Physiology, Nutrition, and Metabolism, 44*(5), 468–476.

Dupuy, O., Bherer, L., Audiffren, M., & Bosquet, L. (2013). Night and postexercise cardiac autonomic control in functional overreaching. *Applied Physiology, Nutrition, and Metabolism, 38*, 200–208.

Eidenmüller, A. (2005). *Ambulante neuropsychologische Rehabilitation. Ist diese in späteren Phasen nach cerebraler Schädigung überhaupt sinnvoll?* [Ambulant neuropsychological rehabilitation. Is it after a cerebral damage useful?; Unpublished doctoral dissertation]. University of Würzburg, Germany.

European Union. (2016). *Regulation (EU) 2016/679 of the European Parliament and of the Council of 27 April 2016 on the protection of natural persons with regard to the processing of personal data and on the free movement of such data, and repealing Directive 95/46/EC (General Data Protection Regulation) (Text with EEA relevance).* Retrieved November 20, 2023 from https://eur-lex.europa.eu/legal-content/EN/TXT/?uri=CELEX%3A32016R0679

Filaire, E., Ferreira, J. P., Oliveira, M., & Massart, A. (2013). Diurnal patterns of salivary alpha-amylase and cortisol secretion in female adolescent tennis players after 16 weeks of training. *Psychoneuroendocrinology, 38*, 1122–1132.

Gaisbachgrabner, K. (2014). *Empirische Untersuchungen zu langen Arbeitszeiten und dem Hypothalamus-Hypophysen-Schilddrüsen-System im Mehrebenenansatz* [Empirical studies on the effects of long working hours on the hypothalamus-pituitary-thyroid-system; Unpublished doctoral dissertation]. University of Graz, Austria.

Goldman, L., Caldera, D. L., Nussbaum, S. R., Southwick, F. S., Krogstad, D., Murray, B., Burke, D. S., O'Malley, T. A., Goroll, A. H., Caplan, C. H., Nolan, J., Carabello, B., & Slater, E. E. (1977). Multifactorial index of cardiac risk in noncardiac surgical procedures. *The New England Journal of Medicine, 297*, 845–850.

Hough, J., Corney, R., Kouris, A., & Gleeson, M. (2013). Salivary cortisol and testosterone responses to high-intensity cycling before and after an 11-day intensified training period. *Journal of Sports Sciences, 31*, 1614–1623.

Institut für Begleitfoschung. (2015). *RecoveryCheck.* Retrieved November 20, 2023 from http://www.begleitforschung.de/de/products/recovery.html

International Organisation for Standardization. (ISO). (2018). *ISO 45001. Occupational health and safety management systems – Requirements with guidance for use.* Retrieved April 22, 2024 from https://www.iso.org/standard/63787.html

International Organisation for Standardization. (ISO). (2020a). *ISO 10667-1. Assessment service delivery – Procedures and methods to assess people in work and organizational settings – Part 1: Requirements for the client.* Retrieved April 22, 2024 from https://www.iso.org/standard/74716.html

International Organisation for Standardization. (ISO). (2020b). *ISO 10667-2. Assessment service delivery – Procedures and methods to assess people in work and organizational settings – Part 2: Requirements for service providers.* Retrieved April 22, 2024 from https://www.iso.org/standard/74717.html

International Test Commission. (ITC). (2018). *Guidelines for translating and adapting tests* (Second Edition, Version 2.4). Retrieved December 12, 2023 from https://www.intestcom.org/files/guideline_test_adaptation_2ed.pdf

Jamison, R., Parris, W. C. V., & Mazson, W. S. (1987). Psychological factors influencing recovery from outpatient surgery. *Behavior Research and Therapy, 25*, 31–37.

Janke, W., Erdmann, G., & Kallus, K. W. (1985). *Der Stressverarbeitungsfragebogen (SVF)* [The Stress-Coping Inventory]. Hogrefe.

Janke, W., Erdmann, G., & Kallus, K. W. (2002). *SVF-78. Eine Kurzform des Stressverarbeitungsfragebogens SVF-120* [SVF-78. A short version of the Stress-Coping Inventory-120]. Hogrefe.

Janke, W., & Hüppe, M. (1994). *Befindlichkeitsskalierung durch Kategorien und Eigenschaftswörter: BSKE (EWL) nach Janke Debus, Erdmann und Hüppe. Test und Handanweisung* [Scaling of well-being using categories and characteristic words: BSKE (EWL) according to Janke Debus, Erdmann and Hüppe. Test and manual; Unpublished report]. University of Würzburg, Germany.

Jiménez, P., Bregenzer, A., Kallus, K. W., Fruhwirth, B., & Wagner-Hartl, V. (2017). Enhancing resources at the workplace with health-promoting leadership. *International Journal of Environmental Research and Public Health, 14*(10), 1264. https://doi.org/10.3390/ijerph14101264

Kallus, K. W. (1992). *Beanspruchung und Ausgangszustand* [Stress and initial state]. PVU.

Kallus, K. W. (1995). *Der Erholungs-Belastungs-Fragebogen* [The Recovery-Stress Questionnaire]. Swets & Zeitlinger.

Kallus, K. W. (2016). *Erstellung von Fragebogen* [Construction of questionnaires]. Facultas.

Kallus, K. W., Blattner, A., & Stelzhammer, J. (2009). *Recovery-Stress-Questionnaire – Social Capital* [Unpublished Questionnaire]. University of Graz, Austria.

Kallus, K. W., & Brandt, J. (2015). RISCO: Risiko-Score für eine dysfunktionale Stressverarbeitung [RISk score for dysfunctional stress COping; Unpublished report]. Institut für Begleitforschung Würzburg/Graz, Germany/Austria.

Kellmann, M., Altenburg, D., Lormes, W., & Steinacker, J. M. (2001). Assessing stress and recovery during preparation for the World Championships in rowing. *The Sport Psychologist, 15*, 151–167.

Kellmann, M., Kallus, K. W., Günther, K.-D., Lormes, W., & Steinacker, J. M. (1997). Psychologische Betreuung der Junioren-Nationalmannschaft des Deutschen Ruderverbandes [Psychological consultation of the German Junior National Rowing Team]. *Psychologie und Sport, 4*, 123–134.

Kiecolt-Glaser, J. K., Page, G. G., Marucha, P. T., MacCallum, R. C., & Glaser, R. (1998). Psychological influences on surgical recovery: Perspectives from psychoneuroimmunology. *American Psychology, 53*, 1209–1218.

Kline, P. (2000). *Handbook of psychological testing.* Routledge.

Krauth, J., & Lienert, G. A. (1973). *KFA. Die Konfigurationsfrequenzanalyse und ihre Anwendungen in Psychologie und Medizin* [CFA. Configural frequency analysis and its application in psychology and medicine]. Alber.

Morales, J., Alamo, J. M., García-Massó, X., Buscà, B., López, J. L., Serra-Añó, P., & González, L. M. (2014). The use of heart rate variability in monitoring stress and recovery in judo athletes. *Journal of Strength and Conditioning Research, 28*, 1896–1905.

Rindskopf, D. (1984). Structural equation models: Empirical identification, Heywood cases, and related problems. *Sociological Methods & Research, 13*, 109–119.

Schulz, P., Schlotz, W., & Becker, P. (2004). *TICS – Trierer Inventar zum chronischen Stress* [Trier Inventory of Chronic Stress]. Hogrefe.

Schuster, G. U. (1997). *Evaluation des integrativen Ansatzes in der ambulanten, neuropsychologischen Langzeitrehabilitation* [Evaluation of the integrative approach in the ambulant, neuropsychological long-term rehabilitation; Unpublished master's thesis]. University of Graz, Austria.

Sime, A. M. (1976). Relationship of preoperative fear, type of coping, and information received about surgery to recovery from surgery. *Journal of Personality and Social Psychology, 34*, 716–724.

Slangen, K., Krohne, H. W., Stallrecht, S., & Kleemann, P. P. (1993). Dimensionen perioperativer Belastung und ihre Auswirkungen auf intra- und postoperative Anpassung von Chirurgiepatienten [Dimensions of perioperative stress and its impact on intra- and postoperative adjustments from surgery patients]. *Zeitschrift Gesundheitspsychologie, 1*, 123–142.

Uhlig, T., & Kallus, K. W. (2016). Recovery-Stress Questionnaire in clinical settings. In K. W. Kallus & M. Kellmann (Eds.), *The Recovery-Stress Questionnaires: User manual* (pp. 215–232). Pearson Assessment & Information GmbH.

Uhlig, T., Seifert, C., Gerlach, K., & Schmucker, P. (1999). Erholung und perioperativer Stress [Recovery and perioperative stress]. *Anästhesiologie, Intensivmedizin, Notfallmedizin, Schmerztherapie, 34*(3), 211–222.

Vallerand, R. J. (1989). Vers une méthodologie de validation trans-culturelle de questionnaires psychologiques: Implications pour la recherche en langue française [Toward a methodology for the transcultural validation of psychological questionnaires: Implications for research in the French language]. *Canadian Psychology/Psychologie Canadienne, 30*(4), 662–680.

van Driel, O. (1978). On various causes of improper solutions in maximum likelihood factor analyses. *Psychometrika, 43*, 225–243.

Index

For Product Safety Concerns and Information please contact our EU
representative GPSR@taylorandfrancis.com
Taylor & Francis Verlag GmbH, Kaufingerstraße 24, 80331 München, Germany

www.ingramcontent.com/pod-product-compliance
Ingram Content Group UK Ltd.
Pitfield, Milton Keynes, MK11 3LW, UK
UKHW020148200926
475702UK00016B/2616
* 9 7 8 1 0 3 2 6 2 0 5 0 3 *